MW01452783

peace

Grateful acknowledgment to the following for permission to use material from their collections
    The Garroway family
    Library of American Broadcasting, University of Maryland
    American Heritage Center, University of Wyoming
    Wisconsin Historical Society

Grateful acknowledgment to the following for permission to use images from their collections
    Paris Day
        for images on pages 9, 24, 51, 55, 77, 91, 129, 157, 188, 228, 262, 293 and 325
    American Heritage Center, University of Wyoming
        for images on pages 34, 47, 66 and 306
    the Associated Press
        for image on page 252
    The Estate of Raimondo Borea, represented by Gartenberg Media Enterprises
        for cover image and image on page 315

This work © 2023 by Jodie Peeler and © 2023 by the Dave Garroway Memorial Trust
    All rights reserved, including the right to reproduce this book
    or portions thereof in any form whatsoever.

Book and cover designed by Midge Wood

Tyger River Books
A division of TigerCo Industries, LLC
Pomaria, South Carolina

ISBN 979-8-9881887-0-4

Library of Congress Control Number: 2023906744

peace

THE WIDE, WIDE WORLD OF DAVE GARROWAY, TELEVISION'S ORIGINAL MASTER COMMUNICATOR

JODIE PEELER
WITH DAVE GARROWAY JR. AND BRANDON HOLLINGSWORTH

TYGER RIVER BOOKS

Acknowledgments

One of the strangest things about a book is that although you see only the author's name on the cover, the whole thing is a massive effort involving a large number of people. One of the hardest things for that book's author to do is name everybody who helped and express enough thanks for everything those people did, because for want of a single one of those people, this book would have been missing something. I may come up short here, but, as Dave Garroway would have said, it's worth a try.

The story of this book is a story of happy coincidences. For years I thought Dave Garroway was a fascinating character, but I couldn't understand why no one had examined his story in depth. There seemed to be a really worthwhile story to be told. It so happened that a search for information about the strange, foot-long microphone he used on that first *Today* program led me to my first contact with Brandon Hollingsworth, who had his own fascination with Dave Garroway. From that first contact came ideas, a partnership, and, best of all, a friendship. So much of this book is the result of information Brandon shared from his own explorations of Garroway's papers, not to mention Brandon's keen insights and valuable perspectives, his sharp eye as an editor, and most of all his sound, steady advice. This book is his as much as it's mine. Brandon, it's a privilege flying with you.

None of this could have happened without Kevin Doherty, either. Kevin contacted me soon after the *Garroway At Large* website went live, and mentioned not only his own interest in Garroway but the work he had done on behalf of the Museum of Television and Radio (now the Paley Center) to preserve Garroway-related footage from the NBC archives. Over the years Kevin and I have had many conversations about our shared interest in these pioneering years of NBC and the people who made them happen, and we even had the fun of sharing a presentation a few years ago at the Mid-Atlantic Nostalgia Convention. Kevin is working on a book about his friend Jack Paar, and I can't wait to read it. Kevin, thank you for everything, and let's please share a panel again soon.

Without Kevin, I wouldn't have made the acquaintance of Ben Alba or James Curtis - and if it hadn't been for those gentlemen, I wouldn't have met two extremely special people I'll mention later. Ben, the author of a magnificent book about Steve Allen and the early days of *Tonight*, and James, the author of several excellent biographies, kept the book you're now holding from being little more than a leaflet. Kevin, Ben, and James, what I owe you is beyond measure.

This book had many allies early on. One of my first contacts was Dennis Hart, whose efforts to preserve the history of NBC's *Monitor* deserve a truckload of awards. Dennis strongly believed Garroway's story needed to be told, and I'll never forget how his response to me was an early encouragement. Throughout the project Dennis has provided materials and insights, and has continued to encourage me.

Another key ally has been Bobby Ellerbee, one of the best friends that broadcast history has ever had, a good friend to this project, and a very special friend to me. Bobby, who either knows everybody or knows who knows everybody, opened a lot of doors for this project and made a lot of very good things happen. Best of all, it's been a lot more fun with Bobby helping and encouraging me, and always making me laugh. Thank you, Sheriff!

Carol Ford played a very important role in this project, too. Carol and two associates wrote a massive, exhaustively-documented biography of Bob Crane that debunked a lot of myths and told his story with honesty, humanity and dignity. I made a point early on of seeking her advice, since the Dave Garroway story involves its own sensitive topics and long-held myths. Not only did Carol provide guidance on handling these things with compassion, but she provided smart advice on the practical aspects of projects like this. Carol's wisdom has guided me through this project, and the example set by her Bob Crane book has been an inspiration.

Mitchell Hadley also saw the value of this project early on, and since I had the fun of first meeting him and Judie at the 2017 Mid-Atlantic Nostalgia convention, we've traded insights, shared ideas, and helped each other's efforts. Mitchell is one of the television medium's most perceptive observers, and his writings often provide perspectives that force me to re-examine my own. He certainly makes me always want to be better at what I do. Mitchell and Judie, thank you for everything, most of all your friendship.

I met a lot of really good folks while working on this project, and along the way made some friends. Dennis Degan gave me the ultimate inside view of 30 Rock one memorable Sunday morning several years ago, giving me the opportunity to visit so many of the places where Dave Garroway worked, and in the years since Dennis has not only provided a wealth of knowledge on NBC's facilities and operations, but has been a good friend too. Gady Reinhold, who gave me the grandest possible tour of the CBS Broadcast Center one unforgettably fun Friday afternoon, shared documents and other items from his amazing archive, and has also been a wonderful source of encouragement. The late Frank Merklein, who was behind one of the cameras on *Today*'s first day, shared stories from his days as a television pioneer, and what was meant as a brief visit turned into a fascinating journey through the lifetime of someone who lived the history that I revere. Frank, I'm sorry my visit delayed your lunch that day, but you were having so much fun reliving those days I didn't have the heart to interrupt you, and I was having too much fun listening. Thank you for one of my happiest memories of this whole adventure.

There have been so many other good people who shared memories, insights and materials. In the course of a delightful telephone conversation Jeff Fleming shared memories of his father and gave me a fascinating, personal perspective of a newsman I wish I could have met. Ed Grosso told me stories of working at NBC in the late 1950s and early 1960s, giving me a feel for those times that has helped inform these pages. Michael Loewenstein told me stories of watching a *Garroway At Large* program from the booth at the old Merchandise Mart studios in Chicago, and how the innovative set designs of Jan Scott inspired his own distinguished career as a set designer.

Some very kind people shared their research abilities and key materials in support of this project. Christine Martuch tirelessly sought out materials, most notably Ed Rothhaar's fascinating master's thesis on *Garroway At Large*, which is a priceless document on the Chicago School in general and Garroway in particular. Bryan Olson provided a steady supply of archival material, including several valuable newspaper pieces and links to video clips. Other kind folks who merit recognition include Mark Nielsen, who is working on some interesting creative projects; Randy West, who chronicled the life of the peerless Johnny Olson; and Cathleen

Londino, whose analysis of the first quarter-century of *Today* was a very handy resource throughout my work. Rick Perlstein is not only one of my favorite historians but is also a lot of fun to know, and has gently encouraged me to remember that my work is better than I often let myself think. A.R. Hogan, whose efforts to chronicle the history of spaceflight television coverage are endlessly fascinating and always inspiring, has provided information and encouragement throughout this whole journey. William Bartlett, who served for many years as NBC's in-house historian (and is author of a beautiful book about NBC's history at 30 Rock), has been a friend to this project in ways much too numerous to count, but all of them appreciated.

One of the sweetest moments was when Meredith Ibey Milliron contacted me about a project she and some associates were planning as a tribute to the Chicago School. The result was a magnificent hour-long webcast, a re-creation of a *Garroway At Large* episode that told the Garroway story, that in its own way captured that Chicago School magic once more. Meredith, my thanks to you, Paul Durica, and everyone else who created something truly beautiful, and thank you for letting me be a little part of it.

You can't do a project like this without a lot of help from archives and collections. There are three major stops for anyone interested in the Garroway story, and I wish to recognize each one in turn. The Library of American Broadcasting at the University of Maryland at College Park houses the Lee Lawrence collection, which includes a great deal of material from her years working with Garroway. The staff of the Library of American Broadcasting was a great deal of help to us both. In particular, Michael Henry was a tremendous help to Brandon during his research visits, and was knowledgeable, affable and helpful without fail. The American Heritage Center of the University of Wyoming, which holds the papers of Dave Garroway and many other broadcast figures, cheerfully supplied material via electronic means when the pandemic prevented me from making the trip there, and the staff was endlessly helpful with my other inquiries and requests. The Wisconsin Historical Society, where NBC's colossal collection of archival documents now resides, is a requirement for anyone who really wants to understand any aspect of the network's first fifty years, for so many marvelous stories just waiting to be told are in those documents. The bonus is that you get to visit a magnificent building and work with a very helpful and friendly staff. Thank you all for your help, and for working with me during a much-too-brief visit. Grateful acknowledgment is made to all three of these institutions for permission to quote from their archival holdings in this work.

Other archives opened for me thanks to some kind people. Jeremy Hunt of the NBC Universal video archive helped me with a key piece of information. Allison Schein Holmes of the Studs Terkel Radio Archive kindly shared with me an advance copy of Terkel's 1974 interview with Dave Garroway before it was ready for public listening. Tricia Gesner made dealing with the Associated Press's photo licensing an absolute pleasure, and Jon Gartenberg gladly made the terrific photo archives of Raimondo Borea available for me, including the beautiful cover photo. Closer to home, I have to thank three libraries that have been part of just about every project I've ever done: the Thomas Cooper Library of the University of South Carolina in Columbia; the Main Library of the University of Georgia in Athens; and the Larry A. Jackson Library of Lander University in Greenwood, S.C. Every time I visit these libraries, it feels like coming home. My employer, Newberry College, has been encouraging and patient as I worked on this project in between my daily chores, and helped support this project and an earlier one with a sabbatical. To my colleagues and my students, thank you.

Nobody can do anything without an inner circle that keeps you grounded, functional and happy. My family never quite understood why I was so fascinated with television history from a very young age, but they tolerated it and my countless other fascinations with good cheer, and always with love. Rob Sherry has continued to be my wise and trusted general counsel in so many things. Ralph Nardone, a writer and historian in his own regard, has known what this project means to me and has supported and encouraged me, with a long and sustaining love.

By my count, I have worked on this book in ten states over the last six years, using quiet hours in hotel rooms to work a little more on the notes or the manuscript itself. Other times, I worked on it at home before heading off to work, and perhaps it's appropriate that a book about Dave Garroway was, much like an episode of *Today*, made ready while much of the world was still asleep. Never, though, was I as productive or contented as when I was at home with the quietly reassuring help of the best assistants I could ever have. From the start, Junior and Smokey sat with me and often competed with the laptop computer for my lap. Junior's mighty heart gave out before this project was finished, but from the great beyond he helped send a little kitten named Gilda to keep us all company, and she quickly took on the role of assistant that he had to leave behind. So much of this book has been written in the wee hours of the morning by the soft glow of my computer's screen, one cat sleeping across my lap and another snuggled next to me. There are far worse ways to work.

Without question, the turning point in this project came from two very special people. In mid-2018, thanks to Kevin Doherty, Ben Alba, and James Curtis, I finally established contact with Dave Garroway Jr. My earlier efforts to contact the Garroway family had not been successful, and I had concluded they wanted to be left alone. I wasn't prepared for Dave Jr.'s request for me to call him, nor was I prepared for what happened when we did talk. Dave Jr. could not have been happier to speak with me or more willing to share memories of his dad. Not only was he interested in the project, but he had made various efforts at writing a book about his dad.

We talked a few more times every now and again. A couple months later, he said he and his sister would be on the East Coast to see after some family business. Would I like to meet? Sure enough, he and Paris spent a weekend in South Carolina, and we had two wonderful, too-short days together, looking through family memorabilia and sharing stories. There were times I couldn't believe my good fortune to have them there, telling stories of their famous dad. At the same time, they were two of the kindest people I could have met, and so much fun to share time with. Meeting them redoubled my vow to tell their dad's story the best, most honest, and most honorable way I could.

Over the next couple of years I talked every few weeks with Dave Jr. He would ask how the book was coming along, share a memory or two of his dad, and talk about what he was up to and whatever else was on a mind that was always in motion. He was always upbeat and chatty when we talked, and always encouraging. His calls became like hearing from a favorite uncle who had a goofy sense of humor and was always working on something.

I had been looking forward to another visit with Dave Jr. and Paris, getting scans of family photos, and spending time with a couple of good people I had now come to know as friends. Those plans became a casualty of the 2020 pandemic. Instead, I stayed home and worked on the manuscript. I delivered the completed first draft to Dave Jr. on Christmas night that year. He was elated. A project he had wanted for years was now a reality. A little more than a month later, he passed away. I am saddened beyond words that he didn't live to see this book in print, but it means the world to me that he knew his dad's story was going to be told, and that he had a printed version of that draft before he passed away. I may have been the one who assembled the various parts of the Dave Garroway story, and Brandon may have been responsible for a ton of the archival work, but this book really belongs to Dave Jr. I am sad that he is gone, but I am thankful for the all-too-brief time I had with him, and for the faith he had in me to tell his dad's story.

After Dave Jr.'s passing, Paris took up the cause that meant so much to her brother. Not only has she provided invaluable help to finish this project, and not only has she shared recollections of her own, but it has been a joy to share company with her and talk about any number of other things. Paris, I thank you not only for your trust in me, but for becoming a beloved friend. I never had a chance to meet your dad, but I am forever grateful to him. Because of him, you, your brother, and so many other marvelous people became part of my life, and the telling of your dad's story has been an journey I wouldn't want to have missed.

To anyone I haven't mentioned, I apologize for not acknowledging you by name, but I hope that as you read this book, you'll see something of your contributions in here. I hope you know that I couldn't have done this without you. I am truly obliged.

Jodie Peeler
April 2023

For

Dave Garroway, Jr.
who loved his dad

and

Ralph Nardone
*for being just what you are
by the dawn's early light*

Introduction

On a morning much like any other in early summer midtown Manhattan, a devoted crowd lined the temporary barricades on Rockefeller Plaza south of 49th Street. Many of them held brightly colored pieces of poster board bearing the same logo, white on orange, a half-circle beneath two arches, bold block letters shouting the common word that was a television program's name. Others held signs hand-lettered with the names of hometowns, the names of loved ones back home, the names of service personnel overseas or causes to promote. At a moment's notice, the crowd, lining the fences several deep, cheered and waved and shook their signs at the television cameras roving inside the barricades, wanting just a second or two of face time on a national telecast, eager to interact with one of the television personalities who had stepped out from the glass-fronted television studio built into a former bank location in the corner of a nearby building.

Rain or shine, summer or winter, since 1994 that corner studio had become a tourist attraction, a magnet for those who wanted to be seen on camera, one of the ultimate "I did that" moments for visitors to Manhattan. For it was in that studio that NBC produced *Today*, the program whose sunrise logo fronted those posters, the most popular morning program on television, and an economic powerhouse for its network.

Nothing about the adjacent Christie's showroom gave the impression it ever had anything to do with television history. Behind its huge plate glass windows were displays of art and artifacts, treasures far beyond the means of most. But on a rainy January morning seven decades before, the exhibition behind those windows was a strange experiment, witnessed by a few thousand set owners on the fledgling NBC Television Network's twenty-six stations, and by a handful of bleary-eyed New Yorkers pausing on their way to work, wondering what General Sarnoff's troops were up to so early on a Monday morning when static or a test pattern was typical television fare.

Inside those windows, dozens of lights had cast an unholy glow on the strangest collection of newsgathering apparatus on public display. The stylish displays of corporate innovation that had lined the RCA Exhibition Hall had, at the direction of a network vice president given to unusual but visionary ideas, made way for clattering teletypewriters, shortwave radios, tape recorders, electric typewriters, newspaper racks, and an explosion of clocks and television screens, as if a cluttered garage had become a television studio. One half of the back wall, clotted with machinery, snaked with spaghetti-like conduit against an outline of the world; the other half had a desk and a large map of the world behind a sofa, a couple of record turntables, and a display of the day's top stories. Everywhere loomed television cameras, even one on a tall platform between the desk and the huge window.

Amid all the chaos, all the clattering equipment and busy staffers, roamed a tall man in a suit and bow tie and round glasses, a foot-long microphone suspended on a hoop around his neck, trailing a long cable. His demeanor serene and charming, his voice easy, his eyes showing a hint of twinkle, he guided the audience through this spectacle with goodwill and good humor, curiosity and amusement and occasional bemusement: one moment speaking of the program as a new kind of television, another moment fascinated with a young writer's electric typewriter, another moment issuing a gentle tease to his smiling co-host.

Seventy years later, the name Dave Garroway would be no more likely to elicit recognition from the crowd outside Studio 1A than would the news that *Today* had come back to its roots within half a city block. Occasionally an older visitor might remember the days of Garroway: the crowd outside the original window; a chimpanzee whose antics delighted youngsters and tormented program staffers; a host's horn-rimmed eyes, upheld palm and peaceful benediction. Such people, however, were the exception. These days, *Today* was pitched to an audience that had known no hosts but its current ones, and knew the program not for its coverage of current events so much as for its rapid-fire segments, the summertime concerts that played out in the Plaza, and the behind-the-scenes personality intrigue that occasionally played out in the gossip pages.

There are no markers outside the 49th Street showroom to note its significance to television history. With the exception of those first few grainy kinescoped moments of the debut telecast seen on retrospective shows, Dave Garroway is a cipher, an answer to a trivia question, relegated to the occasional photo displayed in the hallways of 30 Rock, where he once worked.

Broadcasting is a medium that eats its own, and quickly. It has a long history and a short memory. A personality showered with multiple programs and fifty-year network contracts could quickly fall victim to changing public tastes, lost favor in the corporate suites, or just be surpassed by the next new thing. Whatever the reason, once they were gone they were all too often forgotten, their efforts to reinvent themselves never matching the demands of a new era. Arthur Godfrey, once an inescapable fixture on CBS, is now hardly remembered except for his notorious on-air firing of Julius LaRosa; his genuine contributions to the medium, contributions that nearly every broadcaster since has emulated, no longer register as his. Ed Sullivan, whose variety program dominated Sundays for twenty-three years until he was abruptly punted from the CBS schedule, is now mostly remembered for the times his program hosted four young musicians from Liverpool.

Dave Garroway has languished in a similar obscurity. Now lost in the passage of time, trapped forever in a few moments on a murky film from 1952, it's not possible to readily measure his own contributions to both Today and to the medium as a whole. In his prime, Garroway was as much a symbol of NBC as the peacock, not only on *Today* but on numerous other programs on television and radio. At one point, Garroway could be seen or heard in original programming six days a week: on *Today*, on *Wide Wide World*, on the innovative radio series *Monitor*. He made guest appearances on countless other television and radio programs. He lent his endorsement to dozens of products, a prize for which sponsors gladly put their names on waiting lists. Away from the camera's eye, Garroway fit many fascinations into a day's too few hours: engineering, mechanics, sports cars, astronomy, countless others.

The public face of serenity masked a man fighting many battles: a peerless communicator working himself to exhaustion, a gifted man tormented by addiction, a career frustrated by changing times and unfortunate decisions, and a life brought to a premature end by the depression he could never escape. To co-workers he contained multitudes: endearing, demanding, generous, childish, reassuring, maddening, confident, paranoid, whimsical fun coexisting with profound sadness. But neither *Today* as we now know it, nor the countless programs that have emulated it, would exist without the distinctive, informal, person-to-person style of communication Garroway brought to the show in its first years, and that has been in its blood since.

Dave Garroway has been forgotten by the medium he helped pioneer. The original master communicator deserves better. This is an effort to tell the story not only of Garroway the man but also the times in which he lived and the medium he helped change. The portrait that emerges is of a sensitive and inquisitive man, whose genuine gifts as a communicator and broadcasting innovator are all too often overlooked in favor of the tragedy of his final days.

It took an unconventional man to build what we now consider conventional television. Here is his story.

1

The Garroways were "lower middle class Scotch working people," Dave would remember. His grandfather, born in 1855, was the fifth to bear the name David Cunningham Garroway, a name handed down through the years. His wife, Grace Aitken Garroway, had been born in 1850. They settled in Paisley, Renfrewshire. Their son, also named David Cunningham Garroway, was born there in September 1884. Twelve years later David and Grace, and their sons David and John, had enough of struggling in Scotland and migrated to the United States.

The family settled in Schenectady, a town in eastern New York. Since David Garroway was trained in electrical engineering, he soon went to work as a designer for General Electric, one of the area's largest employers. Garroway ended up in charge of the drafting room, where he helped develop General Electric's first major steam turbine. In a photograph that became a source of family pride, more than a hundred people stood by the enormous turbine, with Grandfather Garroway in the middle of the scene.[1]

The Garroways purchased a farm in nearby Rotterdam Township. Edgewater Farm had a pond formed by a dam on nearby Altamont Road. On those twenty-eight acres, Garroway and sons David and John raised chickens. David's grandson, who himself would bear the name handed down for generations, remembered his grandfather as a "gentle, kindly soul, a little taciturn" and his grandmother as "a wee Scotch wife" who said "better little things, and not much of them."[2]

Their son David went to Union College in Schenectady, and then both he and John went to work for General Electric. David became a designer. Not long after, he fell in love with Alberta "Bertha" Isole Tanner, a young woman in her early twenties descended from the Brockelbank family, which had settled in Massachusetts in 1640. Her father, Albert Tanner, had married a sweet lady named Mary Lackmann and they settled in Schenectady.[3]

David Garroway and Bertha Tanner married in 1910 and moved into a cottage at Edgewater Farm, a short distance from the main house. A few minutes after one on the afternoon of July 13, 1913, at Ellis Hospital in Schenectady, the young couple welcomed a baby boy. They named him David Cunningham Garroway VII.[4]

Dave Garroway's first memory was of being held in his mother's lap, a year and a half or two years old, reaching for a piece of cake. His grandmother wagged her finger and repeatedly said no. His other early childhood memory was of the day the Garroway cottage caught fire. Dave's father, already outside, ran to a window. Bertha tossed the year-old Dave to his father before leaping from the window herself. No one was hurt, but the house was destroyed. Dave remembered being held in someone's arms the next day as the family went to the ruined house. His father poked around in the steaming rubble, retrieving a cache of coin banks filled with ruined, twisted coins.[5]

The now-homeless family moved into the farmhouse with Dave's grandparents, aunts and uncles. Though it was a busy farm and a busy house, there was a lot of love in the family, and Dave remembered those as happy days. The one source of worry was Grandfather Garroway's advancing age. For his safety, his sons had convinced him to let them do the driving. One Sunday afternoon, as the family relaxed on the front porch, they suddenly saw Grandfather Garroway roaring toward Altamont Road in his Model T. Dave's father sprinted from the porch to the middle of the road, waving his father down. Grandfather Garroway swerved to miss his son, and the car plummeted into Edgewater Pond. Dave's father plunged in and retrieved Grandfather Garroway, but the Ford sank to the bottom. "I just wanted to go for a little ride," he explained. Later, Dave's father swam back in and tied a rope to the Ford's rear axle. With the help of all hands and the family's horse, they pulled the car out. After a week's work, it was running again.[6]

For a short time, Dave and his mother went to live with her parents in their house on Stanley Street in Schenectady. Grandmother Tanner was "sweet as a pea to me, and seemed about as big when Albert Brockelbank Tanner was on the premises." Grandfather Tanner had a fierce temper that had ruined an attempt to run a bicycle repair shop. That temper was the terror of the family. Dave remembered Grandfather Tanner as "the family tyrant, beating my tiny grandmother, but never when I was

A young Dave Garroway with his mother. (Paris Day collection)

around." The abuse extended to his daughter. Years later Dave would learn how cruel Grandfather Tanner was to his mother, and "what a wretch he was...how so miserable an SOB could have as neat a girl as my mother, Bertha, I don't really know. Maybe it was because of her father's nature and her rebellion against it."[7]

Although his grandfather was a "brute" to his grandmother, and although the front door of the Tanner house closed "like the gates of hell," Albert Tanner was kind, if a little gruff, to his grandson. "I didn't know Grandpa was a son of a bitch, because Grandpa brought me a present home every day," he remembered. "When he didn't, he'd go out and get one." He would bring David a piece of penny candy, a grapefruit, or something else. He also provided another gift: a basement workshop full of tools that fascinated the young boy. One gift, more than any other, inspired a lifelong passion.[8]

When he was five, young Dave saw a beautiful Chandler automobile that a neighbor had bought. Immediately smitten, he wanted one of his own. Grandfather Tanner disappeared into the workshop and turned some sheet metal, bicycle parts, and a set of baby carriage wheels into a miniature car, just the right size for a five-year-old to sit in and propel it with his feet. "It had a top speed of about six miles an hour if you fed the motor – me – two Eskimo Pies," Garroway remembered nearly half a century later. The fun he had in this first car inspired him to build a larger one with pedals, the first automotive adventure for a lifelong car enthusiast.[9]

Having helped Grandfather Tanner build a car, young Dave asked if he could work for him on one of the roofing jobs he now did. Grandfather agreed, even offering to pay him regular rates. The next day, Dave accompanied his grandfather to the work site, a slate roof atop a three-story house. The little boy, struggling to hold on, slipped and was saved from a fall only by a ladder at the edge of the roof. Grandfather Tanner looked over at his terrified grandson. "You've got to watch that," he said with a laugh. "Don't do that." With that, Dave's roofing career ended.

Although Dave hadn't wanted to move to Schenectady ("That wasn't nearly as much fun as on the farm," he later wrote), he still found things to enjoy. The Tanner home's large back yard provided plenty of room for a young boy to play. Grape vines yielded treats for eating and ammunition for his slingshot. A quart jar of pennies kept by Grandfather Tanner captivated Dave, who often emptied the jar onto a bed and ran his hands through the coins, imagining they were worth at least a million dollars.[10]

In time, Dave and his mother moved back to Edgewater Farm, into the main house with the grandparents "and a few other spare Garroways." There was endless fun for a young boy: chickens to chase around, horses to ride, corn and onions and potatoes to help harvest. At night Dave helped candle eggs, fascinated by the beauty of the eggs and the tiny embryos inside. He loved visiting the chick house, enjoying its warmth as he watched the babies peck their way out of their shells, wondering what each baby chick was thinking about the world it was entering, "just as I had eased my way out of a soft warm friendly shell not too long before, and thanked my lucky stars I was going to have a better break than those chicks." In the winter, when Edgewater Pond froze, Dave watched workers use giant hand saws to cut huge blocks of ice, loading them onto a conveyor chain for storage in a nearby ice house.[11]

With cousins and friends, Dave dug caves and tunnels in the orchard, only getting in so far before the sandy soil collapsed on them. "But never did we go deep enough to get into trouble," Dave said. Along one line of the property, a tall line of trees demarcated the adjoining land of Mr. James, a reputed ogre who stood ready to punish young trespassers with a shotgun blast. The boys didn't really believe the stories, but stayed clear nonetheless. "Never did see Mr. James," he said. "Maybe he was just created to keep us home." Even inside the farmhouse, fascinations could be found. Young Dave's bedroom was an alcove that also housed a complete set of *National Geographic* magazines, which he read over and over again.[12]

Sometimes adventure turned to mischief. Dave and his friend Brewster Gallop figured out the code for torpedoes on the main New York Central Line, which ran near the farm. They had also found a few unspent torpedoes. One day they strapped the little squibs to the track in the correct sequence and ran for cover. Along came a long freight train, on schedule. It ran over the torpedoes, which fired off the code for "emergency stop." To the boys' delight, the engineer locked the brakes and the train groaned to a halt.[13]

From watching the rhythms of nature to turning pages in magazines devoted to adventure, the happy days on the family farm made a lasting impression on Dave Garroway. Long after his career had taken him on adventures beyond a little boy's dreams, Garroway said he felt sorry for any child who had never lived on a farm. "There is no substitute for black earth – for seeing it, feeling it, smelling it, touching it, behind a plough or digging caves in it, rolling in it, even," he wrote. "If you have a few years to watch the cycles of earth and what grows from it, and the changes of the seasons and the stars with them, I think you better perceive everything you'll see later as you grow. I know it's true for me."[14]

Dave also learned those same cycles of nature could be harsh and startling. One fall night, a big thunderstorm blew through and struck the house. Dave recalled "a tremendous bolt of lightning, one which blew a chimney to smithereens…splitting apart beams and going out into the earth by the fireplace, throwing up big stones from the fireplace." Since the house had lightning rods and lightning arresters ("We were very advanced. We worked for GE, didn't we? Yes sir!"), the house was spared further damage. Nor did the lightning strike harm the grandfather clock, reportedly in the Garroway family since 1732, that Grandfather Garroway had brought with him from Scotland.[15]

After Grandfather Garroway passed away in December 1920, Dave and his parents left the family farm for a house of their own, at 13 Van Velsen Street in Schenectady. No matter what else was going on, the marriage between David and Bertha Garroway remained strong. It brought stability to their son's life. His parents, he remembered, stayed in love ("and by love, I mean it in almost a Hollywood B picture sense.") While arguments and affairs split the families of his friends, Dave found peace in his own home, problems always resolved with a love "so strong and deep." He never heard his parents bicker or aim an angry word at each other. Dave felt his parents had "the kind of marriage that two people of good intentions can build for themselves if they really want to."

This love extended to their only child. When Dave was ten his father pledged that he would never strike him. "By God, he never did," Dave wrote, and when he became a father he did not strike his children. Instead, Dave remembered his father as a wise man. Once, a friend told Dave the fourth-grade teacher would give him a hard time. His father counseled him: before you judge anyone or anything, get the facts and then make up your own mind. "I found out the teacher wasn't such a crab apple after all," Garroway said.[16]

So good was the Garroway home that years later, after two marriages of his own had ended, Dave wondered if it did him a disservice. "I came to believe that if two people 'loved' each other and were of good will, then that's all it took to make a marriage work. In later years, I had to modify that notion somewhat, depending on what is meant to each of the parties by 'love' and 'good will.'"[17] Dave himself would spend much of his life trying to achieve that same sort of deep connection with a partner, yet too often ended up frustrated.

The Garroways encouraged their son's curiosity and creativity. Lola Tilden, a family friend, would remember a boy who "really was interested in everything: cameras, marksmanship, books, painting, astronomy, geology, botany, gold, mineralogy, music, mechanics, cars," constantly adding knowledge to his life, believing nothing a person ever learns is wasted.[18]

That curiosity sometimes led to pain. On his way to school one winter morning, Dave walked across the Crane Street Bridge. He paused to admire the snow in the valley beneath. "It looked beautiful," he remembered. "You couldn't see the ground even because the air was so thick with snow." Enraptured by the moment ("just out of love, I guess"), he suddenly had the urge to stick out his tongue and touch the bridge railing with it. His tongue immediately bonded to the frozen metal. Terrified, he screamed for help. Firemen soon arrived. One held a gas torch against the railing, and Dave felt heat creeping toward his bleeding tongue. A few moments later, he was free. Relief quickly turned to agony, as part of his tongue's surface had been left behind on the cold metal. For days after, he could taste nothing "except the bitter flavor of the Crane Street Bridge."

As a doctor tended to Dave's injury, the fire department called his father and warned him not to let his son do it again. "As though I did it every day!" Garroway remembered. Besides, Dave felt he had the real complaint, wondering why the bridge had to be that cold early in the morning. "Why not a heated Crane Street Bridge? I thought. Really, I did to myself, but I kept my mouth shut. After all, I was only in the third grade. And besides, my tongue hurt too much to talk."[19]

One day, Dave's father came home from work carrying a curious item: a cylinder wrapped with a coil, an earpiece attached to it. "This is a radio," he told Dave. "Come over here and we'll listen. There's a program on right now." Dave didn't know what a radio was. His father explained that it let you listen to things from far away, without wires. Would it let him hear his Aunt Elsie up the street? he wondered. No, his father explained; you had to be at a broadcast station. Dave's father slipped the headset over his son's ears, then adjusted a piece of wire called the "cat whisker" on a piece of galena. Suddenly came something Dave would remember the rest of his life: the sound of a violin, "crisp and beautifully clear," as Fritz Kreisler played before a microphone at Union College.[20]

The little radio was a prototype for a set Dave's father had designed to sell to the public. At the time, many people built their own radio sets out of empty Quaker Oats containers. The Garroway radio was smaller and well-crafted, its delicate parts turned on a lathe. Unfortunately, General Electric, always careful to protect possible future product lines, forbade its employees from these kinds of outside endeavors. Still, what he called "the magic of radio" fascinated young Dave, even if he was unable to figure out why he could listen to someone play the violin, but he couldn't talk to Aunt Elsie.[21]

The Garroways' lives were soon disrupted by two developments. Dave's mother developed a mysterious inner-ear condition that often left her confined to a darkened room, her head in a clamp to keep her from developing nausea and pain, a condition that would affect her the rest of her life. Then, after nearly twenty years at General Electric, David Garroway lost his job. He soon got a new job designing industrial circuit breakers, but the family would have to move to Boston.

Dave Garroway wouldn't pay Schenectady a real visit again until 1954. Out of nostalgia, he drove out to what had been Grandfather Tanner's house. The current owners invited him in. Gone were the little things he remembered from childhood: the deer head on the wall, the lamp with beaded fringe. The rose garden his grandfather tended had been replaced with a concrete garage. At the site of the chicken farm, a huge poplar tree grew through the ruins of the cottage. The tree was "so big around that I couldn't even get my arms around it. That's how old I am!"[22]

In Boston, stability seemed out of reach. The job Dave's father had taken seemed in ongoing jeopardy, and the family moved several times. "It almost sounds as though we couldn't pay our rent," Garroway mused.[23]

Dave found escape from those troubles through his education. He found Boston-area schools wonderful and felt engaged by his schoolwork, his enjoyment stifled only by the occasional stern teacher. A tedious geography class had been made bearable by its third floor vantage point, from which students could watch a house being built next door. One day a worker knocked over a bucket of tar and the house caught fire. The children rushed to the windows. The teacher ordered them away. "Every one of you!" she roared. The students went back to their seats "like cowed animals," Garroway remembered. As the flames crackled, as fire engines screamed to the scene, the teacher glared at the abashed children, not even making them study. "She had more sense than that," Garroway said. Just making them miss the fascinating scenes outside was enough. "Oh, I wasted an awful lot of hours' worth of hate on her."[24]

Even with the occasional stern teacher, young Dave's mind was developing and expanding. He was also realizing that he liked to be alone. One of his favorite pastimes was to take a few books to Mount Auburn

Cemetery, between Cambridge and Belmont. There, he would find the gravesite of someone he admired, then sit on the grass by the grave and read. He found particular contentment by the gravesite of Henry Wadsworth Longfellow, which had a grassy area that felt like a couch. "It was very peaceable there," Dave remembered. "I liked being alone with him."[25]

Dave's introversion didn't come from dislike of people. Instead, he felt so many interests beckoning, with new ones always in the wings, and those proved much more fascinating to him. When someone gave him a few foreign stamps, it sparked a brief fascination with philately. Soon after, a family friend gave him a huge stamp collection, full of early American and British stamps. After looking up the stamps in reference books, Dave figured the collection's value at around $6,000. Knowing his family needed money, Dave selected about $1,000 worth of stamps and put them in an envelope, headed for a stamp dealer downtown. Somewhere along the way, the envelope disappeared. He searched everywhere but could not find it. This was the first of the occurrences throughout his life that Dave would call "the unexplainables."[26]

Another lifelong interest began in Boston. The Garroways' landlord lived in a large house full of interesting items. The most fascinating to Dave was a Bausch and Lomb microscope that he considered a work of art. He admired not only its features – the revolving nosepiece, the big eyepiece – but the precision that went into its creation. He yearned to own the great instrument. One day, he told the landlord that he would mow the lawn for two years if he could get the microscope after the first year. The landlord agreed, and both parties kept their ends of the bargain.

The microscope opened a new world to Dave, as he recalled, and even on days when pushing the lawnmower seemed like torture, he never regretted making the deal. Though he would eventually own more expensive and more sophisticated scientific instruments, he insisted he never saw half as much through those instruments as he did through that first microscope. On his eleventh birthday, he received his first telescope, and his ability to look outward matched his ability to look inward. Dave mounted the telescope on a tripod and modified it into a powerful instrument that let him see Jupiter's moons and Saturn's rings "as clearly as though they were cast in crystal before you." Even though his collection would someday include observatory-grade instruments, Dave said "I saw more stars through that one-inch scope than any of the others."[27]

Whether it was microscopes, telescopes, stamp collecting or any other hobby, Dave needed something to do with his hands, something he could do alone, the onset of a lifelong trait. In the basement of their home in Belmont, he built his first workshop, the first of the workshops he would set up wherever he lived.[28]

One particular gadget remained a fascination. The day when his father put the headset over his ears, and the sound of Fritz Kreisler's violin came in through the ether, had sparked something. Soon after, when the family was visiting Boston, Dave asked if they could go to WNAC, whose studio was just around the corner from where they were. He wanted to see the announcer say the station's call letters into the microphone. Up the building's stairs they went. As they arrived, a man sitting in a booth with a microphone was just about to say the four magic letters. Dave was elated. "It seemed a miracle that one man's voice could fly into space in all directions. I'm afraid I was hooked right there."[29]

That afternoon, Dave cleared space in his closet to make his own announcer's booth, hanging blankets on the walls to simulate the sound dampeners he had seen in the WNAC studios. He and a friend from a block over strung a wire between their houses and connected buzzers to each end. Every morning they signed on and, in Morse Code, identified themselves and gave a weather report. When they soon realized they didn't have much to say to each other, the experiment withered.[30]

Even with that, radio's siren song continued to fascinate Dave. He watched his father build a super-regenerative receiver from a set of plans. The radio's tubes, "big as a light bulb, almost," were the first items they bought for the project. Once the set was complete, Dave recalled, it worked beautifully.[31]

2

In 1926 David Garroway's employer reassigned him to Philadelphia. The family moved into a duplex next to a railroad switching yard in nearby Landsdowne. The train yard fascinated Dave: railroad workers expertly moving cars around to assemble giant freight trains, moving them with just the right speed to make the cars couple; the occasional car traveling too fast and derailing, which brought headaches to the engineers and amusement to young Dave. The railroad itself went past his junior high school, so Dave often walked the track each morning, learning how to do it without falling off. He had to do it with one ear open, ready to leap aside if workers came through on hand-operated work cars. "They cared nothing for anybody," he remembered. "If you forgot they were on the track too, you were as likely to get smeared as not."[1]

Within a year Dave's father took a job in St. Louis with the Locke Insulator Company, which made insulators for high-tension electrical lines. It meant financial stability to a family that had struggled. In September 1927, the Garroways moved into a third-floor apartment in a handsome brick building in University City. From their balcony, the Garroways enjoyed a nice view of St. Louis, just to the east.[2]

Just after lunch on September 29, Dave and his classmates heard rain pounding the school's roof. The classroom had no windows, so they had no idea what was going on outside. When school ended for the day, the streets seemed oddly empty. Halfway home, Dave saw a group of people gathered around a radio. From them, he learned a tornado had devastated the city. Dave ran home, grabbed a pair of heavy rubber gloves, and hitched a ride to the middle of town. They couldn't get far in the automobile, so Dave got out and carefully threaded his way past fallen trees and hissing power lines. Any sense of adventure quickly dissolved as he heard the screams of those trapped in demolished homes. "Your curiosity is overtaken by your humanitarian feeling very quickly," he remembered. Dave spent the next several hours helping to free people, working well into the evening, "by which time the screams had ceased." Out of it, he said, came "a deeper respect for the incredible power nature has."[3]

The devastation of that day was an inauspicious introduction to a city for which Dave didn't feel much warmth. To him, the weather in St. Louis felt too hot in the summertime and didn't offer the sorts of cold, snowy winters he had loved in Boston. Worse, the air in town was fouled by smoke from local factories. He often fled to the nearby countryside just to get some fresh air.[4]

His hobbies continued to offer refuge. The one-inch telescope he had received on his eleventh birthday continued to offer endless fascination, "a marvelous help when things were bad, and a great delight when things were good." At thirteen he learned how to grind his own mirrors and used plans from *Amateur Telescope Making* to build his own six-inch reflector. His results, though imperfect, worked well enough. In later years, one of those self-made mirrors became the shaving mirror in his bathroom.[5]

That mirror served as a reminder of a lesson that self-constructed telescope taught him. Looking through the telescope at the heavens, he lost the "illusion of central position," the belief that one is the center of the universe. The best thing astronomy did for him, he later wrote, was providing perspective. "When you look out there to the moon and then the planets, the sun and the closest star, and see how far it is to the first way station, and how many way stations there are beyond that, well, you could only smile and if you believe in God, thank Him for letting you in on the big news." The hours he spent alone with a telescope were special. "Looking through a telescope is essentially another loner's occupation," he reflected. It brought "times very wonderful and sometimes very frustrating. But it's seriously a one-to-one relationship between you and the thing you are looking at."[6]

Astronomy was just one of the ways Dave explored science. For a time, he tinkered with chemistry sets. His parents didn't mind the sometimes-messy results. "They only checked to see that the combustible elements weren't so all-fired combustible they could blow the house across the state line," he remembered. When an experiment went wrong, his mother didn't say anything about the extra laundry she'd have to do or the strange smells coming out of the house. "It's nice to know you're learning," she told him.[7]

Other pursuits brought out a more competitive side. His father had discovered golf at age twelve, and his mother enjoyed hitting an orange ball called a "tiger" when the course was open to ladies. Dave's parents felt he needed to develop the habit of outdoor exercise, and insisted he take up golf. It took well. "Once the bug caught him it was no longer necessary to drive him to the course," the elder Garroway told a reporter in 1932. "The danger now is that it may soon become necessary to drive him away." Soon, Dave was playing rounds with the adults at the Normandie Golf Club. On weekends he joined a foursome match for a game of "dollar-dollar-dollar," at a dollar on the first nine, a dollar on the second nine, and a dollar on the overall score. Since they knew they would cancel out each other's bets if they played on opposing teams, the Garroways played together. "Dad was steady down the middle, and I usually had two or three birdies for picks," Dave remembered. The Garroways became known as a hard team to beat. To avoid confusion with his father, Dave was often called by his family nickname, Dick, in stories about the tournaments. Although Dave downplayed his own golf talents, claiming that learning the game at age eleven meant he learned to swing too late, he worked hard at it. The Garroways played the Normandie course two or three times a week. They played similar styles of golf, and often alternated for best scores.[8]

Dave believed his time on the golf course helped him develop an ability to tell the nature and character of people. "Put them on a golf course with me and I'll tell you all about them after two holes," he said. As a college player, Dave and his teammates watched golfers at the first tee, observing how each golfer interacted with his caddy, how he held the club, and all the other things each golfer did. Before a golfer took his first swing, each teammate estimated that golfer's final score and put quarters down as a wager. After each round, they asked the caddies for each golfer's final score, then settled up. "We were all pretty close," Garroway remembered. "Seldom missed by more than three or four strokes."[9]

Golf provided a safe outlet for Garroway's competitive nature. Others got him in trouble. In junior high school, Dave read a book about probability theory. A section about the odds in dice inspired him to learn how to shoot craps, and he began playing impromptu games against classmates in the boys' room. He eventually won enough money to buy a piano. One day when the family was away, he came out on the wrong end of a $450 wager and lost the piano. Worried about his family's reaction, Dave somehow won enough money to get the piano back. He confessed when they returned. "They laughed," he remembered. "Dad didn't think it was wrong to gamble at even odds, just a waste of time. But he thought if you were doing something where you had a better than even chance to win, as I did in craps...you weren't gambling, you were working."[10]

Dave's skills as a golfer and gambler helped bring in a little more money for the family as the Great Depression lingered. Decades later, he told his own son of how he took helping the family to another extreme during those lean years. At night, he sneaked out with a .22 rifle and shot out the porcelain insulators on power lines. The power company would have to replace the insulators, which were made by his dad's employer.[11]

The new University City High School building was almost complete. Dave spent that summer watching workers put final touches on the new building. He especially loved the school's elaborate new public address system. A console in the principal's office controlled the bells and loudspeakers all over the school. Messages could be sent to the entire school or to a single room. Radio programs could be patched in. Dave befriended the technician who installed the system, learning how the wiring and relays made it all work. The principal soon found out Dave knew the system well enough to repair it. "I had him in my back pocket with this electronic monster, which kept getting a little out of joint every few days," Dave remembered. "I'd get sent for, and it wasn't hard to fix." This knowledge, he said, kept him from getting kicked out of school after he was caught shooting dice in the principal's office.[12]

This relationship with the principal, which Dave likened to "favorite son" status, was his first taste of power. While power in itself didn't interest him, having the run of the school did. One day, Dave found a set of master keys, sneaked into a science lab and stole a bottle of mercury, then quietly returned the keys. He got away with it, but his conscience burned. A year later, a science teacher noticed a bottle of mercury was gone. "I didn't say very much," Garroway remembered, "but felt guilty as hell, mostly because I was." That guilt ended any interest he had in power.[13]

Nevertheless, mischief still beckoned. After he learned how to pop locks open, he sneaked to the garage of his apartment building, popped the padlocks on the sixteen garage doors, and randomly reattached hasps to different locks. He then retreated to an upstairs window to watch the confusion at daybreak. "I can tell you, it was a madhouse," he wrote.

Since most of the victims knew of Dave's reputation as a tinkerer, he kept a low profile for the next few days.[14]

Not all of his tinkering led to bedlam. As part of a contest each Christmas, Dave designed and installed elaborate lighting displays outside the family's third-floor apartment. His 1928 entry took top prize in the children's class, winning him $50 in gold. The following Christmas, his entry was a runner-up and good enough to win the family an urn percolator.[15]

His love for automobiles continued. With a friend, he bought his first car, a Model T that cost them $20. Together, they rebuilt it. "We had it all ready to go when it developed a masterful shimmy and then came apart, nut by nut," he remembered. Although Dave's dad knew the likely problem, he let the boys figure it out themselves. "He didn't want to cheat us of the blissful feeling of accomplishment that came when, by trial and error, we finally breathed mobility into the handsome old thing."[16]

The stage was another discovery. Dave acted in a few plays and became president of the Drama Club, but found stage plays "kind of a bust." He much preferred the company of a fellow Drama Club member, Robert F. Dick, an amateur magician. One summer, Robert borrowed his family's Buick and the two ninth-graders, along with an assistant, spent six weeks touring their act through Missouri, Arkansas and Oklahoma. The troupe would come into a town, paste up some billboards, rent space in a church or an empty bar, and hope some curious townspeople would stop in. Invariably, the patrons were met by the pigeons that Bob kept for the act. "Bob, I think, paid the pigeons more than he paid us," Garroway wrote. "Or he fed them better, anyhow." Bob helped Dave develop a mind-reading act. Dave turned a pair of pajamas into a costume, donned a homemade turban, and read minds as the Swami Uganda. After the show, they'd catch a nap on the floor of the hall they'd hired, then go off to the next town. If they made enough money for gas and a bite to eat, it was a success.[17]

By this time Dave Garroway was maturing into a handsome young man, the features that would be familiar to a generation of viewers already apparent: the strong chin and jawline, intense but twinkling eyes behind round eyeglasses, his slender frame reaching his full height of six feet two inches. Appearances in school plays, a light opera, and the magic show helped him build a stage presence and an ease with performing.

For all his confidence on stage, though, Dave could not build confidence in things typically closer to a young man's heart. "I was scared stiff of girls," he said. Dave had started to notice them while living in Boston. He yearned to talk casually with them, the way he saw other boys doing. But he couldn't. Instead, he turned green, unable to break the ice. "It was all right if they said the first word," he said, "but they never seemed to do that." Unable to work up the courage to speak to one girl he particularly liked, he wrote her an unsigned note, asking her to meet him in the auditorium's projection booth after school. He slipped the note inside her locker, then stood a short distance away, trying to look nonchalant. The girl went to her locker, gave the note a quick read, then crumpled it and tossed it aside.[18]

The older Dave got and the more his friends started to date, he felt he should do likewise. Not sure how to begin, he asked a girl he knew to teach him the proper way to get a date. She taught him all the things to do: pick her up at her house, hold the door for her, buy the movie tickets, take her for a grilled cheese sandwich and a Coke after the movie, and then take her home. At the end of the session, Dave confessed that he didn't know if he should kiss the girl goodnight or not. "I can't handle that one for you," she said.

On a tip from her, Dave asked out a pretty blue-eyed girl from school. They went to see *Hell's Angels* at a movie theater. Everything seemed to be going well. "I could hear low bass violas playing in the distance and tiny piccolos a hundred miles up," Dave remembered. Thus inspired, he asked her out a couple nights later. She turned him down, for her steady boyfriend, Jack Norwine, was back in town. Dave was crushed. He was in love with her, and carried her picture in his wallet. Sometimes she would go out with him while Jack was away. This hurt even worse. As Dave remembered, she "didn't help any by keeping it faintly alive." Sometimes when Jack was visiting her, Dave would park three or four houses away, sit in his car, and stare at Jack's Model A roadster, thinking about Jack being inside with the girl Dave loved. "I recognized that it was romantic love," Dave said, "but I couldn't deny that it was real. Because the tears came coursing down my cheeks. You can't even see through them." Worse, Jack wasn't the only young man in her life. Each afternoon as school ended, she would climb aboard a big blue Rolls-Royce driven by a scion of a wealthy local family. Unable to compete, Dave sat on the steps of the school looking on, envy chewing at him, both over the car and over the girl who "couldn't see me for a low-grade bean." Someday, Dave vowed, he'd have a car like that.[19]

A few years later Dave saw an ad in the newspaper for a Rolls-Royce. He went to the garage to inspect it, and bought the rough-looking car for $75. Once he got it home, something seemed familiar about it. With a razor blade, Dave started scraping through the layers of paint, eventually finding a layer of robin's egg blue. A check of the registration confirmed it was the same car he used to see pull up outside the school every day. Dave painted the car aqua. "It revolts me to think of it now," he confessed years later. "I did awful things to that car. Maybe it was a desire to chop it up, destroy it."[20]

Girls continued to perplex him. He later recalled that when he was about to enter college, "I realized that something was not maturing normally in me sexually." He just wasn't very interested. "I would have liked to have slept with some of the girls, but not with the ones I was fond of …because you didn't take nice girls like that to bed. What you slept with were the other kind." Dave didn't want to sleep with anybody like that. "Besides, the closer I got to it, the less I needed it, it seemed." When a girl who had undressed for him asked what he wanted to do, "I would say, half laughing and half not, nothing really. 'Put your clothes back on.' Somehow, they didn't think that was funny." Dave would still be a virgin when he left St. Louis.[21]

Even if Dave couldn't figure out romance, he was successful elsewhere. Years of coaching from his dad had turned him into an excellent golfer. The two men became fixtures of the annual Father-Son Tournament held each year by the St. Louis District Golf Association. This tournament operated on an "alternate-stroke" format, with each member of a pair taking turns playing the same ball. It baffled some entrants, but was perfect for the Garroways. The two men played a similar game and were of similar ability, although Dave's height made him a better driver, and his father's experience gave him more finesse and more skill at putting. Father and son also had a rule: no matter how well or poorly they played, they would say as little as possible to each other.[22]

It worked. The Garroways won the inaugural tournament in 1930 and took the next four annual tournaments. They also played in doubles tournaments, and sometimes against one another, with father defeating son by one stroke to win the 1933 club championship. When fellow Normandie members developed a game called "bridge-golf," combining the rules of contract bridge with golf, the Garroways joined in the fun.[23]

The Garroway men claim another golf title. (Paris Day collection)

    Dave went on his own adventures in match play. Eliminated in the first round of the 1933 Missouri State Amateur, he was invited to play in a "consolation flight." The winner got a silver cup, while the runner-up got a set of Bobby Jones clubs. Dave wanted the clubs, so he talked his opponent into playing each other's balls. The switch made them play harder. Dave brought home the clubs. After Dave became a student at Washington University in St. Louis, he joined its fledgling golf team, and was there when it was officially adopted as a minor sport in 1934. Dave represented Washington University at the national intercollegiate golf tournament for three years.[24]

Golf was one of the few ways Dave felt he fit in at Washington University. Most of his classmates joined fraternities and sororities, but as a self-described loner, he didn't like the idea of pledging. He already knew most fraternity members from when they were high school classmates. He was content to live with his family, two blocks from campus. His refusal to pledge left him branded a "barbarian," not invited to dances or other social events on campus. "This embittered me somewhat, a lot in fact," he later wrote. "And I signed off from my contemporaries." Instead, Dave spent hours in the university library reading everything he could. He signed up for extra courses, earning enough credits to choose from majors in English, fine arts, abnormal psychology or history. "I got over the bitterness when I found out how much fun it was to go to class," he said. There, he didn't feel ostracized. Sometimes the courses he auditioned led to lasting connections. One instructor, art teacher Fred Conway, helped Dave understand the artistic mindset, which differed from his own scientific mindset. Conway became his "principal instructor, I would say, in life. He taught me more about living than any instructor I had in college, before or after."[25]

Another interaction led to another of Garroway's "unexplainables." He mentioned to a psychology professor that in high school, he won some money in a dice game. That night, during a sleepwalking spell, he had put the money in a book. The next morning, he couldn't find the book anywhere. The professor put Dave under hypnosis, helping him reconstruct the moments when he hid the money. When Dave woke up the next morning, there was dirt on the soles of his feet and smudges on the bed sheet. Next to him was a book. Inside the book was the missing money.[26]

Other encounters were less happy. Dave signed up for an astronomy course, hoping for a chance to see the stars through a beautiful six-inch Alvan Clark telescope in the university's observatory. Unfortunately, the instructor "hated astronomy with a thoroughness that must have taken all of her life to accumulate," and the class never visited the observatory. Dave was stunned to find the magnificent telescope sitting in a room with an unlocked door and broken windows, open to the elements, an easy target for thieves. When he voiced his concerns to the instructor, she "put me down like a ton of bricks." The self-taught astronomer's hopes for an easy A gave way to the reality of a C. "She didn't like smart-aleck students," Garroway remembered. "Or even smart students, in a subject she abhorred."²⁷

In that class, Dave developed a crush on a girl who sat in the back row. Adele Dwyer "had a twinkle in her eye that wouldn't go out," Dave remembered. He couldn't work up the nerve to talk to her. One November evening, the class went out to the countryside, away from the bright lights of the city, to watch the Lyrid meteor shower. On their backs, watching the show overhead, Dave worked up the courage to chat with her. They struck up a friendship and went out a few times, but weren't an item. A couple of years later, she told Dave she was engaged. This broke Dave's heart; he had become very fond of her. Eight months later, she called. The engagement was off. "I'm not busy New Year's Eve. Are you doing anything?" As Dave said, "I'm absolutely sure that that was the happiest moment of my life. *Was* and *is*. I was more delighted in that instant than I have ever been." They remained a couple until he graduated in 1935. He was twenty-one. Right after graduation, the family headed for Boston, where Dave's father had a new job.²⁸

Garroway's feelings toward Washington University in St. Louis were complicated. Stung by his ostracism from social life and frustrated by opportunities he felt closed to him, his resistance manifested itself before graduation. He refused to pay the required $5 to have his photograph in the university yearbook. Yet he continued to play on the Washington University golf team after graduation, participating in national tournaments in 1935 and 1936.²⁹

In 1960, a writer for the Washington University alumni magazine contacted Garroway about an interview. He warned the writer off; his comments wouldn't be that favorable. When the writer persisted, a quarter-century's worth of resentments poured out. The fraternity system upset him a great deal, Dave said, because he couldn't afford to both join a fraternity and play golf, and his refusal to participate left him "a social outcast. It ostracized me." For that, he held the university itself responsible. Its support of a fraternity-sorority system, a non-campus phenomenon, made this possible. "The school has control over whether or not the student belongs to such a system," Garroway said. "I believe the system should be abolished."

His frustrations spilled over into the academic realm. "I did not have to work hard enough," Garroway charged. Instead of a stimulating environment, he felt Washington University had given him "a continuation of high school," which could have been fixed "by employing competent educators." His feelings, he admitted, had governed his relationship as an alum. "I have been concise and not overly cordial in my relations with the University because, frankly, I shall never forget the quality of education which I purchased there. I hope it is much better today." Six years later, however, Garroway appeared on a quiz-bowl program as part of an alumni team and helped win $15,000 for the university.[30]

After Dave graduated from Washington University, the family decided to move back to Boston. The senior Garroway arranged a transfer to his employer's office there, and that summer the family moved to Watertown.

Through a connection his father had made, Dave was hired by the Chance Piston Ring Company of Kansas, which sent him a selection of its products and appointed him the company's sales manager for the New England area. The grand title seemed like a joke to him, but with all the earnestness he could muster, Dave visited garages and auto supply houses, doing his best to convince mechanics and managers to try Chance piston rings. It quickly became frustrating. Every shop already had a favored piston ring, so an upstart brand from a factory in the Midwest didn't interest anyone. Dave quickly became convinced it was a dead-end job, and not even a visit to the company's annual convention in Missouri helped his prospects. "I never did unload one single piston ring on anybody. Not one," he remembered. "Couldn't even give the samples away, in fact."[31]

As Dave's prospects as a piston ring salesman grew more hopeless, another family connection came to the rescue. Fred Tilden had been a friend of Dave's father since childhood; they had served together in the National Guard, and their families had remained close over the years. One of Tilden's interests was the English language, and he had written a small, self-published paperback book. *You Don't Say...Or Do You?* listed about five hundred commonly mispronounced words, used within the context of a story told in brief chapters. On the left-hand page, the individual chapter of the book was printed. On the right was a list of the commonly-mispronounced words, along with their correct pronunciation.

Tilden wanted schools to order his book, and he employed a clever strategy for building interest. He would show up at a school and ask to see the principal, knowing that a visit from an intelligent stranger might be an interesting break in the principal's otherwise dull day. After some small talk, Tilden showed the principal a copy of the book, and offered a deal: if the principal could read a certain sentence from the book without mispronouncing a word, every teacher in the school would get a free copy of the book. The principal would take the wager, only to fumble a word. His point made, Tilden then explained how the book was put together and how to use it correctly. Then he left a box of books with the principal. Give one to each of your teachers, he said. Let them examine it for a few days. Then they can either bring it back, or buy it for fifty cents. With that strategy, Garroway figured Tilden got into ninety five percent of the schools he visited and sold about half the books he brought.[32]

Tilden hoped to move into bigger territory, but he needed an assistant. He offered Dave a sales position. Borrowing his father's Buick roadster, Dave followed Tilden as they ranged through the cities of New England and sold books. In time, Dave was earning $100 in profit per week, nearly what he had made playing golf.

Having conquered New England, the two salesmen saw New York as a ripe market. There were five boroughs and dozens of schools, and the prospect of months and months of profitable work covering each one. They based themselves out of the YMCA on 63rd Street in Manhattan, working the schools in the daytime and sleeping on cots at night. Their efforts had "books cooking gladly in the schools. It seemed to presage a couple years of profitable work."[33]

3

One evening, tired from a day of going from school to school, Dave stopped by the YMCA's front desk to check his mail before heading to his room. A familiar face from St. Louis caught his eye. It was Jack Norwine, who had dated the girl Dave had lusted after. Surprised to see each other, the two men renewed their acquaintance. Norwine couldn't stay long, for he was on his way to play bridge. They needed a fourth. Did Dave play, too?

For the rest of the night, Dave and Jack and a few others played bridge and drank whiskey in the apartment of Jack's friend Barbara Biermann. At 1:30 a.m., Biermann called a halt to the game. She had to be at work the next morning. "I have to fire twenty page boys at NBC and hire twenty more."

Suddenly Dave was mesmerized. "Friend, when she said NBC, those three letters came out as though they were gongs that Big Ben strikes, or even louder," Garroway remembered. "I could feel them and their tune."

"NBC?" Dave asked.

"Yes," Barbara responded. As assistant manager of guest relations at the network, she was in charge of hiring and firing page boys. In the morning, she explained, she would fire twenty of them and hire their replacements.

"Nineteen," Dave replied.

Biermann was puzzled. "What do you mean?"

"You just hired me."

He was dead serious. He didn't know at that time that NBC recruited employees in vital positions through the page system. Nor did the meager salary of $15.55 a week bother him. Dave Garroway just wanted to be affiliated with the great network, and he wanted to live in New York. They talked the rest of the night, then reported to 30 Rockefeller Plaza in the morning.[1]

Dave Garroway could hardly believe his eyes. Out of the elevator stepped Lowell Thomas, one of the most famous men in broadcasting, whose newscasts were a staple of the NBC network. Now, that famous voice was directed to him. "Where am I this morning?" Starstruck, his eyes bulging, Garroway grasped for words. The floor's chief page, DeVere Engelbach, came to the rescue: "Studio 3F, Mr. Thomas." The great broadcaster turned and walked toward his studio.

"Gee," Garroway stammered. "That was Lowell Thomas."

It was a heady start to his first day. Only a few hours before, he had been a book salesman talked into being a fourth at a bridge game. That morning, Biermann had taken Garroway to be fitted for his page uniform. From there, it was off to training, learning how NBC wanted its pages to walk, act, answer questions from guests. After an inspection by a supervisor, Garroway was assigned to the third floor of the Studio Building, where Engelbach would train him in his duties, including the finer points of directing the network's famous people to their studios. In time, Garroway wouldn't get as starstruck when he saw famous people get off the elevator, but he never really lost all of his awe. "Not all of it," he confessed decades later. "I'm still impressed with big-name people, just a little bit. And I hope I never lose it."[2]

Garroway's sudden change of employment, however, left Fred Tilden spending the next few days trying to retrieve the money and returned books from the schools Garroway had visited. The old family friend didn't hold it against him, though. "It was the last of Fred's many kindnesses for me," Garroway remembered, for Tilden died soon after.[3]

Advancement came quickly. After two months as a page, Garroway became a guide. Six months later, he was training new guides. This role literally opened doors for him. As a trainer, Garroway could now walk into any office that intrigued him, claiming he needed to know what happened in there so he could explain it on the tours. Along the way, he befriended several NBC employees, some of them in such important places as the master control room on the fifth floor.[4]

Not only did he meet famous people who worked for NBC, but sometimes celebrities not affiliated with the network wanted a tour. Kirsten Flagstad, a famous soprano, put in one such request. Garroway, who had become fond of attending the Metropolitan Opera and was so enraptured by his first hearing of *Tristan* that he could hardly move for five minutes, was chosen to give her a personal tour. When Flagstad thanked RCA chairman David Sarnoff for the tour, she made kind mention of the young man who had guided their visit. After that, Sarnoff had Garroway lead his personal tours, and "we became chatty friends," he remembered. "Good fellow to know, I figured."[5]

Most of the time, those whom Garroway showed around were tourists and the otherwise curious who wanted a glimpse inside the network. To these groups of thirty-five or so, Garroway showed off the studios and technical facilities within the RCA Building, offering what he called "about an hour's worth of odd erudition." Sometimes when a broadcast or rehearsal was in progress, Garroway brought the tour group into an observation booth above the studio, where they could look through a soundproofed window at the action below. On another part of the tour Garroway demonstrated techniques that produced sound effects: crinkling cellophane to mimic the sound of a crackling fire, a pair of coconut halves making the sound of horses' hooves. One tour stop let each person speak into a microphone and see their voice on an oscilloscope. Sometimes they would be recorded. Seldom, Garroway remembered, did anyone like the sound of their own voice when they heard it played back.[6]

Page duties also meant helping with live broadcasts. None were more prestigious than those of the new NBC Symphony Orchestra, conducted by Arturo Toscanini. The network took great pains to spare the notoriously temperamental maestro anything which might annoy him, designating a special elevator and certain corridors for the conductor, and changing tour routes to keep the public away from him.[7]

Garroway sometimes served as the "stand-in" page for Studio 8H, the giant auditorium studio where Toscanini's performances would originate. As stand-in page, he held the door so no one could leave or enter mid-performance. In those hours Garroway watched the great man and his orchestra prepare for their on-air debut, and he was present during the orchestra's first network broadcast on Christmas night, 1937. Hundreds of audience members in movable chairs lined the studio floor, while scores more watched from the balcony. Each guest received a program, printed on silk to prevent the sound of rustled pages from fouling the broadcast or, worse, annoying the maestro.

Still, the unexpected could happen. One night, in the middle of a concert, a woman in the middle of the audience began to feel sick. Unable to escape, she retched on the studio floor. The smell spread through the studio. Toscanini, not missing a move with his baton, turned and shot a glare toward the audience. Quickly, quietly, the pages grabbed sand buckets and cleaning items. At intermission, they put the stricken woman in a wheelchair, a cloth bag over her head to hide her embarrassment as she was wheeled out. The pages then cleaned up the mess.[8]

Sometimes the unexpected things Garroway witnessed came from the performers themselves. Fred Allen's comedy show also originated from the cavernous 8H, and one night his guest was "Shipwreck" Kelly, famous for sitting atop a flagpole. Stagehands installed a flagpole in the studio for Kelly's act. Rehearsals had gone fine, but during the live broadcast, Kelly began chatting with an attractive young woman in the audience. He missed his cue from Allen. Too late, Kelly realized he was on and replied with the wrong lines. The show's director went behind the curtain, yelling out Kelly's correct lines so the show could continue. After the show, the annoyed director left Kelly atop the flagpole, unable to climb down, still trying to figure out what had gone wrong.[9]

New York offered much to the young man from Schenectady. In his off hours, Garroway wandered through the galleries at the Metropolitan Museum of Art and saw performances at the Metropolitan Opera. Even the people of the great city – a city he considered "haughty, so full of life, and yet so full of a serene hauteur that made her seem untouchable, almost" – could fascinate him, a scene unto themselves. He might sit on the great steps of the Metropolitan Museum, or a bench near the Plaza Hotel, or the lobby of the Algonquin, or even squeeze into a niche between the Hotel Astor and a shoe store in the great crossroads of Times Square, and spend hours just watching people walk by, imagining where they were from. In the upstairs apartment he shared with other NBC pages, Garroway drilled a hole in the floor just large enough to allow a view into a nightclub on the first floor. The "Garroway No Cover Charge Floor Show Viewer" let the young men lie on their stomachs and peer into Leon and Eddie's to watch the nightly shows. He even had time to play a little golf, winning a June 1937 tournament organized by the NBC Athletic Association.[10]

As a youngster in Boston, Dave Garroway had been fascinated by watching the announcer at WNAC speak into the microphone. Now, he wanted that same job. He saw his opportunity in an announcers' class NBC offered to pages and guides.[11]

The course required four hours of classes each week. Students were drilled on anything and everything an announcer might face. They practiced foreign languages, refined their diction, learned to correctly read copy, mastered musical terms. Since an announcer's voice was the personification of the network itself, excellence was demanded. Those who passed could get hired by NBC affiliates around the country, or even as a junior network announcer. Garroway enjoyed the course, imagining himself becoming one of those voices that spoke for the great network.[12]

Those thoughts of glory were quickly dashed. A 100-watt station in West Virginia needed an announcer, and Garroway tried out. He was twenty-fourth of twenty-five applicants. Chief announcer Pat Kelly assured him it wasn't the error Garroway thought it was. "That's just where you stand," Kelly said. Garroway retreated, feeling he didn't have the talent to be an announcer. "I had no natural voice, no deep baritone voice, which would have been a great advantage," he remembered. "Just an average voice, average speaking voice." He reflected years later, "Right there I should have been discouraged, but I just couldn't believe I was that bad." Instead, he developed a plan. Hard work, late hours, and access to NBC's vast facilities would give him what nature didn't.[13]

Each evening after work, when the studios were mostly empty, Garroway went into one of the smaller radio studios on the eighth floor and adjusted the microphone. He then went to the third floor and connected the studio's feed to a wax cylinder recording machine. Garroway started the recorder, went back to the eighth-floor studio, and read whatever copy he could find: practice copy from the announcing class, commercial scripts from other shows, or anything else that was handy. Twenty minutes later, he went to the third floor and listened to the result. "It's difficult to do it yourself, and monitor it yourself, and judge yourself," he remembered. "But who else could I ask to do it?" For months on end, Garroway spent three to five hours reading pages and pages of copy, listening to himself, developing his style, turning himself into an announcer. To him, the style most announcers used didn't work so well, and he labored to avoid developing what he called the "hundred-watt chant" of most announcers. "I wanted to sound like a human being and still get the message across," he said.[14]

He got another chance. KDKA, a 50,000-watt station in Pittsburgh, told Pat Kelly that the station was one announcer short. No one at the station was a good candidate. Kelly had several announcing class stu-

The aspiring network announcer, 1938.
(American Heritage Center, University of Wyoming)

dents ("five or six whizzes in the class and twenty ordinary kids," Garroway remembered, placing himself among the latter) try out for Derby Sproul of KDKA. Dan Russell, who instructed the course, had each come before the microphone and speak. At the end of the audition, the phone rang. Russell answered. A moment later, he looked at Garroway with astonishment. "They want you upstairs." Garroway couldn't believe his ears. He and a second candidate went upstairs to meet the visitor from Pittsburgh. The two announcers made recordings that Sproul could take back to KDKA. Station manager Al Nelson listened to the recordings and liked Garroway's style, which an NBC publication later likened to "the well-known Ford Bond." It earned him an on-site audition.[15]

On the morning of March 3, 1938, Garroway walked into the KDKA office. The audition began with some routine announcing chores and a couple of news items. Then Nelson asked, "Can you ad-lib?" Garroway said he could.

"Okay. You're covering a parade."

Smoothly, confidently, Garroway set a scene of crowds lining the streets, bands marching, cars and carriages bearing smiling honorees and dignitaries, his words painting a vivid picture. He looked through the window at the engineer, who scratched his head and gave him a "keep going" signal before disappearing for a moment. Garroway kept going, filling time by demonstrating a little of the French and German he had picked up, the tough-to-pronounce names from classical music he had mastered in Dan Russell's class. A few minutes later the engineer came into the studio, Garroway still in full song. "Okay, knock it off," he said. The audition had only been seven minutes. Nelson and his associates had left a few minutes before, their minds made up. No one had told Dave to stop. Garroway was KDKA's newest hire, his $35 a week salary more than double his pay in New York. That afternoon, he announced his first program, then left for Boston to visit his mother. KDKA promptly issued a press release announcing that Garroway "is single and is the author of a book on pronunciation and sounds."[16]

As Garroway would later tell it, his debut as an announcer did not go well. He had been given rushed training on how to run the turntable used for playing commercial announcements. A fifteen-minute program was coming to a close. Garroway turned on the microphone, gave the identification, and then played the commercial. As his hand came down, he hit the arm of the turntable and made the record skip. "Shit," he said. Then he realized the microphone was still on. Although he heard about it the next day, he remembered no fuss was raised over it. "They were a kindly crew down there," he said.[17]

Garroway quickly found a room near the Duquesne University campus, then moved into an apartment in the Squirrel Hill neighborhood, "over a one-car garage, so you can imagine how big it was," he remembered. "But it was all mine." He also bought an "artillery-wheeled" Buick coupe to get around in. The car had seen better days, and when he drove it to Boston, he worried it wouldn't make the trip back. He left the Buick there. Back in Pittsburgh, he bought a secondhand Packard, a model nicknamed "the yardstick" because it was reputed to be the car other Packards were measured by. The bright yellow car made Garroway look like he was living beyond his means. In reality, he had paid little for it and did his own maintenance. Working on it, he insisted, gave him as much pleasure as driving it.[18]

4

KDKA's newest announcer joined as the station prepared to move into new studios. A partnership with the *Pittsburgh Press* allowed KDKA to put a new studio in the *Press* building. Now announcers could give instant news updates and provide the latest developments during newscasts. If a celebrity or dignitary visited the *Press* newsroom, they could stop in the studio for an interview.[1]

This new broadcast facility opened in Garroway's second full week at the station. As the studio was formally opened, writer Maxine Garrison smashed a bottle containing water from Pittsburgh's three rivers against a microphone. During an inaugural program, Garroway roamed the newspaper's telephoto room, interviewing the paper's chief photographer about how the photo they were receiving was transmitted over the wires from Washington. He later talked to KDKA's chief technician and to a "newsreeler" who summarized the news. Though hired as a studio announcer, Garroway was now billed as "the Roving Announcer," going from place to place to talk with anyone, as host of a series titled *The Parade of the People*. Steadily, Garroway became an interviewer and newsman in his own right.[2]

Experience brought more opportunities. He hosted a two-hour Sunday morning program, *Happiness Trails*, which played recorded music. In between, Garroway offered suggestions for afternoon road trips, places to see and things to do. Other times, the Roving Announcer was on the scene at special events, one day originating special broadcasts from a custom-built booth at the Electric show, or the next covering the rededication of a community clock in a nearby town.[3]

Soon he had a new program: a quiz show called *You Don't Say*, inspired by the book. Previous press releases had mentioned Garroway's connection to the book, but when the radio program commenced, a Pittsburgh columnist stated he had written it under the pen name F.F. Tilden. Even though Garroway was two years removed from his sales job, the little book refused to die. On occasion, an advice columnist recommended a letter-writer send off to Garroway for a copy of the book, or a columnist repeated the embellished story of Garroway as author. Other times, Garroway gave away copies of the book to contestants on the program.[4]

On occasion Garroway's duties required personal appearances around the listening area, at church socials or club meetings or other gatherings. Once, he was asked to present *You Don't Say* to a church group in a nearby small town. Garroway arrived at the church at 7 p.m. to get set up. No one was there. Fifteen minutes later, the woman who had hired him for the church arrived. By 7:30 they had arranged all the chairs, set up the public address system, and were ready for the program, which was to begin at 8 p.m. At the appointed hour, there was no one in the audience. Things were no better an hour later. Garroway felt so sorry for the embarrassed woman that he gave back the $100 in appearance money.[5]

A few years before, Garroway was all but told to forget about an announcing career. Now he was hosting his own programs and earning praise in diction competitions. He volunteered with local charities, lending his voice to broadcasts on behalf of the Milk Fund. He had grown into a tall, serious-looking young man in wire-framed glasses, hair slicked down into the part he would carry for years, wearing a standard necktie.[6]

In June 1939 Garroway became KDKA's director of special events. Although he would still announce, now he would also oversee field work and remote broadcasts around the area, such as interviewing workers along the Pittsburgh riverfront as the first summer vacation packet departed, or talking to Civil War veterans gathered for a memorial concert.[7]

Not everything went so well. That July, Pittsburgh's Billy Conn fought Melio Bettina for the light heavyweight championship at Madison Square Garden in New York. Garroway had supervised the local station breaks during the network broadcast. Just as the fight announcer was about to present Conn as the new champion, Garroway went back to normal programming. The pre-emption of a hometown hero's triumph sparked local outrage. "Pittsburgh didn't hear its champion," local columnist Si Steinhauser complained the next day. "Garroway might have waited just one minute to give Conn a chance to be heard here. Perhaps he didn't realize it was a special event. Plenty of radio fans did and they're irate, and justly so."[8]

Sometimes the assignments put Garroway in more danger than he had bargained for. For one broadcast, he was to meet up with a man who was following the trail of Lewis and Clark, and was navigating the Allegheny River in a dugout canoe. Garroway was to join him in the canoe for the remote. Fitting all the remote equipment in the tiny boat was another matter. They had to unload half of the canoe to make everything fit. There was only room enough for Garroway, and the engineer had to stay on shore. Off they went into the Allegheny. As Garroway conducted the interview, the explorer struggled against the strong current. They finally had to request a tugboat to pull them to the other side of the river. At one point, Garroway thought about falling overboard as a gimmick. The idea passed when he realized the current was too swift, the Allegheny was very deep, and the transmitter he was wearing couldn't be taken off that quickly. "But temptation is a funny thing. It comes and goes very fast. And sometimes you act on it, as you know. I often wonder about that temptation." Another remote had Garroway aboard a Navy submarine submerged at the confluence of the Monongahela and Allegheny rivers, where the Ohio River begins. It was a windy, choppy day, and the dive was limited because there was a risk the submarine could get stuck in the mud, so it mostly stayed near a hollowed-out basin. The half-hour broadcast won a local award.[9]

Sometimes the risks came from above. KDKA was relocating its 700-foot broadcast antenna, and the station milked the event for all its spectacular worth. The ever-inventive Garroway decided to climb the tower and cover the removal of the first bolt, interviewing the workers overseeing the dangerous job. He would then ride down on the first section to be removed. It didn't take him long to regret it. With a forty-four pound transmitter strapped to his back, he found the climb long and difficult. He couldn't find a comfortable climbing position, so his climb became a slow crawl to the top. He had to start the climb well in advance of the 2 p.m. air time so he wouldn't be out of breath when the program began. He also hadn't anticipated how cold it would be at the top.

At last, the top section was unbolted and a crane started to lower it. Happy to be moving, Garroway began his narration, telling the audience that a better signal would soon come from KDKA's new tower. The tower segment had moved ten feet when a cable on the crane jumped a pulley. Everything suddenly stopped. Garroway dangled in midair in the cold winds while workers tried to fix the crane. Two hours later, with the tower segment lashed to another section of the tower, Garroway climbed down and the special broadcast ended. The next day, the crane had been repaired and Garroway rode down on the first section, then gave updates throughout the day as each section was lowered.[10]

Other special broadcasts weren't as death-defying. Three weeks later, Garroway climbed into a special swing to broadcast alongside riveters working on a new bridge on Wilmot Street over Panther Hollow, part of Mayor Cornelius Scully's city improvement plan. For another broadcast, he and newspaper reporter Charles Danver of the *Post-Gazette* helped clean the ornamental eagles on the Boulevard of the Allies. "If that Garroway feller ever tires of radio work," Danver wrote, "he shouldn't have much trouble qualifying as a trapeze performer – the way he shinnied up the pylon with a bucket in each hand and a microphone between his teeth. And one of the smoothest spielers I ever heard, rattling the whole thing off without a note." Another remote took him to Buhl Planetarium to tell listeners about the planetarium's sophisticated machinery, while another had him broadcasting live updates from the National Contract Bridge Championships at the William Penn Hotel.[11]

Sometimes the Roving Announcer's responsibilities stacked up. On Halloween night 1939, Garroway was helping get the KDKA studios in order for an event the following Sunday. Suddenly, he looked at a clock and saw he had to get to the William Penn to announce a program from there in fifteen minutes. He was dressed in overalls, which wouldn't be acceptable to wear at the function. Garroway grabbed an overcoat and put on a hat before he scrambled off to the hotel, where those present at the broadcast thought his outfit was a clever prank.[12]

Garroway's efforts were getting noticed and rewarded. That November, he won the H.P. Davis Memorial Announcer Award, which brought a gold medal, a $150 prize, and a mention in NBC's house publication. "Dave's progress as an announcer has been rapid and steady," read a notice in the *NBC Transmitter*, noting Garroway "has firmly established himself both professionally and personally as a lad of outstanding personality and intelligence."[13]

More opportunities followed. Garroway became master of ceremonies of *Greater Pittsburgh Speaks*, inspired by the popular *Information Please* program hosted by Clifton Fadiman. It became a local hit, and sometimes it threw him the unexpected. On a February 1940 broadcast, a team of meat salesmen competed against fish salesmen before a hundred invited guests. Garroway asked the first contestant a question. To his chagrin, the man pulled a master script from his pocket and gave the answer. He then passed the script to the next contestant, and the pattern continued throughout the quiz. The irritated Garroway ignored the script in the final round and made up new questions on the spot. The fish vendors won the match, which NBC's in-house publication quipped was "appropriate enough since it was just before Lent anyway."[14]

That April, a solar eclipse allowed the avid amateur astronomer to bring his knowledge to radio. Garroway chartered an airplane, put a transmitter aboard, and persuaded a staff member of the Buhl Planetarium to fly with him to transmit a live account of what the eclipse looked like, and compare notes with ground observers. "Well, everything was great, except the cloud cover was so thick we couldn't see the sun at all," Ted Kenney recalled in 1966. "But Garroway with that terrific encyclopedic mind of his just recounted step-by-step what an eclipse was supposed to look like. He even fooled the scientists."[15]

On another occasion, Garroway had to cover the Pittsburgh visit of the Twenty Mule Team in conjunction with a motion picture premiere. Garroway took the air at the appointed hour, only for him and the crowd outside the Palace Theater to see no mules and no stars. For one long, awkward hour Garroway kept talking. Every so often, he looked over at the engineer and silently signaled, "Don't they want it back?" No, Garroway was told; you're doing fine. As the hours passed, the crowd dwindled. Garroway talked about anything and everything he could think of. After three long hours of ad-libbing, some of the stars showed up, delayed because the mule team had broken down en route. Too tired for an interview, the stars went off to bed. The next day, Garroway rode through downtown atop the mule-drawn covered wagon, the antenna on his portable transmitter just clearing the trolley wires overhead.[16]

Other broadcasts brought brushes with greatness. A classical music series, *Musical Americana*, originated from KDKA with sponsorship from Westinghouse. The series brought distinguished conductors and performers to play alongside the Pittsburgh Symphony Orchestra, and eighty-eight NBC stations carried the program. As Garroway recalled, the program's producer didn't like the announcer hired for the commercials and contacted KDKA for help. All of the available announcers were auditioned, and Garroway won out. He was quickly fitted with a white tie and tails, and that evening he was sitting alongside Milton Cross, the famous announcer for the Metropolitan Opera's broadcasts from New York, whose broadcasts Garroway had listened to for years. After the broadcast, there was a three-hour intermission before the repeat for the West Coast. Cross invited the young announcer to dinner. Garroway, in awe, eagerly accepted. For the next thirteen weeks, the two went to dinner at the Hotel Schenley. Each time, Garroway ordered the same oyster soup that Cross ordered.[17]

Garroway's duties on *Musical Americana* occasionally extended beyond just reading the announcements. Pianists Arthur Austin Whittemore and Jack Lowe performed Ravel's *Bolero* but needed someone to play tympani. Quickly, Garroway learned how to play the big drum, right down to the ascending note at the end. He also found he could parlay his connections into opportunities for mischief. In May 1940, the high-profile Pittsburgh Club asked him to give a presentation. Garroway, presenting a radio-style program, worked from an *Information, Please* script. Everything went well until Garroway came to the commercial message, when his smooth, cool delivery suddenly deserted him. In desperation, he asked if anyone in the audience could help. A stocky man in glasses volunteered. No one thought much about this unremarkable-looking man until he began to read the script. As his voice, clear and with perfect diction, rang out in the room, the crowd went silent. Then they broke into applause as they realized it was Milton Cross, whom Garroway had planted in the audience as a practical joke.[18]

In between his high-profile assignments, and all the other special events – interviewing movie stars who visited town, carrying a live broadcast of the first solo flight by a fellow announcer who was taking flying lessons, hosting human-interest reports – Garroway remained an avid golfer. Since he mostly worked evenings, he had afternoons free to visit the course. At the Stanton Heights club he refined his game to the low seventies and high sixties. Golfing in black silk pajamas ("they are very cool and delightful, if you can stand the kidding, which never bothered me very much"), he defeated the state champion in the first round of the Pennsylvania Amateur, and the runner-up in the second round of the tournament.[19]

A routine chore wiped out any ambitions of a tournament-level golf career. One day at his apartment, he bent over to wash his hands. A sharp pain through his lower back sent him to the floor. On the way down, he hit his chin on the porcelain sink and knocked himself unconscious. He came to in the adjacent living room, unable to move. In time he was able to pull his telephone off a table and summon help. His doctor diagnosed him with a disc problem. Dave spent the next few weeks on crutches. When he was sufficiently healed to try golf again, his game wasn't the same. Dave finally gave up the game in 1954, although he would join the Winged Foot Golf Club in Manhattan and play recreationally with the likes of Tommy Armour and Claude Harmon. When Garroway's back finally healed years later, Harmon's son gave him lessons in California.[20]

For Garroway, KDKA was part of a plan to eventually make it to the full NBC network. The network's chief announcer, Pat Kelly, realized this. "He probably will succeed if he continues along the same high level," Kelly wrote.[21]

For a moment, that dream was about to come true. Comedian Ransom Sherman, whose *Club Matinee* program originated in Chicago, had an unusual sense of humor that fascinated Garroway. Although KDKA didn't carry the program, Garroway listened to it over a network feed at the station. He didn't want to miss a moment of Sherman's antics, even if it meant sacrificing time on the golf course.

On vacation in Chicago, Garroway attended a *Club Matinee* performance and met Sherman afterwards. At that same broadcast were representatives for an agency casting for a new soap opera. When one of them heard that Garroway was an announcer in Pittsburgh, they invited him to audition as their new program's announcer. Dave cut a recording and, a few days later, found out he had the job. He would have to go to New York, where the program would originate, to sign the paperwork. Dave's big dream seemed to be coming true. But since no one had played the audition record before sending it on to New York, they weren't aware of a slight whistling sound when Garroway said the sponsor's name, Crisco. When the record was played for the account executives in New York, that whistling sound cost Garroway the job.

Back in Chicago, a disappointed Garroway told chief announcer Bill Kephart what had happened. "Open your mouth," Kephart said. The announcer felt around Dave's teeth, then took him to a mirror. A small piece had broken off one of Dave's teeth, causing that whistle. Kephart told him to go to the dentist and have it repaired. Garroway was disappointed that the network opportunity was gone, but Kephart asked him to make an audition record they could keep on file if WMAQ had an opening. Garroway cut the disc and returned to Pittsburgh, not keeping it in mind. His eyes were on New York, not Chicago.

Two weeks later, the phone rang. It was Jules Herbuveaux of WMAQ. "We've got a place on our announcing staff. Would you like the job?" It was $65 a week, twice what he was making at KDKA, and WMAQ was a powerful NBC affiliate. As he looked back years later, Garroway thought of how the soap opera announcing job might not have lasted that long, and of the career successes that all began with an unfortunate whistle. That chipped tooth, he concluded, was the best break he ever had.[22]

Garroway had long been enamored of the number thirteen. He liked pointing out that he had been born on July 13, 1913, at 1 p.m. (or 13 o'clock), and had lived at 13 Van Velsen Street in Schenectady. With thirteen as his lucky number ("It's a number that he plays and hits," one newspaper notice said), Garroway insisted that his new life in Chicago begin on September 13.[23]

At NBC in Chicago, Garroway joined a large announcing staff that included such giants as Charlie Lyon, Ford Pearson, Louis Roman and Bob Brown. Garroway believed that as a new hire, he didn't have much chance of big-time work. He thought he'd caught a break when he tried out as an announcer for the daily *Alka-Seltzer News of the Air*. After a good audition, Garroway entertained visions of living a high life off the job's $720-per-week salary. One week in, he learned that he was merely a substitute for the vacationing Charlie Lyons. "But it was fun, being a rich man for a minute," he remembered.[24]

Garroway had wanted to expand into commercials. In those times, when sponsors maintained control over the programs, they also approved the announcers who delivered the commercial messages. Despite many auditions, Garroway was never selected. Parker Gibbs, who had left a musical career to get into radio production, auditioned Garroway for many commercials, but "the client always thought he was too casual and not enough 'hard sell.'"[25]

Most of Garroway's duties were not as prominent as the role of a program announcer. One of his most frequent chores was to give the network identification ("This is the National Broadcasting Company") at the end of a program, then push buttons on a box that sent a system cue to the network's affiliates to signal local breaks. For most programs this was not complicated. Paul Rhymer's continuous-plot comedy *Vic and Sade* was another matter. Garroway had to keep himself from laughing out loud during the program. Almost everyone involved in the program faced the same problem: actors in between their own lines, announcers listening in between cues, and even the staff in the control room. In time some of the program staff, including director Charlie Urquhart, Paul Rhymer, and their wives, became regular dinner guests of Garroway. Sometimes Rhymer and Garroway would do crazy things, like drive down Michigan Avenue in Garroway's green Rolls-Royce with dollar bills stuck in the bands of their straw hats, Paul with his feet hanging over the edge of the car, tossing dollar bills to passersby, people chasing after the car, Dave keeping just ahead of them so they couldn't catch up.[26]

Adele Dwyer, Garroway's friend from Washington University in St. Louis, had moved to Chicago about the same time he had. They got in touch and caught up. Adele had broken off an engagement, and the two began seeing each other. For Garroway, who had never expressed love to anyone, this was a new experience. He and Adele discussed their feelings, and they decided that being in their late twenties, they should do something about being single. Getting married, Garroway believed, was something you were expected to do when you had reached a certain point in your life, a mark of adulthood. Over the next several months, they talked about the prospects of life together, about their similarities as people, their shared experiences and philosophies.

In December, Adele went back to St. Louis to see her family. A couple of days before Christmas, she called Dave in Chicago. Alone in his apartment, caught up in holiday spirit, he proposed and she accepted. The engagement was formally announced by Adele's parents in mid-January. On February 15, 1941, Dave and Adele were married in a "full-size, formal wedding" at a St. Louis church. The next day, Dave was back to work at NBC.[27]

Dave and Adele moved into a large granite coach house built by a lumber tycoon. The huge garage had extensive hardwood decoration and room for twelve cars, a turntable, a gas pump, a lube rack, and a workshop. It had two apartments, one on the second floor and another on the third. Dave and Adele lived on the third floor, which Dave redecorated in a Hawaiian motif with grass matting on the floor, plants around the room, and walls painted the exact color of the walls of the Pump Room at the Ambassador East. (The publicity agent for the hotel, a Garroway friend, supplied the paint formula.) Dave installed his own workshop, where he and Adele cut gems and made jewelry. For Dave, it was the start of a happy era, "not ecstatic, but the nice kind of gentle happiness we hoped for," he remembered of those years.[28]

The special events programs Garroway had done for KDKA had occasionally been fed to the NBC network. Abe Schechter, NBC's Director of Network and Special Events, took note. On occasion, Garroway was assigned to help cover a special event for the network, such as the National Corn Husking Contest in Davenport, Iowa.

In September 1941, the American military staged a series of war games over 30,000 square miles in Louisiana. The maneuvers, which involved soldiers, armored vehicles and aircraft, tested the readiness of the American military on the eve of American involvement in the new world war. Correspondents were accredited to cover the action for major news outlets, and Dave Garroway was assigned to the Second Army. Colleague Bob Stanton, along with a field engineer, was assigned to the Third Army. The two were to file ten-minute reports each weekday afternoon during the thirteen days of the war games. In keeping with the games' realistic nature, the reporters wore uniforms and insignia, and could be captured by the opposing force. NBC had reporters on standby in case Garroway or Stanton were captured.[29]

Garroway was suddenly in the company of such distinguished reporters as John Charles Daly and Eric Sevareid of CBS. He remembered Sevareid's pieces as "beautifully written, poetic," while Daly "seemed to think he was in India, and most of his maneuvers were British in type." A couple of tents over were columnists Robert Kintner and Stewart Alsop. Garroway felt the reporters "looked down their long noses" at the young announcer from Chicago. He tried not to let it get to him. Instead he focused on his reports from the field, covering maneuvers in which tanks were represented by trucks with the word "tank" on the side and soldiers marched with brooms instead of guns. Garroway covered General Ben Lear's Red forces as they faced off against the Blue forces of General Walter Cramer. One day, Garroway happened to be at the broadcast headquarters at a local school when the Red soldiers captured General Cramer. Because Garroway had air time scheduled before the other correspondents, he got General Cramer on the air first, much to the consternation of the other reporters.[30]

That night the press moved to a new headquarters in a different

*On assignment for NBC, circa 1941.
(American Heritage Center, University of Wyoming)*

building. Garroway and two other correspondents were assigned to a large bedroom with three single beds as sleeping quarters. As the other two reporters snoozed away, Garroway had trouble sleeping, bothered by little crackling sounds. Suddenly, "in one magnificent piece," the entire plaster ceiling fell on them. The two other reporters awakened, startled and bloody and sputtering, while Garroway tried to get the dust out of his eyes. "I'm sure they thought this was my doing, too."[31]

Garroway noticed that a half-hour before an engagement, the Coca-Cola trucks would show up, ready to hand out cold drinks to the soldiers. He noted that although the security forces of both sides tried their best to hide what was coming, the Coke trucks somehow had good enough intelligence to beat them there. He had picked up on other things, too. During a break in the action near Shreveport, Garroway dined at a local restaurant, so taken by its remoulade sauce that he asked to speak to the chef. As they talked, the chef mentioned the war maneuvers had gotten on his nerves. In particular, the firing of a certain artillery piece kept him awake. Garroway made a bargain: teach me how to make that remoulade sauce, and I'll have the gun silenced. "I was safe in saying it,"

Garroway confessed a dozen years later, after he had dazzled countless dinner guests with the same recipe. "I knew this gun was to be moved the next day."[32]

One night Garroway, in a swampy location, described for the microphone how unpleasant it was to be in a war, marching through the muck. He heard the footfalls of an approaching company. At about 150 yards from him, they softly began to sing "Onward, Christian Soldiers." Garroway went silent and let the sounds of their voices and marching feet tell the story. The last of them marched past just as Garroway's air time was completing. He quietly did his close and went off the air. "It was as though we had planned the production for six months," he wrote.[33]

When the military staged similar maneuvers in North and South Carolina two months later, Garroway and two other NBC men covered those for the network, filing ten-minute reports each day for two weeks. What Garroway witnessed did not fill him with confidence about the nation's defenses. "After five days I find that the men in the field are not the only ones who've been learning lessons," he said. "Once again, our Army system of communications has more or less broken down, has been shown to be far below the standard that we must establish if we are to compete with other armies. Again, we have failed to provide that absolute essential for effective tank action – plenty of good old infantry to follow up the tanks and to hold the ground that they can capture but cannot keep."[34]

Back in Chicago, Garroway was put on WMAQ's overnight shift, with an occasional assignment to cover a special event, such as the national corn-husking contest. Sent to a farm near Tonica, he and another announcer reported from wagons drawn behind tractors, reporting back to another announcer who sat in a booth at the starting line.[35]

Overnight duties on a program dubbed the *Milkman's Music Hall* set a course for his future. Starting at 1 a.m. and lasting five hours, the *Music Hall* was a leisurely program, free in form. Not many people thought of radio at that hour. "If we were up," wrote Indiana columnist Paul Damai, "we were either reading in bed or trying to draw a jack in the middle of an ace-high straight." Gripped by insomnia one night, Damai tuned in the *Music Hall*, a program whose listing he had once viewed "with the detachment of looking at the Pole star, or as one would consider the crown jewels: very pretty, interesting, but totally unobtainable."

What Damai heard was a program created more or less on the fly, because they acted like no one was listening: the announcer reading from joke books, chatting with the engineer, and then playing a record. "They give vent to gales of laughter as they break said record in front of the mike." This could be followed by a half-hour concert "while they go out and smoke eight cigarets," Damai speculated. "They're back, at concert's end, with another joke book, and the procedure is repeated. All the while, mind you, they dare not hope anyone is listening. That's why lighthouse keepers go slowly mad. That's why Dave Garroway, who works this shift on WMAQ, is sooner or later going to pay a visit to an eminent Chicago psychiatrist."[36]

Time on the overnight shift left afternoons free for Garroway to work on his golf game, and on occasion work and pleasure coincided. Garroway not only covered tournaments on assignment for NBC, but in the July 1942 Tam O'Shanter Open, Garroway played in the tournament and covered it for NBC, a feat that ended when Garroway lost in the amateurs' third round.[37]

Other assignments followed, including helping report the results of the 1942 elections in special two-minute updates on election night. That December, Garroway remembered his friends back in Pittsburgh with a special Christmas gift: a large, beribboned box containing a single coffee bean.[38]

5

With the United States fully involved in the world war, Garroway had a feeling he would soon be called to service. Perhaps recalling his experiences during the Louisiana and Carolina Maneuvers, he did not want to be drafted by the Army. Instead, he requested to join the Navy. Through a special Navy program, college graduates could go through accelerated training and be commissioned as officers. Although Garroway had signed up for Navy service, his orders took a while to come through. Finally, it happened: report for training in Cambridge, Massachusetts.[1]

Adele had planned to remain in Chicago, but the separation proved too much. Three months into training, he got a tearful call. "Please let me come and live with you," she asked. "I can't stand it here alone." She joined him in Massachusetts. Garroway had a hunch his orders to an active unit would come sooner rather than later. Before he was shipped out, "a strong, very strong urge arose in me to have a child." He and Adele drove up into Maine for a few days, where they dug for precious stones they could use in their jewelry-making hobby. Along the way, they spent a night in the town of Paris. Not too long after, Adele learned she was pregnant. She went back to Chicago to prepare for the baby. Dave remained in Cambridge to finish training. After graduation in early July, he awaited orders. Some of his peers went out relatively soon, but Garroway sat around Cambridge and wondered when he'd leave.

Garroway's lifelong habit of tinkering followed him into the Navy. This time he got into watchmaking and watch repair, carrying all the necessities in a small bag. One morning he was walking across the campus with the school's commandant, who glanced down at two books Dave was carrying: the Navy's *Watch Officer's Guide*, and the *Watch Repairman's Guide*. Although Garroway didn't think he was good at repairing watches ("I think I probably stopped as many as I started"), it gave him something to do with his hands, which to him was very important.[2]

Garroway was officially commissioned on December 29, 1942, twen-

Ensign Dave Garroway with wife Adele and his father, 1943.
(Paris Day collection)

ty-six weeks after reporting to Cambridge. Now he was ordered to report to Alameda, California, via first available transportation, to join the minesweeper USS *Devastator*. Garroway took a cab to the airport and spent the flight to San Francisco dreaming of war adventures, imagining the ship with the ferocious name "tugging at its hawsers, at the dock, waiting to go and eat up those Japs. Just waiting for me." At San Francisco, the eager young ensign hurried to a ferry across the Bay to Alameda, then by cab to the General Engineering shipyard. It was a Sunday, and the yard didn't look very busy. Garroway asked a watchman at the gate how to get to the *Devastator*. The watchman put down his newspaper, checked a board behind him, and pointed Garroway to a shipway far to his right. In an instant, Garroway's visions of imminent action vaporized. The *Devastator*, only a few weeks into construction, wouldn't be ready for action for a while.

Garroway quickly grew bored waiting for his ship to be commissioned. He applied for membership in the International Shipfitters, Riggers and Welders' Union, bought some tools and safety gear, and asked to help construct the *Devastator*. The shipyard was happy to oblige. Garroway helped move the minesweeper's steel plates into place and did some welding. One day, a co-worker accidentally dropped a heavy steel plate on Garroway's foot. Instinctively, he retracted his toes. The steel plate neatly severed the end of his steel-toed boots, but Garroway's foot was unharmed. With his toes intact, with new skills in his repertoire, with some income stashed away from his shipyard work (some of it sent back to Adele to help care for the forthcoming family), and with the ship ready for launching, he left the shipfitters' union.

Garroway lived in a public housing area of a few hundred apartments. Most were empty, reserved for officers whose wives were with them. To get around this, Garroway had a young woman from the Junior Officers' Club pose as his wife. The apartment was unfurnished, so, as with his earlier apartments, Garroway decorated the place in a Hawaiian motif. He carried on an affair with the woman who, he remembered, spent time "teaching me each day how wonderful sex could be, each day more than the day before." A few years later, after he had achieved nationwide stardom, Garroway grew wistful, telling an Oakland reporter about "'the girl who got away,' the one with whom he was in love," and the dreams he had of marrying her and settling in the Bay Area as a radio announcer.[3]

In the marriage he presently had, a baby was on the way. When a telegram said birth was imminent, Garroway got emergency leave and hurried to St. Louis. The baby refused to appear. Garroway got one more day of leave, but was then ordered back to Alameda immediately. While he was over Denver, Adele gave birth to a daughter they would name Paris, after the town in Maine where she had been conceived. "Beautiful little girl, although I didn't see her for two years."[4]

After its launching in April 1943, the 221-foot *Devastator* was towed to a pier for completion. Garroway had to adjust his daily routine for the ten additional miles to the pier, rotating duties among six cars to make sure he had enough ration stamps to get to the shipyard from his quarters. One day, he stepped aboard the ship. Something felt odd and got worse. After five minutes aboard, he raced to the side of the ship, heaving. The wake of a passing boat, just barely rocking the moored 900-ton minesweeper, was all it took. Recalling that he'd gotten seasick almost any time he'd been boating in the past, Garroway believed he'd adapt once the ship put to sea.

Which it soon did. Garroway, in a crisp uniform, felt proud as the ship he'd helped build made the long-awaited turn toward the open sea, ready for trials. Then the first crested rollers started to come in. The bow started to plunge just enough. As his crewmates gazed up at the Golden Gate Bridge, Garroway was at the side, again heaving. Once the ship was on the open sea, the communications officer was in constant agony, unable to do his duties. "The sea and I were not friendly," he told an interviewer years later. Even after he'd thrown up everything in his stomach, the dry heaves continued. Only sleep brought relief.[5]

The *Devastator* ambled along the California coast, crewmen testing the ship's systems in preparation for Pearl Harbor and the war beyond. Every moment at sea worsened Garroway's agonies. The ship's captain tried to encourage him. "It's all in your head, my boy," he said as his stricken communications officer lay on the deck, blood coming out of his mouth from torn stomach muscles. "You'll get used to it." Garroway hoped it would go away, and in port, he studied diligently for his duties.

The long voyage to Pearl Harbor in March 1944 finally destroyed any hopes of naval heroism. Constant seasickness left him unable to do his duties. "I was required to come to the bridge, but I would collapse. I was too weak to stand," he recalled. When his watch ended, shipmates helped Garroway to his bunk, where he'd try to sleep off as much as he could before suffering through the waking hours. A few days later, realizing just how serious his condition was, the captain excused him from further watches.

Passing the agonizing hours in his bunk, Garroway wondered how much he could take. He knew how long the voyage was. "And I knew how far it was to the fantail of the boat and just step over. A lot of suicides are like that. They don't want to die. They just can't take the pain for that much longer." Finally realizing that he'd made it this far, Garroway willed himself, "minute by minute," through the rest of the voyage. At the pier, an ambulance was waiting to take him to Aiea Naval Hospital and its seasickness ward. Garroway later said he was put in next to a man who had died during the night, not having gotten treatment in time for internal hemorrhaging induced by seasickness.[6]

His own malady put Garroway into a group to study the effectiveness of seasickness remedies. "I took enough pills of an experimental nature during the time I was sick to drop dead from them," he recalled. None worked. After six weeks in the hospital Garroway was put back into the officers' pool. Walter Timmons, whom Garroway had befriended in the Navy's communications training course at Harvard, was in charge of the pool. He showed Garroway a long list of possible jobs, telling him he could have any one he wanted. One Timmons chose at random was as officer in charge of the Pacific Fleet Yeoman and Stenography School. "On solid ground right here," Timmons said, calling it a steady job without too much supervision. Garroway had no idea of what the job would involve, but since he liked solid ground and not too much supervision, he immediately accepted.[7]

Garroway reported to Camp Catlin, where he would oversee the training of personnel for secretarial and clerical chores. Theirs was a drab building with eight classrooms, each overseen by a chief petty officer, typically men who had been experts in a field in civilian life. His chief typing instructor was Albert Tangora, named the world's fastest typist seven times, able to type more than 140 words a minute under championship conditions. When Camp Catlin's commanding general had a distinguished visitor, Tangora was often asked to show off his typing skills for the visitor. Having the brass around so often brought challenges for Garroway. Tangora "kept the pressure on a little bit because he was such an attraction," Garroway recalled.[8]

The easygoing Garroway soon learned the challenges of being in charge. His chiefs would sometimes try to influence him so they could get time off. One left an expensive gold writing pen with a notecard in his desk. Garroway never saw the gift, which ended up shoved to the back of his desk drawer. The chief, not seeing return on his investment, started becoming hard to get along with. Garroway suddenly had to become a disciplinarian, and after a little while the chief's attitude returned to normal. At war's end, preparing to go home, Garroway emptied the desk drawer's contents into his baggage. When he unpacked in Chicago, Garroway found the pen and realized why the chief had become so difficult. Garroway offered to return the pen, but the giver told him to keep it.[9]

As an officer in charge of a unit at Camp Catlin, Garroway had membership in the Marine Officers Club. He soon tired of "sitting around looking at a lonesome drink." One day, while ambling around downtown Honolulu, he stopped in at NBC's affiliate, KGU. It and CBS affiliate KGMB were the only stations in Honolulu. KGU had been started by Marion Mulrony, a Navy veteran who had built the station out of sheer determination. That determination was accompanied by an arbitrary, idiosyn-

Garroway (front row, third from left) as officer in charge of the Pacific Fleet Yeoman and Stenography School. Champion typist Al Tangora (fourth from left) stands next to Garroway. (Paris Day collection)

cratic nature. "If he went to the movies and saw Dinah Shore wearing a low-cut gown, her records were no longer played on KGU," longtime staffer Ed Sheehan remembered. "He also hated sopranos, and that was that – no sopranos and no discussion about it either...He also insisted that we produce an annual memorial program to Robert Browning on the poet's birthday. He thought Browning more important than anything Truman, Marshall or MacArthur were doing right then."[10]

At KGU, Garroway asked if the station needed any announcing help. In Garroway's recollection, the man he spoke with stood up, shook his hand, and put his arm around him. "You're an angel from heaven, aren't you?" the man asked. "What's your name?" Garroway introduced himself and said he worked at NBC in Chicago. The man introduced himself as the station's program manager. He complained that his station was shorthanded because Navy jobs paid more than his station could afford. He was one of two people left to run the station, and had to stay there "all day and half the night." The manager hired Garroway on the spot, telling him to be there at nine that night, run the station as long as you want, and then go home.[11]

Left with no instructions except to improvise, KGU's newest hire started a free-form program that ran from nine to midnight. Garroway spent the first few evenings searching through the station's record collection. He found himself intrigued by Peggy Lee, Tommy Dorsey, and the young Frank Sinatra. After some thought, Garroway decided to focus primarily on jazz. "I didn't know too much about jazz, but I liked it," he remembered. The lively new style became the centerpiece of his program, though he sometimes threw a symphony record into the mix. "We called those musical shower baths," he said. "We played a Bach harpsichord solo after some of the big bands to kind of wash yourself off."[12]

As Garroway spent the late night hours alone at KGU spinning records for his listeners, he began to develop the intimate style that would set him apart, and adapted some techniques he had used on the overnight shift at WMAQ. "When you talk into the microphone, if you talk right to it, and this is just as true for the camera eye, you are talking to one and a half people," he later explained. "It's just one person and more, but not two people," he said. "You know there's a plus in there, but you can concentrate on one person and talk directly to one person."[13]

Garroway began to vary the patter between musical numbers. Having lived in so many different places during his life, he began imaginary walking tours of cities he knew. One night he might take his audience on a walk from Burton Place in Chicago down to the Merchandise Mart, calling out landmarks such as the Tallahassee Fruit Store, the Swedish Club, and Delsey Street. "And that store over there, I saw June Travis one morning, who I thought was the prettiest girl I'd ever seen up to that point."[14]

At first, Garroway didn't know if the program was working. "I was depressed. I didn't think anyone ever listened to the show, so I began to drift away, saying whatever came into my mind," he remembered. But it was working. His unusual style resonated with homesick service personnel, and KGU had a hit. "All of a sudden, the phone began to ring, the mail started arriving. It was a new approach for me, this casual attitude that was born of depression. But out of a bad break came a good one. I'd found my style, my own particular trade mark. But for it, I'd probably still be announcing on a local station."[15]

Off the air, he learned to deal with Mulrony's eccentric, frugal nature. Mulrony not only took home the station's garbage each night because he didn't want to pay for trash service when his home garbage service was free, but he walked the station's hallways turning out lights. Sometimes Garroway was plunged into darkness in the middle of writing copy. One night, as Mulrony walked down the hallway turning off light switches, Garroway walked toward him with two large lighted candles, stopping long enough to wish him a good night.[16]

Right when it seemed Garroway's life had equilibrium – an easy job in the Navy, a popular radio show by night – she came along.

Her name was Betty. Years before she had too much to drink and fell asleep in the sun. The severe burn damaged her skin, and she wore pancake makeup to cover the blotches. Garroway "got hit in the head" with her and the resulting relationship "caused me more agony than anybody I've ever met."

Neither professed love for the other. It didn't matter. Garroway remembered them as "inseparable." They often sparred "like tigers," but Garroway felt that her injury had made her angry, and that kindness was what she most needed. As he recalled, "She was funny and exceedingly intelligent, and very wise, and could be very tender." They finally resolved their tensions enough to spend an evening without a fight. About that time, the war ended, and when Garroway was shipped home, so did the relationship. Garroway remembered Betty as being "desolate" when he left Hawaii.[17]

Garroway put both his sense of humor and his craftsmanship to work. To commemorate his service in a rear-area support job, he formed a piece of brass welding rod into a tiny gold brick that could be pinned to a ribbon on his Navy uniform, a parody of the campaign stars that combat veterans wore on their service ribbons. He created two more, giving them to colleagues who joined him as the first recipients of the Order of the Gold Brick. "They gave it to themselves for outstanding goldbricking in the line of duty," Dave Jr. wrote years later.

When one of the Gold Brick recipients was married, one of the bride's guests was Vice Admiral Theodore Wilkinson, whose own uniform bore numerous awards. As Garroway and his associates went through the receiving line, they found themselves face to face with an admiral who was puzzled by the little embellishment to their award ribbons. In embarrassment, wondering if official reprimand or worse was in their future, the men retreated to a corner and removed the little gold bricks. After the new bride explained the award to Wilkinson, an order came down. The next day, Garroway presented Wilkinson with his own gold brick, which the admiral proudly pinned to his own American Defense Ribbon.[18]

After the Japanese surrender in September 1945, Garroway prepared to return home. His time in Hawaii had brought him new opportunities in broadcasting, expanded his horizons, and left him with a love for the islands that would linger. "My life up to that time had been an amazingly happy life, incredibly happy," he remembered. He wondered how long this happiness would go on. "I was about to find out."[19]

6

The long voyage from Hawaii at an end, Garroway stepped ashore in San Diego. Adele had driven out to California with little Paris to meet him. Garroway told her to meet him on a street corner that he knew in town, the better to avoid the crowds at the pier. With great anticipation, he headed to that street corner, "my Navy gear in one hand and a big smile on my face."

Anticipation quickly turned to anguish. As soon as he locked eyes with Adele, Garroway's head began to ache and a feeling of depression overwhelmed him. Perhaps it was the release of anticipation. Perhaps it was guilt over the affairs he'd had in San Francisco and Hawaii. Whatever the cause, the pain didn't go away, not even as they talked. "My head felt incredible," Garroway wrote, remembering "an intense headache without any pain." Aspirin made no difference. "The pain was not unbearable, not intense. In fact, I recall, in a sense there was no pain."[1]

They headed back to Chicago by way of St. Louis, a pall over the threesome. The silent miles passed. No one knew what to do. Despite Garroway's best efforts, he couldn't stifle the misery he felt, and he told Adele what was going on. "She was understanding, as she could be under the circumstances," he remembered. "I tried to be normal, but I wasn't a good enough actor, I guess. Although I learned to be after a while."[2]

Back in Chicago, resuming his employment with NBC, Garroway undertook two tasks: an increasingly urgent campaign of want ads seeking an apartment for himself and his family, stressing his NBC connections; and finding a psychiatrist, starting a process that stretched three decades. "Until March 1976 I never got off the couch, except long enough to change doctors," he later wrote. The first doctor he visited was matter-of-fact, saying his problems were either anxiety or depression. "I don't care what you call it," Garroway replied. "What do we do about it?" The doctor gave him a prescription, but the medication didn't help. Another psychiatrist prescribed more pills, but to Garroway the prescription "might as well have been salt tablets."[3]

At the house they rented on Pratt Boulevard ("with enough rooms to house half of the Yeoman School," he remembered), Garroway tried to rekindle his relationship with Adele and got to know his two-year-old daughter. Proximity to his family only made the pain worse, no matter what he did. He slowly began to distance himself from Adele. He struggled in conversation with her, then steadily began avoiding her. "I was fond of my wife as ever," Garroway said, "and yet I could not stand to be close to her."

To most people, Garroway seemed fine. His troubles didn't affect his duties at NBC, where work eased the agony. "All the time the work I was doing was quite satisfactory, and no one seemed to know," he remembered. "It did not show to other people, nor did it affect my work on the air." When he was around Adele or little Paris, the pain, which he likened to a steel band around his skull, and his depressed feelings intensified. "This damn near broke my heart," he said. Desperate to salvage his life and his marriage, Garroway went from doctor to doctor seeking answers. "As I switched from psychiatrist to psychiatrist, and they began to talk in terms of two-year psychoanalyses, things didn't look any better. Guilt feelings built up at having practically abandoned my wife and child by withdrawal, and without being able to give any reason. Here I was with some mysterious ailment with no known cause and nothing to do about it that I could find."[4]

It only worsened as time passed. Garroway tried to explain that it was a sickness, that he was seeking help. It didn't get better, and his misery affected the rest of the family. Adele decided to head back to St. Louis with Paris, "which I thought was a wise move while I tried to come to and get ahold of me or find me again." Distance didn't heal the marriage, though, and Dave and Adele legally separated in March 1946. That September a St. Louis court granted Adele a divorce, with incompatibility the cause. Garroway, represented by counsel, did not contest it. Adele was granted custody of Paris, and Garroway was ordered to pay alimony and child support. Although their marriage failed, they eventually settled into a relationship he characterized as "good friends." Garroway visited with Paris when he could, and regularly exchanged letters with Adele. She remarried in 1954 and, Garroway later wrote, "this time got lucky."[5]

WMAQ initially put Garroway back to work on odd announcing

chores, covering parades and other special events. On occasion, he was selected for a special assignment, such as when sportscaster Bill Stern requested Garroway to help him cover a golf tournament. When nothing special came along, Garroway was just one of the announcers, sometimes taking some ribbing for his facial resemblance to Chicago newspaperman Paul Gallico. Alone, his evenings free, he spent hours on end playing bridge with friends and colleagues, continuing the pastime that had inadvertently led to his big break at NBC a decade before.[6]

Garroway hadn't been much of a drinker. One evening while playing cards at the home of his friend Charles Urquhart, Garroway mentioned he had the ability to decide if alcohol would affect him before he drank. A doubting Thomas at the game scoffed, challenging him to drink a quart bottle of Scotch. Garroway downed the contents and played on, amassing a considerable sum. He wasn't drunk, he maintained. Alcohol never made Garroway feel good, he wrote; instead, it just made him sleepy. At another late-night card game, though, Garroway made a discovery that would lead to the most productive time of his life – and, eventually, would help ruin it.

The game had gone on for hours, Garroway in tense struggle with a surgeon. Both were feeling fatigue set in, not to mention the many drinks they'd had. The doctor glanced at the clock. It was four in the morning. "I've got to be in surgery in three hours," he said. Garroway was astounded. In his condition, sleep-deprived and under the influence, how could this doctor conduct an operation? The doctor reached into his bag and pulled out a bottle. He shook out a couple of white capsules and took them. He then gave two to Garroway. Within an hour, he was wide awake, sharp and alert. Dave Garroway had just been introduced to Dexedrine.

Brought into mass usage during World War II to keep soldiers alert in combat, Dexedrine staved off fatigue and improved reaction time. It seemed like a new wonder drug. After the war it became widely available, even over the counter. No one yet knew of the devastating effects that its sustained use would have on the body. Garroway liked what Dexedrine did for him, but he suspected it would eventually be outlawed. He went to a pharmacy and ordered three kilos of Dexedrine ("enough to last him until he was one hundred and eight, probably," Dave Jr. would say years later). The pharmacist had it ready for him that evening. No doctor ever prescribed Dexedrine to Garroway. The doctors who treated him throughout the years were aware that he took it, although Dave Jr.

said his father never mentioned how his doctors felt about it.

A normal dose of Dexedrine was ten milligrams a day. However, prolonged use of Dexedrine makes the body require more to get the same effect. During the *Today* years, Garroway would be up to a gram a day, enough to drive an average person up the wall. But between Garroway's prolonged use and his physical constitution, it helped him get out of bed and plow through a professional life whose demands became increasingly heavier. It gave him the energy to keep going and the alertness to keep up with what was going on. Over time, though, the less pleasant effects of his Dexedrine use would become increasingly apparent to himself and those around him. It cost him professionally and personally, and eventually contributed to his premature demise.

Garroway took his Dexedrine in different ways, but the one most associated with him was a liquid solution of Dexedrine and Vitamin E. He kept some in a little bottle that he carried, taking a pull when he needed a pick-me-up. He called this solution "the Doctor." Sometimes he shared it. Once, an NBC staff musician told Garroway he was stricken with a cold, barely able to breathe. The host pulled out the little bottle and told him to take a swig. "Almost immediately," the musician told Chicago broadcasting historian Rich Samuels, "it seemed as though Studio G was spinning in circles." Then came the cue; they were on the air. "I don't remember anything after that," he remembered. "But the following day, my drummer told me I'd never played better."[7]

Both "the Doctor," giving Garroway the power to burn midnight oil, and his love of automobiles played a key role in what was coming. So did a key relationship he established.

At WMAQ, Garroway and two other announcers were put on the late shift. The other two announcers did not own cars and had to use the elevated trains to get home. The last train ran at midnight, but the station remained on the air until 1 a.m. Since Garroway's automobile meant he wasn't tied to the El schedule, he got the midnight shift. It was an unsponsored "fill" hour of symphony music. When a dance studio bought a half-hour of time for a rumba program, it moved sign-off to 1:30 a.m.

Stuck with this uninspiring time slot, and not wanting a mass audience that only sought background music, Garroway wanted to adapt what had worked at KGU. He decided to aim at "a theoretical person and a half that had the same interests that I did, sink or swim. I didn't think myself so strange that such a show, by a generalist and for a generalist, would begin to actually listen to the words, and the music that the words were mostly about." For the midnight program he adapted the name of a popular song, "11:60 P.M." Not sure he could come up with enough material for *The 11:60 Club*, he offered a young writer for the Carolyn Gilbert show fifty cents per script. Out of this began Garroway's close, enduring friendship with Charlie Andrews.[13]

Charlie Andrews had fallen in love with jazz in his hometown of Fond du Lac, Wisconsin. When jazz bands played at the dancing pavilions, he was entranced by their stylish suits, their smooth style, and how it all stood in contrast to the plain aesthetic of his working-class environment. He befriended many of the musicians, and they introduced him to books and music that represented a whole new realm to him. It made him hungry for more, and it led him to Chicago, where he began working for an advertising agency.

When Andrews first heard Garroway on *The 11:60 Club*, he was hooked. "Dave had a very catholic taste," Andrews remembered. "He liked a little bit of everything, so it was a fascinating show to listen to." He began to write material and took it to Garroway ("Here's a little story you can tell about this record, or a little piece about this"), knowing that he constantly needed new material. Garroway began to use some of it, and soon Andrews got to know Garroway on a personal level. He quickly learned Garroway didn't trust writers. "He didn't like the idea of anyone putting words in his mouth," Andrews recalled. "But he liked the idea of having ideas put in his head." He also came to know Garroway's solitary nature. "Dave was a strange guy," he recalled. "He was a loner, pretty much." It was soon after his separation from Adele, which had left him with a large house that was mostly empty. Andrews needed a room, so Garroway let him move in. There was little furniture in the house, but countless albums arranged in Garroway's own system. "He just lined them up, up and down, through all his rooms," Andrews said. "When we'd play records at night, if he'd want to find a Sarah Vaughan record, he'd just walk along until he saw it on the floor."[9]

Three decades later Garroway remembered *The 11:60 Club* as "the best show that I will ever do." From a shaky beginning Garroway and Andrews created a program that featured what Garroway called "an impressionist style. It wasn't formalized. It was free flowing talk, often without sentence structure, just useful adjectives and useful nouns, and other forms."[10]

As it happened, Garroway was creating a show around a music genre he didn't fully understand. "I didn't know the first thing about jazz," he confessed after he had found network stardom. "For that matter, I couldn't carry a tune in a well-constructed basket." To fill in the gaps in his knowledge base, Garroway relied on Andrews, as well as record collector George Hoefer, a well-known jazz enthusiast who had written for *Down Beat* since 1935 and had helped establish jazz record departments in local department stores. Hoefer lent Garroway music from his collection of more than 7,500 records. Garroway didn't take listener requests ("If I do, it'll be your show, not mine," he told them). Once, Garroway spoke on the air about an angry young caller who berated him after she had called three times with a request and he hadn't played it. "I have the record right here in my hand," Garroway said on the air. "But I'm not going to play it because it's too corny. Listen a minute and you'll hear me break the thing." The next sound was of a record being smashed. Audience members wrote in, an overwhelming majority of them applauding Garroway.[11]

The lone exception to the "no requests" rule was a friendly rivalry with listeners to write in with the title of a jazz record they had. If the record was added to a show's playlist, the listener would be invited to bring the record and appear on the program. Mike Rapchak, a jazz enthusiast who worked at a soap factory but dreamed of a radio career, requested Artie Shaw's version of "Stardust." Impressed, Garroway invited Rapchak to visit. After the show, their conversation swung to Rapchak's radio aspirations. With Garroway's encouragement, Rapchak enrolled in courses and began a radio career that eventually made him one of the leading personalities in the medium. Another listener, Wisconsin sophomore Loring Mandel, turned the offer on its ear. He and his roommate wrote parodies of song titles and sent them to Garroway. This too yielded an invitation to the Merchandise Mart studios, the first of several visits Mandel would make to see Garroway. At one point, Mandel asked if he would consider paying him and his roommate to write for him. Garroway dashed these hopes with a shake of his head: "If it pleases you to write it, it pleases me to use it."[12]

Garroway also adapted the rambling style of his program in Hawaii. The relaxed style, he said, had originated with a high school friend, Jim

Campbell, who was known for his low-pressure demeanor and stylish verbiage. To that, Garroway added jazz slang he picked up from visiting local clubs and listening to the performers; when he'd hear a gag he liked, he wrote it down and worked it into his on-air persona. Publicity man Dave Meany suggested one more touch: addressing the listener with unusual terms of affection. "Well, hello there, old incandescent," Garroway might purr at the start of a broadcast, while at another point the same listener might hear themselves called "my ancient" in that same cool, carefree voice. "This is Garroway, David, going for some free-breathing records like we do most nights along about the witching hour, when the hands of your clock get so intimate. Yes, the ductile time of the day has come again, and we'll do it while you sit there, feet up, eyes closed, long white throat back...." Two decades later, Garroway admitted it was all a gimmick. "It worked. I got the attention. Then I dropped it." Sometimes it worked too well. A young singer named Patti Page, already intimidated by how her life was changing as her star ascended, made her first disc jockey show appearance with Garroway. "He frightened me, all the words he used," she remembered. At a loss, she looked at her manager and asked, "What do I say now?"[13]

Along with the slouched style and unusual vocabulary, Garroway developed another trademark. Some time before, he had listened to Father Jealous Major Divine, a charismatic Black evangelist. Father Divine ended his famous high-energy sermons by abruptly calling out, "Peace! It's wonderful!" That benediction had stuck with Garroway. One night at the end of his show, Garroway's director signaled that he had ten seconds left. "I just held up my hand and said 'peace,'" he remembered. In 1956, when the benediction had become nationally famous, Garroway explained that it had been used as a farewell and a greeting for many centuries, and that "it has no superstitious meaning for me. It's just something I started to say." Sometimes, Garroway styled his farewell as "some love...and peace." He explained it came from something an old girlfriend would tell him. "It places love within some reasonable limits – a definite amount of love, which is what she used to wish me. After all, people can't go around giving all their love to everyone. We save the best part of our love for those who are closest to us."[14]

The "new" Dave Garroway was a conscious construct, and he admitted as much to Mandel, who was surprised to find Garroway's off-air voice "higher, brighter, faster." As a record played, Garroway told Man-

Garroway and his record turner, Joe Petrillo.
(American Heritage Center, University of Wyoming)

del that he had studied the audience he wanted to read, decided to slow his speech and lower his own-air voice, and use a distinctive vocabulary. Between segments, Mandel noticed Garroway doodling on his script, absently creating in the margins "a series of disks that looked more than anything else like blood corpuscles." Mandel was surprised to find that what seemed "oddly private" for the listener was instead "a thoroughly calculated personality," and he left the meeting feeling as if he had met "two Garroways, the real and the constructed."[15]

Also helping Garroway create his distinct style were the talents of his "record turner," Joe Petrillo. The nephew of James C. Petrillo, the powerful head of the American Federation of Musicians, Joe was present because of a requirement that all records played on the air had to be spun by a union member. A trombonist in his own right and about Garroway's age, he understood what the host was trying to do. Petrillo also had uncanny accuracy with the phonograph needle. If, after a record was played, Garroway wanted to highlight a particular moment in the performance

– for example, a trombone solo – while he was talking it up and saying "Listen while he blows it again," Petrillo would know the exact spot to place the needle. "I don't think he missed one in four years," Garroway remembered. Other times, he might have Petrillo play the record twice: once at normal speed, and then at another speed, all the while providing commentary about what the listener could hear in the song. Sometimes Garroway might have Petrillo play two records at once, or blend records in a segue. As Garroway worked through the songs on his list, he poked a pencil through the paper. On the desk were newspaper and magazine clippings, and a notebook containing his thoughts for the show. Sometimes, those notes would simply be how long he needed to ad-lib.

"Garroway, talking like a man with a slouch in his voice, simply eased his way to the very top rung of the ladder," a writer observed in 1950. "It was his relaxed voice, vocabulary and urbane comment between the records that caught on with late-night stay-ups." It took time, though, to show WMAQ management that it all worked. Rumors circulated that *The 11:60 Club* wasn't pulling in enough sponsorship or enough listeners. "I don't think this jazz is going to go over," a program manager told Garroway. Sponsors dropped out except for a small jazz club called Jump Town, known as a musicians' hangout.[16]

One of Garroway's colleagues, Peter Lucas, stopped by to talk. The old house he had been renting a room in was to be torn down. Out of the conversation came an idea. They couldn't conduct a phone survey at 1 a.m. to gauge the show's reach. But what if they invited the listeners to a house-wrecking party? "There's not much that they can do to a building that's due to be demolished the next morning." At about 12:30 that night Garroway told his listeners the story of Lucas' doomed home, and wondered aloud if anyone was listening that late. He gave the address and instructed anyone who wanted to come to bring their own food and drinks. "My private guess was that between one hundred and two hundred would show," he remembered.

Garroway signed off at 1:30 and headed for the old house. The streets were jammed. "Some ninny on the radio told his listeners to go to an address on North State, that he was giving a party to wreck the joint or something," a cop told Garroway. "It's one hell of a mess." When he finally got to the house, Garroway looked out on a massive crowd, "not unfriendly and not boisterous." He saw a couple drinking from flower pots, each with a finger inserted into the hole in the bottom. Garroway was struck by "the number of people who really felt that I was speaking to them. In fact, several were slightly offended that other people were there too. Somehow they had felt the occasion was strictly for them alone." The point was made. After six weeks with Jump Town as the lone sponsor, after the house party established that Garroway had a following, after fan mail began to pour in from listeners as near as Chicago and as far as North Carolina, able to listen as WMAQ's powerful signal reached far away, the tide turned. "Before long we had more commercials than we could accommodate," he remembered.[17]

Decades later Garroway remembered the Chicago days as "beautiful." He was the subject of fan clubs and mail from far away. One writer called Garroway "the idol of late listeners in the Midwest. On any day of the week in Madison, for instance, you could hear comments that ranged from the university professor's 'I really enjoy his sophisticated chatter and subtle ad libbing,' the housewife's 'He's so nice and unassuming,' to the high school student's 'Gee, Garroway's hep.'" Some listeners wrote repeatedly, and he sent responses in the same jazzy style he employed on-air. "Over-sized alohas for those incandescent phrases," he wrote a young woman who sent an adoring letter. "Do you have any idea how abstract and unreal it is to talk night after night into that little rectangular tin demon and how warmly vivifying it is to realize that someone is talking to you? Real warm, real vivifying." WMAQ had *11:60 Club* membership cards printed and Garroway, styled on the card as the club's "eagerest beaver," signed and sent them to fans who wrote in.[18]

Columnists picked up on the Garroway phenomenon. There was his strange chatter on subjects that spanned the spectrum, delivered in a tone "as intimate as a toothbrush," delivered without a script, on topics ranging from "nuclear fission, Hawaiian Okelehao, Bilbo, eavesdropping, and the snarle [*sic*] and delusion known as woman"; the discourses that a particularly exciting record "grabs you right by the eyeballs" or that Teddy Wilson "plays a mighty intellectual piano for my dough"; his insistence that "we don't play corn on this hassel, Honey." They pointed out the tortoise-shell eyeglasses that became his trademark, replacing the thin wire-rimmed glasses he had previously worn; his taste for checkered sport coats with contrasting pants; his preference for loud bow ties; his lack of a hat; his love of exotic automobiles. And, whether through intent on his part or the efforts of writers and publicity agents, the Garroway mythology took root: the coincidences in his life that involved the number thirteen; his stint as an assistant at Harvard being conflated into having taught astronomy there; his time as a book salesman transforming into having actually written the book.[19]

With radio stardom came influence. The new role of the disc jockey meant the power to promote new genres and new artists. Hugh Downs, himself just getting started at NBC in Chicago, recalled Garroway as "one of the best that ever was. Dave came along at the turning point in radio, when the disc jockey became a powerful influence." A play of a record on his show could turn a song into a hit. Or a song by a "square" act could be ridiculed as "cheesy," and listeners could hear Garroway feed a Guy Lombardo or Vaughn Monroe record to a mouse (named "Meager Beaver" after he held a listener contest) that he claimed lived in the studio.[20]

Part of that influence gave him and his fellow disc jockeys the power to promote acts, both on the air and off the air. A group of jazz enthusiasts called the Hot Club of Chicago, which had ballooned from six members to 450, enlisted Garroway to emcee a performance by drummer Gene Krupa and his band. It was the start of a second career as a concert organizer and emcee, as Garroway launched a series of *11:60 Club* concerts at local venues, featuring top stars and up-and-coming acts. When the Hudson-Ross department store signed on as an *11:60 Club* sponsor, it not only brought newspaper advertising for the show, but Garroway made personal appearances when artists appeared at the stores for record signings. Between air play on his nightly show and his influence in getting acts booked at local clubs, Garroway played an important role in launching the careers of George Shearing, Nellie Lutcher, Anita O'Day, Harry Belafonte, Matt Dennis, and Jackie Cain and Roy Kral.[21]

One morning in 1946, Charlie Andrews was downstairs playing some new records he'd brought. "Hey, Dave, listen to this one," he called out. Garroway walked out to the stair as Andrews dropped the needle on a record titled "If You Could See Me Now." Mesmerized as the first chorus ended, Garroway started down the stairs, only to miss two steps and tumble down the staircase. Unhurt but still transfixed, he collected himself at the landing. "Who in the world is that?" he asked Andrews. It was an artist neither had heard of, a young jazz singer named Sarah Vaughan. "We both knew that one of the great voices of our generation had come along," Garroway wrote. Garroway played and replayed the record several times that day, and used it on his radio program that night. "The number and quality of phone calls that night told me we were on the right track." While Garroway said many people had credited him with the success of Sarah Vaughan as a performer, he maintained that she had more to do with the success of *The 11:60 Club*.[22]

In March 1947 Garroway asked her to appear at one of his concerts in Chicago. She wanted to, but protested she had nothing nice to wear. He handed her a $50 bill. "Buy yourself a gown," he told her. In his shy way, the disc jockey was smitten with her, and with her talent. Out of it developed a special friendship. His frequent promotion of her music boosted her salary from $250 a week to $750 a week, enough to help her buy a car, which she later gave back when she couldn't keep up the payments. Sometimes Garroway drove her around Chicago, at speeds so fast it frightened her, and she'd threaten to kill him.

On evenings when his radio duties kept him from her nightclub shows, he had her sing to him over the phone, invariably asking her to sing his favorite of her songs, "Tenderly." Garroway loved playing her music on *The 11:60 Club*, sometimes having Petrillo replay a single word or phrase over and over, discoursing on Vaughan's ability to add meaning to a song by sculpting a vowel or massaging a phrase. So high was his esteem for her singing abilities that Garroway gave Vaughan her lasting nickname, "The Divine One."[23]

7

In early 1947, NBC programming executives were at work on the summer schedule. The big network programs typically ran on a thirty-nine week agreement. The thirteen weeks of summer often became an audition for promising new acts in a low-risk environment. Garroway was chosen for a six-week trial run of a musical variety program, in the Sunday afternoon time period normally occupied by *Ellery Queen*.

It wouldn't be the *11:60 Club* format, though. The music would be performed live by NBC-Chicago's thirty-five piece orchestra, conducted by Joseph Gallicchio. Jack Haskell and Vivian Martin, who performed on two other NBC programs, would be the singers. Director Parker Gibbs spent a lot of time with Garroway and Charlie Andrews, looking for different ways to present music. "If in rehearsal or on the air, something happened that warranted comment, we would stop the show and do it again with comments by Garroway," Gibbs told Ed Rothhaar in 1958. The idea was not to make up the unusual, but look for it when it happened. Out of it came a program with a loose format. It was up to Garroway to make it work. "We supplied him with the raw ingredients of music and stories, and inspirations of the moment put the whole thing together," Gibbs said. Nor were they afraid to puncture the conventional wisdom of radio. Most broadcasters hated long pauses. Garroway wasn't afraid of them. After a musical number, it was common for Garroway to be quiet for a few thoughtful seconds before his low purr segued into his next observation or anecdote. It was another expression of his cool, contemplative style.[1]

Suddenly, the obscurity that the devoted had stayed up late for was something anyone could listen to, and not even the format change could blunt the appeal Garroway had to an audience. One review, describing Garroway's voice as "soft as a chocolate bar on an August afternoon," told that his fan mail included praise from cleaning women and Broadway stars. WMAQ eventually had to designate a clerk to handle letters from admirers. A *Billboard* review saw great potential. "Oh, brother, what a relief" for those "who just want to listen, who are tired of being hit over the head with kilocycles," reviewer Cy Wagner said. Garroway could fit in explanations of how and why music was played, "neither pedantic nor maudlin," then digress on whatever came to his mind, making even a mention of astronomy fit the show. "That's the funny thing about Garroway," Wagner wrote. "He can be talking about modern music one minute, science the next and somehow draw a line of natural transition between both. It takes an unusual guy, with unusual talent, but that Garroway is, and that Garroway has." Wagner warned that it would take "an unusual sponsor with courage" to pick up a show so unconventional, but "for the three who have the stuff, here's a program that could become the popular musical show of the year."[2]

Influential *New York Herald-Tribune* radio columnist John Crosby wasn't sure what to make of Garroway's "strange chatter and even stranger ideas." Baffled by his hep talk, of phrasings such as "old tiger" or "my incandescents," Crosby confessed, "I don't know what he's getting at any more than you do." Crosby called Garroway "as weak on nouns as he is overdeveloped on adjectives. He scatters the word "thing" around in all directions, applying it indiscriminately to music, singers, and even his own program, which he describes as 'a low pressure thing.'" To Crosby, Garroway's style was like "skating around the English language with his characteristic, but misguided assurance."[3]

The ratings, though, spoke for themselves. In August, NBC announced *The Dave Garroway Show* would remain on Sundays. All the while, Garroway would maintain his *11:60 Club* hosting duties, as well as his responsibilities as a concert organizer and host. Even the strange vocabulary entered the common vernacular. The word "hassle," meaning a conflict or a problem, useful both as noun or a verb, started to be heard in common usage. And a popular song from earlier in the decade would find new life. From the late 1940s on, "Sentimental Journey" would be Dave Garroway's theme song.[4]

His sudden fame started a pattern that dogged Garroway for the next decade and a half, as he juggled multiple responsibilities among several programs and sponsors, along with outside obligations. A typical day might see him making a sponsor appearance for Hudson-Ross stores at 8:30 a.m., then going to a theater rehearsal an hour later. At noon there was a luncheon address, then he was off to an appearance at a veterans' hospital at 2:30. Then it was back to WMAQ for an afternoon radio series, and then preparations for *The 11:60 Club* at midnight. In between, he might put in a guest appearance on another program, and after *The 11:60 Club* finished for the night, he might go to the local jazz clubs to catch some performances. Something had to give in this schedule, and all too often it was rest. By 1949 Garroway estimated he was down to two hours' sleep per night. A quick sip of The Doctor every now and again, his increasingly frequent remedy, kept him energetic and alert.[5]

As a concert promoter, Garroway produced concerts at venues around Chicago, featuring acts he'd discovered or found worthy: Jackie Cain, Clark Dennis, LaVerne Linroth, Charlie Ventura, Jose Melis, Dick Farney. At some performances he had emcee help from a competitor he'd befriended, Studs Terkel of WENR, whom a columnist described as having a "tough guy voice and manner but the soul of an intellectual," and whose *Wax Museum* show "ranges from Bach to boogie woogie and back."[6]

Sometimes the club owners sought Garroway's advice. Lipp's Lower Level had boomed during the war years. Now it was a sleepy place where "the three-piece band that ground out dance music was playing for its own enjoyment," manager Frank Holzfeind recalled. As a dedicated listener to *The 11:60 Club*, he wondered if a nightclub couldn't attract patrons with the same kind of music. With no dedicated jazz clubs in Chicago, it could provide a way to stand out. One night, Holzfeind asked Garroway for advice. To get jazz, Garroway said, the club needed to be completely integrated. This, too, would be a first, for no club in the Loop allowed the races to mingle freely. The place needed a new name, too. Taking Garroway's suggestions to heart, Holzfeind reopened the club in late November as the Blue Note, the name taken from a cafe on the radio series Casey the Photographer. Despite its location in a leaky, low-ceilinged cellar, the club became very popular. Garroway kept an interest in the place and suggested acts that Holzfeind could book, including a young Harry Belafonte, who was experimenting with jazz. Holzfeind credited Garroway's "uncanny ear for the unique" with much of the club's success. "He was plugging Sarah Vaughan's records, for instance, when nobody else was paying any attention to her. It was on his recommendation we hired her, and you know the rest. From the Blue Note she went right to the top."[7]

Through deed and word, Garroway was making manifest his belief in equal rights. He could not understand the prejudice that pervaded the country, and readily championed Black performers including Belafonte, Sarah Vaughan, Earl Hines, Ella Fitzgerald, the twelve-year-old Toni Harper, and many others. To Garroway, the cure for racism was in educating the next generation. "Educating the adult who hates Negroes because they are colored is a pretty thankless task," Garroway told an interviewer for a student newspaper. He blamed parents' thoughtlessness as a key cause of racism. "You must start real young. After about first grade, the kid has 'set,' as psychologists say, and his habits and thought patterns are firmly settled." To Garroway, "the hope for the solution of this prejudice problem is not with the adults, but with the kids of America."[8]

Sometimes racism evidenced itself in horrifying ways. At a concert he produced at the Chicago Theater in 1948, Sarah Vaughan had just begun singing when a fusillade of tomatoes rained on her, hurled by bigots in the balcony. Startled, Vaughan fled for the safety of backstage. Incensed, Garroway marched on stage and hushed the audience. The anger in his voice could not be concealed. "Yes, now you know," he growled into the microphone. "Now you have seen in capsule form the hate which poisons the heart of America. It started the last war, and even now is starting the next. Today, hate-mongers stopped you from enjoying a great artist. Tomorrow, if you don't halt them, hate like this, magnified into war, will kill you and your children, too." Stirred by Garroway's sermon, the crowd cheered for Vaughan to return to the stage, where she continued her performance. After the concert, his anger still burned. That night, Garroway told his *11:60 Club* audience what had happened. Listeners deluged Vaughan with letters, telegrams and flowers.[9]

Garroway's belief in equality became well-known. While attending a jazz festival in New Orleans, Garroway stopped in at a nightclub. When he stepped outside for a moment, a group of irate White people confronted him. "So you're a nigger lover, huh, Dave?" one of them growled. As they began to menace him, the band leader, a friend of Garroway's, gave a signal to his players. The group marched out of the club, still playing, and formed a human shield around Garroway. "Dad was forever grateful to his friend," Dave Jr. said.[10]

At WMAQ, Garroway helped a young Black man, Harold Mason, who aspired to be an announcer, taking him as a protege and helping him learn announcing technique. He participated in a music festival at Comiskey Park, benefiting thirty churches in the Chicago area, featuring a 1,000-voice choir, the music of Ella Fitzgerald, and a four-year-old prodigy named Margaret Harris. He hosted a radio contest for the benefit of the American Brotherhood organization, and also got involved with the Chicago Urban League. With fellow radio hosts Studs Terkel, Linn Burton and Oliver D. Edwards, Garroway hosted a benefit for the Chicago Urban League at the Rose Bowl Ballroom.[11]

In his off hours, Garroway frequented clubs where Black musicians and entertainers gathered, drawing on his extensive list of contacts to help them get opportunities. He earned invitations to speak before Black social clubs and lodges. He urged them not to settle for the role they had borne for so long. "Too long have you scratched your head and played the part of tired and lazy folks on the Mississippi levee that the bigots want you to play," Garroway told one group. "And if you continue this role without questioning its character, then the label of Uncle Tom that has been yours to bear will be a fitting epitaph written on your tombstone. I am with you and you know this, but I am only a voice crying out to you to pick yourself up off the ground. I can stand here and talk against prejudice and discrimination for as long as you will listen. But when I am through, the task will still be up to you to do something about it." The crowd stood in applause.[12]

A decade before, Dave Garroway couldn't give away the sample piston rings in his salesman's case. Now he had a fifty-two week deal with NBC and a sponsor for *The Dave Garroway Show*. The National Guard's sponsorship not only underwrote its $3800 weekly budget, but helped get the program picked up by the entire network. Garroway's duties as *11:60 Club* host continued, and he continued to promote popular concerts. He maintained an interest in the Blue Note as its booking agent. Rumors of a television offer started to circulate. Even Hollywood was calling, with Columbia signing him for a cameo in *I Surrender, Dear*, released in 1948. All of it was managed through the help of his trusted agent, the five-foot-four-inch "Biggie" Levin, once described as "a nervous little man in chronic bad health" but also "one of the toughest, shrewdest agents in a field that attracts only the tough and shrewd." Levin's clients included Charlie Andrews, puppeteer Burr Tillstrom, and Studs Terkel.[13]

Garroway was bringing in $1,500 a week ("it chokes me to mention it," he told an interviewer). He lived in a bachelor apartment in Oak Park, decorated in a Hawaiian motif that he said made it look "more like the

Tiki Bar in the Moanana Hotel in Honolulu than it did a one-room apartment," his roommate a Siamese cat named Natch. Increasingly frequent profiles in newspapers and magazines detailed his eccentricities: his custom glasses and oversize wristwatch, the bespoke outfits that ranged from professional to eye-popping. One writer said Garroway "talks like an uninhibited professor of surrealism" who "wears clothes like a cross between a Camus character and Bond Street dandy." He became known for his casual demeanor before the microphone, flopping in a chair and tucking his feet beneath him, or sometimes walking around the studio barefooted.

Wealth also let him expand his collection of automobiles, for which he served as chief mechanic. Among the rolling menagerie was a peacock-blue Lincoln with a custom cut-down top of his own design and Harris tweed upholstery, from which Garroway made a matching blazer that he wore while driving the car. He still had the Rolls-Royce, which he had reupholstered in black patent leather, and had added a four-seat British roadster and a 1923 Model T Ford that he bought "because it was falling apart and I felt sorry for it." Garroway spent hours working on the cars at a North Side shop that he called the Tree House. One day a friend and fellow tinkerer, NBC announcer Hugh Downs, came over to visit. "The guy looked crestfallen," Downs said of Garroway. "It seems the front bumper of his Rolls-Royce was too big for Dave's chrome-plating vat."[14]

In 1949, Garroway bought the car that would be his prize possession for nearly thirty years. The 1938 Jaguar had started life as a gift for a Rumanian crown prince's nineteenth birthday. Somehow, it ended up in Lincoln, Nebraska, then in St. Louis, where Garroway bought the car for $2,500. Thus began a project that never really ended. Garroway not only loved the Jaguar's looks and handling, but he used it to satisfy his love of racing. In 1949 he raced the car at Watkins Glen, New York, and at a hill climb in Vermont. While airing it out on the Studebaker test track at South Bend, Indiana, the car's engine let go at 110 miles per hour. Four months of persuading later, Garroway convinced Jaguar to sell him a larger XK120M engine. Garroway extended the car's engine compartment to fit the big engine.

It was among countless modifications he made. After tearing up the original aluminum fenders during a race at Watkins Glen, Garroway hired an eighty-year-old Finnish body specialist to make replacements from steel. He installed larger headlamps. He tore out the original uphol-

Working on the Jaguar, with the Rolls-Royce waiting inside.
(Paris Day collection)

stery, replacing it with imitation alligator skin and beige velour imported from Italy; a few years later, he redid the work with six genuine alligator skins.[15]

The Jaguar was Garroway's love, and it prompted envy. Mel Torme tried to persuade Garroway to sell it to him. Over the years it carried countless of Garroway's celebrity friends as passengers. It never failed to draw attention. Some admirers took their interest too far. Inevitably someone would try to open its hood to look at the engine. Too often, the offender did not undo the latch in the middle, but pulled on the corner of the hood. This bent the thin sheet metal and required a body shop to straighten the hood out. This usually happened when Garroway wasn't around and it "just drove him nuts, literally," Dave Jr. said. One day while Garroway was in a bar with the Jaguar parked across the street, he saw an admirer begin to pull on the corner of the hood. The incensed Garroway ran right through the bar's big plate glass window and out into the street to stop the man. The startled admirer scurried off. Although Garroway wasn't injured, he did have to pay for a new window. As Dave Jr. observed, this "just might have been cheaper than sending his hood out to be repaired."[16]

His star ascended. For two consecutive years, a *Billboard* poll of disc jockeys named Garroway the favorite in their profession. *Radio Best* magazine named Garroway "The Most Original New Radio Personality of 1948," and had Peggy Lee present the award on his show. One reviewer praised Garroway's program as "rare and certainly refreshing," with chatter "amusing and intelligent," and suggested that other variety show hosts could learn something from Garroway's style. His fans included high school students in Chicago and university students in North Carolina, who stayed up late to catch the WMAQ show in the wee hours ("Won't say the show is better than the sack time," went a review in *The Daily Tar Heel*, "but it's among the few better things"). Earl "Fatha" Hines gave thanks with a new tune titled "Blues for Garroway." And Garroway's name became a powerful marketing tool for everything from a limited-edition record of new jazz favorites, to a method of fighting baldness.[17]

Not everyone was charmed. Critic Dale Harrison, who called disc jockeys "the Skidrowdies of radio," blasted Garroway as a sign of "cultural wastefulness" that was becoming "stronger than the forces which once provided fine, intelligent entertainment for a nation." He lampooned Garroway's much-discussed sartorial choices, saying they gave him the look of "a dispossessed hillbilly." Harrison wrote of a correspondent who said she never tuned in Garroway because she said the sound of his name "gives me the feeling of having a file run up and down my spine." The critic replied, "I've got a better reason for not tuning him in. My reason: I tuned him in once."[18]

Living alone in Chicago, busy with his broadcasting and promotion career, Garroway had little time for companionship. He had occasionally been linked to names such as Jane Skinner, who had been seen riding around Chicago with him in his custom Lincoln. Of all the names Garroway was linked to during his Chicago years, though, one stood out.[19]

Tallulah Bankhead was in Chicago to appear in Noel Coward's *Private Lives*. A night owl, she had discovered *The 11:60 Club* and was taken by the man with the seductive purr in his voice. One night, a staffer stuck his head in the studio. "Dave, I know you don't take phone calls, but there is a lady on the line who just won't let go." It was Tallulah Bankhead, he said, "and you'd be anxious to speak to her." An amused Garroway told him to take her number, and after he signed off, he called her back. Bankhead raved about the program for several minutes. "I'm up half the night, you know, and you're sensational, dahling." Garroway told her that they wanted her on the program but she had been unavailable. She promised to be on the program if they could record her in advance.

The next afternoon, Garroway and a recording engineer arrived at Bankhead's room. The actress continued her enthusiastic praise for Garroway's program, amazed that the show ran five nights a week. She had her assistant bring them wine. All the while, Garroway recalled, the great actress was "never still for a minute, skedaddling around the room." For most of an hour they recorded "an uproarious interview, during half of which Tallulah interviewed me." Garroway and the engineer packed up their equipment and prepared to leave. At the door Bankhead asked Garroway, "Why don't you pick me up after the show tonight?"

That night Garroway and Bankhead went around to several clubs, seeing Duke Ellington and his band perform at the Blue Note and visiting a few other places. Garroway was getting tired but decided there was one more place they needed to visit, a club where Louis Armstrong was performing. Garroway had reserved a good table for them. Armstrong spotted Bankhead and started "blowing those golden sounds right at her from the stage." As the great jazzman played, Bankhead shouted her encouragement to him. At the end of the set, Armstrong joined them at the table and Garroway watched the two engaged in entertaining conversation, each with their own distinct vocal style. "Of course, they had known each other before, but what a reunion scene they put on, Tallulah dancing in the aisle and Louis on fire until the last number had been played."

While Bankhead reveled, Garroway fought off sleepiness, and eventually persuaded his famous companion to call it an evening. At the Ambassador, he accompanied her back to her room. "I want you to come in," Bankhead said. "I'm very happy with you and very lonely without you." That was when Garroway said he met "another Tallulah, quiet, refined, almost like a lonely child." She went to her refrigerator and took out two large glasses of iced coffee, offering him one. "I always have one of these before I go to bed," she said.[20]

From this, Garroway remembered, came an ongoing relationship that lasted about half a year. Sometimes he would pick her up at the stage door; other nights, after his air shift ended, he would go up to her room and find her reading. Sometimes they went back to Garroway's place for the night. "She was an absolute delight," he wrote, "in private funny, pensive, discursive with amazing scope, good in bed, unspoiled and wise," a contrast to the "raucous" Tallulah the public knew.

One morning he awoke to find a blister on his hand. Garroway was convinced it was an insect bite, but Tallulah said it was a blister. "Look at your sheets," she said. Under the sheets, they found a small black hole in the mattress. Tallulah's cigarette had fallen from her hand, burned a hole in the mattress beneath the two of them, and come out where Garroway's hand had been. "Sacre bleu!" she cried.[21]

It didn't take long for the rumors to circulate. "The cocktails-at-seven set is chattering about Tallulah Bankhead's alleged romance with that lad named Garroway," columnist Dorothy Kilgallen claimed in September 1947. Other gossip columnists joined in, claiming that many of Garroway's on-air endearments were coded messages to Bankhead.[22]

When Noel Coward visited Bankhead in Chicago, Garroway watched the two friends chatter away. Suddenly Coward was seized with the urge to go on a roller coaster: "I simply must!" When Garroway said there was one in Riverview Park, Bankhead had the idea of making it a picnic, calling room service to order food and drinks. They piled into the Rolls-Royce, Bankhead and Coward talking all the way to the park, their conversation carrying on even as the roller coaster started to move. Garroway listened to them carry on, even over the thrilled screams of everyone else on the ride: "Their conversation was not interrupted for a second, nor was it on the next dip or the one after that." But one ride wasn't enough. "Let's go again!" Bankhead shouted, telling Garroway to open the picnic basket. "We'll have lunch on the rickety old thing." As the ride pulled away, Garroway handed out the sandwiches and cans of beer, and somehow Bankhead and Coward munched away as the ride climbed and dove. Garroway was laughing too hard to eat.[23]

One night Bankhead asked Garroway and Charlie Andrews to help her roll some cigarettes. "I just can't seem to do it." She got out a supply of rolling papers and a bag of material to roll in the papers. "What's this?" Andrews asked. "Tea," she responded. The two men rolled the cigarettes as requested. From time to time, Bankhead's housekeeper/assistant came through the room.

In 1951, that housekeeper/assistant filed a lawsuit against Bankhead for unpaid overtime. Garroway, who had just been hired for *Today*, felt "as though the earth opened up." He worried the housekeeper's testimony could mention the time he and Charlie Andrews rolled marijuana cigarettes for Bankhead, testimony that could prompt NBC to terminate his new contract. Soon after, Bankhead reached a settlement with her assistant. There would be no potentially damaging revelations. Garroway later claimed that "without a word to me," Bankhead had "paid $30,000 to, beyond any reasonable doubt, save my job on the *Today* show." At a party years later, Garroway tried to thank her. She took his hand and squeezed hard as she replied, "What the hell are you talking about?"[24]

8

The coaxial cable connected Chicago to the fledgling television networks in January 1949. Before then, television programs from New York had to be brought in by kinescope, a crude process of making motion pictures off television monitors. Stations in Chicago, St. Louis, Detroit and Milwaukee had put together their own network in those early days, but the original programs staged in Chicago for this little network couldn't get national distribution. Now, with the coaxial cable, stations in Chicago could send original programming to New York and the full network.[1]

Chicago television operated as a sort of island. There was a different audience, and the stations had to work with lower budgets. What Chicago lacked in resources and big-name talent, though, it more than made up for in creativity and resourcefulness. Puppeteer Burr Tillstrom created a program called *Junior Jamboree*, focused on a clown named Kukla and a one-toothed dragon named Ollie, who interacted with a friendly human portrayed by Fran Allison. The gentle and inventive program, which relied heavily on improvisation, had been developed for children but quickly developed an adult following. It found sponsorship and a slot on the NBC midwestern network as *Kukla, Fran and Ollie*, and became a hit when it joined the national NBC network in January 1949.[2]

"Chicago can't compete with New York or Hollywood for top-name talent," said Ted Mills, program director of NBC's Chicago affiliate. "Our economic position doesn't permit it." Instead, Chicago thought its way out by creating new programs that reflected "a frame of mind, an attitude, a way of looking at television entertainment. This approach produces shows that are warm, friendly, relaxed, simple." There was another difference. New York had what Mills called "the cynical approach. Their shows are money-built. They quiver with pace and rock with speed, lushness and excitement. They are of the zim-zam-zowie variety." In contrast, as another Chicago television veteran explained, "We don't mind a New York comic doing pratfalls. We just can't imagine ourselves behaving that way." Critic Robert Lewis Shayon, after observing ABC and NBC operations in Chicago, concluded, "Sophistication does not preclude taste, imagination, nor even simplicity. In the case of Garroway and *Kukla*, it is sophistication working for the essential, the honest."[3]

Isolated by half a continent from network and advertising executives, the denizens of the Merchandise Mart studios displayed a proud independence and inventiveness, able to exercise a rare freedom. "Those Chicago days were wonderful," Bob Banner remembered a decade after the Chicago School had dismissed. "We did more or less what we pleased. We were willing to try almost anything and our programs had a freshness and a spontaneity." The lack of ratings pressures, Studs Terkel remembered, also fostered inventiveness. "At that time, TV was in the hands of creative people, people who were willing to experiment."[4]

The result was a stable of programs unlike any other: sometimes eccentric, sometimes gritty, always unique. In addition to *Kukla, Fran and Ollie*, there was Terkel's improvised slice-of-life program, *Studs' Place*, set in a tavern where a group of regulars interacted based on whatever was on their minds or whatever happened on the set. There was a soap opera, *Hawkins Falls*, and a children's program, *Ding Dong School*. All of them shared an intimacy, "the approach that made people feel as if you were talking to them alone," Terkel remembered.[5]

Before long, the orthicon tube would summon Garroway. Ted Mills, as Charlie Andrews remembered, didn't know Garroway that well but wanted to do a show with him because he was popular on radio. Since Mills had some musical talent already available, an idea formed around a variety show, perhaps done from a theater on Michigan Avenue in the traditional grand variety show style. Charlie Andrews talked Mills out of it. "He's never going to work out standing in front of a theater audience," the writer said. "Why not do a variety show without an audience, and let the cameras move around and show the background? That's interesting, it's all new." Mills saw the potential and decided to do the show, which Andrews remembered as "a very courageous thing for him to do."[6]

Garroway was reluctant. "I used to damn the word television," he said in 1961, "because I could see it coming and didn't know what the hell to do about it." When NBC asked Chicago for a half-hour program, though, its top radio host was a logical choice. Out of it came a show with a weekly budget of $5,000 featuring music, variety and light comedy. While most variety programs featured a studio audience, Garroway's wouldn't. An audience would have destroyed the intimate style that was his trademark. "A performer should aim his stuff not at several hundred people gathered in the studio, but rather at the three people gathered around the set at home," Garroway maintained. Already he understood the new dynamic of television, while so many other programs were trying to televise vaudeville. Home viewers, he believed, "won't even chuckle at the same thing that will cause an earthquake if told in a theater. They just like to sit back and be entertained." Garroway thus forbade a studio audience. "I am aiming my show at the people at home."[7]

Nor would the program hide that it was a television show. It wouldn't be afraid to let Garroway amble between set pieces, or to let viewers see props and equipment in the background. The trappings of televised stagecraft, and the behind-the-scenes people who made it happen, would become part of the show. The intent was a program that wasn't stuffy, that despite hours of preparation and hard work seemed spontaneous and unrehearsed. "We did some things first because, like Columbus, we got there first," Garroway said in 1975. "We were pioneers. How could you lose?"[8]

Some of Garroway's staff from his radio program would carry over: trusted writer Charlie Andrews, orchestra leader Joseph Gallicchio, comedian Cliff Norton. They would be joined by two female singers, Carolyn Gilbert and Bette Chapel; a male singer, Jack Haskell; and a song-and-dance group called the Honey Dreamers. Occasional guests, such as Louis Armstrong, Duke Ellington, Buddy Ebsen and Henry Morgan, were worked into each episode. Edith Barstow, who became a choreographer after a career as a dancer, would oversee the dance numbers.[9]

The camera, standing in for the viewer, became a character itself. Inventive staging and directing techniques would transform the once-static box into an instrument. Set designs by Jan Scott made effective use of forced perspective and other techniques, giving depth and substance to the program's surroundings. A new device called a Sanner crane, one of four NBC owned, allowed overhead camera shots that were previously not available. Columnist Harriet Van Horne compared the Garroway camera to a panther, for "It stalks a picture, brings you toward it with stealth – then pounces," or a great bird "that swoops and darts and has known no confines save the dome of the sky." To Van Horne, the Garroway show made the camera "an artist in the company of artists."[10]

The result, which debuted at 10 p.m. Eastern on April 16, 1949, was a variety program "as far removed from all other variety shows as Milton Berle from Ed Sullivan," John Crosby wrote. Aside from not originating from New York, *Garroway at Large* differed in having no studio audience ("It's nice to see that someone is trying to get rid of that audience. We'd best get rid of it right now or it'll become the curse of television as it was of radio") or other "useless trappings of the big variety show." This allowed the cameras to wander "like inquisitive children, getting odd, striking glimpses of the dancers, the singers, the orchestra and, of course, of Mr. Garroway." Between acts, Garroway roamed the set, talking to the camera in his intimate purr that Crosby felt symbolized the program. "The whole show is conducted almost in a whisper," he wrote. In July, the acclaimed program moved to Sunday nights at 10 p.m. Eastern, which meant Garroway's radio series was then moved to Monday nights at 11:30 p.m.[11]

The Garroway program played with the new visual potential of television. As Carolyn Gilbert sang a tune titled "Take Your Shoes Off, Baby, And Start Running Through My Mind," a pair of bare feet began scrunching the singer's hair. Another number, titled "Rhapsody for Camera and Orchestra," featured several cameras running wildly through Joseph Gallicchio's array of musicians. Those cameras, and other elements of what happened behind the scenes, were part of the show in Garroway's world. One night, Garroway introduced the audience to a man named George Shafer, whom he described as "a celebrated leaf-dropper." The camera panned up to show a crewman on a platform, slowly dropping leaves onto a set below. The camera followed the leaves down, until they fell on a young couple who began singing "Indian Summer."[12]

Holding it all together was Garroway, whom one writer described as "six-feet-two of husky nonchalance" who wandered the stage, helping with the props, talking to stagehands, praising musicians in the studio orchestra for an inspired flourish, taking the mystery out of the new medium. For instance, while explaining the difficulties that lighting directors faced in eliminating heavy shadows, he might point to his own shadow on the floor. "Now go away," he would direct, as another bank of lights came up and took away the shadow. "This is typical Garroway," one observer wrote. "It gives audiences the impression of a show that has never been rehearsed, and Garroway "hopes it looks like that. Actually, forty hours of rehearsing go into each show." Garroway's own comments were ad-libbed. The scripts merely noted how long Garroway was to talk, and the host edited his comments on the fly. During rehearsals, Garroway watched the cast and staff go through their numbers, fret over the technical details, and awaited his summons. When he was needed, he ambled over, said "And then I say so, so, so and so, and then I walk over here, and say something about the product, and then I step over this cord here and walk to this setting and introduce the next number," then strolled off the floor to his chair and relaxed again. Choreographer Edith Barstow remembered how easy Garroway took it: "You could always tell around the studio when it was show day instead of rehearsal day. On show day, Dave wore shoes."[13]

It wasn't as easy as it looked. "The more relaxed you want to look on TV," Garroway said in 1971, "the more casual, the harder you have to work to achieve it – much good writing and rehearsal." Radio was the opposite. "You walk in there purposely unprepared and almost free-associate. If you've got a few notes on the funny things that happened that day, you usually wind up with more material than you need." As a result, Garroway found himself labeled a comedian. He disagreed. "I'm not funny at all," he said, insisting his style wasn't a setup. "If I want to say something, I say it. I just talk as if I was talking to myself and don't try to aim it up or down." Garroway didn't even like the word "emcee." Instead, he described himself as "just like the grocery clerk: when everybody has bought everything, I'm the guy who wraps it up."[14]

NBC asked Garroway to guest-host *Texaco Star Theater* while Milton Berle was on vacation, but when told he couldn't use his own cast and he had to retain Berle's format, Garroway refused. The broad style of Berle's humor clashed with Garroway's low-key, dry humor that rewarded the viewer for paying attention. "The comic elements sort of sneak up on you before you know it," Kay Gardella wrote. On one episode, Garroway kept walking past a man in a chair who looked like Henry Morgan, a comedian known for his acerbic wit. As he walked past, Garroway would glance over, bemused, but said nothing about the man. As the show ended, Garroway finally asked, "Aren't you Henry Morgan?"

"Yes!" he replied.

As the show ended, Garroway announced, "This program came to you from Chicago."

Morgan bolted from the chair. "*Chicago?*" he yelled, running out of the studio.[14]

Garroway could also puncture the show's own material. On one episode, Jack Haskell was to sing the song "I Love You." Just before the song, Garroway read the lyrics, illustrating to the audience just how little substance a song can have. "Now you know what the man wrote, and this is what Haskell can do with it," he said. Haskell went into the song. As he ended, the camera revealed Garroway at a blackboard, thirty-nine chalk marks denoting each time Haskell sang "I Love You." The host looked over to the singer. "Jack, I need one more to even it out." Haskell complied and Garroway made the final mark on the board.[15]

Cliff Norton's comedic sketches tended toward low-key absurdity. In one, he depicted a man studying a book of magic. Trying to make a flag of many nations, the man misread "bandana" as "banana," with predictably messy results. More sublime were the musical and dancing sketches Charlie Andrews thought up. In one, a boy and a girl at the beach changed into bathing suits. As they took off their glasses to swim, the cameraman knocked the shot just slightly out of focus. The two young people met on the beach, played ball, fell in love, and agreed to meet up for the bus ride home. They went to change back into their street clothes, and put on their glasses. The camera shot went back into focus, too. Now, though, the boy and girl didn't recognize each other and went their separate ways. Other numbers included a presentation of "Slaughter on Tenth Avenue" that Will Jones called "a beautiful thing to watch," and the witches from *Macbeth* singing "Rag Mop."[16]

Special visual effects became part of the repertoire. They were the work of Weeland Risser, manager of staging services, and Ralph Doremus, a scenic designer who had once worked with magician Harry Blackstone. Their inventiveness helped Garroway shatter a camera lens with a golf ball (a trick achieved by fastening a mousetrap, loaded with a steel ball and a piece of stiff wire, to a sheet of glass) or depict underwater dancers by putting an aquarium one inch from the lens. A skit with Cliff Norton as a pitcher and Garroway as a catcher depicted trick pitches with a baseball suspended by a fine piano wire, maneuvered by stagehands. Charlie Andrews thought up a sketch about a trip to the dentist, with the camera lens depicting the mouth of the viewer as dentist Norton brought dental tools to the camera lens, and sound effects represented exaggerated scraping and drilling. One day, cameraman Bob Haley brought in a glass brick; when held to the lens, it created dozens of simultaneous images. They worked it into the program, producing a kaleidoscopic effect that prompted NBC to ask where this strange "image multiplier" had come from. (After the staff refused to say, NBC finally demanded an answer. "We just mailed them the brick," Bill Hobin said.)[17]

At times the comedy put Garroway himself in peril. In one sketch, he was to play a soda jerk whose necktie got caught in a malted milk mixer. The tie was to be cut away on cue. When someone misplaced the scissors, Garroway was nearly strangled. For the dentist sketch, which needed the sound of a drill for full comedic effect, a plug failed to connect, nearly losing the audio. For several minutes Garroway crouched out of camera range, holding the plug in place at the wall, "in mortal fear of being electrocuted." A gag to have Garroway appear in the clouds at the end of a number ended with Garroway stuck twenty-five feet above the studio floor. The host remained stoic, not speaking about his peril. "It would have spoiled the show," he said. Sometimes the mishaps became part of the comedy. A story Garroway was telling about a businessman with a fly on his nose was to end with Garroway putting a fly on his nose. When the punchline came, Garroway couldn't find the fly. "We spent ten minutes looking for the fly, the staff came out, we were all on our hands and knees, looking for the fly," he said. The cameras stayed on the scene until the show ended, after which the tiny prop resurfaced.[18]

For the most part, NBC left them alone. "Oh, I guess there were pressures," Garroway said two decades later. "Chicago was sort of an island out there. We didn't even get the telegrams from New York." Not that NBC was that worried. Chicago's lower production costs, only $4,500 per episode, reflected considerable savings over New York-based productions.[19]

The lone constraint was that all programs originating from Chicago end with a spoken notice to that effect. It annoyed the staff. Director Bob Banner asked why they had to say it when the shows from New York didn't announce their city of origin. The response: "Because you are remote. New York is television." This answer irked the Garroway staff so much that they started having fun with it. They worked it into a post-credits portion of the program called "the snapper," the very last thing before the program faded out. One program ended with Garroway informing the audience, "This program came to you from Chicago, where the laws of gravity are strictly enforced." Garroway then disappeared upwards, a twist on the Hindu rope trick. In another sign-off, Garroway announced the program had come via coaxial cable. He then picked up a hatchet and chopped a piece of water hose painted to resemble a cable.

The screen went blank. Garroway then put the ends back together and the picture returned. In another instance, Garroway announced, "This program came to you from Chicago, the friendly city." He turned around and walked away, revealing a knife in his back. The antics annoyed New York, but Garroway's staff didn't care. They kept doing it. Garroway, content with the relaxed Chicago style, wanted to keep the show there. "In New York we'd all be subject to a lot of annoying outside influences – backbiting and what goes with it," he said. "Maybe later, when we are even a more tightly knit unit, we'll move East."[20]

It took very little time for critics to fall in love with *Garroway at Large*. "Nobody yells at you and the cameras have finally caught on to the tricks they can do," Walter Winchell wrote, calling the program "the first with a professional flavor. Big-time all the way." Harriet Van Horne called it "so imaginative, so rich in the small, original touches that make or mar a video production, that no one working in the medium can afford to miss it. It is pure television, in the sense that it is derived from no other form of entertainment," and Van Horne wondered why New York couldn't produce something so fresh and enjoyable. John Crosby, glad that Garroway had toned down for television "perhaps the most exasperating prose style ever heard in radio," assessed the program more as an experiment, and "a pretty successful one, than as a program." To him, the show couldn't be put on in any medium except television. "It appears to be directed at pleasing a few people in a living room, not at provoking wild shrieks of laughter from a studio audience. The orchestra, the singers, and Garroway are all toned down to a point where they won't wake the baby. And, of course, you won't hear a single handclap." Chicago columnist Larry Wolters pronounced it "Grade A television fare" and "proof that top grade video doesn't necessarily need to originate in New York or Hollywood." The *New Yorker* called the program "a strangely boneless half-hour," with Garroway presenting acts and telling stories "as though he were walking in his sleep. In fact, he manages to project this feeling so effectively that on several Sunday evenings I have had the uncomfortable sensation that I was asleep myself." The reviewer found the Garroway show "a conscious rebellion" against most variety shows, which seemed "designed to blow up your television set, if not your whole damned house...in the world of television, Garroway is a tiny oasis of peace and quiet."[21]

Garroway's fellow performers lauded his style, and even those skeptical of television found *Garroway at Large* a breath of fresh air. Comedian

Fred Allen, who saw the networks' slashing of radio budgets as a recipe for compromised standards, was interested in moving to television. He cited both *Kukla, Fran and Ollie* and *Garroway at Large* as examples of what could be done with the medium, and he puzzled why Garroway hadn't landed a sponsor. "Whoever does that show is turning out real television. He's creating something for television," Allen said. "Berle isn't doing anything for television. He's photographing a vaudeville act. That's what they're all doing." Allen made known he wanted a show like Garroway's, based on a loose, informal format.[22]

Audiences loved it, too. Garroway's fan mail included almost daily requests from female viewers: married women wanted to run off with him, and one woman sent him a love note twice a day by special delivery. Even tiny changes in his voice could concern his fans. One mother, thinking she heard congestion in his delivery, offered to cure the cold she was sure he had contracted.[23]

Success brought security. Despite interest from sponsors including General Foods and appliance manufacturer Admiral, *Garroway at Large* had yet to land one. However, CBS expressed interest in hiring Garroway. NBC, still smarting from how CBS had recently swiped several big NBC stars through huge deals, secured Garroway to a five-year contract for radio and television. He would earn $5,000 per week, a rate that would increase once his program found sponsorship. That finally happened in December, when flooring manufacturer Congoleum-Nairn bought *Garroway at Large*. He also briefly added a five-minute television program called *Reserved For Garroway* to his workload, five nights a week.[24]

Garroway's new responsibilities went beyond television. The radio networks were exploring daytime program formats beyond soap operas. Both ABC and CBS had moved toward more variety shows during the day. CBS in particular had a powerful morning presence with Arthur Godfrey's radio show, a folksy and relaxed variety program with a regular ensemble. Now NBC counter-programmed Godfrey with Garroway. A soap opera called *Dr. Paul* was axed from the 11:15 slot to make way for a weekday fifteen-minute show called *Reserved For Garroway*, recycling the title of his earlier five-minute television show. The new radio program loosely mimicked the Godfrey format but turned it on its ear. Lampooning the audience-giveaway segments of other morning shows, Garroway and Andrews inflicted spur-of-the-moment interviews with audience members and hatched "Garroway's Giant Crackpot Question," in which

Garroway in his Hawaii-themed apartment. (Paris Day collection)

the winner might be rewarded with their choice of one dollar in cash or sixteen bales of fresh Illinois hay. Musical interludes came from the Art Van Damme Quintet and a pianist, Giovannini; they were soon joined by singers Connie Russell and Jack Haskell. Charlie Andrews popped up from time to time with wry observations.

In between numbers, Garroway offered commentary on items he had noticed in the news, philosophical musings, or anecdotes about the cast members. Or he might offer advice, ranging from the practical to the bizarre. When a listener wrote and told of getting a nasty note from a bank teller after overdrawing his account by a few dollars, Garroway suggested a way to respond:

> First, go to the store and buy a mackerel, a good, medium-sized one. See that the flesh is firm and fresh-looking. Have it wrapped up well. Then go to the bank and tell the man you want to rent a safe deposit box. He will give you a key to it,

and you will be the only one with a key to it. That's the law. That box is yours. Now carefully take your package, unwrap it, and place the fish neatly in the safe deposit box, and lock it in. Then walk out of the bank and go on a nice long vacation – say, in Alaska. After a few days up there, you can really enjoy a good rest. Spend as much time as possible thinking about that bank, and the new atmosphere you have created there.[25]

Reviews noted the contrast between the extroverted Godfrey and the "untense" Garroway, favorably comparing him to Henry Morgan, "but without Morgan's satirical vein." *Variety* called it "an enjoyable combination of bright music interspersed with some amiable patter by emcee Dave Garroway, all nicely tailored for the daytime audience." John Crosby, still sorting through his feelings about Garroway, didn't know if his "bonelessness" would ever truly compete with Godfrey; despite reining in his eccentricities, Crosby felt the ultra-casual Garroway remained "a special taste, possibly a little fey for wide esteem." Indeed, some of his tendencies, such as having the studio audience of his radio show express their appreciation by snapping their fingers instead of applauding, might have struck many viewers as the opposite of the folksy Godfrey.[26]

Industry insiders lauded Garroway. He remained the top disc jockey among a *Billboard* poll of disc jockeys, and radio editors of newspapers and magazines voted him the most promising male star in television. *Ross Reports*, a television industry journal, noted that Garroway and Godfrey were considered the top male stars on the air, and that leaders in the business made a point of watching Garroway. Like *Kukla, Fran and Ollie*, they considered *Garroway at Large* a show that could only work on television, taking full advantage of its possibilities.[27]

Women, in particular, fell for Garroway. Columnist Bob Goddard wrote that in an informal survey, women of "reasonable age" had "an overpowering urge to mother him. I don't know whether any other television star can make that statement or not but it's certainly not going to do Garroway any harm." After an appearance in Philadelphia, Garroway was in a station waiting for a train to Chicago when an elderly woman came over to him and began doting on him like a mother, prompting slight embarrassment.[28]

Not everyone was charmed. "A great many people are decidedly cool to this very cool guy," Crosby noted. "In Chicago, where Garroway first got his foot in the door and from which he still broadcasts his network shows, Garroway attracted many devout admirers. There were others, quite an impressive band too, who would like to wring his neck." Another reviewer noted, "Fans either blow hot or cold on Garroway. They either like him a lot or can't stand him." One critic even accused Garroway of stealing Henry Morgan's act, even though the two men had appeared on each other's programs and NBC had even considered pairing their series in the same television hour. Another review said Garroway stood no chance against Godfrey. "We rise hastily and turn off Garroway's program the minute we hear that irritating whistle that is his signature. We don't like his voice, his records, or anything about him! Godfrey or nothing, on Monday mornings when we are at home."[29]

On July 10, *Garroway at Large* lampooned the Red Scare. "Today, no matter who you are, or what you're doing, there's always the possibility that you may be investigated," the number began. "I'm not intimating that you're doing anything wrong. I'm not even saying you have to do anything. Just read your paper, make your car payments, stay home with your family...and the first thing you know, the FBI." There followed a song: "Don't ever hurry, no matter what you do / Someone will say you're 'rushin'' / And they may investigate you!" Over the course of the number, Garroway and singer Carolyn Gilbert dropped numerous references: the Alger Hiss case ("never be seen in the company of pumpkins...and Heaven help you if you own a Woodstock typewriter"), loyalty oaths ("Never, never admit to having been or being now, the life of any party"), and the Red Scare ("Even the good old *Harvard Crimson* may be under suspicion one of these days, simply because of its color"). The number closed with a suggestion that the current investigations could lead to an average citizen being jailed for using red ink, seeing *The Red Shoes* at a movie house, stopping at a red light, or being seen with Red Skelton. "Lock all your doors / Cut off your phone," went the closing bars. "Never trust anyone, stay all alone / Don't move a finger, so help me it's true / Or they'll investigate you, too."[30]

The next day, FBI assistant director Clyde Tolson received a memorandum about "a scurrilous television program last night" that "indicated smear on the FBI tactic." The memorandum cited not only the opinions of two agents, but a representative of the Office of Naval Intelligence.

"It is suggested we have the Chicago Office ascertain the background of the people involved in this program." A subsequent follow-up went into detail about not only Carolyn Gilbert but about Garroway himself ("has the general reputation of being a 'screwball,' that Garroway attempts to create this impression for professional advertisement") and his numerous ties to the Black community (his Black tailor; his promotion of Black artists on his programs, especially Sarah Vaughan). The report included a rumor, passed along by an informant, that Garroway was homosexual (a rumor that Garroway was living with a blond secretary, according to this informant, was that there was nothing immoral with it because "Garroway had nothing to do with women anyway"). Concerned viewers also wrote to the FBI. "This program is the most thinly veiled Communist propaganda I have ever seen," a Pennsylvania viewer wrote. "Fun was poked at the recent spy trials, the F.B.I., Senator Hickenlooper, in fact at all the decent things now being done to safeguard our country. You would do well to look into the motives behind some of the characters who put on this show."[31]

Inside NBC, the response had been rapid, and angry. "I saw the show at home and started calling people," an NBC Chicago executive reported to New York. "There is no excuse to offer." Those responsible for clearing the material for broadcast, he wrote, "realize they used extremely bad judgment...I could fire one or both of these men, but it would not serve a good purpose. I am certain there will be no recurrence of this type of material." Public statements were made. "It won't happen again!" an NBC spokesman assured.[32]

While the matter was forgotten by much of the audience, the FBI would remember. Two years later, when the McCarran Committee requested information on Garroway and several other entertainment figures, the controversial musical number and the rumors about his sexuality were among the information provided. The Bureau also closed itself off to him. When *Today* producer Abe Schechter requested having cameras visit the FBI for the morning show in connection with National Crime Prevention Week in March 1952, he was turned down. Appeals from the network brass cut no ice. "I told Julian Goodman, who called me, that we could not do anything on this," L.B. Nichols told Tolson in a memo. "We were very fond of Abe, would do anything we could to help Abe or NBC, but we would not be a party to anything connected with Dave Garroway. I then referred him to the Saturday night program that occurred a few years ago wherein a tirade was entered into against the Bureau in connection with a song and quotes that followed the Communist Party line."[33]

The financial bonanza of his new contract and stardom increased Garroway's ability to live comfortably: the $210 suits, a new Cadillac convertible, an apartment in the Ambassador East. It also brought new worries. His numerous shows – his two morning programs, the late-night program, the Sunday television series – squeezed his time. With so many demands, his sleep dwindled to two hours a night, and he leaned on the Doctor to keep him going. He worried that the Sunday television series ate into the quality of his radio programs. "Dave used to talk a lot about musicians who turned out good records when they were still struggling, but became leaders of mere 'commercial' bands when they hit the big time," one journalist wrote. "It might well be that the same thing is in store for him." Even after *The 11:60 Club* and the local television spot were sacrificed, Garroway's time remained at a premium.

One cost hurt the most. Television, he told an interviewer, had taken from him "one of my most precious possessions, anonymity. I can't roam around now without people stopping me." Radio had suited him much better. "Radio is like a bank," he said. "You sit back, nothing happens, and you get rich." As a faceless voice he could have fun wandering around, not being bothered. Now, television made it impossible. In New York, he was stopped on the streets and asked if he was indeed Dave Garroway. Incidents like these, and the episode in Philadelphia, "unseat his serenity," Val Adams wrote. "He fumbles for just the proper response, and sometimes he's embarrassed." It didn't sit well with a man whose casual on-screen nature was a refined and rehearsed version of his own inherent nature. "Dave is essentially a quiet fellow," one writer noted. "Once in a while he does become animated, when the spirit moves him; he can laugh at a bawdy joke, and at times he blows his top. But even at an informal party of old friends, where the toasts are flowing freely, Dave's casual nature still outshines anything on the raucous side."[34]

Sometimes Garroway punctured the ballyhoo that had been constructed around him. A group of young people in Chicago invited him to the first meeting of a Garroway fan club they formed. The excited teenagers watched their hero walk into the room. Suddenly he barked, "Why did you come here? Don't you know you've spoiled a dream?" Shocked silence quickly dissolved the young fans' excitement. After a moment, Garroway returned to his usual kindly demeanor and explained the lesson behind his feigned rudeness. "I, too, used to have my own little private fantasy about famous people in the world, and what would happen when I met them," he said. "I was always disappointed when I found out they were just plain people, not big, rich, famous celebrities."[35]

Nor was Garroway afraid to take the air out of himself on his programs. Greeting French actress Mariette Voigt on *Garroway at Large*, he tried to impress her by speaking in high school French. She replied in her native tongue. Garroway smiled, unaware that her response had been, "I've seen your show many times and often wondered if you knew what you were doing...and now that I'm here, I know that you don't." He also owned up to mistakes. On a Mother's Day episode, Garroway waxed philosophical on the day's significance as he strolled over to introduce violinist Eddie South. "Do you think your mother's watching tonight?" Garroway asked him. South responded gently, "Dave, my mother is gone." Garroway swallowed his embarrassment. "I'm sorry. I didn't know." He then retreated as South began to play.[36]

Inside, something continued to gnaw at him. In March 1950, he confessed to a reporter that a chronic sadness would not let him go, and it defied his attempts to understand it. "If I had sat down ten years ago and tried to blueprint what I would want to be and have at thirty-six," he said, "the chances are I would have wanted things exactly the way they are now. But, generally, I'm pretty miserable. I guess some people are born somewhat melancholy and they're gonna stay that way, no matter what." It was the first time he had spoken so openly of his depression, and he discussed the many ways he had tried to flee from the sadness – how neither golf nor playing cards nor gem cutting had satisfied the need within. "The thrill of it went away," the writer said, "and left him, as usual, bereft of knowing why." The sadness even manifested itself in a painting Garroway had purchased for his apartment, "a protoplasmic thing called 'Pensive' by Robert Philippe. Its mood is pretty woebegone."

In 1961 Garroway called this period "miserable," saying: "I couldn't see people and enjoy them, so I isolated myself pretty much in my work. I took psychotherapy, but it didn't help. There was nothing I could do to help myself. Then, very suddenly, the depression went away. Within a few days. I still don't know why." There would be happy times, but the cloud would never be far away.[37]

New York struck Garroway as a strange place, its formality a stark contrast from the unpretentious ways of Chicago. He had gone there to tend to some network business, including a stint guest-hosting NBC's *Broadway Open House*. Unable to find an apartment, he had holed up at the Waldorf-Astoria, where the staff got upset when he used a hotel towel to polish the Jaguar. With no apartments available, he didn't dare leave the hotel. And, he told newspaperman Mark Barron, a group of friends he dined with were all insisting he accompany them to a performance of *South Pacific*.[38]

From New York, he drove to a Sports Car Club of America meet at the Studebaker proving grounds in South Bend, Indiana. On the second lap of a six-lap race, the Jaguar's engine blew up. At that night's awards banquet, Garroway joked that he'd lost interest in salvaging the poor car, instead shopping for a sailboat. He started lobbying Jaguar to sell him a larger XK120M engine. The carmaker didn't want to sell him one, but Garroway was persistent. Four months later, he got it. It took a lot of work and a few modifications to squeeze the big engine into the car, but soon the Jaguar was back in action.[39]

Garroway's most prominent admirer, Fred Allen, was still looking for a television format that suited him. He came to Chicago, where he conferred with Garroway and did a guest appearance on *Garroway at Large*. Allen told Garroway the small studio had no room for an audience ("If you would bring one in, they would have to applaud up and down, not sideways") and complained that the audience in his own studio consisted of eighty three sponsor and network executives and "fat mamas who climb onto the stage with fat children they want autographed. And the kids hand us their popcorn bags to write our names on." The network wanted Allen to use a variety format, but he wanted a show more like Garroway's, believing it would last longer. Allen blamed a faulty ratings measurement method for making both radio and television dull. "Someone should have covered and smothered television," he complained. "That's the trouble with fellows like Marconi. They invent something and leave everybody else with eight million ulcers."[40]

The Chicago method astounded those new to it. Robert Ruark, having sat in on many television productions in New York, said it was "almost embarrassing" to sit in on *Kukla, Fran and Ollie* and *Garroway at Large*, that in comparison to the tightly-controlled and scripted productions in New York, the loose, improvisational nature of both shows "commit few sins." He particularly praised the work of Mills and Hobin, who "discovered the TV camera as a friend and ally, rather than as an enemy." New York's programs, Ruark believed, were "a good two years behind Chicago." Meanwhile, personnel in New York, proud of their higher ratings, referred to their Midwestern rivals as "The Charm School." Comic Jack Carter returned from a visit to Chicago insisting that Garroway's partisans gave him the impression they considered him out of date. For his part, Garroway didn't believe there was such a thing as Chicago television. "It's just that out there, there is more chance for individual experimentation. There is less tension and less crowding." He predicted that even though New York and Hollywood were dominant, Chicago would continue as a video production center.[41]

Garroway was on top. One evening he went into the men's room on the nineteenth floor of the Merchandise Mart. At an adjacent urinal was Studs Terkel. "They love me," Garroway told his friend. "General Sarnoff called me."

"Dave, you are very popular," Terkel replied. "You've got a very good program, and you're not hurting NBC at all. They love you because you're very valuable to them. Protect that, Dave."

"Oh, they're wonderful people."[42]

Garroway at Large entered its second season as inventive, and as irreverent, as before. During a visit by cartoonist Al Capp, spoken dialogue gave way to superimposed comic-style balloons that contained their words. In a sketch, as Lil' Abner was about to marry Daisy Mae, Capp suddenly interrupted the proceedings, declaring the finale was to be saved for the comic strip. On a show before Thanksgiving, Cliff Norton depicted a chef who would demonstrate how to stuff a turkey. The joke was that Norton would spoon-feed corn to a live turkey. All went well at rehearsal, but on the live show the bird shook itself free from Norton's grasp and ran around the studio, knocking Garroway down. Viewer complaints about the treatment of the turkey prompted NBC to order an investigation, but Chicago responded that Garroway suffered more harm than the turkey.[43]

Stories also circulated about Garroway's effectiveness as a salesman. One told of a woman out to buy some wall covering. A salesman told her it was twelve and three-quarter cents a square foot. She replied, "Oh, no you don't, young man. Dave Garroway says it's only thirteen cents a square foot and that's all I'll pay!" Another observer noted that Garroway "walks right out of the lens and flops down on the arm of your sofa and unfolds that sample of floor covering. If you aren't careful you find yourself pouring him a cup of coffee while you sip your own. You feel you'd know him any place in the world, and what's more, he'd recognize you, too." Paul Gallico wrote that although he didn't need any of the items Garroway sold, his style of simple salesmanship "makes me wish I did so that I could show my gratitude by rushing out and getting what he sells...You see, he doesn't deafen you or annoy you. He just talks about his business and then shows you that it's better than the other competing kinds."[44]

The program's sponsor felt differently. Congoleum-Nairn didn't like that the show's costs were going up, or that ratings weren't meeting expectations. In its first season, *Garroway at Large* was budgeted at $4,500 per week. Its second season was budgeted at $10,000 per week. Now, NBC raised the figure to $18,500 per week. Although the show remained popular in Chicago, the overall ratings for *Garroway at Large* were low. In New York, which represented a fifth of Garroway's line-up, stiff competition from a celebrity show on CBS and a mystery program on DuMont had cost him ten ratings points between the start and end of 1950. Ratings in Philadelphia echoed the drop.[45]

NBC executives discussed ways to help Garroway's ratings, but more problems emerged. Celebrities were easy to snag for appearances on New York shows, but persuading them to visit Chicago was a hard sell. The program's planning, usually three weeks in advance, further complicated guest booking and advance publicity. The increasing fees paid to television guests, which one NBC executive complained "have gotten tremendously out of hand," also limited the program's budget for special appearances. NBC tried to work with the McCann-Erickson advertising agency to improve Garroway's ratings during the mid-winter ratings period, but it wasn't enough.[46]

Worse, not all markets carried it live, which ruined the show's effect. Viewers in Ames, Iowa, having read the critical acclaim that *Garroway at Large* had received, watched the program. More than five hundred viewers registered their dissatisfaction, and the Ames station pulled it from the schedule. The fault, one observer said, was that it was on kinescope. When seen live it was "the most original and relaxing program of the weekend," a Des Moines columnist wrote, but a filmed *Garroway at Large* just wasn't the same. Iowa viewers were also puzzled by the way Garroway wandered around the set.[47]

By April rumors were circling that *Garroway at Large* had sponsor troubles, that Congoleum-Nairn was about to drop the show, or that the show would move to New York, to a larger studio and a larger budget. At the end of that month, Garroway admitted Congoleum-Nairn was reviewing its advertising and would likely cancel at the end of June. "We'll probably be back in the fall," he said. "There are four options on the program." He also denied a move to New York was in the works.[48]

Garroway's prediction about the program's present sponsorship proved correct. Congoleum-Nairn's option on the time slot expired, and NBC sold the time to Procter and Gamble for a series starring Red Buttons. Congoleum-Nairn still had an option on the program itself, but blanched at the higher cost. When Congoleum-Nairn finally let it go, Armour, whose Dial soap division already sponsored *Dial Dave Garroway*, took an option on *Garroway at Large*.[49]

The end of Garroway's second year on television ("Two years! Sometimes it seems as though we'd only been on for twenty!" he had cracked a few weeks earlier) came in late June, and he closed the season with viewer-requested favorites from the show's previous episodes. In his closing remarks, Garroway said little about the loss of his sponsor, only that he would be back on another day of the week, at another time. After his traditional "peace," the televised Garroway faded into an uncertain future.[50]

In the summer of 1951 Garroway and Andrews took a trip to Europe. Dial liked the momentum Garroway's daily radio program had built and didn't want him gone for that long, but Garroway insisted on a tour of Europe. Andrews helped broker a compromise: Garroway would tape daily segments and have them flown back to Chicago, one set of reels on a plane and a safety duplicate on another. The recordings would be played between musical segments on *Dial Dave Garroway*.[51]

The two began their tour of Europe on July 9, using what one columnist called a "Huckleberry Finn-Tom Sawyer" adventure. Listeners heard Garroway's musings about coffee in Paris ("I don't think they start with coffee in the first place. And French waiters are sneaky. Before you can stop them, they've diluted the stuff with an equal amount of milk – burned milk") and visiting a champagne bottler in Rheims ("They give you all you can drink free. Some American tourists have been here since early 1947"). Watching the Follies Bergere, Garroway mused over the elaborate costumes the girls wore ("The skirts, trains and headdresses must have cost at least $5,000 per costume, though the top part of their dresses, I'd judge cost about twenty-five cents.")[52]

When they tried to record at the Eiffel Tower, a Frenchman in a fancy uniform grew suspicious of the equipment Andrews took into the elevator. "He points at me and yells a lot of French," Andrews said. "I try to push past him carrying the equipment, and right away he tries to make a federal case of the thing." Just in time, Garroway arrived, and was able to speak enough French to get Andrews out of trouble. They couldn't take the tape recorder up with them, though. Later, Garroway wanted to record inside the casino at Deauville so listeners could hear the sounds of the great gambling hall. The management told him he couldn't, and requested that he leave. A short while later, Garroway returned, played and lost a round of roulette, then took out a camera. Five men marched over, took Garroway in hand, and delivered him to the manager's office. Garroway identified himself and said he just wanted to take some pictures. The manager stripped the film from Garroway's camera and gave it back to him with a warning: "Good sire, please do not return to this establishment." ("I think he meant it," Garroway said.)[53]

At one point during their Paris stay, Garroway's funk returned and he holed up in his hotel room. Andrews urged him to get up and get out, but Garroway protested that he had no energy. Andrews bought a guidebook, typed out a few sentences about landmarks for Garroway to refer to, and recorded Garroway in the room, acting as if he were actually at the site he was describing. For a visit to Napoleon's tomb, Andrews had Garroway stand over the bathtub to provide an echo, as if they were standing in the tomb itself. Word came back: send more like it. For the next week, Andrews scrambled for more landmarks that they could fake from within the bathroom. At the end of the week, Andrews flushed the toilet at the end of the recording, making no comment. Parker Gibbs, back in Chicago, figured it out. ("Unidentified sound at end of tape. I cut it out. I hope I did the right thing," he wired Andrews.)[54]

After Paris, they rented a sports car and drove to the Riviera, where Biggie Levin would join them. Along the way, they stopped for gas. They recorded Andrews' efforts to talk in French to a gas station attendant. "*Je* want *cinq* liters of gasoline," Andrews said. The attendant looked on in puzzlement. "Look, buddy, *mon cheri. Une, deu,* three, four, *cinq – cinc* liters." As the tank filled, Andrews observed. "Watch it, buddy, you're getting up to *cinq*." From France they drove to Switzerland, enjoying the sights along the way. One afternoon, they pulled up at a hotel in Zermatt. Too tired for much else, they trudged to their rooms and promptly went to sleep.[55]

Back in New York, NBC had telephone operators scrambling to get in touch with Garroway with an urgent message. All they knew was that he was in Europe. For twenty eight hours, the operators worked to track him down, finally connecting with him at the hotel. When he picked up the phone and answered, he heard cheering in the background from the operators, whose search was over. The cheering then gave way to sobering news.

After the call, Garroway walked to Charlie Andrews' room. The writer was startled to find Garroway by his bedside, waking him up. "I want to show you one of the most thrilling sights in the world," Garroway said. He took Andrews to the window, where he threw open the curtains and revealed a breathtaking view of a huge mountain bathed in morning sunlight. "Here is the Matterhorn at dawn."

"Dave, that's beautiful."

"Our show has been canceled."[56]

Armour had dropped its option on *Garroway at Large*. It had scheduled the series for 10:30 p.m. Eastern, a time slot already controlled by Armour on NBC. It solved the time slot problem, but opened two new ones. Some smaller markets only had one television station, and thus offered programs selected from all the networks. Garroway's live slot would conflict with boxing matches on other networks, which audiences wanted to watch only when they were aired live. Although these affiliates still wanted Garroway's program, they would have to take it via kinescope. Other stations without boxing matches to think about would only take Garroway via kinescope, too. With only eleven stations carrying the show live and forty-five taking the show on kinescope, Armour couldn't run effective seasonal campaigns. Ads promoting hams for Easter, for instance, might be seen in some cities two weeks after Easter had passed. Promotions for Thanksgiving turkeys might suffer the same fate. It didn't help, either, that Cliff Norton had signed a deal to perform at a Chicago hotel. NBC would have had to find a new time slot for Garroway, and Norton's performance contract would have needed renegotiating.[57]

Garroway came home with his prospects for a new sponsor and another evening television slot looking dim. With NBC's nighttime schedule mostly full, it looked more likely that Garroway would move to the mornings, perhaps taking over Rudy Vallee's 11 a.m. slot. Vallee wasn't obligated to NBC, so Garroway's contract with the network gave him priority. "If Garroway switches to an early niche," Kay Gardella speculated, "he'll have to alter that easy, yawning style so appropriate to late looking."[58]

9

NBC was already thinking about reworking the morning lineup. Behind it was an idea from the network's forward-thinking vice president in charge of television, Sylvester L. "Pat" Weaver. A Dartmouth alum who had worked his way up through Young and Rubicam to head the agency's radio holdings, the innovative Weaver had a vision of what broadcasting could become. After CBS lured several top NBC stars to jump networks and sign lucrative production deals, NBC needed to find a new way forward. The network felt Weaver's new ideas could help, and hired him to lead NBC's fledgling television efforts. This he was prepared to do in his characteristically unconventional way.[1]

"Television – the most exciting, the most dynamic medium of transmitting information ever developed – eventually will be the major entertainment force for ninety-five per cent of all our people," Weaver wrote in 1951. There would be more than entertainment, though, in his vision. Weaver believed viewers should get "adroitly-done information" and that television must "expose them to the personalities of the people who are making contributions to our life and times so that they may stimulate broader interests in the people and a new adulthood. That is the pattern of any good mass medium." Weaver's vision was that "every member of the audience has a box seat as the cream of the entertainment world performs, and becomes an informed spectator of the times in which he lives."[2]

Weaver also argued that when sponsors and agencies owned and controlled the programs, and made deals with the networks to buy the air time, it shut out advertisers with smaller budgets. Weaver instead wanted a system in which the networks oversaw the programs and sold "participations," thirty- or sixty-second spots during commercial breaks. More affordable access to network shows would open up more possibilities for smaller advertisers, and generate more revenue.[3]

Weaver took particular interest in an unscheduled block between 10 and 11 a.m. Eastern. He proposed swapping that back to the affiliates in exchange for a two-hour block between 7 and 9 a.m. Eastern. Those two hours would be filled by a "rise and shine" program sold in quarter-hour units, with certain segments the affiliates could sell locally at their own rates. Weaver imagined a televised *Breakfast Club*-style program with a small studio audience, featuring news as well as music and comedy, a "morning communications show in a studio with both sound and sight" meant to "start a habit of tuning in *Rise and Shine* as the first stop in the morning before going to brush the teeth."[4]

Another proposal suggested a midday program called *Today*. The daily fifteen-minute program would present hard news, told with the help of film and photos, briefing the viewer on the day's events, a program that "dramatizes the things, events, people and places which make up the day's news in absorbing, diverting techniques, stemming out of the vivid dramatic potential of television." *Today* would also be a showcase for new records, books, magazines, films, radio programs, and virtually anything else going on that day, covering "the whole realm of audience interest," meant to "condense attractively what is being offered the public today via all media." The host "will have to be a person of curiosity and humor" with "wit, lightness and geniality." A concept by scriptwriter Charlie Speer called for "a couth, knowledgeable, amusing and friendly personality. He should be an Arthur Godfrey, but with shoes on. He should have some of the bland, 'off the cuff' geniality of Bing Crosby, yet he should be as impeccable as Lucius Beebe."[5]

Through the summer of 1951 Weaver's team sketched out ideas for the new morning show. In late July, producer Mort Werner outlined a two-hour program. Originating from the RCA Building's Studio 8G with a small "drop-in" studio audience, it would be treated as a televised radio show. The "continually changing audience," Werner wrote, would not sit and view the program "but will 'glance' but LISTEN." A recurring news segment with scheduled updates would give each new shift of viewers the latest news, while recorded weather reports would come directly from the United States Weather Bureau. Entertainment would come from a boy singer and a girl singer, a ten-piece orchestra, a four-piece Western ensemble, and from a comedian who "will wander in and out of the show" (Werner suggested Jack Kirkwood, Doodles Weaver, New York morning radio comedians Gene Rayburn and Dee Finch, or the similar team of Bob Elliott and Ray Goulding). The announcer would double as the newsman.

Werner wrote that "the whole show will be carried on the shoulders of the MC." This person "must be a guy who has tremendous stamina, who can talk about anything at any time, and who can stand out in 'one.'" Werner warned that this person should not be a comedian, but should "have the stature and dignity to talk about news, to interview people, to narrate over film, and to have a real selling personality." For the role, Werner strongly recommended Johnny Olson, then heading up a noon program on DuMont, or Mel Venter, a popular San Francisco broadcaster who hosted *The Breakfast Gang* on the Don Lee Network. Weaver wanted a high-energy host, since there would be so much to cover in so little time. As he remembered years later, he envisioned "a buttoned-up hard-hitting guy climbing up walls and taking us up to date all over the place," and thought rapid-talking Rush Hughes, famous for his *Hughesreel* synopses of current events, would be an ideal host.[6]

In early August NBC sent a memorandum about *Today* to its salesmen. It was tentatively scheduled for a fifteen-minute block at 12:30 p.m. weekdays. As "a new concept in news presentation," the new program would give attention to ten or so features from across the news spectrum each day. "The show's format, through its flexibility, can be instantly translated into a program dominated by one theme, giving that theme a *March of Time* treatment," Rud Lawrence wrote, using as an example how the show could adapt to breaking news such as a cease-fire in Korea. "We will have top people doing the scripts for the show, and as much importance is being attached to this program as to the many other programming conceptions that NBC introduced."[7]

Back from his European trip, stung by the loss of *Garroway at Large* and with no new prospects in the offing, Dave Garroway pondered his professional future. He still had time on his NBC contract, and although his show was off the air he was getting $10,000 a week. Chicago had plenty to tempt him. He had bought an apartment in the sleek new "Glass House" designed by Ludwig Mies van der Rohe and being constructed on Lake Shore Drive, and Garroway was already planning a décor that would be "more modern than tomorrow afternoon." Hawaii still beckoned, and he had frequently voiced a desire to move there by the year 1952. He had his cars to keep him busy. Romantically, he had been linked to Rosemary Clooney, her sister Betty Clooney, and to Peggy Lee. There were rumors of wedding bells. One columnist teased that Rosemary Clooney had included the line "a tiger's not a tiger if he's tamed" in a recent song, and wondered if it was a sly reference to Garroway. Though Rosemary admitted she was fond of Garroway "and there's no one else in the running," she wanted to keep singing for a few more years first.[8]

Still, the loss of Garroway's television series left him stung. One September morning he went to the Pump Room, the stylish restaurant on the Ambassador's ground floor. As he waited for his breakfast to arrive, he noticed a copy of *Variety* that an earlier patron had left in the booth, and started leafing idly through. Past screaming headlines about the movie industry outperforming the previous year's pace, past a multi-page ad for a contest centered around the new science-fiction film *The Day The Earth Stood Still*, it was another day in the entertainment industry. That is, until a headline about halfway through the issue captured Garroway's attention:

NBC-TV'S "GET HEP" FORMULA
Early-Morning, Zingy Sked Set

Sylvester L. (Pat) Weaver, NBC's television veepee, is putting the finishing touches to a unique programming idea, which will start the network's television day at 7 a.m. On the agenda for a Nov. 1 kickoff is a two-hour "wake up" cross-the-board show designed for all-family viewing which, under a new sales pattern evolved by the network's TV chieftains, will permit for a gross billings potential in excess of $2,500,000 a year.

As Garroway read on, learning that the "get hep" aspect of the new program would include "continuing sequences" of news, weather, new books and magazines, new records, and other material of interest to viewers as they began the day, he got excited. The article stated Weaver's belief that "with a proper application of showmanship based on a 'service to the waker-upper' formula," the new program would build a steady and dedicated audience, avoiding the hard luck that befell DuMont's efforts at early-morning programming.[9]

To a man of a thousand interests, reeling from the loss of his television series and looking for a new prospect, the "get hep" proposal seemed like a call. "I was built to do this show," Garroway said on *Today*'s twenty-fifth anniversary program in 1977. "All my training has been as a generalist, to specialize in nothing and know something about everything. This show was made for me." As soon as he could, Garroway called Biggie Levin. The NBC morning proposal seemed tailor-made for his touch, Garroway said, pleading with Levin to convince Weaver the show wouldn't work with a comedian as host. With each entreaty from his excited client Levin replied, "We'll see."[10]

Mort Werner hadn't considered Dave Garroway. Having seen him only on *Garroway at Large*, the producer thought Garroway's style too relaxed for a fast-paced morning program. His telephone rang. It was that relaxed voice from Chicago: "I understand you don't really feel I'd be right for the *Today* show." Werner admitted his misgivings.

"Mr. Werner, what do you know about me?"

"Well, I've seen your program -"

"What do you *know* about me?"

Stumped, Werner conceded Garroway's point. Garroway suggested they talk before Werner made up his mind. "I'm in Chicago and you're in New York," Garroway said. "What are you doing for dinner tonight?"

Within hours, Werner was on a plane to Chicago. Around midnight, the much-delayed flight reached Midway Airport. There, Garroway was waiting to drive the tired producer back to the Ambassador East. They went up to Garroway's room. "I thought you'd be hungry," he said. Out of the kitchen came two cans of baked beans and two warm bottles of root beer.[11]

They talked into the morning hours. Garroway spoke of his years of broadcast experience, the many stations he'd worked at, the stories he'd covered, and even that he had won the Chicago Open golf tournament. Werner came to realize how much he had underestimated Garroway's knowledge and abilities. "I really fell in love with the man on a one-to-one basis," he admitted two decades later.[12]

Soon after came Garroway's summons to Manhattan. On October 12, he met with producers and executives at the RCA Building. Charlie Andrews vividly remembered the meeting in Pat Weaver's office high above the Rockefeller Center skating rink, the city's skyline stretching forever, making a "simple, midwestern guy" feel overwhelmed. As Weaver began to describe the concept for *Today* – futuristic studio, advanced communications facilities, instant direct reports from overseas – Andrews felt excitement. "I'm sitting there thinking to myself, 'This is the most incredible damn thing I've ever heard about. Please, God, let us get in on it!'" Garroway recorded a twenty-minute audition, trying out the roles of newsman and interviewer in a simulated program segment. His audition impressed many, most of all the program's architect.[13]

Pat Weaver had known about Garroway for years. "I had always liked his casual style," he remembered, "especially after he somehow maneuvered his way into a show of his own." Weaver also appreciated Garroway's experience in Chicago, where stations did their own programming much as had the stations Weaver worked with on the West Coast. As Weaver talked with Garroway, his thoughts of a high-energy host melted away as he realized the wide range of subjects to be covered on the program would work better with a relaxed host. "Dave understood what we were trying to do," Weaver told Tom Brokaw on *Today*'s twenty-fifth anniversary program. "I realized that his command and his serenity in what was going to be a very difficult and live three-hour-long thing would have a secret chemistry that I really hadn't thought about." In an October 15 meeting, it was made official.[14]

A few weeks later Tom McAvity, NBC's director of talent and program procurement for television, suggested to Weaver various salary and incentive packages for an offer to Garroway: $2,000 per week for *Today*, incentive money for each segment that sold on the program, and fees advanced against guest appearances on other programs. If *Today* flopped, McAvity suggested a "flexible arrangement" in which Garroway could be used on another program until his earnings satisfied the guarantee. Levin had insisted *Today* could sell for $1,500 per fifteen-minute segment and that Garroway should get an initial guarantee of $300,000 plus additional potential earnings, while the sales department felt that $650 per segment was a more likely prospect but could be raised if the program caught on. McAvity suggested an approach that combined Garroway's financial interests with his career goals. "We think he is equally as interested in his career as in money," McAvity wrote. "Biggie's not worried about his career – only money. The fact that Dave in this project would be, as in other projects, a pioneer, should appeal to him."

The pioneer signed as *Today* host on November 12.[15]

To some, the loss of Dave Garroway was a sign that Chicago was on the way out. Another sign came in November when the beloved *Kukla,*

Fran and Ollie was abruptly cut to a fifteen-minute show. Though NBC claimed this was "to improve the show," those fifteen minutes were sold to another sponsor. Burr Tillstrom, who hadn't been warned of the plan, found out while visiting a station in Milwaukee. Scuttlebutt in Chicago said it was a deliberate move to cripple the Second City as a production center, prompted by insecure New York producers who were jealous that Chicago won such acclaim on lower budgets. Jules Herbuveaux denied that Chicago was on the way out, saying the half a million dollars NBC was about to spend on a new studio signified a commitment to Chicago as a source of network programming.[16]

Others didn't buy it. "The public be damned and let it eat cheese," wrote Ohio columnist Truman Twill, who believed NBC had a "scheme" to strangle Chicago's productions. "It's just too darned bad if anyone has formed an attachment for the Garroways and Tillstroms. It's also too darned bad if some people happen to prefer to live outside New York City. They should know better." To Ted Mills, it was an omen. The "intelligence, common sense, integrity and sweetness" of Chicago programming was defeated when the city's sales office and clients snubbed home-grown offerings and kept taking their business to New York. For him, the cancellation of *Garroway at Large* was the last straw. "I could almost hear the Chicago structure tumbling around my ears," he wrote. "If we built some sensational shows now, there would be no place on the network to put them. I therefore felt, as I do now, that the possibility of Chicago's building into a major origination center was hopeless." Mills left for New York, a producer with nothing to produce.[17]

On North Michigan Avenue, a billboard with Dave Garroway's picture had promoted his NBC programs. As 1951 ended, one observer noted how Garroway's picture had faded and now seemed so far away.[18]

Weaver's concept for early-morning television met with no end of skepticism from columnists and critics. "The only thing that looks good at that hour is a cuppacawfee," Walter Winchell wrote, later suggesting it "should attract a large audience of roosters." Jack O'Brian added, "Someone please try to convince us there's an audience big enough and available at that alarm-clock hour?" Another writer said the daily early-morning schedule, five days a week, "indicates NBC is in search of a pound of flesh for their investment!!!!"[19]

Weaver's own promotion of the concept reached lofty heights. "*To-*

day will be a milestone in the social history of this country," he told a breakfast meeting of advertising representatives and network executives at the Waldorf-Astoria. "The program is in the temper of the times. It has been in the planning stage for over six months. All means of communications yet invented will be employed to bring this show to the public." Garroway proclaimed it the most exciting thing that has happened in a decade of broadcasting. "We're going to try to inform the public without being stuffy about it. If you believe, as many, that an informed public is a free one, then you realize what a great responsibility and a great challenge *Today* is going to be." The buildup, through advertisements and official network proclamations, reached such heights that one television columnist wondered if he shouldn't have his ten-inch screen reinforced before *Today* made its debut.[20]

Not everyone was biting. A hardware salesman from Kentucky had gone to Chicago for a sales convention. In one session, a product Garroway had promoted on television received frequent attention. The salesman didn't have a television and had never heard of Garroway, and grew more irritated with each mention. "Who is this Garroway character?" he asked the man sitting next to him. "I've never heard of him, and I hope I never hear of him again. He certainly can't be here. He would have drowned in the syrup by now." When the master of ceremonies asked Dave Garroway to say a few words, the salesman was mortified when the man to whom he had been complaining stood up and went to the lectern. Garroway told the story of what had just happened and pointed the embarrassed salesman out to the crowd. With no way to sneak out, the salesman apologized to Garroway after the speech.[21]

The *Today* unit had to put together an on-air team to support Garroway. There had been talk of hiring Fred Allen as Garroway's on-air partner, but producers decided to play the show straight. The first hire was Jim Fleming, a journalist who had covered the Middle East and Russia during the Second World War. Disgruntled with how he was treated by Soviet censors, Fleming tore up his credentials and was ejected from the country. Hired by NBC in 1949, he had worked on a number of projects, including the radio series *Voices and Events*. An intelligent and thorough reporter with an ability to ad-lib, which would be especially important if a story broke while a program was on the air, Fleming had been considered as host of the fifteen-minute *Today* project. Fleming began putting together a staff for the news department.[22]

Jack Lescoulie was hired to do commercials and announce. Lescoulie, the son of vaudevillians, had created and hosted *The Grouch Club*, a West Coast program in which people aired humorous complaints about their lives, and that spawned a series of short films. While reporting for *Stars and Stripes* during World War II, he had flown on the Ploesti oil field raids. After the war Lescoulie created a program with comedian Gene Rayburn for early morning radio, but got into producing. "I had quit the entertainment world in disgust," he claimed, only to be back in two years when a television producer spotted him in a restaurant. "You're Jack Lescoulie, the man I want with Dave Garroway," the producer said. When he learned *Today* was to be a "television newspaper," Lescoulie spent time in a New York paper's city room. One employee stuck in his mind: a young man with the ability to kid everyone on the staff just enough for them not to resent it. One writer described Lescoulie as "a fresh-faced tall, blond fellow with a wild, off-beat sense of humor and inborn irreverence whose yeasty comment often saves the program from disastrous monotony."[23]

At 36 West 49th Street, across from the RCA Building, between a bank on the corner and a parking garage entrance next to the Center Theater, a curious glass-fronted showroom three stories tall had been built as part of the Rockefeller Center complex. Before it was constructed, Garroway had often walked across the vacant lot as a shortcut to his job at NBC. In 1945 RCA leased the showroom and turned it into a public showcase of the company's technological achievements. There, visitors could view exhibits on global communications, marvel at a fifty-foot tall revolving "theme mast" displaying the company's achievements in miniature, and even step in front of a television camera to have the exotic experience of being televised. Along a back wall a stylized map depicted the continents, with transoceanic circuits represented by spaghetti strands of conduit. The Exhibition Hall championed not only RCA's industrial and technological might, but also took care to display the latest of its consumer wares, the record players and radios and televisions it meant to make essential in postwar homes.[24]

As planning continued for the new program, something about those large windows stuck in the mind of Pat Weaver. Members of the team had half-joked that they'd have to share studios with *Howdy Doody*. The original concept had put the new program in Studio 8G, but that indoor studio didn't fit Weaver's vision of a studio that arrested the eyes and lit the imagination. He imagined morning sunlight falling on a set designed by Norman Bel Geddes, spectators gazing through giant windows to watch a newsroom in action. While the RCA Exhibition Hall wasn't the Bel Geddes masterpiece he had envisioned, half a city block of twenty-seven-foot-tall windows was too good to pass up. "I had grabbed it the minute I found out it was available," he later remembered. "I loved that ground-floor studio with its windows on the sidewalk, inviting passersby to watch and listen." It took some persuading, both of RCA and of the Rockefeller Center landlords, to use the western end of the showroom as the home of the new program, but Weaver thought it would pay off as a "conversation piece" that "will become the number one tourist attraction of New York visitors." Walter Winchell wagged that NBC was "putting glass walls on their 49th Street studios so that pedestrians can be late for work."[25]

Charlie Speer's proposal for the midday *Today* called for "a simulation of a tele-communications center" that would have "the utilitarian features of a commentator's desk and its equipment" in an "ultramodern, sleek, smart and appealing" format. The basics of a newsroom would never be far away, with Speer's mocked-up script calling for teletypes ticking away in the background, bulletins and magazines and papers on the communicator's desk, and teletype bells punctuating each new headline. In the background would be a large-scale wall map, chairs, a sofa and a coffee table. This was adapted for the morning program's new studio. The western half of the Exhibition Hall was curtained off and cleared out, leaving a studio space twenty-two feet deep and sixty feet wide. In went desks, typewriters, teleprinters, radios, recording equipment and seemingly any other form of newsgathering apparatus. Two tape recorders would constantly record what was going on, and any of twenty overseas telephone circuits could be switched in and recorded as well. On one end a large, curved desk was built for the master communicator's station; behind it rose a tall console with monitors and an array of clocks. Nearby was a couch in front of a large polar-projection world map with a clock built into it. This studio, soon to be dubbed the "communications center," looked impressive, but the design was careful not to make permanent modifications to the space just yet. Behind the teleprinters and recording equipment, the spaghetti-strand map of

RCA's communications reach remained intact, against the possibility of the new program laying an egg.[26]

Down the ramp that led to the lower level, a space became a control room filled with monitors, switching equipment and camera control units. (Not everything could be handled from this tiny control room, so filmed segments would have to be inserted from a coordinating studio inside 30 Rock.) Hundreds of feet of cable were strung through the building. Camera positions were determined, including one atop a tall platform near the windows, and camera crews were designated for the new program. Frank Merklein, who joined NBC after returning from World War II, headed up one of them. In his four years with NBC Merklein had operated cameras for everything from *Howdy Doody*, *Texaco Star Theater* and *Broadway Open House* to being present at Republican campaign headquarters as Governor Thomas E. Dewey, the Republican presidential nominee, learned of his defeat on Election Night 1948. For two years Merklein and his crew had specialized in covering sporting events and other happenings away from the studio. Now NBC designated Merklein's crew for what was essentially a remote from across 49th Street. Decades later Merklein would remember field work being a factor in Crew 12's selection. "We were chosen because of our large amount of experience," he recalled with a twinkle in his eye. "Also, we were available."[27]

The scope of the ambitious effort meant numerous delays. The debut, originally set for November 1, moved to January 1, then January 7, then back yet another week when workers needed just a little more time to install equipment in the Exhibition Hall studio. As construction wound down, the *Today* staff began testing the new communications center in a series of "dry run" programs. All the while, Garroway was pulled in several directions. He not only had to take part in planning meetings and dry runs, but he had to see after the affairs of getting settled in Manhattan, moving his possessions to a new home and disposing of some that couldn't make the trip. Among the sacrifices were some of his treasured automobiles. The Rolls-Royce, he said, had been left "like an abandoned baby, on a doorstep. It looked like a little orphan Rolls-Royce, if you can imagine such an impoverished object." The Jaguar and his Hillman Hinx were kept at a garage just outside New York City, while the rest were to be sold. Garroway also had to restyle his wardrobe, with only conservative clothes allowed in his new role.[28]

On top of that, Garroway had to promote his new show, making personal appearances, speaking at luncheons and advertiser meetings, and making guest appearances on NBC evening programs to promote *Today*. Stopping by Fred Allen's program, the veteran comedian asked Garroway, "Who is going to see the program? Roosters and milkmen?"

"Housewives," Garroway said.

"I hear," Allen said, "that housewives have other things to do at that hour."[29]

Though Allen's mockery of his friend was tongue-in-cheek, it reflected a broader skepticism. Jack O'Brian suggested that as Garroway prepared to command the "new news-chatter mishmash," his Christmas gift should be "a medal for bravery as he prepares to take on the most durable opponent in the history of entertainment – warm beds." Another writer insisted that if Garroway could make the show popular, "he will be a better man than Gunga Din." On the eve of the program's debut "to a startled and probably sleepy populace," John Crosby suggested that NBC's buildup of the program's power and grandeur had prompted "the tendency among the more timorous of us is to flee to the hills before this shattering enlightenment is thrust on us." More directly, Bill Henry suggested a more appropriate title for *Today* would be "This Way Lies Madness!"[30]

10

Accustomed to the strange early morning hours after weeks of practice runs, Garroway arrived at the Exhibition Hall at 2 a.m. on January 14, 1952. Some staff members, sustained by afternoon naps, had already been at work four hours. Even if anyone had time to sleep, apprehension was likely to foil rest. Jim Fleming, driving in from Greenwich along deserted roads, tried to quiet his nervous feelings. Producer Dick Pinkham, after a night tossing and turning in a Yale Club bed, came in three hours before air. A policeman saw Mort Werner near his home in Scarsdale and asked why he was out at 3 a.m. Werner explained he was waiting for a ride to New York, where he'd help put on a television show at seven that morning. The cop scoffed. "You must be out of your mind."

By 5 a.m. all hands were present. They made ready for a last rehearsal, a fifty-minute run-through at 6 a.m., before *Today* began at 7 a.m. It would be a three-hour program, but only the first two hours would be carried in the Eastern time zone; affiliates in the Central time zone would pick the show up at 8 a.m. and carry the third hour. Anxiety chewed at producer Abe Schechter. He nervously watched the run-through on a monitor near the downstairs control room, muttered when a shot wasn't to his liking, and scrambled up the ramp to the studio floor to correct the offending cameraman. By the time he arrived on the floor, the director had switched to another camera, rendering Schechter's advice useless. Schechter returned down the ramp to the monitor, only to be dissatisfied about another shot and run back up the ramp just as another switch happened. The pattern repeated not only throughout the rehearsal session, but through Schechter's tenure on *Today*. Crewmen soon dubbed it the Schechter Ramp Dance.[1]

As Schechter grimaced and scurried, as tension gnawed at a sleep-deprived and nervous crew, Garroway serenely glided through the last moments before air. Pinkham, sagging after his restless night, thought Garroway seemed "fantastically relaxed." He asked the host how he could be so calm. Garroway noted that Pinkham seemed to be tired, and offered a sip from his bottle of The Doctor. "God knows what was in it," he said years later, "but I drained some of it and felt much better." While the rest of the team scrambled and agonized, the master communicator proceeded through the countdown with no strain. "Either I am Fearless Fosdick or I am too dumb to be scared," Garroway later wrote, "but I sat behind that kidney-shaped desk qualmless as the red second hand rolled around slowly."[2]

Outside the RCA Exhibition Hall that dark January morning, a cold rain licked lazily at the midtown streets. Early morning traffic motored slowly along 49th Street. A handful of people paused in the damp chill to stare through the Exhibition Hall's huge windows at the curious, brightly-lit scene unfolding inside. On occasion, a spectator waved at Garroway through the glass and got a wave in return. A pigeon paced in front of the window, oblivious to it all. Meanwhile, in the handful of cities in the Eastern time zone where NBC had a presence, a few early-rising viewers switched on their sets. New York viewers heard WNBT's low-key announcer read promotional copy for Richard Harkness's lunchtime newscast. A station identification card faded to black as the new hour began.

Inside the Exhibition Hall, the stage manager counted down the last seconds before air. Garroway settled in behind his desk. Jack Lescoulie, at his own desk, picked up his copy and leaned toward his microphone. On cue, the cameraman on the tall platform began a steady pan of the busy newsroom floor as the picture faded in.[3]

The opening scenes of that first *Today* program – the camera's slow rake of the busy Communications Center floor, the stylized program logo, the purr of Jack Lescoulie's introduction, Garroway's genial first words ("Well, here we are, and good morning to you"), the early zoom lens swiftly homing in on Garroway with a slight bobble, the bespectacled master communicator standing in front of his desk with an enormous microphone around his neck, predicting that *Today* heralded "a new kind of television" – would be shown time and again in decades to come, a mandatory part of any retrospective on *Today*'s past.

That momentary clip from a grainy kinescope deceives modern viewers into thinking the first *Today* program went smoothly. Despite all the careful planning, the first telecast was full of things that didn't work. A dramatic rooftop shot from the top of 30 Rock was spoiled by low clouds;

viewers saw only the skyscraper's ventilation system belching steam. A remote from Chicago, where Jim Hurlbut interviewed two stony patrolmen in a squad car, was abruptly interrupted by a station break, then lost its audio. The first weather report was a one-sided conversation, as Weather Bureau meteorologist Jim Fidler's voice didn't come through on the studio circuit; Garroway, stretching a phone receiver's coiled cord to its limit, had to repeat Fidler's forecast for listeners as he sketched out the forecast on the map (having first had to erase the forecast left from an earlier run-through). Cues were missed. In one instance, Jack Lescoulie began a report about the Dodgers' Roy Campanella right before a station break, and continued talking on as the program went to commercial. During another break, a spot for savings bonds rolled without sound, and scenes of busy factory workers appeared over a chorus of the studio's clattering teletypes. ("If I'd known that, I would have whistled 'Dixie' or something," an amused Garroway told viewers after the break.)

Innovations had teething problems, too. A combination news/time ticker at the bottom of the screen appeared and disappeared throughout the morning. The teleprompter system didn't stay in sync with Garroway, who asked Mort Werner on air to tell the cue people "they're running about three inches high." With his experience on *Garroway at Large* having long demolished the fourth wall, it was in the host's nature to be forthright about the problems throughout the morning. Early in the program, Garroway shared an associate's observation that "we're like a play in New Haven for the first week getting ready to come into the big town."

With NBC News hoarding its best resources for *Camel News Caravan*, *Today* had to be innovative. Not only did was the set equipped with wire service machines and wirephoto printers, but producers worked out agreements to get front pages from prominent national newspapers, either flown in that morning or sent by wirephoto, for display on set. The morning's first news story (charges that Soviet anti-aircraft guns were being used in Indochina) came not from NBC, but from the front page of the *New York Herald-Tribune*. Wire service photos illustrated much of the rest. A story about Captain Henrik Kurt Carlsen of the stricken freighter *Flying Enterprise* used footage from a newsreel service. An update about an investigation into flammable rayon sweaters was illustrated with crude diagrams shown with an overhead projection technique called Viewgraphic.[4]

Garroway spoke by transatlantic circuit to NBC correspondents in

London and Frankfurt, only to glean more conversation than news. Remote feeds from five mobile units brought live scenes from Washington, Chicago, and Grand Central Station, but showed merely the bustle of morning commutes or overcast city skylines. Correspondent Ray Scherer, outside the Pentagon, tried to get military notables to speak on camera. Some were more cooperative than others. Intercepting Chief of Naval Operations Admiral William J. Fechteler, Scherer asked for an update on the state of the navy. "When I left it yesterday, it was in pretty good shape," an unimpressed Fechteler replied. These demonstrations of the program's technical abilities, in the absence of a story to use them on, quickly felt gratuitous. Even Garroway grew bored with how little the remotes showed; after the third viewing of the vast parking lots outside the Pentagon, he griped off-camera that he was a little tired of seeing cars.

Since *Today* was meant to be listened to as much as watched ("We don't expect you to sit there with your two pretty eyes glued to the screen," Garroway told viewers), the program paused at intervals while popular records of the moment played. As they did, the platform camera panned across the busy newsroom, capturing the bustle below as staffers puffed cigarettes, tended their gadgets and prepared for the next segment. Before one such interlude, Garroway was quickly called to the overseas circuit to speak to Romney Wheeler in London; the veteran correspondent predicted the next song would be Tony Martin's hit "Domino," which he said was very popular in London, and the song was promptly cued up for the audience. (In his post-mortem on the first week, Weaver cited the long-distance song intro as not the wisest use of resources.)

Sometimes, though, that technology was put to better ends. NBC had arranged for two Army sergeants serving in Korea, Mickey Sinnott and Bill Cassidy, to speak with relatives from Brooklyn. A crew captured the conversations on film, then the film was flown back to New York. In the studio, Garroway interviewed the soldiers' parents, then screened the films of their sons in Korea. Another *Today* staple, the author interview, began when Garroway interviewed Fleur Cowles about her new book about the Peron regime in Argentina, *Bloody Precedent*.

As Garroway's interview with the Sinnott and Cassidy families was wrapping up, Northeast Airlines Flight 801, with thirty-three passengers and three crew members aboard, took off from Boston. The twin-engine Convair spent the next hour plowing through rainy skies. At 9 a.m., just as NBC's east coast stations left *Today*, Northeast 801 was cleared to land at LaGuardia. Three minutes later the plane bellied into Flushing Bay, just over half a mile from the end of Runway 22. Passengers and crew scrambled out of the sinking airliner, all rescued by nearby boats.[5]

At 9:22, the Associated Press dispatch moved over the wires. A minute later, Jim Fleming informed *Today* viewers of the crash. Within minutes, a Viewgraphic map was up showing where the crash had occurred, and Fleming stayed with the story throughout the remaining hour. (*Today*'s coverage not only beat other networks but even beat WNBT, which, along with other Eastern time zone stations, had resumed local programming at 9.) It was *Today*'s introduction to breaking news.

After three hours of demanding on-air work, Garroway watched the stage manager count down the last seconds of the first *Today* telecast. The master communicator bade his audience a good morning and raised his right palm in the familiar "peace" gesture. The program faded to black, the tally light on the camera went out, and the stage manager signaled "clear."

Life photographer Peter Stackpole, documenting the morning's activities, snapped a photo of Garroway just after the program went off the air: chair at full recline, head back, face alight in a relieved smile, arms hanging by his sides, a massive weight gone from his shoulders. Almost immediately the assemblage in the Exhibition Hall erupted into applause. Staffers and executives rushed over to shake his hand. "I remember it as though it were now," he told Tom Shales years later. "I remember the great feel of it. I was delighted with it. I felt pleased with myself as I perhaps never have before. And when it was all over, the whole crew applauded. It was the best sound I ever heard."[6]

They'd shown it could be done. Now they just had to do it again, and do it better.

The reactions were strong. *Broadcasting*, stating that the promotional buildup to the debut of *Today* suggested "the program would be of greater historical consequence than the invention of the printing press," opined that "Gutenberg's reputation is not threatened." It complained that the format, trying to accomplish too much in a limited time, too severely truncated news, features and music. The setting, *Broadcasting* noted, seemed "designed by the producers of *Captain Video* or *Space Ca-*

det," and its busy and crowded nature would resemble "St. Vitus' dance brought to the screen were it not for the restorative presence of the man who now saves the show and can, with proper support, establish it as an important television feature." *Broadcasting* praised Garroway as "imperturbable" and suggested *Today* would be successful only if the rest of the program were tuned to more closely match Garroway's calm demeanor.[7]

Some critics felt the show was repetitive, showing the same headlines over and over. A Chicago columnist said that despite *Today*'s lofty ambitions, it was "an incompetent imitation of CBS's *See It Now* technique." Si Steinhauser suggested the shot from the top of the RCA Building, showing its ventilation system steaming in the cold morning fog, was actually "'blowing its top' because NBC was spending its money so foolishly." Others disputed that the show was as effective by ear as it was by picture. "If a program isn't designed to be watched, it isn't a TV program," Cincinnati columnist John Caldwell wrote. "It is more for radio or a party-line telephone." Though Caldwell said the program could work out some of its problems, "my best advice of yesterday was to follow their advice and not look at the show." Writer Art Cullison in Akron doubted that Garroway could compete with morning radio news, or even with a little more sleep. "I hope not, but don't be surprised if Dave is kayoed."[8]

New York critics were not charitable. Jack O'Brian said *Today* was about what he had feared: "big, sprawling, confused, shallow and not quite satisfying." He poked fun at the set ("looked like a command post for an invasion") and the large staff ("seems more a visual exercise in keeping a staff working in plain sight of several (prospective) million viewers"). O'Brian wrote, "It was not so much that this mountain of communications brought forth a TV mouse. Rather, it fathered a whole parade of mice; or maybe ant hills would be the better analogy. Certainly it had all the ant marks – the hurry and scurry visible, the real purpose buried somewhere in the purposeful confusion." Though he praised Garroway's easy demeanor and considered the program's intent noble, "we had to go get a newspaper to see what actually was happening beyond our *Today* screen."[9]

Bob Lanigan of the *Brooklyn Daily Eagle* liked the program but complained that it took him too long to get up in the morning, and "I refuse to lug my TV console into my bathroom's limited space. Even if I could, it would be too dangerous. I splash around a lot, and if some water hit my cathode tube I might short-circuit myself." He chided the program's slow start on a newsless Monday morning, where the big news was snow in Frankfurt. "Then it happened – wham! The dream of every newscaster had come true. Big, black headline stuff! A giant airliner attempting to land at LaGuardia Field crashed into the East River! No details, just the news flash, but excitement – WOW! Unfortunately for *Today*, the accident took place twenty three minutes after Garroway signed off."[10]

John Crosby called *Today* an "incredible two-hour comedy of errors perpetrated as a 'new kind of television.'" The remotes, Crosby said, were "a triumph of communication over content," with little of substance actually being conveyed on a slow morning. "What hath God and NBC wrought, I kept thinking, and what for? I found out a few minutes later, when Garroway had Romney Wheeler cue up 'Domino.'" Of all the items in the studio, from the technical equipment making possible the remotes to a needle-threader Garroway demonstrated, Crosby compared what he saw to "small boys, playing with gadgets." In another piece, Crosby compared the show's cast and staff to "passengers in a space ship which has lost its pilot, passengers surrounded by a lot of gleaming dials and instruments whose purpose they didn't comprehend." To Crosby, *Today* was a triumph of hoopla over substance. "If one-fifth the money spent on cameras and technical crews and long distance phone calls and telephoto machines had been spent on writing, research and editing, NBC might have had something of value to say between 7 and 9 every morning." Though he praised Garroway as an effective and intelligent host, "it seems a shame he has nothing to get his teeth into. If he wants a place to sink his teeth, I suggest Sylvester L. 'Pat' Weaver, who dealt this mess, who is largely responsible for 'the big television' theory with which NBC is now obsessed, and which may wind up squeezing all the common sense and humanity out of NBC television."[11]

Anton Remenih criticized the "cluttered up" format and suggested the show simplify and focus on its strength, Dave Garroway. "Give the news but don't make such a fuss about it. Throw the gadgets out. Read the headlines and tell us if we need galoshes to get to work. Play a few quiet records. In between platters and headlines permit Dave to nudge us gently into another day by telling us one of his little stories." Chicago columnist Larry Wolters believed Garroway was "constricted by slithering cables and other communications gadgets that cramp his easy, breezy style."[12]

Those with the show knew it had problems. Garroway agreed. "In the beginning, we were pretty pompous, terribly impressed with our technical devices," he remembered two decades later. "We called ourselves 'The Center of the World' and claimed we were in touch with every place. Actually, we weren't in touch with anybody except the engineers." Part of the job, he recalled, was "to get rid of the claptrap. We had it all gimmicked up and you don't need gimmicks. We learned to concentrate on people rather than things." But he took exception to the more acidic comments. "My goodness, if you went to the opening of a new building and some things didn't work, you wouldn't say it was a bad building," he said in 1977. "You'd say the faucets on the fifth floor dripped and the john didn't work. You'd say there were a few things that had to be fixed. A television show has to be built, and it took us a year to get things fixed."[13]

A week after the premiere Weaver sent a seven-page memorandum, written in his characteristic wandering style, to all *Today* personnel. "You have done well in the first week," he wrote, noting that the public seemed to pick up on what NBC was trying to offer. He chided the critics, taking aim at Jack O'Brian's "mountains labor and mouse emerges" comment, saying that such a view "fails to realize that we bring mice to people who have only heard of mice hitherto, people whose letters thank us for showing them at last mice, for giving them a new horizon where mice will be commonplace. All this, before the fact that in addition to mice, we are and shall be bringing elephants." That said, Weaver saw room for improvement: interviews seemed pointless, technological capabilities were mis-used ("We do lay ourselves open to criticism if the best we can think of to hear from London is to start a record"), a sense that content was being changed to fit a style.

Weaver warned that the show would not catch on if it drew only a loyal fan base, but needed to become a service that could fit into the lives of most people, and that straightforward presentation of material would make the program stronger. He suggested some adjustments, both in content and in technology (recommending a new map format for the screen, Weaver scorned the projection system used on the initial programs as "those damn big things with phoney animation"), and reminded the unit that "this show cannot continue unless it is sold," suggesting that the sales unit approach coffee, cigarette, orange juice "and other naturals for this program." Still, Weaver felt positive about the potential. "I can't help but feel that from a creative point of view, the *Today* unit should be bursting with projects that are beyond their means, in terms of getting information that will have available to the public, the full measure of our world that we live in, the cities, the rivers, together with our solar system, etc. and a way of making it relevantly included in the *Today* Show whenever it comes up in the news."[14]

Publicly, NBC acknowledged the show was trying to settle down, and that changes were already being made. Some hiccups came from the pressure of getting *Today* on the air, but the second week would provide an opportunity for the show to "loosen up." Although the program debuted with only two sponsors, expressions of interest had come in from several prospects and local stations had reported some success with spot commercial inserts. NBC said thirty stations were carrying the program, many of them showing a full two hours. Some critics were willing to give the show room for improvement. "Dave Garroway and company are entitled to a little time to work things out," Bill Henry wrote in the *Los Angeles Times*. "They're just groping around right now, like anybody else who gets up before 7 o'clock on dark winter mornings." Walter Winchell wrote that *Today* "has the makings of a good show" and was "zippy in spots plus many imaginative touches," but "it has to improve."[15]

Today also learned early that, as the first program in the morning, it could break a story to the American viewing audience. On February 6 the show was less than an hour and a half from air when the wire service machines rang out with a bulletin: King George VI had died. The program was quickly reformatted. Garroway led off the program with the solemn news, then spoke via transatlantic phone with Romney Wheeler. Veteran journalist H.V. Kaltenborn came in and helped Garroway and Jim Fleming cover the morning's developments. They did the best they could, even if they had only a few old pictures on hand to show between bulletins and wirephotos. In the follow-up, Mort Werner ordered that *Today* follow the practice of major newspapers and work up an obituary for all prominent world figures, ready to use on the air at a moment's notice. The following week, *Today* carried coverage of the funeral proceedings. With no live television pictures available, the sound of Big Ben tolling and of the horses' hooves as the cortege left Westminster Hall for the burial at Windsor Castle, carried by shortwave, provided an impressive and haunting aspect to the coverage.[16]

NBC worried that too many potential viewers still didn't register that *Today* was out there. Frank McMahon had an idea. "You have an almost captive audience during the middle half-hour of Caesar-Coca," he wrote Weaver, suggesting a cross-promotion with the popular *Your Show of Shows*. "Twenty million people – the same people you are trying to get to watch *Today*." McMahon suggested having Sid Caesar switch the audience mid-show to the Communications Center because most viewers hadn't seen "one of the most exciting developments in television. If you want a reason for the switch, I can have just blown up the RCA Building for another *Today* exclusive." Garroway could then interview Caesar and Imogene Coca as part of a special showing of *Today*, and that might persuade viewers "to get the Garroway habit." The idea was adopted, though instead of interrupting *Your Show of Shows* NBC instead scheduled the special half-hour program for the last Monday in March, pre-empting *Lights Out* in between a musical program and *Robert Montgomery Presents*.[17]

One of the hardest markets for *Today* to crack was Philadelphia, where comedian Ernie Kovacs hosted an anarchical morning program with a devoted following. Word that *Today* would displace Kovacs prompted angry responses. "We have had a lot of things forced on us by TV – football blackouts, boxing blackouts, baseball blackouts – and now practically a Kovacs blackout," one viewer wrote. "The more I see of the Gestapo methods of TV, the more I'm beginning to appreciate radio." Another complained, "Once again Philadelphia has to take a back seat for New York. You'd think we were a suburb instead of a city with its own TV stations." Kovacs himself offered awards to *Today* viewers. "Anyone who can watch television for at least ten hours a week must be rewarded," he said. "It calls for real endurance." NBC's efforts to persuade Philadelphia viewers included sending a publicity man to walk around on the streets wearing a convict's uniform. The man changed out of the outfit to have lunch at his hotel, returning to his room just in time to ward off a maid who was about to have the police summoned.[18]

All the while, *Today* was building a following. Just a few days into its run, a one-minute commercial on *Today* brought its sponsor 16,000 responses. The Florida Citrus Commission bought ten weeks on *Today* at $100,000. A company promoting a weight-loss plan signed on for a campaign in which a Brooklyn housewife would weigh in each day, allowing viewers to keep track of her weight loss. Even *Time* magazine, which had panned *Today* in an early review, signed on as a sponsor. NBC urged companies to strike early, "when the brand buying of the day still lies ahead," and before their competitors could buy into *Today* before them, encouraging them to buy into the eighty low-cost sponsorships *Today* offered. By the end of *Today*'s first thirteen weeks, the program had eighteen sponsors.[19]

One key factor in selling *Today* was Garroway's known power as a salesman. "I do my own commercials on television because it feels good," he said, "and it feels natural. Besides, I like to do them." So in demand was he by sponsors, executives worried that making the host do so many commercials would not only reduce the role for which Lescoulie had been hired, but would take the program out of character and "spoil Garroway's usefulness to the program as a star performer."[20]

The real signs came as audience skepticism and curiosity gave way to a new habit. In its first thirteen weeks *Today* went from a 4.8 rating to a 7.6. In a week, the staff received 1,500 favorable letters and only five that didn't like the show. "We have had about 70,000 letters," Garroway said, "about 42 percent from housewives, 38 percent from children and 20 percent from men. They say we have changed their living pattern." One housewife wrote, "To sit down with a cup of coffee and you, Dave, is all I ask. It's wonderful."[21]

Some complained the suggestion that the show was effective for listening as well as viewing didn't work in practice. People were drawn to the set. One man, tired of making the trek between his kitchen and the living room when something piqued his interest, knocked a hole in the wall so he could see. Another viewer arranged a system of mirrors so they could watch from another room. Anton Remenih wrote of a viewer whose travels back and forth between rooms, breakfast in hand, left a trail "clearly marked with coffee, cereal, egg and juice stains. It's beginning to look like U.S. 66 after a summer's tourist traffic has passed over it. Have you priced rug cleaning lately?"[22]

The program wasn't attracting viewers just to the small screen. From the first morning, the big windows of the RCA Exhibition Hall had drawn onlookers curious about the goings-on inside. From the first week, the cameras had turned around to show the onlookers. In no time, the big windows became a place to see, and be seen. Some characters quickly turned it to their own advantage. One morning in the second week, as the camera panned along the crowd outside, two men raised a sign urging viewers to tune in Herb Sheldon's morning radio show. The camera quickly moved off them. ("It was really nothing at all," Sheldon said. "The sign cost me four dollars.")[23]

More often, the onlookers' motives were benign, merely people on the way to work looking in for a moment, others waving to the camera, a few waving to Garroway himself. Crosstown buses paused along 49th Street to let passengers look at the studio, until the bus line made them end the practice. Tourists began to show up with cards with the names of their hometowns. Shutterbugs liked taking pictures of themselves off the monitors in the window. One morning the cameras spotted Frank Sinatra outside. First daughter Margaret Truman occasionally looked in, waving at Garroway, once making faces to get him to break up, only to be caught in the act on camera. Garroway joked that he'd thought about standing in the crowd during a vacation break, "but I'm just too tired to get up that early."[24]

For others, it was an opportunity to connect. An Ohio salesman on a trip to Manhattan stopped outside the Exhibition Hall each morning, waiting for the cameras to turn toward the sidewalk crowd. As everyone else waved, the salesman used sign language to say hello to his mute mother, who was watching in Atlanta. A distinguished executive stopped by each morning on the way to work to wave at his four-year-old son, watching at their New Jersey home. A young girl living in upstate New York wrote to tell Garroway she hoped to stand in front of the window on an upcoming visit so her mother, living in Florida, could see her for the first time in a year. When she showed up outside, Garroway talked to her in the studio. That night, she called her mother, only to learn the program hadn't been seen in Florida that day. When he learned of this, Garroway had her return the next morning. A young beauty named Marion Stafford, visiting New York with her mother, had been hired as a model after the camera lingered on her one morning.[25]

The Garroway style was seeping into mainstream culture. A commission of the National Council of Churches of Christ, U.S.A. published a booklet full of advice for ministers who would appear on television. One suggestion was to study Garroway, as well as Arthur Godfrey, to inspire "spontaneity, friendliness, a sense of humor and a warm, open approachableness" in their telecasts. Garroway was also taking the stigma from eyeglasses. Dorothea Dix, responding to a writer upset that her husband turned out to be myopic, suggested, "Look at Dave Garroway or Steve Allen on television. Their popularity isn't hurt by them. Believe me, most girls would welcome a date with either of them and feel very romantic about it....Better get a little closer to that man of yours before some other girl who admires the horn-rimmed type takes him away from you."[26]

Garroway not only ruled morning television, but continued as a presence on radio. *Dial Dave Garroway* had moved with him to New York, with Skitch Henderson and his orchestra taking on the musical responsibilities. Garroway continued the same format, offering wry suggestions to listeners, such as brightening up the daily commute by intently reading a book with blank pages, laughing at intervals, underlining parts of the non-existent text in pencil. If someone asks if it's a good book, "just say, 'I enjoy the book but they sure loused up the movie!' Then leave. This will enable you to study human reaction. You will find out how soon people lose their tempers, how angry they get – and how hard they hit."[27]

Other duties popped up, such as guest-hosting *Your Show of Shows*, which gave Garroway a chance to play once more with his gentle style of humor, including some gags reused from *Garroway at Large*. Word circulated that the much-missed show could return in the fall prime-time schedule. And Garroway, along with a few other stars, was enlisted to co-host coverage of the New York Easter parade.[28]

His income afforded Garroway a Park Avenue penthouse apartment once occupied by NBC president Merlyn Aylesworth. He had an architect redesign the apartment, incorporating a two-story opaque window that provided light for the living room and balcony. He decorated the front of the fireplace with tiles he made himself. Garroway didn't put in much furniture ("I want just enough to be comfortable") and filled the shelves with books, records and other odds and ends. A balcony above the living room held a small office. Although it was a nice apartment, Garroway didn't want to do much entertaining: "Perhaps it's because each guest is too important to me, each one an intensely individual human being with ideas fighting for expression." When he could entertain, he relied on his housekeeper, Cornelia Thomas, to help.[29]

Not that he had much time to entertain. His work day started early, prompted by an elaborate device whose alarm not only sent out a waking tone, but started a radio and set off a coffee percolator. His alarm was set for 4 a.m., but the device started working at 3:45. From the Park Avenue apartment he could walk to work. "New York at dawn is like a stage set in an empty theater," he rhapsodized. "Everyone you see at that hour

Garroway and daughter Paris, captured in a Polaroid photo, gaze down on Park Avenue from his penthouse apartment. (Paris Day collection)

seems like a stagehand strolling on and off the set." One morning, one of them stopped him. "You'd better give up those late hours and start getting some sleep," the admirer said. "That early show of yours is going to be rough!"[30]

Once at the Exhibition Hall, Garroway spent the next two hours or so in rehearsals, catching up on late developments and trying to shake off remaining drowsiness with the help of coffee and The Doctor. At 7 a.m., the show went on. Three hours later, it was off to a staff meeting that lasted until noon. At 12:15, he was off to a radio studio for *Dial Dave Garroway*. The afternoon was spent in meetings with sponsor and agency representatives ("after lunch, there were a thousand things to do") until heading home for dinner at 7 p.m. He considered *Kukla, Fran and Ollie* his "good night" show, but "sometimes I get reckless, go the whole hog and sit up for Dinah Shore." Most nights, he was in bed by 8 p.m. "It's not hard to get to bed at 8 p.m. if you have to be up by 3 a.m.," he said. Eventually, this stretched out to 11:30 at night. "After the first year it was enough for anyone," he said. "I never minded it except for the first ten minutes from 3:30 to 3:40. I never got used to that ten minutes."[31]

On the increasingly rare occasions when he could relax, Garroway tinkered with his cars, once getting himself ticketed in Connecticut for driving the Jaguar twenty miles an hour over the speed limit. Though he loved driving, his days as a racer ended. In one race, he was doing ninety miles an hour "and something went by me going fifty miles per hour faster." He finally quit when he spun the Jaguar during a race at Watkins Glen, coming to a halt inches from a fence. "I was scared as hell," he remembered. "I just got out and walked away. I never went back, nor had I any desire to."[32]

Nevertheless, Garroway's well-known love of cars worked its way into *Today*. One morning, the staff put together a feature involving an array of sports cars cruising along 49th Street. Abe Schechter looked out the window. "What the hell are we showing sports cars for?" Somebody reminded Schechter that sports cars were Dave's hobby. The producer wasn't moved. "Well, fuckin's mine, but I ain't putting *that* on the air."[33]

As he had elsewhere, Garroway's name was attached to many potential love interests, though he insisted his strange schedule got in the way of serious romance. Betty Furness, famous as a spokesperson for Westinghouse, had been spied in Garroway's company during *Today* rehearsals. A knitter, she had made many pairs of socks for him, but denied anything other than a good friendship. Rumors continued that he and Rosemary Clooney were an item. More substantial were the rumors that he was romancing model Nancy Berg. On at least one occasion, columnists noted him on the town with Adele, his former wife, with whom he maintained a strong friendship and often exchanged letters.[34]

Fred Allen tweaked Garroway's early hours in a special appearance as *Today*'s floor manager ("Someday I hope to manage the ceiling, and that would put me at the top of the television industry"). When Garroway asked why Allen was on the show, he replied, "Dave, I haven't seen oatmeal in thirty years. I just got up to see once again what oatmeal looks like." Garroway was courting trouble with the program, Allen said. "Your *Today* is based on the assumption that something will always happen. If it doesn't happen newspapers will be blank, newsboys will stand on corners with their mouths wide open but in absolute silence, and Dave, if you just stand around saying and doing nothing you might get arrested for vagrancy." Allen suggested vignettes and odd items Garroway could keep on hand for mornings with little news, his ideas making Garroway laugh so hard he had to turn from the camera.[35]

The program's prospects seemed so tentative, went a joke within the network, that NBC should "cut the budget in half and call it *Yesterday*." Garroway had no illusions about the program's prospects. One morning, a technical error made the picture go out mid-show. When they were back on the air Garroway quipped, "This program has been in the red for so long, it's a pleasure to see it black even for a little while."[36]

There was hope. John Crosby noted that the show no longer seemed amazed at itself and now ran smoothly: "That is, mostly it does." The show, he said, "seems destined to stay with us." So it was. In mid-May NBC announced that *Today*, now carried on thirty-one stations and having signed twenty-four sponsors, would remain on indefinitely. With *Today* showing promise, NBC detailed Mort Werner to develop a concept for the other end of the day, a nighttime counterpart called *Tonight* that would extend the broadcast day to 1 a.m.[37]

At first the show had two directors, Jac Hein and Mike Zeamer, directing alternate hours. Soon, the job proved so intense that Mort Werner instituted a "first team" and "second team" system, with Hein and Zeamer alternating days. The flurry of activity in the downstairs control room meant the director had to juggle several live feeds, including studio cameras or remote pick-ups, enough film to run uninterrupted for an hour, and thirty-seven possible audio positions (about twice the number of most programs). A script girl had to keep track of four stop watches. Rehearsals were of limited value, so the show was often improvised while in progress. "Our commentators have legs," Hein said. "They have to, to keep up the fast pace we set for them."[38]

Sometimes things broke. One morning as a lengthy film sequence was being piped in, the film's sound failed. For five minutes Jim Fleming ad-libbed, with no notes or preparation, flawlessly narrating three important stories. As the film ended, applause erupted in the studio from Garroway and the program staff.

Other technical problems were self-inflicted. Since the telecine machines used to show filmed segments required a few seconds to get up to speed, the control room had to start them in advance so they would play on time. This required the on-air talent to stick with those portions of the scripts exactly as written, as certain words in the script served as "roll cues" for the control room. Unfortunately, Garroway and Fleming had a propensity to ad-lib, thus not providing the roll cues. When the film didn't follow, they would stammer to viewers that they didn't know why the film wasn't coming up. For writer Gerald Green, this was an ongoing source of irritation. No matter how often he reminded Garroway or Fleming to read the roll cues, the problem continued.

One day Green was at home watching *Today* as his daughter sat nearby playing on a rocking horse. As Fleming blew past another roll cue and was greeted with dead air, Green began shouting: "Run it! Run the damn film!" A few evenings later, he heard yelling from the den. It was his daughter in front of the television, watching *Felix the Cat.* "Run it!" she shouted. "Run the damn film!"[39]

Other technical difficulties were handled with grace, thanks to Garroway's calm style. In the middle of a *Today* segment, there was a loud bang and a blank screen. When the picture came back, Garroway pointed over to technicians quickly replacing a blown image orthicon tube on the stricken studio camera. Garroway displayed the expired tube to the audience and invited viewers to write in if they would like to have it. Hundreds of letters later, the winner was determined to be an Ohio man whose letter had been postmarked within minutes of the tube blowing. The blown tube was promptly sent to him.[40]

Garroway's easy, loose style made him an ideal host, Lescoulie said. "Dave was the ideal man to talk to people early in the morning," he remembered in 1982. "He moved like molten glass, slow and easy. I always said if you stepped on his foot, he wouldn't say ouch for five minutes." After about a year and a half of learning Garroway's timing and reacton style, "then I really could cut loose with some comedy. After that, it was marvelous. He'd play along absolutely straight and it would work out fine." The trust was mutual. Garroway issued a standing order to Lescoulie: if he ever felt a segment or an interview was getting slow or stale, come in and save it. In other segments, they played off each other for laughs, as when Lescoulie shot an arrow through an apple on Garroway's head to mark the anniversary of the William Tell Overture. Such was Garroway's trust in Lescoulie that he presented him with a gold ring, a replica of a silver ring Garroway wore. Inside was an inscription: "To Jack Lescoulie, for being just what you are by dawn's early light." Lescoulie wore it the rest of his life.[41]

Others on the staff understood how well Garroway went with the early hours. A young production assistant, Estelle Parsons, found him a pleasure to work with. "He's so relaxing, and the other hosts always seem so uptight," she said. Jim Fleming, a determined newsman, also understood the Garroway approach and adapted to the early hours. "I realize that many persons are at their grouchiest, so I have to practice a special approach," he said. "What is it? Oh, it's no secret formula; it's just that I never try to shake the rafters. I try to be easy-going and informal. And, as a matter of fact, so does everyone on this program."[42]

For as well as the team worked, costs and other factors threatened the stability of the on-air ensemble. While reviewing the costs of the program, Pinkham worried that Lescoulie's use on the program, "announcing the show, doing a few commercials, sports and some features," didn't justify his salary. Lescoulie was working on a week-to-week contract, yet to be signed to a longer deal.

Of equal concern was Fleming, whose excellence as a newsman resided alongside a determined temperament. In addition, according to his son Jeff, Fleming may not have been fully comfortable in an on-camera role. "It could have been that it wasn't his element, or that his personal standards were so high, which is why he could seem stiff," his son said. Whatever the issue, Fleming had worn out his welcome with producers, who decided not to pick up his option. Pinkham wanted Chicago newsman Clifton Utley, but realizing he probably couldn't start for a while, suggested NBC veteran Merrill "Red" Mueller as a replacement if Fleming quit in protest. Mueller would replace Fleming in March 1953, and not long thereafter Frank Blair, a low-key South Carolinian who had been working for NBC's Washington bureau, moved to New York and became the resident newsman, a role he retained until 1975.[43]

As plans moved ahead for Fleming's replacement, Pinkham suggested holding off on a replacement for Lescoulie, since replacing both would make the program seem troubled. Even Garroway's future had a cloud over it; negotiations on his new contract were hung up, as Biggie Levin didn't like NBC's reduction in money for guest appearances.[44]

While Garroway, Lescoulie and Fleming were the public faces of *Today*, there were dozens of people who kept the same hours and put in the hard work to keep the show going, to book the guests, to dress the set, to give stage directions, to get the pictures on the air and make the show run. Only occasionally were some of them seen on the air. They kept the same hours as Garroway, and it took its toll on their lives and their families. Jac Hein told a writer, "My kid doesn't know who I am anymore," while Mike Zeamer said his kid thought he was a cat burglar. Some members of the staff used the same support Garroway did, using The Doctor to help keep them going. After three hours of grinding, demanding work, many in the crew walked across 49th Street to Hurley and Daly, a tavern adjoining the southwest corner of the RCA Building, for a brief decompression before heading back to the *Today* offices for a production meeting. When that meeting finally broke up around 1 p.m., several of them adjourned to Toots Shor's restaurant for a lengthy session of the Telop One Club, a drinking group named after the technical term for the program's title card.[45]

Out of necessity, the fledgling *Today* program provided opportunities for women and minorities, setting precedents that changed lives. Estelle Parsons had been on a visit to New York from her home in Massachusetts. Through a connection in her roommate's family, she met Mort Werner, who told her about a new morning television program that NBC was starting. She joined *Today* in September 1951 as a production assistant for the news department, doing a little bit of everything. One of her jobs was to compile the morning weather report and prepare it for Garroway, drawing the forecast on the chalkboard map with red chalk that wouldn't show up on monochrome cameras; all Garroway then had to do was trace over the red chalk with his white chalk.

Another job was to prepare book features for the program, typing notes about the book to give Garroway talking points for author interviews. One day Garroway said to her, "You know more about this book than I do, so why don't you talk about it?" Producer Dick Pinkham liked the segment, so Parsons was soon doing on-air segments, going on remotes and even doing some reporting on Estes Kefauver's political campaign. It wasn't her passion, as she admitted years later: "I wasn't really interested in the job. It was just my nine to five." In the evenings, she booked singing engagements and worked toward her real ambition. Garroway once asked her what that ambition was. Years later, as he remembered, "I thought 'Poor thing. Hasn't anyone ever told you that you aren't pretty enough to be an actress?' But fifteen years later I watched that girl, Estelle Parsons, win an Academy Award."[46]

Another of the early-risers was Muriel Kirkpatrick, who hoped to get into television as a dancer but ended up as a secretary to Gerald Green.

Her jobs included compiling scores for Lescoulie's sports segment, trivia for *"Today* in History," and compiling temperatures for the temperature chart shown on the air, giving the weather in cities where *Today* affiliates were located. The last slot on the chart was blank, and the *Today* staff began filling that slot with an actual town with an unusual name suggested by audience mail, a job that eventually became Kirkpatrick's. On the centennial of the Paris Exposition, she had the idea of filling the chart with towns in the United States that bore the name Paris. Garroway intercepted the chalk and added one more entry: "Paris Garroway, Temperature 98.6."[47]

One of the hardest workers on the staff, regardless of gender, was Mary Kelly. A Connecticut native, she had been on vacation in New York a few years earlier when she asked the *New York Times* if they would hire her as a copygirl. They did. From there she worked as a lawyer's secretary, a promotion expert at a news syndicate, and then as an assistant on *Broadway Open House* and a publicity worker for the Cancer Fund. When *Today* came along, she joined up. Among her many jobs was one of the most crucial: making sure guests got to the Exhibition Hall on time. A writer said, "It is a task that on occasion makes agility of a greyhound, the tenacity of a bulldog, and the diplomacy of an ambassador. Mary, who usually sets out on her morning patrol in a rented limousine, has all these qualities in abundance. Her native cheerfulness is also a big help in calming ruffled guests who have an idea it is bad for the nerves to look at the sun before noon."[48]

Most of the time she succeeded, despite the risks. Waiting in a hotel lobby at 6 a.m. for a famous guest, she was accosted by a house detective who suspected her of being a call girl and called NBC to verify her credentials. On another occasion she went to pick up Ava Gardner at her hotel, only to get no response. Defeated, she went back to the studio, only to learn later that Gardner, having temporarily mended fences with Frank Sinatra, had cast aside her obligation to *Today* to be with him. (Garroway decided to press on with the interview, instructing Estelle Parsons to portray Ava Gardner.) The death of Joseph Stalin sent her on an abrupt journey to locate Alexander Kerensky, who had headed the Russian provisional government in 1917 and now lived in New York. Working on the barest of information, she tracked him down after checking apartment after apartment on the same street. "Some of the people I woke up were pretty mad," she said, "but they cheered up when I told them Stalin was dead."[49]

Fred Lights had returned from wartime service to find his hometown of Chicago had gone crazy for Garroway. When his show came on, Lights remembered, "You couldn't talk. You listened. And then, when his television show came on, he was like a god – to Black people, especially. It was just fascinating." Hired as a librarian by NBC in New York, he wanted more fulfilling work. "They knew I was restless in my job," he remembered, "and they would send me on different interviews."

A couple of days before Christmas 1953, his supervisors sent him to observe a *Today* broadcast. As he took in what was happening, the stage manager took off his headset, put it on Lights' head, and left the program. "I don't believe I moved from that spot the whole morning," he remembered. "I was in shock." Lights wondered if the high-stakes *Today* job would really be his, but he showed up the next morning. It was the start of a position he held for seven years on *Today*, the first Black stage manager on network television.[50]

It was a large and diverse team that labored behind the scenes, and each member of the team was important, from Garroway in front of the cameras, to the technical staff in the downstairs control room, the writers and staffers who provided material and made sure everything was in place. Looking after them all was the white-coated Major Dumas, whom frequent guest host Faye Emerson wrote "has one of the most important jobs of all. Major is the man who greets the crew when they come in the middle of the night to rehearse, with coffee, doughnuts, Danish pastry, and all sorts of goodies. Every time I do the show I drink at least fifteen cups, and I will make a flat statement that Major makes the best coffee in the world." It was an opinion shared by no less an authority than Duncan Hines, who tried Major's coffee during a *Today* appearance and presented him a special badge of merit.[51]

As the program's first year ended, reviewers looked back on how much the show had matured into something of value. "Anyone wanting to write a book describing the political and social developments of 1952 could save themselves years of research by gathering kinescope recordings" of *Today* "and taking notes on what he saw," Merrill Panitt wrote. "*Today* presents, as no other television show does, an accurate picture of modern American life." The program had changed viewing habits. More than thirty-two percent of viewers reported they ate breakfast in front of the television, either taking their food with them into the television room or putting their televisions on carts rolled into the kitchen. It had people knocking holes in walls or setting up mirrors so they wouldn't miss a moment of the show. One "mirror viewer" wrote to ask Garroway to "do something backwards" every so often. A viewer started getting up a half-hour earlier so she could have breakfast cooked by 7 a.m., while another viewer extended the legs of her television set so she could watch while still in bed.[52]

Today had an audience of two million viewers. Even so, rumors persisted that the ratings were still too low, that it wasn't earning enough money, that its future was tenuous. Something was needed to make *Today* a program people wouldn't miss.[53]

11

It started with a trip to buy pet food.

Roy Waldron and Buddy Mennella met at NBC after World War II. Both were veterans, both were NBC pages. Both were performers; Roy danced and Buddy sang. While on tour with a traveling show, they visited a pet shop in Glen Rock, New Jersey. The owner mentioned the shop was for sale. Both men loved animals, so they became business partners and bought the store. One day they drove to New York to visit an importer who supplied them with specialty pet food. The importer showed them a baby chimpanzee, thirteen weeks old, that a big-game hunter had brought back. He could be theirs for $600. The shop wasn't making money, and Mennella suggested they needed something to draw people in, so the chimpanzee came home with the two men. They devised a contest to name the little chimp, and put announcements in the local newspaper. A nine-year-old submitted the winning entry, naming him Mr. Muggs. "His face looks like a mug to me," the boy said.[1]

A few weeks later, Buddy's father was in a New York City hospital. With no one to watch the store or look after Muggs, the two men put him in winter clothes and carried him along. Waldron and Mennella had some extra time, so they decided to stop by the RKO Building, across 50th Street from the RCA Building, to visit a friend. At about that time, in the *Today* offices on that same floor of the RKO Building, writer Len Safir was at work. He had seen a *New Yorker* cartoon depicting a monkey leaving a news desk and a human taking over, saying "And now, for the human side of the news." This gave Safir an idea for periodic cutaways to a monkey, dressed in a suit, banging away on a typewriter as a quick visual gag. Staffers had called around to local pet shops, but hadn't found a monkey.

Charlie Speer ran into the office. There was a chimpanzee in the building, he said, out by the elevator. Safir walked out to see Waldron and Mennella holding Muggs, "about the cutest-looking thing you've ever seen." The men were offered $20 for a one-time appearance by their chimpanzee. They asked for $50. They were brought to the *Today* offices and left with an agreement for multiple appearances, at $200 a week. Muggs made his debut on February 2. A bemused Garroway, just returned to the program from a bout of pneumonia, welcomed his new on-air assistant. At a loss for what to say, he ad-libbed a first name for the chimpanzee that gave him an air of distinction. From then on, he was known as J. Fred Muggs.[2]

Safir reasoned that keeping Muggs on the program would help the show's ratings: that children would want to see the monkey, and parents would realize *Today* offered quality content worth tuning in for its own sake. It worked. "Len Safir, bless his soul, made like a hundred million dollars' profit for NBC," Dick Pinkham remembered, crediting Muggs with the ratings increase. "Until then, I thought they would cancel the whole damn thing and I would be back in the newspaper business."[3]

Soon Muggs was getting more than a hundred fan letters a week. People sent him packages containing gifts: toys, a high chair, clothing. Many of the fan letters were from adults. And, of course, he was a particular hit with children. "I have wanted a baby sister for a long time," a little girl wrote, "and now I would like to have one who looks just like you." Children protested when parents tried to change the channel. A Louisville grade school turned on a television each morning so students could watch Muggs; the move, they claimed, also reduced tardiness. When Muggs' televised birthday party was interrupted by technical difficulties, five thousand angry calls flooded the NBC switchboards.[4]

Not everyone loved Muggs. A New York viewer mailed him a piece of rope with a threatening letter enclosed. Unsubstantiated rumors circulated that Garroway didn't like Muggs, that on the advice of a zoologist the host had physically threatened Muggs to get him to understand the show's pecking order. John Crosby wrote that neither Garroway, Lescoulie nor Fleming were happy about the addition and chided "what great brain over at NBC dreamed this one up," calling Muggs' debut "an orgy of cuteness" and "nonsense." But NBC saw the potential for ratings growth, and the day-to-day deal for Muggs' appearances turned into a thirteen-week contract.[5]

Like everyone else on the show, Muggs' day began at 4 a.m. He went to the studio, then after the program went with his owners back to the pet shop. Mennella denied they wanted to turn him into a trick chimp; instead, they wanted him to know he was loved. They trained him to brush his teeth, use a toilet, eat with a spoon and drink with a cup. They refused to keep him in a cage. The "J." in "J. Fred," Mennella later maintained, stood for "Jack of all trades" because Muggs was so versatile. The young chimpanzee was generally well-behaved, although he preferred to be around humans and dogs instead of other apes. His unpredictability made for interesting moments. Garroway believed that "the best stuff on television is the unpredictable," and said suggestions in production meetings about ideas for Muggs often ended in laughter. "At that point we have to stop and laugh," Garroway said. "Because we can't make Muggs do anything. He truly is unpredictable. We never know just how he will respond when the cameras are on him." Early on, Garroway had to change his plans for a segment when Muggs went to sleep in his chair.[6]

Other programs and stations tried to cash in on the Muggs phenomenon. Some programs tried direct imitations. One station, trying to promote its upcoming airing of *King Kong*, sent someone to stand outside the Exhibition Hall window in a gorilla costume with instructions to get Muggs' attention. When the chimpanzee saw the giant gorilla outside, Muggs screeched, pounded the glass, and ran around frantically. The director prepared to cut away, but Garroway stayed calm, asked that the cameras show the promotional card the gorilla was carrying, and said the press agent deserved credit for his ingenuity.[7]

Some foresaw trouble. "When Dave Garroway's television chimpanzee grows up to weigh 120 pounds," one columnist wrote, "we want to see Dave lugging it around in one arm like he does now. Or better, maybe the chimp will lug around Dave, Charlie McCarthy style." A columnist who vacationed in New York was surprised to look in and see Muggs acting less well-behaved, his episode culminating in knocking Garroway's glasses off, "at which point he was hauled aside and given a small spanking." The crowd outside buzzed with ideas on how to handle chimpanzees' behavior, "but I never had a chance to ask Muggs his on how to handle people."[8]

Staffers had to learn how to work around Muggs. Those who were gentle and talked sweetly with him usually fared okay, but on occasion he turned on a friend. Most mornings, as writer Paul Cunningham scurried into the studio with the script just before airtime, he would see Muggs sitting in a corner, sticking out his hand for a handshake. Cunningham would greet Muggs and shake his hand. One morning, in a bad mood, Cunningham spurned the handshake and told Muggs to get lost. Not two minutes later, an angry Muggs hopped over to Cunningham's desk and smacked him across the back, nearly knocking him out of the chair.[9]

It didn't take long for Muggs to use television for his own advantage. He made an association between the red tally light that lit up when the camera was active, and his own behavior. When the light was on, he wasn't scolded. Muggs realized he could play for the camera, pull Garroway's glasses off or tweak the host's nose, and get away with it. "His masters are now giving him an intensive course in proper chimp decorum while on television," Dick Kleiner wrote. "His is a simple psychological problem: delusions of being human."[10]

Muggs' increasingly spirited behavior inspired the producers to get him out of the studio more. Marlin Perkins of the Chicago Zoo, a familiar Chicago television face from *Zoo Parade*, agreed to host a birthday party for Muggs. As the arrangements were made, Perkins asked if Muggs had been checked for worms, saying the chimp couldn't visit the zoo if he had worms. Pinkham, aghast, asked Perkins how he could tell. Put Muggs face-down on a table, Perkins said, and examine his rear end. Pinkham thought to himself, "I have a B.A. in English from Yale. What the hell am I doing?"[11]

A *Today* visitor summarized the show: "It is the only place in the world where you can shake hands with a former prime minister of the Soviet Union and a chimpanzee at 7 o'clock in the morning."[12]

While J. Fred Muggs helped *Today*'s ratings, the heroic work of Matthew Culligan brought the program's ledger into the black. NBC's sales staff had been treating the morning show almost as an afterthought, concentrating instead on the marquee programs in prime time. Pat Weaver put former magazine publisher John Kingsley Herbert in charge of reviving *Today*'s fortunes. The program was on pace to lose $1.7 million by the end of its first year. In late 1952 Herbert hired Culligan, whom he knew from the magazine sales realm, to oversee *Today*'s ad sales.[13]

Today staffers were skeptical that Culligan could turn the program's finances around. His optimism, charm and confidence soon won them over. When Muggs showed the program's viewership potential, it gave Culligan's pitches more strength, as did the talents of the program's host. "I was so impressed with Garroway as an engaging personality," Culligan told historian Jeff Kisseloff. "I picked potential advertisers and challenged them." Culligan went to the marketing director at Fram Filters, offering to pay for telegrams to fifty of its distributors asking their opinions of Garroway. Thirty-five wrote back saying they liked him. It convinced Fram leadership. Culligan leaked that story to the press, and in a primitive form of viral communication it persuaded others to consider *Today* as a marketing vehicle.[14]

Culligan persuaded advertisers that their ad buys went farther on *Today*, and at a lower cost. It worked. Big names – Dow Chemical, promoting a new product called Saran Wrap, which Garroway demonstrated by holding a piece across the camera's lens to show its transparency – and smaller names, like Rennit junket, signed up. Garroway himself got involved, courting sponsors and talking with them about how the low-pressure *Today* program could be an effective forum for their products. By May 1953, the program was grossing $350,000 a month. The following year, *Today* set a one-year record for all forms of entertainment by grossing $11 million.[15]

As *Today* began, Garroway "felt like I was in a revolving door. I wasn't sure I would ever get anywhere." Now, a year later, he was going places. He began 1953 by getting a one-year extension with NBC, then departed for a vacation in Florida, with Bob Elliott and Ray Goulding helping Lescoulie and Fleming those two weeks. The program continued to expand its reach and capabilities, covering breaking stories, stretching the muscles of television. Press releases from NBC's publicity department constantly promoted *Today* as an important force in informing the public. "There appears to be an existing need for visual news at breakfast," Pinkham was quoted in one release, "and the fundamental objective of *Today* is to provide people with a television newspaper." This prompted one columnist to write, "I can't get over thinking of Dave Garroway as the managing editor of television newspaper, or that chimpanzee they have on the show sitting in on the city desk and answering the telephone. There are more things on heaven and heart, Horatio, than are dreamed of in your philosophy. Or in yours too, Mr. Pinkham."[16]

Sometimes the conflict between *Today* as televised newspaper and *Today* as entertainment was inescapable. In March 1953 *Today* carried live coverage of an atomic bomb test in Nevada. The pictures from the desert showed the bomb's explosion giving a rapid, otherworldly sense of dawn in the early morning darkness. Chet Huntley, reporting from the forward zone at the test, could only say, "All words are too puny and too fragile to be used at a time like this." After the test it was back to the studio, where Garroway resumed holding court with Muggs. "There certainly had been nothing too startling to keep us from enjoying our grapefruit, toast, cereal and coffee," a columnist wrote of the incongruous scene.[17]

The clash between news and entertainment rose to the level of international incident two months later. As Great Britain prepared for the coronation of Elizabeth II, CBS and NBC made elaborate plans to cover the big event. At the time, there was no real way to get live television pictures across the Atlantic. The best the networks could do was fly reels of film across the ocean for broadcast that afternoon. Shortwave radio broadcasts and wirephotos would have to suffice until the films arrived. CBS and NBC arranged for their films to be flown to Goose Bay, Labrador on the same jet bomber; the films would then be flown to Boston, the farthest-north origination point on the two networks, aboard speedy planes each network had hired in hopes of beating the other. NBC had also secretly arranged for a Canberra jet bomber, due to be delivered to Venezuela, to fly a set of films over, potentially providing a two-hour scoop on CBS.[18]

Today took the air at 5:30 the morning of June 2, starting NBC's daylong coverage. Shortwave radio provided the sounds; still photos transmitted by a crude wirephoto process called Mufax, which took nine minutes to transmit, provided muddy images from the scene. ("The Queen's face seems to be in a shadow," Frank Blair told the BBC's Gibson Parker via shortwave hookup. "Can you recall the expression on her face as the picture was taken?" Parker: "As a matter of fact, she is smiling directly at the camera in the original.")[19]

It didn't go as planned. NBC's strategy, announced on-air with what one observer called "some gloating," to have a two-hour scoop via the "secret weapon" Canberra was foiled when the plane turned back to England. More concerning was that the solemn ceremony was interrupted by commercials, which cut away from important developments that CBS did carry. Another reviewer complained that the BBC's restrained commentary "was too often interrupted by commercials or aimless chatter by time-fillers such as Dave Garroway."[20]

The commercial interruptions irritated the BBC, which had agreed to make coverage available to the American networks if the Westminster Abbey ceremonies were not interrupted by commercials or used as a basis for sponsorship. The BBC particularly protested the antics of J. Fred

Muggs, seen in the midst of a solemn ceremony, goofing around with Garroway. At one break in the coverage, Garroway walked over to Muggs, who was sitting on the sofa, and asked: "Ah, don't you wish that you, too, could be a king in the far-off land where you originated?" A photo of Garroway and Muggs appeared on the front of the London *Daily Express*, shown in a way that implied Garroway had crowned Muggs "in a bold burlesque of the coronation ceremony." Even though Garroway hadn't crowned Muggs, the impression remained. The networks "booted their responsibility through poor taste in presenting the coronation as an advertising backdrop," wrote one observer. "Sooner or later the networks will discover that there are some ceremonies which do not lend themselves to moneymaking and should be presented as a matter of public service. The coronation definitely is one of these."[21]

At least one dignitary found Muggs a source of amusement. On a visit to New York, former president Harry Truman, out on a morning walk, paused at the Exhibition Hall while *Today* was in session. "Who is the fellow with the baby?" he asked. Told the "baby" was a chimpanzee, Truman laughed heartily and continued on his way.[22]

Garroway took two weeks off in June for a tour of Europe. While at a customs office between Switzerland and Italy, a refugee from Romania spotted Garroway holding his passport. The man, "with pathetic eagerness," pleaded with Garroway to let him hold his passport for a moment, "as though, in holding it, he came a little closer to the elusive freedom and opportunity he had been seeking since fleeing his native land." It prompted Garroway to think about how many Americans took passports, and their freedoms, for granted. "I think everyone should get a passport, just to have it even if they're not planning to go somewhere, so they can look at it once in a while, knowing it is their passport to freedom."[23]

The influence of the program he helmed was inescapable. Booksellers found that a Garroway mention of a book prompted calls wanting to know if it was in stock. Even NBC had to give in, moving its own press relations department to a smaller space to give Garroway's staffers more room. Charlie Andrews, thinking about how far he and his friend had come in less than a decade, looked around Garroway's new, large office with its three windows. "It's a rule here that you have to get $10 million in billings before you get a window," Andrews said. "Dave, you finally made it." Success only went so far, though. One day as he left the studio, a woman stopped him. "Say, mister, when does that fellow Garroway come on? I watch him every day in Louisville."[24]

There was more Garroway to be watched. In September 1953 he helped his Chicago friend Burr Tillstrom, who presented a special color edition of *Kukla, Fran and Ollie* as the first publicly-announced broadcast of a network program in RCA's "compatible color" system. It was a first-class operation, with the Kuklapolitans staging a presentation of *St. George and the Dragon*, the NBC Symphony providing musical accompaniment. Garroway served as host, gently lampooning Metropolitan Opera announcer Milton Cross as he gave the opening and closing announcements.[25]

It coincided with the expansion of Garroway's empire. Ever since Garroway moved to New York, there had been rumors NBC might bring back *Garroway At Large*. His appearances as a substitute host on *Your Show of Shows*, in which he brought back some of the offbeat humor the Chicago series had specialized in, had added substance to the rumors. After each appearance, critics acclaimed the return of Garroway's style of humor. "You think, by golly, this is the old Garroway back in form again, just like he used to be in Chicago," one reviewer wrote of a *Your Show of Shows* appearance. "Television can be pretty good on occasions such as these."[26]

In mid-1953 it looked like *Garroway at Large* would indeed return, with Pontiac interested in the series if a time slot could be found. "He might as well take it," Si Steinhauser suggested. "Has to get up in the middle of the night for his morning *Today*, so why bother with sleep? He can only kill himself overworking and what he gets for doing so is only money." Garroway himself was open to the idea. "When you're already doing thirty-five half-hours," he said, "what's one half-hour more?" Some stories suggested Garroway would leave *Today* and concentrate on prime time, backed by many of the players in his Chicago troupe.[27]

This was easier said than done. Connie Russell had gone off to Hollywood, Bette Chapel had remained in Chicago, and Jack Haskell had moved to Texas. Only Cliff Norton was in New York. While Norton was able to return, a new ensemble had to be built. Skitch Henderson took over musical supervision, and a new cast was assembled: Ken Spalding, Diane Sinclair, Shirley Harmer, and a seventeen-year-old singer, her looks reminiscent of a young Judy Garland, from a little mining town in Pennsylvania. A recording of her singing had been sent to Columbia

Records impresario Mitch Miller; she had been summoned to New York, where she auditioned for Miller, Arthur Godfrey and Dave Garroway. In the end, Garroway hired her for the prime-time show, and changed her name from Norma Jean Speranza to Jill Corey.[28]

Years later Corey looked back on the whirlwind that led to her overnight stardom, chronicled in a *Life* cover story that followed her from hometown sendoff to television debut. She remembered feeling overwhelmed by the offers from record labels and television producers, by the barrage of questions from reporters. One opened by asking, "Well, Cinderella, how does the slipper fit?" She remained stunned by the question years later. "What do you say to a question like that if you're seventeen and you've never been out of Avonmore, Pennsylvania except to go once to Pittsburgh?" After the interview she asked her new agent if she was considered a star. He said she was. "Well, I never want to do another interview."[29]

The Dave Garroway Show premiered October 3 in its Friday evening time slot, with help from guest star Wally Cox. "Garroway came home to his native evening habitat Friday night as casual, simple and intelligent as ever, in as smart a concentrated musical revue as you are likely to locate anywhere on TV," one review said. "Welcome home, good taste; you'd been away just long enough." Another reviewer wrote that Garroway "seemed more at home" on the evening show "than he does on *Today*...The program was breezy, simple and in good taste. Garroway doesn't care if the home viewer sees a camera or a floor manager. Neither do we." Although the new cast drew favorable responses, one in particular got attention. "Dave would seem to have found a real charmer in a pert, honest-eyed songstress, Jill Corey," wrote one review. "She's a cinch to be a star." Jack O'Brian predicted "Dave Garroway's pert thrush Jill Corey will make it big. Maybe big as Judy Garland."[30]

Others felt something was missing. Anton Remenih of the *Chicago Tribune* wrote the new show "just can't recapture the zip and sparkle it radiated from Chicago," that "an intangible something is missing now... The Dave Garroway show goes thru the Chicago motions, but the spirit is missing." John Crosby said that though the new program was "a fairly close replica of the old show" and Garroway's humor "is still wry and adult and just about unique on television," the show was "a little disappointing, largely, I think, because we expected too much." What had been innovative in Chicago four years before had become standard practice, making the program "a little mild for contemporary tastes."[31]

The network left him alone. "I guess I bring enough billings into NBC," he said. "They haven't even offered any suggestions." Nor did they insist on an audience or a laugh track, both of which he hated. (Once, appearing as a guest on *Texaco Star Theater*, Milton Berle asked Garroway why there were no laughs on his show. Garroway: "We have no audience. What's your excuse?") The program provided a relaxed format, which was "harder to do in a way. That type material is hard to get. And the very fact that it's simple makes it hard." But the effort, he said, is "to bring the cast into your home instead of taking viewers into a theater."[32]

Sometimes the bizarre intruded on Garroway's world. One morning early in November, the genial *Today* host had an unmistakable black eye and scratches on his face that makeup couldn't conceal. "I was in a cab accident," he told a reporter; he was taking a young lady home when his taxicab was hit by another car. Who was the young lady? "Nobody you'd know," he frowned. The reporter, curiosity piqued, called the police station nearest to the site of the accident. They had no record of any accident. A few days later, Walter Winchell told readers the likely culprit was "a thrown highball glass at a Halloween party," a tiff between Garroway and his girlfriend, whose swollen jaw from the same incident "cost her $1000 in cancelled foto assignments."[33]

A couple of weeks later, a chance meeting almost gave Garroway a tremendous interview. Back in New York on another visit, Harry Truman again paused in a morning stroll to look in the Exhibition Hall for a few moments. Garroway waved to Truman, who waved back. This time, they brought Muggs outside to meet the former president, who shook hands but backed away laughing when Muggs tried to put an arm around him. "I don't let people get so intimate with me," Truman joked. A producer asked if Truman would like to come inside to talk with Garroway on the air. The former president turned to George Jessel, who was part of his entourage that morning. "What do you think, George?" The comedian, who had a show on ABC, replied, "The president is too busy and I'm on another network." Truman and his group went on their way. Years later Gerald Green was still irked about the incident, calling Jessel "the biggest schmuck that ever lived."[34]

At other times the bizarre was the doing of Garroway himself. During the 1953 World Series, Jac Hein went over to Garroway's apartment. Garroway had the game on television, but with the sound off. The audio came from a shortwave radio that was picking up a French broadcast of the game. Hein asked him why he was doing it. "Sounds funny this way," Garroway said. Another time, Garroway and Charlie Andrews were talking about dating. Andrews griped that he when he took girls to lunch, they chattered inconsequentially. He wondered what it would be like to take a girl to lunch who wouldn't say a word. "Let's do it," Garroway said. They hired two beautiful women from a modeling agency, extracted promises from them to maintain silence the whole time, and then went to a hotel dining room. Garroway allowed the women to order their own food, but that was it. The two men talked throughout the whole meal about anything and everything while the two models sat in silence. When the meal was over, Garroway and Andrews paid the models their fee, shook hands with them, and went on their way.[35]

On New Year's Day 1954, Garroway wondered aloud how many people were watching *Today*. Within days, 8,000 responses had flooded the mail room. They appreciated not only the show's content, but the taste Garroway brought to the proceedings. One viewer wrote in praise of how Garroway handled an interview with a man who used a swear word, by immediately cutting away from the interview and playing a record. The viewer wrote that while they long appreciated Garroway's unflappability on air, "that time he proved himself to be more than that. He showed discernment, a sense of the fastidious and ability to make a quick decision. I am convinced more than ever that we need more gentlemen of Garroway's type on television."[36]

John Crosby called the two-year-old *Today* program "a howling commercial success, though hardly equal to its press releases." It was now on fifty-one stations, reaching six million homes and supported by ninety-one sponsors, ranging from dessert mixes to Florida citrus to Pepsi-Cola to Polaroid cameras. At its peak viewership point on any given day, it was watched by more than a million and a half families. It grossed more than $5 million in ad revenue. It covered any topic under the sun, from the profound to the sublime, from the serious to the amusing. J. Fred Muggs kept children amused ("Mother is too busy to change the channel," said Jac Hein). It was successful enough to spawn hints that other networks were working on their own morning shows.[37]

A good part of the credit was given to Garroway for his casual style, but he denied he was casual. "To me, I'm working my head off all the time, and it's very hard work as far as I'm concerned," he told an interviewer. "But people think I show up just at air time and ad lib my way through a show off the cuff. Ad-libbing requires intense preparation. The words may be ad-libbed, but not the ideas and situations into which they are fitted." He also downplayed the attention he got for his early hours. "There are sixty-five people on that show who get up as early or earlier than I do," he said. Garroway also denied rumors that J. Fred Muggs lived with him, or that his was a glamorous life. "I'm not a big wheel in the town's mad social whirl. After thirty-one half-hours of TV weekly, the only thing I could do at a cocktail party would be to go to sleep standing in a corner." More often, "Cheese, baloney and milk out of the ice box are my speed when I eat at home. On the rare occasions when I'm brave enough to open a can of chili to heat it up, I get trapped on the telephone and the chili burns."[38]

In mid-February, taking some time to rest in Florida, Garroway was filming a Pontiac commercial for the Friday night show. In the middle of a demonstration of the car's power steering, looking at the cameraman alongside him, Garroway plowed through a stop sign on Key Biscayne and was broadsided by an oncoming car. "Garroway has remarked to me several times that he never had an accident while racing sports cars," the commercial's director said. "And he has this kind of luck while driving a Pontiac twelve or twenty miles an hour." Hospitalized, a three-inch laceration above his left eye from cutting his head on an open vent window, Garroway clowned around for press photographers, taking the pulse of a nurse while he lay in a hospital bed. Though he said he could do that week's prime-time show, doctors insisted he remain in Miami for a few days. Garroway's return a few days later was to the relief of at least one viewer. Akron columnist Art Cullison wrote that while Jack Lescoulie was "pleasant enough" as substitute host, he didn't possess Garroway's "nonchalance." He mused, "Without Garroway, I'm afraid the audience would swing over to another station offering the same type of program."[39]

That was in the works. CBS had long been rumored to be at work on a morning show, and in mid-February announced Walter Cronkite and Charles Collingwood would host it. "The existence of one newspaper," said CBS programming vice president Hubbell Robinson Jr., "doesn't mean there can't be a second." He said the new program would be different and attractive. "Given an opportunity in any field, people like to shop around and we're giving them this chance in early morning television."[40]

When *The Morning Show* debuted on March 15, the similarities to *Today* were unmistakable: Cronkite as the easygoing host, news breaks from Charles Collingwood, music played from records. In place of Garroway's chalkboard weather map was a high-tech weather map with flashing lights and other effects that one reviewer said "looks like something swiped from Coney Island." In place of a chimpanzee, *The Morning Show* had Bil and Cora Baird with two puppets, Charlemagne the Lion and a "disk doggie" named Humphrey. John Crosby wrote, "If imitation is the sincerest form of flattery, then CBS-TV's new program, *The Morning Show* is the nicest compliment that has ever been paid to its two-year-old opposite number on NBC called *Today*. The chief difference between *Today* and the *Morning Show* is that Walter Cronkite has a moustache and Dave Garroway hasn't, and Garroway wears glasses and Cronkite doesn't." Anton Remenih was not impressed at all: "Who, pray tell, wants to sit in front of a television set at 7 o'clock in the morning and watch puppets? Video, what hast thou wrought?"[41]

The principals of *Today* looked on in the spirit of good sportsmanship, sending Cronkite and Collingwood a telegram: "Abandon all hope ye who enter here." The following week, Garroway was waiting to speak at an NBC function, listening to a network official ahead of him on the program drone on and on. When Garroway finally took the microphone, he said, "One more word and we would have had to give equal time to Walter Cronkite."[42]

Cronkite, Collingwood, the Baird puppets and a pinball-machine weather map could not duplicate *Today*'s appeal to viewers old and young. Nor could they match the fascination that one *Today* cast member held for viewers old and young, who celebrated a milestone that spring. On April 20, *Today* threw an on-air party for J. Fred Muggs. "May we do it with humbleness. May we do it with dignity and restraint," Garroway solemnly announced as Muggs ran a finger through the icing of a birthday cake. As Garroway, Blair, Lescoulie and Mary Kelly applauded, Muggs put both hands into a bowl of marshmallow fluff and smeared the foursome with it. Two months later, Muggs signed an on-air contract extension on the air, making a giant "X" on the paper to Garroway's great amusement. He was loved by viewers, who were always eager to see him. Once, when a *Today* delegation arrived at the Charlotte airport, Garroway and other cast members were barely noticed by the crowd, but

Muggs was besieged with attention, including an interview with a reporter. ("We are pretty sure this episode proves a point, but we just can't think what it is," one editorial read.)[43]

While Muggs was popular with viewers, his behavior became an increasing concern. Unable to process what was happening around him, perhaps frightened or bewildered by much of it, he became increasingly prone to acting out. A woman in an elevator with Muggs gave him a friendly glance, only to suddenly feel him kick up her skirt with his foot. On *Today*, Muggs shook hands with Miss America, then pried a diamond ring off her finger and put it in his mouth. During a rehearsal for Martha Raye's television show, Muggs sank his teeth into her arm, sending her recoiling in agony. Her understudy, Vicki Carlson, also suffered a bite. On a remote with Dean Martin and Jerry Lewis in Atlantic City, he took a bite out of Lewis. Faye Emerson, who had also suffered the wrath of Muggs' teeth, attributed this not to meanness but "like any other child, if frightened, he reacts instantly. Jerry tried to do what I tried – pick Mr. Muggs up from the back when he wasn't looking." She warned Muggs that the last person he should bite is Lewis: "He very well might bite you back." In November 1954, Garroway hosted Little Miss USA on *Today* and asked what she'd like to have. The four-year-old girl, sitting on Garroway's knee, replied, "J. Fred Muggs." The chimpanzee loped out and, with one of his long arms, knocked her off Garroway's knee. Garroway gasped as the girl tumbled to the floor. But, unhurt, she stood up and went back for Muggs, who gave her a gentle kiss. Actress Kim Novak sat Muggs on her lap. He promptly groped her; she ran away screaming. Producers asked actress Jane Powell to be a guest and be kissed by Muggs; her response was a firm "No!" When Muggs accompanied the *Today* staff to the 1956 Democratic convention, a political coordinator asked Gerald Green if Muggs could be restrained from biting any political figures. Green assured the worried staffer, "If he bites a Democrat in Chicago, he will bite a Republican in San Francisco next week."[44]

Stage manager Fred Lights defended Muggs. He said that many people ignored Mennella and Waldron's advice to let Muggs come to them. "Muggs was gentle and friendly," Lights said. "He certainly was not vicious." Muggs' behavior, which Lights admitted was "frightening" at times, wasn't his own fault. Part of the problem, the stage manager said, was that as Muggs grew older, "he didn't know his own strength." Muggs took to Mary Kelly, seeing her as a foster mother. "If I come into the room and don't go over and let him kiss me, he throws a fit," she said. Even she could get her fill, though. When she was assigned to chaperone Muggs on a round-the-world trip, he escaped from her Beirut hotel room, sending her chasing after while wearing nothing but her slip. "I never want to babysit for a chimpanzee again," she said.[45]

Still, some were getting tired of Muggs' act, including some of the staff members. The production team worked on ways to use of Muggs without having him in the studio, sending him out on more remotes and trips. In the summer of 1954, NBC sent Muggs on a five-week world tour, with Mary Kelly as his chaperone. It was a publicity bonanza for NBC, but some observers wondered about the message it sent. "As publicity for the United States at this ticklish moment in history, I kind of wonder about it," wrote Pittsburgh columnist Fred Remington, citing "skepticism across the globe as to America's competence to be the leader of the non-Communist nations. And one wonders if a touring chimpanzee with a retinue of attendants is quite the device to soothe these fears."[46]

When Muggs returned in late August, *Today* made a big production of welcoming him back. The trip hadn't changed him in the least. "He still isn't amenable to direction," wrote C. E. Butterfield, "and actually seems more pesky than ever. The sole reason for J. Fred in the program, of course, is the fact animals are amusing." Butterfield wondered if the weekly fee Muggs earned for his owners was fully earned. "Personally, I'd like to see him do a trick occasionally, rather than just try to eat up the script."[47]

There was tacit acknowledgment from producer Bob Bendick that Muggs was becoming a handful. In January 1955 a female chimpanzee named Phoebe B. Beebe was introduced as an understudy. "She does all the childish sorts of things Muggs did when he was first on," Bendick said, while also insisting Muggs' job was safe. "Muggs is not being eased off the show. He is going to travel more, go out and meet people, coast to coast, and spread good will." The writer doubted these reassurances. "It is obvious that he is being eased out, like the main-office salesman who gets hotheaded and must be shipped off to the suburban branch. Poor Muggs. Too big for his bristles!"[48]

How Garroway himself felt about Muggs has been a point of contention. In later years, after an unhappy Mennella and Waldron had sought legal action against Garroway and NBC, he had been careful in his comments about Muggs, instead sticking to humorous references to vaccination cards in the NBC infirmary. On the air, Garroway was generally philosophical and gentle toward Muggs, keeping a smile on his face even on occasions when Muggs was taking a bite out of him. As Robert Metz later wrote, "It was an open secret at Radio City that the two were on-again, off-again pals." Once, when Muggs was on Garroway's lap, the host slipped on a fright mask while Muggs was looking away. When Muggs saw the scary face, he screeched in terror. When a smiling Garroway took off the mask, a relieved Muggs embraced him.[49]

Sometimes Garroway was concerned about the way Waldron and Mennella disciplined Muggs. One *Today* guest and a few viewers grew so concerned that the American Society for the Prevention of Cruelty to Animals sent an observer. "An animal like Muggs is high-strung and when he's petted or teased, he can very easily run wild," said Raymond Mulligan of the ASPCA. Although his trainers tried to make him behave, "the way it's done looks pretty bad on camera. After the show, they can do what they want. We've recommended that nobody touch him when he's on camera." The ASPCA worked out an agreement with Mennella, Waldron, and Gerald Green, distributed to all hands: "Be very careful not to give commands, pet, or in general play with him." One writer called it the "supreme test of his TV career." Now that none of the cast could support him, Muggs would "have to demonstrate if he's really of star caliber!"[50]

Television, between the daily *Today* program and the Friday night program, had left Garroway's radio efforts forlorn. The daily programs disappeared from the NBC schedule, replaced with a new two-hour weekly program. Its format was freeform, letting Garroway cover whatever topics he was interested in and giving him a chance to have longer-form interviews with interesting people, the kind of discussions he liked. NBC set up a dedicated studio that remained ready for Garroway at all times; when he had a few moments, he could record a segment. Much of it was recorded each morning after *Today* was finished. The studio also had shortwave circuits, allowing interviews with people in Europe.[51]

Originally slated to air on Friday evenings, NBC moved it, and *Sunday With Garroway* made its debut April 18. Garroway described it as "a magazine of the air with a news format." Jim Fleming, who produced the program and provided live news breaks, emphasized that the show would not imitate *Today*. However, the program would feature highlights from interesting segments on the previous week's *Today* programs. These were inserted among conversations with newsmakers, interviews with celebrities, and visits with interesting people. Garroway, concerned as the Cold War churned and the specter of the hydrogen bomb and instant annihilation lurked in the background, often spent time with scientists, philosophers and religious leaders who tried to put the unsettling times in perspective: for instance, asking Bertrand Russell about "how mankind may best maintain a civilized pose and equanimity in the age of hydrogen." It was a reflection of a concern that increasingly dominated his thinking as the decade continued. Other times, he poked fun at himself; in an interview with NBC supervisor of announcers Pat Kelly, for whom he once worked, Garroway re-enacted the audition for which Kelly had flunked him sixteen years before.[52]

It was a gentle program, a contemplative side of Garroway not often seen on *Today* and seldom seen in his earlier radio programs, and in a way he showed more of his real self on *Sunday With Garroway* than he had before. There were no audiences, no cameras; only Garroway, talking about what was on his mind, in the intimate format he loved. One reviewer said *Sunday With Garroway* presented a "mellow, don't take it too big, mood" that "taken in judicious doses, it is pleasanter listening than the glorified deejay show it might be suspected of resembling." Although the entire two hours "could leave dialers slumped as deep in their chairs as Garroway," the program "can be nibbled at random with an excellent chance of hitting a tasty tidbit." Magee Adams was less impressed, saying the program gave him "the uneasy sense of being left at a loose end. Despite all the diverting snacks, you wind up the two hours with the feeling of having missed a full meal."[53]

Sunday With Garroway was finding a home, but the Friday night *Dave Garroway Show* was endangered. Its ratings weren't superb, but the program had found a dedicated audience that felt NBC wasn't making the most of it. One viewer, bemoaning that "little attention has been paid to Dave Garroway's Friday night musical," called it "a pleasant, easy-going program and should be praised to the skies and beyond because this is the sort of program we need much more of." As the season concluded, Pontiac executives said they loved the program but were concerned about the low ratings. One representative asked why Garroway didn't tell jokes like other hosts. "We've developed a style that Dave is comfortable with, and besides, it's very hard to do jokes without an audience," Charlie Andrews argued. The representative responded, "You've put your finger on it. We need an audience." From that point on, Andrews felt, "we were doomed."[54]

Pontiac's agency demanded other changes. Not only did they want a live audience, but the cymbal crash into "Sentimental Journey," Garroway's opening trademark since 1949, was to go; the carmaker insisted a vocal group open the show with the Pontiac jingle. Garroway was to play to the studio audience, no longer breaking the fourth wall and wandering from set to set between segments. Andrews complained that these changes limited Garroway greatly. "The people you have to answer to in television don't trust the audience at all," he said. "If you have a guy like Garroway who was just amusing, never funny, they were never sure. 'How do you know people are amused?'" In the end, Pontiac didn't renew its option, citing low ratings.[55]

Garroway felt the New York version of his program suffered from a poor time slot and too much advertiser and agency meddling. "They almost took the show over at times, censoring numbers, putting in ones we had nothing to do with but assuming no responsibility thereafter," he wrote years later. In one instance, Pontiac vetoed an appearance by Frank Sinatra, citing "moral reasons." Garroway also lamented that the freewheeling, experimental mindset of Chicago, typified by the "let's try anything" approach of beginners happy to be working on television, was gone. That *esprit de corps* had given way to "many more prima-donnas than in Chicago." In a way, Garroway had become a victim of his old program's inventiveness; the things that had seemed innovative and witty in 1949 had become standard fare in 1953.[56]

Edith Barstow concurred. Success, with its busier schedules and increased salaries, had spoiled the formula. "Although everyone was congenial, we had many differences of opinion," she said. "Consequently, no one's complete idea was as well carried through as it had been in Chicago." Garroway himself wasn't discouraged, attributing the program's problems to competition from ABC's *Ozzie and Harriet* and CBS's *Mama*. "I'd sure like to take another stab at it next year," he said. Despite occasional rumors that the program would come back, it never did. With no more televised Garroway on Friday nights, the radio show moved and became the ninety-minute *Friday with Garroway*.[57]

Profiles of Garroway made much of the trappings of fame, the Park Avenue apartment, the national stardom, his claim he owned more than thirteen hundred bow ties but only one four-in-hand (for when he went incognito, the story went). His name was linked in gossip columns to glamorous women, and thousands of female viewers maintained a serious crush on him. Some wrote him letters claiming that he was talking to them alone. A few wrote lengthy letters insisting they were married to him; others claimed that they were to have met up, but he had jilted the writer at their planned rendezvous. One even showed up in Chicago, registered at a hotel as "Mrs. Dave Garroway," and opened accounts in his name.[58]

Garroway denied his life had any glamour at all. "This show takes all my waking time," he told a writer in 1954. Not only did the on-air work take up a lot of time, but so did rehearsals and client meetings and other matters incidental to his responsibilities. He had little time for anything else, let alone a satisfying evening on the town with a potential suitor. "If I'm feeling really reckless, I can tear around 'til ten." So exhausted was he that when vacation time came up in mid-1954, Garroway stayed in New York, catching up on lost sleep and giving time to his many hobbies that had gone neglected.[59]

For all his ease in front of a camera, Garroway was happiest when he was alone. Shy around people, he enjoyed times when he could watch people from an anonymous spot. He found New York a terrific place for just that, and had ever since his days as an NBC page. To him, there was "no greater miracle than God's ability to shape a billion faces, all different," and he was likewise fascinated by the human brain's ability to recognize the subtle differences that allowed someone to tell one person from another. Garroway had loved people-watching from that little gap in Times Square near the Hotel Astor, in hotel lobbies, and in Greenwich Village. Now, flush with income from his NBC contract, Garroway rented an office on the second floor of a building on Fifth Avenue. From that office, he could people-watch to his heart's content. He brought in his beloved Questar telescope, "a marvelous little extension of your powers of vision," so he could watch people heading home against the evening sun.[60]

Sometimes his introversion seemed rude to those who didn't know him well. One evening, leaving the studio after an episode of the nighttime program, Garroway's mellow mood dissolved into gloom. His longtime associates, knowing the signs, quietly took their leave. One assistant, who had made the move from Chicago, didn't want to leave her

The man who seemed at ease in front of millions of viewers was happiest when he was by himself. (Paris Day collection)

boss in such apparent distress. For a long time she sat with him as he maintained a stony silence. Finally, Garroway got up and headed outside. She followed. It was the deep of night in a tough neighborhood, Park Avenue and 106th Street. The two stood there, the assistant standing by as her boss stood silent. After several more moments of silence, Garroway hailed a cab. "Good night," he said to the assistant as he climbed into the cab, leaving her to fend for herself. She was stunned, and yet forgave him. One Christmas Day in the mid-1950s, Mike Wallace was walking along Park Avenue. Among those out and about, he saw a large, familiar-looking man wandering the sidewalk. It was Garroway, "wearing an old pepper-and-salt duster and a disreputable cap, peering into holiday-decorated shop windows like a man who didn't have a friend or a dime."[61]

Every once in a while, Garroway's melancholy came out on the air. In 1952, on a *Today* program just before Easter, an electric incubator had been brought in to show baby chicks hatching. As one chick took its first look from a tiny hole in its shell, Garroway warned, "Don't come out! It isn't worthwhile!" A year later, one day after he marked his fortieth birthday, he commented on his mixed feelings to the *Dial Dave Garroway* audience. "I can't quite make up my mind how I feel today," he said. "I have every reason in the world to feel happy, and I've got a very good reason for feeling sad, too. Yesterday was my birthday." He talked about the reasons he had for being happy: a great job, kind people, that he had "maintained as much saneness, I guess, as is possible in the crazy world we live in today." At the same time, he said, he also thought about T. S. Eliot's observation about measuring out life in coffee spoons, and about the signs of aging: graying hair, earlier bedtime, getting a little winded when climbing stairs. But, he said, he thought about all the good luck he'd had. "If I'd sat down twenty years ago and said where I'd like to be today, it wouldn't be more than about an inch from where I am right now."[62]

His closing note of optimism was in line with the Garroway the public read about, through interviews and magazine articles that were often heavily ghostwritten for national magazines: a man who seemed not only quietly amused by his celebrity and good fortune, but glad to be a droll participant in a medium plagued by absurdities, recounting his misintroduction of ballerina Maria Tallchief, about to dance the Firebird Suite, as "Maria Firechief," or the time he introduced Marguerite Piazza as "Marguerita Pizza"; the live demonstration of a sponsor's pudding mix that failed to yield recognizable pudding, causing him to frantically ad-lib until someone discovered half the pudding mix had stuck to the inside of the box; the time a sponsor's cake was ruined before the commercial and a prop man re-frosted the cake with shaving cream, only for Garroway to go off-script, take a bite of the frosting and react in disgust; the time *Today* originated from his apartment and he did a soap commercial from his shower, but the director failed to tell him when the camera was off him, leaving him afraid to come out. Or he was the Garroway of the off-center ponderance, once suggesting that if history had been different, the English explorer Sir Martin Frobisher might have discovered the American continent first. "Just think, we would now be living in the United States of Frobisher; in baseball we'd have the National League and the Frobisher League; we'd celebrate I Am a Frobisher Day; judges in Atlantic City would select Miss Frobisher of 1954; there'd be a House Un-Frobisher Activities Committee; in the tobacco auctions they'd yell 'Sold Frobisher!' and absconding bank tellers would fly down to South Frobisher. All in all, it was a pretty close call."[63]

Garroway presented himself as a voyager through a world where anything could, and would, happen, and he was no longer surprised by any of it. "It's a crazy life – and I love it!" read an article under his byline in *The Saturday Evening Post*. "Just one show, for instance, brought into my studio a dozen kids in bizarre costumes, a bearded press agent with an ostrich, a former Russian prime minister, a kiwi bird (stuffed) borne by Miss New Zealand (stacked), two members of President Eisenhower's Cabinet, Yogi Berra, and the world's greatest French-horn player – to say nothing of me and my chimpanzee companion, J. Fred Muggs." Other times, staffers gave free rein to press agents who came up with unbelievable pageant winners, whose titles sounded like things Charlie Andrews himself might have written: Miss Concrete Life Preserver, Miss Portable Swimming Pool, and even a Miss Square Salami. "The salami was square, the girl was rounded at the edges. I think the girls were rather sweet to go through with some of these things," Garroway remembered.[64]

Jack Lescoulie had many roles on *Today*. One of them was to be the resident kidder, out to get a chuckle when he could when sent on a strange assignment. During a remote from the Bronx Zoo, he conducted an interview with a penguin, spoofing the Kool cigarettes penguin mascot by asking the zoo's penguin which brand it preferred. Once, he wrestled a walrus, losing in two falls. As the resident sports correspondent, Lescoulie poked fun at the self-seriousness of sportswriters by presenting "Fearless Forecasts" about upcoming games. At times his efforts to leaven the mood struck some viewers as needling; one viewer felt his kidding of newsman Frank Blair "seems awfully edgy to us."[65]

Sometimes the staff blew off steam on the air. One morning as Garroway was doing a commercial for an apple grower, Mary Kelly was seized with a goofy mood and grabbed the fruit off the desk, gleefully hurling apples at two assistant directors, who then threw them back at her.

On occasion the live commercials came close to disaster for reasons beyond the staff's control. Seconds before a live commercial for dog food, a stage manager put a puppy on the table next to a food bowl. The little dog promptly squatted and relieved himself. The stage manager froze in shock. Mort Werner briskly walked over, scooped the pile of dog waste into one hand, and ducked out of the way just before the commercial went on. The happy puppy chowed down on live television, with no sign of the crisis that had just been averted. Out of earshot, Werner walked over to the stage manager and displayed the mess in his hand. "I just want you to see," Werner said, "what the difference is between being a stage manager and a producer."[66]

Viewers stuck with *Today*. CBS, not getting the results it hoped for, retooled its morning show and brought in a new host, Jack Paar. "In a way, it's a quiet victory for NBC since Paar is a lot closer to Garroway than Cronkite was," wrote John Crosby. "Paar is a pleasant, glib, slow-spoken, self-assured individual with a sense of humor distinctively his own." The sly, emotional, unpredictable Paar provided a counterpoint to what had become an institution in *Today*. Jack O'Brian compared the two: "The Garrowaycast has a sort of functional, stainless efficiency but who wants functional fare when you can have fun?"[67]

If that wasn't enough, Garroway made a temporary return to prime time in December when *Producers' Showcase* presented a color version of the musical *Babes in Toyland*. Alongside Dennis Day, Wally Cox and the Baird marionettes, Garroway anchored the program as a weary department store Santa. It met with critical acclaim, and one writer suggested the program "should become as much of an annual classic for TV as Charles Dickens' *A Christmas Carol* for radio."

At Christmas Garroway, known for bizarre greetings during the holidays, sent his friends an official-looking document that resembled a legal summons. Only when they opened the document did they see it was a gag. "Many a recipient didn't have the strength to do that until the oxygen tent arrived," Dorothy Kilgallen wrote.[68]

12

Today began its third year atop the morning ratings, financially secure, about to expand its reach further with the impending start of full West Coast service via a "quick-kine" system that would allow viewers in the Pacific time zone to see all two hours of *Today* on a filmed delay. In January the program celebrated its birthday with a week in Miami Beach, sharing resources as Steve Allen's *Tonight* program also originated there. It came very close to not happening; a union dispute, settled at the last minute, threatened the broadcasts of both programs.[1]

Bad luck also plagued associate producer Lou Ames. For one show that would feature a professional alligator wrestler, someone suggested having Jack Lescoulie wrestle a fake alligator. Ames couldn't find one. He finally tracked down an inflatable alligator in New Jersey and had it flown to Miami. On the way from the airport, two armed men hijacked Ames' car. Ames pleaded, "Take my money. Take my car. But please let me have the alligator!" The men dropped him somewhere in the Everglades and drove away. Ames found his way back to the remote, minus the alligator. Police found the car the next day, with the alligator still in the back. As promised, Lescoulie wrestled the fake alligator on the program.[2]

Within weeks, Garroway suffered a deep professional loss. His trusted agent and adviser Biggie Levin, the man whose counsel and wisdom had guided him to the position he now occupied as the face of NBC, suddenly passed away. "Biggie was one of the best business managers around, and a nice guy, too, which is a rare combination," a stunned Garroway said. He returned to Chicago for the funeral, then made arrangements to continue paying Biggie's ten percent commission into a trust fund for his adopted children. Although Garroway signed with the prestigious William Morris agency to manage his affairs, the loss of Biggie's personal touch denied Garroway profoundly valuable counsel that could have kept him from making unfortunate decisions years later.[3]

There also came a more urgent edge to *Today* in its third year, as matters of the world's precarious geopolitical state began to weigh more heavily on Garroway. One morning, as he chatted on the air with people on the sidewalk along 49th Street, Garroway brought up tensions in the Far East and asked if the United States should defend Chiang Kai-Shek's Chinese Nationalists in Formosa, even if it risked starting a war with mainland China and the Soviet Union. Each person Garroway spoke with said the United States should do so. A columnist wrote, "Garroway searched the crowd in vain to find one person who would say that we should not use such force and risk such a war, even if it came to the use of atom and hydrogen bombs."[4]

Garroway's increased concern about the world was further reflected when he went to cover an atomic bomb test in the Nevada desert in late April. He would cover the test from a trench less than two miles from the blast, huddled alongside a group of soldiers. NBC turned the coverage into a full production, with *Today*, *Home* and *Meet the Press* represented in the NBC contingent. The plan called for splitting the screen during the detonation, with the fireball on one side of the screen and the trench containing Garroway and the soldiers on the other. "We think it will be just about the most exciting picture ever shown on television," an NBC executive said. Afterward, a model would tour the destroyed village to show the bomb's effects.[5]

The networks cooperated, but the weather didn't. Daily wind storms delayed the test seven times. Dozens of television people lingered around Las Vegas, looking for things to do. Worse, as delays continued, the technical requirements for the remote interfered with setup for a Liberace special NBC had paid $25,000 to broadcast. Though Garroway was accustomed to being an early riser, day after day of being up at 11 p.m. to be in the trench on time took its toll. "These delays are enough to drive us into a psychiatrist's office," he told a reporter. "It's an emotional strain working yourself into the proper frame of mind each morning. No one knows what will happen in the trench and we have only six minutes to evacuate the area. That's why everyone is getting edgy with all the delays which, of course, we know are necessary." Having had enough, Garroway went back to New York. The atomic test went off the next morning.[6]

Garroway's "peace" trademark seemed more relevant than ever. In June, he explained his thinking in an article for *Better Living*. "Peace is a malleable force," he wrote. "To many people it means freedom from war, while others it represents a peaceful atmosphere. I'm trying to be a peace-bringing 'friend in the house' – that's what hundreds of my fans have called me in their letters, and I think it's the highest compliment they can give me." Some viewers saw it differently. One viewer wrote to an editor, "Would you agree that it is far more fitting for Dave (Peace) Garroway to end his programs with 'peace with honor,' as so well put by President Eisenhower? We don't want just 'peace.' We want 'peace with justice.' How about it, Dave?"[7]

Even in the midst of the sobering world *Today* covered with more frequency, there was still time for humanity. In late March, *Today* told the story of a New York bus driver who was struck and killed when he stopped to help a motorist. Garroway asked viewers to each send in a dime to establish a fund to help the widow and seven children. Within a week, and with only half the mailbags opened, more than $20,000 had been raised. By mid-May the fund was at more than $60,000, with contributions still coming in.[8]

Friday With Garroway was about to make way for another of Pat Weaver's innovations. Having revolutionized television by opening the early morning and late night time slots, having made participation-style sponsorship an increasingly popular model for the economics of broadcasting, Weaver now sought a new role for network radio, left behind as television grew more popular. Weaver put Jim Fleming in charge of a project to reinvent network radio, a continuously-running forty-hour weekend service called *Monitor*. The program would include content on anything and everything, hopscotching from segment to segment, presenting live pickups from around the nation and around the world: interviews, music, breaking news, regular news on the hour. Portions of the fifth floor of the RCA Building were restyled into "Radio Central," which had not only studio facilities but equipment that could bring in transmissions from any point on the planet. A great glass window would allow visitors on the NBC studio tour to see inside, and those lucky enough to visit on weekends could witness *Monitor* as it was going on the air.[9]

The Weaver style was everywhere – the fantastic studio, the wide-ranging format, even the otherworldly beeping signal, the "*Monitor* Beacon," that became the program's trademark. Weaver, employing his trademark argot, described the new program as a "kaleidoscopic phantasmagoria," available anywhere – in the car, at home, at the beach, anywhere there was a radio. As John Crosby said after hearing the initial description of the program, "If that isn't a kaleidoscopic phantasmagoria, then I don't know a kaleidoscopic phantasmagoria when I hear one."[10]

From the start, Weaver had wanted Dave Garroway for *Monitor*. When Weaver's assistant approached Garroway about it, the host begged off, thinking the idea wouldn't work. Later that day, the assistant returned with a request from Weaver: would Garroway do it as a personal favor to him? "Well, if he wants me to do it, I'll do anything for Pat." From there, Garroway served as the first host (or to use Weaver's preferred term, "communicator") on the concept recording that was produced for affiliates and executives. When *Monitor* made its debut on June 12, in a broadcast simultaneously presented on NBC radio and television, Dave Garroway presented the first news headlines. Later on that first program, he presented an interview with Marilyn Monroe and poetry from Carl Sandburg.

Weaver's high concept didn't quite land at first. Jack O'Brian felt the segments, in the "vignette" style the show presented, were "injected so hurriedly" and "chased off the air so quickly that it seemed a series of offhand notions" that sought to be different just to keep the listener attentive. "By attempting far too much, the effect was far too little." Jack Gould believed the Marilyn Monroe interview showed Garroway "is not the best of interviewers," but hoped "at long last network radio is going to receive a shot in the arm." John Crosby wrote, "This program is aimed at all of us on the beaches and in our cars all Summer long, but I know a couple guys on the beaches who, after about fifteen minutes of this, are going to tune in Guy Lombardo and just stay there the rest of the afternoon." Will Jones believed there was "an overlay of cuteness" about the whole enterprise, and that even Garroway didn't seem comfortable with the fancy term "communicator."[11]

Garroway would add a regular *Monitor* shift to his schedule, anchoring Sunday evenings until the end of his NBC tenure. He joked about it. "You name it and that's what I am. I'm the guy who takes you there...I'm a guide...I'm a communicator (oops, no, that's just for *Monitor*)...I'm an emcee...I'm a switchpoint guy," he said in a run-up for his next role, another Weaver innovation. "One thing for sure. I'm an armchair general bar none because I'll be taking people all over the North American continent and I'll never leave Manhattan."[12]

For Pat Weaver had another idea: demonstrate the power of live television by showing pictures from all over America, as they happened.

This special, to be titled *Wide Wide World*, was the result of two years of planning and would be presented as an installment of *Producers Showcase* on June 27. Dave Garroway was to be its narrator. The program had a simple premise: showing what people were doing on a summer evening. "Just add boiling water to this program," Garroway said, "and you'll have enough summer vacation to last a lifetime." Viewers of the ninety-minute special saw live scenes of a nation as the day ended: from people going to theaters in Times Square, to Chicago at dinnertime, to people going home from work in Denver, to swimmers in San Diego, then back to Washington and the Lincoln Memorial. The special bounced around: a jazz concert near Washington; a Shakespeare festival in Stratford, Ontario; skiers at Mount Hood; the comedian Cantinflas spoofing matadors in front of an arena crowd during a Mexico City fiesta; then closing shots of Manhattan at twilight and San Francisco in the afternoon light.[13]

The *New York Times* called the special "superb entertainment" and hoped for "another chapter. The first part of *Wide Wide World* was just great." The *Baltimore Sun* said the program "left much to be desired" as entertainment, but showed the technical possibilities of television: "The engineers – the unbilled stars – did so well that they pointed the way to new achievements almost beyond the reach of present-day imagination." Will Jones called *Wide Wide World* "the dullest and longest travelog ever" and wondered why NBC was showing what other people were doing on a summer evening. "When I saw the people skiing in Oregon, it occurred to me I was being pretty stupid spending any part of a summer evening in front of a TV set." John Crosby wrote that "television has just completed a full circle. This is what TV used to do before it had any money or any shows. The cameras would just prowl around and take pictures of things that were actually taking place." Crosby hoped, "If NBC can get some advertisers interested – and several are – there will be more *Wide Wide World*s."[14]

Weaver continued to see Garroway as an ideal instrument for his concepts: a man one writer described as "sort of a Gary Cooper with enunciation" who could demonstrate interest in anything, whose indescribable charm "is like trying to describe why Louis Armstrong's baritone voice is thrilling. It's a style that makes the viewer feel like Dave is one of the family. The nice one of the family." In October he joined Sid Caesar, Nanette Fabray and Wally Cox in a special that Weaver ordained, showing what life would be like in the year 1976: a world of push-button conveniences, more playtime, more information. When *Wide Wide World* made it onto the fall schedule as a Sunday afternoon series, Garroway was tapped to host, a self-described "utility infielder" who would be "the narrator, sort of the glue that puts the piece together." He liked the program's premise, believing life television "has a quality film will never have. You feel a softness, a dullness in film. Live TV has a tension and drive that are essential in maintaining the pace of a show." Nor did he mind that it added more work to an already crowded schedule. "I guess you might say I'm the kind of guy who's miserable when he has nothing to do."[15]

Wide Wide World had its series debut on October 16 with Garroway perched on a stool, a lighted globe slowly spinning behind him, a majestic orchestral theme by David Broekman in the background. For ninety minutes, Garroway was the easygoing guide for an afternoon of live remotes around the theme "A Sunday in Autumn." There were live shots of the Grand Canyon, of the Texas State Fair, of crowds going to Radio City Music Hall, of mermaids swimming at Weekiwachee Springs in Florida, of scenes from a camera mounted in a cable car plying its route through San Francisco. With apparent ease Garroway narrated as the pictures on the screen effortlessly cut from scene to scene, hundreds and thousands of miles instantly traveled with the flip of a switch.[16]

That ease and informality concealed the reality that the eleven pickups during the program had required tremendous preparation. Garroway had spoken during the program's first minutes about the seventy three cameras, the 41,000 miles of telephone lines, the 1,800 technicians that were making the live pictures possible. That didn't begin to cover just what those 1,800 technicians had to do to make the program happen. A single four-and-a-half-minute sequence produced by the St. Louis affiliate, for example, had required more than a month of preparations and planning; coordination with the Air Force for a fighter jet flyover at the precise moment and altitude, and with the Army for the use of one of the last active sternwheeler riverboats and a television-equipped airplane; cooperation from lock masters along the Mississippi River to hold up towboats during the pickup; coordination with the telephone company for video and audio relays, and a week's worth of seemingly endless rehearsals participated in by all parties. The actual sequence as aired went well, and then it was off to the next pickup, watching the fishing fleet at Gloucester. Not everything went as well in other pickups. Rain in Manhattan ruined plans to show ice skating star Dick Button perform on the Rockefeller Center rink, and an attempt to show Donald Campbell break a speed boat record on Lake Mead was ruined when the boat sank. An underwater sequence from Weekiwachee, Florida had nearly come to grief when someone forgot to connect an oxygen hose and killed all the tropical fish in the giant aquarium; an emergency truckload of fish saved the day.[17]

"We took a trip yesterday," began one review. "We spanned the nation, saw more than most tourists could see in a lifetime, and never left the comfort of our living room. *Wide Wide World* proved as fascinating and exciting as a Hollywood thrill drama, yet what we saw was actual places and things, all unstaged and live." Another review called out Garroway's implication that "everything was going to be delightfully impromptu. This, of course, was pure buncombe." Instead, the review said, the most impressive bit was the very first remote, a live shot of the Grand Canyon, "which is a miracle itself and so vast it defies any effort at staginess. Best actors here were burros. Next best were the Rockettes during an actual performance in Radio City Music Hall. Here, the usual show was being given and no attention paid to TV acting." Will Jones grumped that *Wide Wide World* was "another cross-country mish-mash of live pick-ups by NBC-TV. About all it proved is that the network sure does have a lot of cameras." Nor did he care for the words Garroway was given to speak, "as he waded through all that drivel by some Rockefeller Center drone with delusions of Carl Sandburg. Slop! To gum up the sinews of our civilization!"[18]

Wide Wide World would be Weaver's last achievement for the network. At ongoing loggerheads with RCA chairman David Sarnoff, Weaver was promoted to NBC chairman, which took away his operational influence. One writer, counting up Weaver's innovations in television, wrote that "Weaver was going to make people a little better for watching TV, instead of just a little amused, and a little inclined to spend money which had been the main objective of radio. He was going to slip in culture on the sly and educate with fifty-six roving cameras...he was the man who was going to set television on the highest cultural level ever attained by a mass medium." His legacies would live on for a while. *Wide Wide World* continued for a few more years, and *Monitor* lasted until early 1975, although its format gradually transformed and its time slot shrank so much that, by the end, it was *Monitor* in name only. And, of course, *Today* and *Tonight* would remain long-lasting and reliably profitable mainstays on the network schedule. But NBC would never again be as innovative, or as daring, and Garroway had lost another of those who believed in him.[19]

As 1955 ended, Garroway reprised his role as Santa in a re-staging of *Babes in Toyland*. For Christmas, he had a six-foot toy tiger flown in from Germany as a special present for Paris, and gave alarm clocks to his fellow workers on *Today*. To a reporter, he listed his resolutions for the new year: "I will not go to any cocktail parties. I will wear my green suit. I will get out of my rut. I will brush my teeth after every meal. I will lose thirty pounds. I will find out what it is I am looking for. I will love more people."[20]

13

Today in 1956 was a smooth, well-operating program, well into vanquishing its CBS counterparts. CBS had jettisoned Jack Paar in favor of a new show, *Good Morning!*. It was hosted by Will Rogers Jr., who had once served as a *Today* guest host while Garroway vacationed. *Good Morning!* would occupy only part of the time; CBS also planned a children's program called *Captain Kangaroo*, which in time proved the only serious competition *Today* faced from CBS.[1]

Today, meanwhile, had diversified. Former Miss America Lee Ann Meriwether joined the cast, a formal acknowledgment of how much women mattered to the program. She wasn't always content to just be the "girl next door," though. In May, after rumors circulated that Soviet leader Nikita Khrushchev and premier Nikolai Bulganin might visit the United States, Garroway did a man-in-the-street interview outside the Exhibition Hall. Most people outside were against the idea of the visit. Back inside, Meriwether told Garroway that she didn't think a visit would be such a bad idea: "I'd like them to see life inside an average American home." Frank Blair quickly disagreed, warning Meriwether that they would get a lot of letters. "Well, that's just her opinion," Garroway dismissively said. A columnist wrote that Meriwether had a point: Americans should not be afraid of the Russian leaders, and should let them know as much. "And it would not hurt the Russians to know that we can raise girls like a Lee Meriwether, who dare stand up in front of the whole country and say what's on their minds."[2]

Today continued to break news, often scoring beats on the competition. When the passenger liner *Andrea Doria* sank after colliding with the liner *Stockholm* in July 1956, Mary Kelly raced to the West Side piers to meet the liner *Ile de France*, which had rescued hundreds of survivors. An amateur photographer who had captured scenes of the sinking *Andrea Doria* recognized Kelly and gave her his film, which was shown on *Today*. Unfortunately, the grim news of the sea disaster was presented around other segments that included Lescoulie and guest Jayne Mansfield parodying a scene from *Caesar and Cleopatra*.[3]

Wide Wide World continued on, although its efforts to stretch the capabilities of live television inevitably bumped against the demands of time, not to mention the constraints of commercial television. A live presentation of Shakespeare's *Richard III* was ruined by station breaks (as an act ended, a cut to Garroway on his stool, throwing to commercial: "The crown is within reach now. How uneasy lies the head that bears the crown, we'll see in a moment...."). Another writer accused *Wide Wide World* of "hopping about rather like a nervous grasshopper during its Sunday afternoon travels." The writer complained, "The format becomes downright annoying when Dave Garroway interrupts a wholly inadequate visit at some colorful spot to rush on with the afternoon's crammed itinerary. Maybe ten minutes or so is sufficient for some of the program's stops but it doesn't begin to do justice to a Williamsburg or an Indian pueblo."[4]

It was also a tense job for Garroway. "Every show is a nerve-racking ordeal because there are about three hundred word and music cues in each script," he said. "If one cue is missed by five seconds, a chain reaction is started that jams up subsequent scenes." During a given show he had to keep an eye on two monitors, two cameras, a teleprompter and a stage manager. Sometimes he had to be prepared if things went wrong, so he read up on each program's subject. On one episode, a seven-minute segment disappeared due to technical issues, so Garroway delivered an impromptu lecture to the audience, not even appearing to break a sweat. Another time, a piece of equipment blocked his view of the teleprompter, leaving him unable to read the script and give the exact switch cues. "And there I was, trying to make fifty million people think that I didn't have a care in the world."[5]

Still, there were moments of power, as when an episode devoted to American military strength featured live pictures from simulated Army maneuvers, from military aircraft in flight, and from a submarine as it submerged. Jack Gould called it "one of the most extensive and fascinating uses yet made of live television" which was "well worth both the trouble and the expense." If parody was any indication of cultural relevance, Steve Allen spoofed Garroway on his program in a segment called "Big Fat World," which one reviewer called "one of the deftest, subtlest impersonations I've ever seen." Garroway's closing, in which he quoted

Edna St. Vincent Millay, drew a jibe from Mort Sahl ("He sits on that stool with the world behind him and says, 'No higher than the heart is high.' I wonder if the folks out in Des Moines dig that line?"). Garroway's use of a stool, prominent on *Wide Wide World*, was credited, or sometimes blamed, for a "stool craze" among other personalities including Ethel Merman and Jimmy Durante, Frank Sinatra, Mike Wallace, Perry Como and Tennessee Ernie Ford.[6]

Monitor, with its booping-and-bleeping audio trademark, continued to boop and bleep its phantasmagoria through the weekends, with Garroway the soothing Sunday night communicator, engaging in interesting conversations. One evening, he interviewed announcer Norman Brokenshire, who confessed he never wanted to sound like anyone else on radio until he heard Garroway. He had tried to imitate Garroway's style, but failed. Referring to *Monitor*'s frequent use of pickups from faraway locations, Brokenshire said, "We didn't have those kinds of facilities." The veteran announcer mentioned how *Monitor* featured remotes from places such as Timbuktu and Tibet. "Your remotes are ridiculous," he told Garroway. Other times, Garroway's interviews on *Monitor* had been recorded in advance by NBC correspondents, with their questions edited out so that Garroway could seem to be interviewing the subject on the air. John Chancellor, then a young radio reporter in Chicago who drew many such assignments, recalled being urged to get interview subjects to say "Well, Dave" so the responses would seem more personal when Garroway "interviewed" them on *Monitor*.[7]

For Garroway, his success as NBC's jack-of-all-trades was enshrined in a new ten-year contract with the network, which he signed in March. His services with individual programs were covered under separate agreements. Jack O'Brian wrote that under the deal Garroway could leave *Today* in 1958, "but he'll probably stick with breakfast-before-dawn for the sake of the $5,000 a week." The breakfast-before-dawn schedule meant good money, but left him with little social life. "It's sort of like entering a monastery. You force yourself into isolation," he said. "Having to get up at 4 a.m. five mornings a week is rather like withdrawing from the human race. So few people keep those hours any more – not many farmers, I believe." He sympathized with others who had to keep similar hours. When his friend Bill Cullen got an early morning show on a New York radio station, Garroway called him each morning to make sure he was awake. Garroway reported to work at 5:15 and remained at NBC until

4 or 5 p.m., then often went to a garage on 64th Street and worked on his cars. Then it was back home, where he would read, or record thoughts into a tape recorder, until late at night.[8]

Every once in a while Garroway found time for some fun, when he invited a few friends over to play some music. The little Dixieland combo featured Garroway on drums, Jack Lescoulie on trombone, Lescoulie's friend Jackie Gleason on trumpet, Jac Hein on trumpet or drums, and occasional piano or tuba provided by Steve Allen. Once, when *Today* was in New Orleans, Lescoulie played trombone with Paul Barbarin's Dixieland band. He was stunned when Garroway and Frank Blair began eating lemons in front of him.[9]

Garroway remained competitive as ever when it came to games of any kind. Once, traveling to California for *Today*, he was playing Scrabble with Dick Pinkham when the plane developed engine trouble over the Rockies. He was down $100 when the plane made an emergency landing in Phoenix. A six-hour delay later, he had erased all but seventy-five cents of the debt. John Moss, a sometime opponent in poker games, said Garroway's self-discipline made him a man who "never does anything without a reason" and "a man who has won entirely too much of my money" through his "calculating, unemotional" style.[10]

In 1954 Dave Garroway attended a dinner party at Billy Rose's house at Mount Kisco, New York. There he met Pamela Wilde. The daughter of a film studio executive, she had lived in Paris for many years. She had been a ballet dancer and an actress, and had also helped produce films. She had also been maried before, to a French marquis, with whom she had a son. Pamela remembered in 1959 that although she hadn't heard of Dave Garroway, "I flipped the minute I saw him." They struck up a conversation after the dinner party, talking about books. The next week, he sent her a book of Roald Dahl short stories they had discussed.[11]

Three days later, he invited her to dinner at the Rainbow Room. They told each other their stories, talked about their interests and previous marriages. On their next date, Garroway had her over to his apartment. His attempt to cook for her didn't work well at all. The next time they got together, she cooked him an elegant French meal. "Dave's story is that he knew he wanted to marry me the moment he found out I could cook," she said. A gradual courtship ensued. "It took quite a stretch of crepes suzette before he told me he loved me – and another stretch before he asked me to marry him. Suddenly, one day he said, 'I bought you a ring. Would you like to wear it?' Then he added, 'You had better tell your bosses that you are going to quit your job this summer.' That was his proposal."[12]

Pamela said in 1959 that Garroway had eventually told him of that night at Billy Rose's party, "As you walked into that room, I was fascinated immediately." Garroway remembered that he found her "utterly charming and attractive," and that he had explained to her the problems he had about falling in love. Pamela, he maintained, gently increased the pressure to get married. The rumors circulated through late 1955 and into 1956, sometimes teased by Garroway himself. Larry Wolters asked Garroway when he was getting married again. "I'm working on it now," Garroway told him. In March 1956, Pamela explained the lack of a set date to a reporter: "It'll be the second time for each of us and one should take one's time." There was talk they would marry in Paris during Garroway's summer break. In the end, they were married at City Hall by an acting city clerk on August 7, 1956, with only Pamela's parents present. "Then, because we were all hungry we went home and I cooked dinner," she said. The newlyweds had a day together, then Garroway was off to San Francisco to cover the Democratic National Convention.[13]

In time, Pamela's son Michael, from her previous marriage, came to live with them. Garroway found him "a sweet boy, but timid." He went to a parents' day function at Michael's school but was not impressed with the headmaster. Garroway moved him to a different school, where, he claimed, Michael "brightened immediately, and we became friends." The new family lived in the Park Avenue apartment, but Garroway felt they needed a place to be together and relax. He hadn't thought much about not living in the city. "I like to see the country from a rapidly moving automobile, and for about two days," he had joked. Soon after he married, however, Garroway purchased a beach house on Westhampton, Long Island. It was fully furnished, and had a kitchen that could at best accommodate one person at a time. Nor did it help when a family of rabbits burrowed in and chewed the labels off the food cans in the pantry. "You want apricots for breakfast and you wind up with chili con carne," Garroway said. He nicknamed the home Nemo Point, after a broadcasting term for a program not originating from the studio.[14]

Garroway later questioned his wisdom in getting married. With the pressures of *Today*, *Monitor* and *Wide Wide World*, he was constantly busy. Five days a week he started out at 3:30 a.m. and didn't get home until at least six in the evening, if not nine. There was barely more time on weekends. "I only had two or three hours a day to be a husband and a father," he reflected years later. "No sensible man would have taken on those responsibilities under such conditions, but I was not sensible, I was polite."[15]

As *Wide Wide World* began its second season, its producers wanted to move from emphasizing the technological marvel to telling stories with it. "Electronic miracles no longer interest us," Pat Weaver said. "*Wide Wide World* is now concentrating on people, not places." Producer Barry Wood called the program's format "a blend of newsreel, documentary and travelogue techniques with major improvements. It's timelier than a newsreel, more entertaining than a documentary and a lot more imaginative than the dreary travelogues that have been emptying movie houses for years."[16]

Sometimes it didn't work as producers hoped. Jack Gould wrote that a September installment was "too energetic in its self-conscious pursuit of visual poetry," and "the narrative prose delivered by Dave Garroway sometimes was fearfully lush." John Crosby warned the show was "getting appallingly pretentious, especially in the prose department...the whole show was punctuated with his Gads-the-Wonder-and-Mystery-of-It-All sort of prose which sounded as if it had been written by a man whose mother had been frightened by Carl Sandburg. An hour and a half of this sort of thing can get mighty tiresome." Another reviewer felt the series was "on the brink of trouble" and advised, "*Wide Wide World* would do well to offer once again casual glimpses of its subjects, woven together by simple, lucid, descriptive narration." Meanwhile, a CBS competitor, *Odyssey*, won praise for just settling down to spend an hour telling the story of Virginia City, the silver town in Nevada. "It was a pleasure to bypass Dave Garroway's nation-hopping for a TV travelogue that didn't keep you moving," a reviewer wrote. "This viewer got out of the habit of looking at Dave Garroway's program some time ago because of all its hopping."[17]

Today continued onward. Lee Ann Meriwether, wanting to focus on her acting career, bade farewell in December. Singer Helen O'Connell joined the cast as an editor and fashion specialist, and provided a song every now and then. "I haven't given up singing, but I wasn't hired as a singer. I was hired as a talker, a pleasant switch," she said. Garroway parlayed his stardom into the merchandising realm: a record album, *Getting Friendly With Music*, sought to educate listeners about the finer points of musical concepts. It was the first of several Garroway-themed albums to come. Just in time for Christmas came a *Today* board game, which one ad promised would give "all the fun of actually producing the show in the simulated studio and on remote pick-ups." The fun didn't extend to Garroway himself. He did the Christmas Eve show in pain, after a recurrence of the old back and leg injury that ended his golfing career two decades before, and within days was confined to two weeks' bed rest.[18]

14

Today was a sponsor and ratings juggernaut. It was carried on 113 stations, brought in more than $30 million in sponsor revenue, and had a staff of more than a hundred. With *Good Morning!* now on the ropes, *Today* was vanquishing its challenge from CBS. *Today* had become "a pleasant program in which to get the skimmed news, weather, mild interviews and a neat geniality," wrote Jack O'Brian. TV writer Marie Torre said the "spectacular gamble" of 1952 had "revolutionized the nation's morning viewing habits and helped put the family TV set on wheels."

Today and Garroway were so much a part of the American landscape that they became the subject of a take-off in the upstart humor magazine *Mad*. In it, the titular host of *The Dave Garrowunway Show* dealt with an array of strange people watching from the sidewalk, a grinning co-host trying to wrangle an ill-mannered chimpanzee named J. Floyd Gluggs, a live remote from an atomic test that ended badly, and a weather report that proved a little too accurate. At the end the hapless Garrowunway ended up as one of those people watching from the sidewalk, locked out of the studio in the middle of a downpour, his place as host taken by the chimp. The real Garroway loved the spoof and happily promoted it on *Today*.[1]

Big changes were on the way, though. In January, just after celebrating the program's fifth anniversary, Jack Lescoulie departed for the opposite end of the broadcast day. With Steve Allen leaving *Tonight*, NBC reformatted the late-night program into a format that mimicked elements of *Today* and *Wide Wide World*. The new *Tonight! America After Dark* would feature live remotes from various night spots around the country, showing top performers, and featuring live segments featuring entertainment columnists around the country. Lescoulie, signed as the studio host for *Tonight!*, would begin his duties on January 28. He compared leaving *Today* to "leaving your own family," and credited Garroway with helping him develop the skills to become a host. "Being with Dave Garroway is like getting a Ph.D. on the air," he said. "He taught me everything I know. If Yale is lucky enough, I suggest that if he ever wants to leave TV, they grab him as a teacher." Frank Blair would take on Lescoulie's sidekick role.[2]

The other departure, announced within days of Lescoulie's, was that of J. Fred Muggs.

Publicly, NBC put a happy spin on the chimp's departure. "Like so many before him who have reached star status, Muggs feels that he has outgrown his supporting role and is now ready for top billing," the network stated. Garroway added, "Muggs' ad-libbing and zany antics have broken up more than one show and taken the pressure off long hours of telecasting. It will be a different world around the set without him. We all wish him well."[3]

Behind the scenes, it was a nasty divorce. Mennella and Waldron accused *Today*'s producers of limiting Muggs' part on the show and not letting him perform an act they had developed. They claimed Garroway spiked Muggs' coffee with drugs and intentionally kept a studio door open when Muggs had a cold. Mennella claimed Garroway had encouraged Muggs to climb around near electronic gear in hopes the chimp would be electrocuted ("ridiculous," Garroway countered).[4]

NBC denied any ill intent. A network spokesman said that although they hated to lose Muggs, "he's getting awfully big and fat around the middle. He's less playful, too." It was no secret, of course, that Muggs had tried the patience of cast and crew. "Muggs is reaching maturity," Garroway told a columnist, "which is to say he's biting everyone nowadays. Pretty tough to admire him under those circumstances." Lescoulie, who once endured Muggs ripping his desk away from him in mid-program, talked of having to smile through moments when Muggs gnawed him on the air. "I was just a teething ring for J. Fred Muggs," he said. "A lovable animal, but sometimes I felt like throwing him through that glass window." Though Frank Blair kept his thoughts to himself, years later he called Muggs a "real pain" who threw furniture. Some staffers claimed Muggs' owners used an electric shocker, or sometimes beatings with a rubber hose, to keep him obedient, allegations strongly denied by Waldron and Mennella.[5]

On Muggs' last day, he was given a lavish send-off. "Write if you find work," Garroway told him as "Give My Regards To Broadway" played in the background. ("Charles Darwin lived a century before J. Fred Muggs," wrote an astounded columnist.) Two weeks later Muggs' replacement, an eighteen-month-old chimp named Kokomo Jr., made his debut. Dressed in a white shirt, gray trousers, a bow tie and gold cufflinks, Kokomo Jr. ran errands for Garroway, taking paper to a wastebasket, rubbing his head as if he had a headache, and breaking into applause at the end of his first day. The new chimpanzee had a sweet and gentle disposition, more likely to plant a kiss on Garroway than sink his teeth into him, yet old habits died hard: from time to time Garroway slipped up and called him "Muggs."[6]

The spurned chimpanzee, and his owners, wanted the last word. One day that September, photographers captured a scene of Muggs, dressed in red pants, a windbreaker and sneakers, climbing out of a cab and walking up the steps of the state Supreme Court building. Inside, he handed a fifteen-page legal complaint to an astonished clerk. "In forty years, I never saw anything like this," the clerk said. The $500,000 lawsuit against Garroway, Lescoulie and producer Jac Hein charged not only that *Today* failed to renew Muggs' contract and thus cut him out of a $1,275-a-week job, but that their public pronouncements about him had kept Muggs from getting work. Newspaper writers had a field day. One suggested Muggs "needs the services of a law firm with some such name as Gibbon, Rhesus and Rhesus."[7]

The suit dragged on for several years, eventually ending in an undisclosed settlement, but the bitter feelings never really subsided. On occasion, reporters would do follow-up stories about what had happened to Muggs; a 1971 *Wall Street Journal* article found him part of the Waldron and Mennella animal menagerie in New Jersey, with two dogs, five other chimps and a mynah bird. Now four feet tall and about 175 pounds, resembling a "junior-sized King Kong," Muggs was still working thirty-five weeks a year, jumping up and down and screeching inside his cage when a stranger walked in ("He's just doing his routine," Mennella assured the visitor). Invariably, the topic would come up; the old accusations and responses would resurface. On anniversary shows, when Muggs was mentioned, Garroway, Lescoulie and Blair would joke about being careful about what to say next, lest they get sued again.[8]

There was also a big change in Dave Garroway's life. Pamela was expecting.

With a child on the way, they needed more space than the Park Avenue apartment had. One Sunday at the Westhampton house, Garroway found a listing in the *New York Times* for a remodeled five-story brownstone on 63rd Street near Park Avenue. Thirteen feet wide and a hundred and five feet long, the building was fully furnished, had a full basement and garage and a small backyard. According to one story, the house was once owned by Rudyard Kipling's brother-in-law, and Kipling himself had reportedly stayed there on a few occasions. The next day, after *Today* was finished, Garroway took the short ride over to 63rd Street for an inspection. He called Pamela in to have a look. She, too, liked the place. It was listed for $100,000, but the owner sold it for just under $98,000 in cash. The closing was completed the next night.[9]

At the time the Garroways bought the townhouse, it had been subleased. Two of the tenants were packing their belongings when Dave and Pamela came over a week later. As Dave recalled later, one of them said, "Good luck and I hope the poltergeist doesn't bother you." Garroway laughed it off. He and Pamela walked through the house, which had recently been redecorated in a dark gray motif and had a dark feel throughout. He said Pamela, who had been tense throughout the day, yelled, "I'm not going to redecorate this place! Get yourself a decorator!" She then called a cab.[10]

Garroway said the house had once been remodeled by a man who ran out of money halfway through the job. It left the home with several eccentricities, including a wall safe in one bathroom, and a wine cellar and an aquarium built into the basement wall. Right next to the dining room entrance was a shower. The garage floor had a drain three inches above floor level. The back yard was solid rock. He did appreciate one touch: an observatory that had been built on the roof. Otherwise, it needed help, so Garroway hired John Grissin to redecorate the house. Since it was so narrow, one wall of the living room was covered in mirrors to give an illusion of more space. The home was furnished in contemporary style with furniture from prominent designers, decorated in shades of yellow, pink, blue and black. In an upstairs room, Garroway set up his model trains. The basement became a workshop, with a sign over the door reading "Wit's End." The garage was large enough to house the Jaguar and the Rolls-Royce. Since it was so narrow, Garroway cut a hole in the floor between the garage and workshop so he could work beneath the cars. "It has been suggested that we call it 'Garroway's Narroway,'" he said. Out back, Garroway had several tons of dirt trucked in to cover the stone.[11]

Soon after moving, Garroway claimed, strange things happened: lights and appliances turned themselves on in the middle of the night; furniture seemed to rearrange itself; the front door, secured by three separate locks, would mysteriously be wide open, letting snow in. Sometimes books fell off shelves for no apparent reason. Other times, Garroway would just have an eerie feeling. "He would feel uncomfortable, like he was being watched," Dave Jr. said. Garroway didn't worry much until one evening when he and Pamela were in their bathroom, preparing for a night on the town. According to Garroway, a plastic hairbrush sitting on the sink launched itself across the room and shattered against the wall. A shard from the hairbrush flew back and nicked Pamela in the leg. As he saw the blood on his wife's leg, Garroway exclaimed, "That is *it*!"

The next day, Garroway hired a medium to drive the spirits from the townhouse. As part of the process, the medium did some research on the building and determined that a previous owner, a stockbroker who had lost everything during a market crash, had leapt to his death from the roof. The spirit of this poor stockbroker, the medium said, was probably the source of the supernatural mischief. At the medium's recommendation, Garroway arranged a séance to drive the spirit from the house.

The séance took place some time later, after Pamela had died. Garroway wanted to test the credibility of the medium. Some important documents were kept in a safe deposit box. Only Pamela had known where the key was hidden. Garroway asked the medium to ask Pamela where the key was. The medium told him to look under the third step of the ground-floor staircase. Garroway took a crowbar to the stair and found the key, as promised. "Dad was impressed," Dave Jr. said. Now satisfied with the medium's credentials, Garroway let him proceed with the séance. The solution, he was told, was to get angry with the ghost when he felt its presence. "This is no longer your house!" Garroway was to shout. "Get out!" This, he claimed, did the trick. Fifteen years later, on a vacation drive around California, he told Dave Jr. these stories. "He made sure to mention that after all was said and done, he did not necessarily believe in ghosts, but that he was just reporting the facts to me like the true journalist he was within," Dave Jr. said.[12]

Publicly, though, all appeared well, and those reading profiles of the Garroways believed Pamela had adapted well to her husband's strange schedule, the strange contraption he built to guarantee he would wake up on time (a phonograph playing Frank Sinatra, then an alarm clock within arm's reach, then a second alarm clock – and, if he wasn't up by then, a very loud alarm that required a key to turn off). She prepared his breakfast, slices of three oranges in the juice of two more oranges. He ate breakfast, then took a cab to NBC at 5 a.m. ("That cab driver is an extraordinary fellow," Garroway said. "I don't believe he's spoken more than half a dozen words in the five years he's been driving me to the studio. I guess even cab drivers don't feel like talking at 5 a.m."), and then she took a nap. He came home that evening and had a simple meal, then worked in the garage until midnight. "A garage mechanic goes home from a day's work, turns on his TV set and forgets all about engines," he said. "I leave the studio, go over to the garage to work on my new engine, and forget all about television." Then it was off to bed. Garroway claimed, "Actually, all I need is four hours sleep. More than five and I get groggy." Much hay was made about a man who once earned $65 a month as an NBC page, but now made more than $340,000 a year.[13]

They seemed like a happy couple in the carefully-presented profiles in magazines, the ghostwritten pieces that appeared under their bylines in prominent publications, a blissful twosome showing Ed Murrow around their home on *Person to Person*, Pamela saying that she still got dinner for David because "I think he'd be very unhappy any other way," that their occasional disagreements never devolved to door-slamming but instead were expressed in quiet, gentle statements. Pamela, along with Helen O'Connell and the wives of three staff members, participated in a maternity fashion show on *Today*.[14]

There were no signs of the turmoil beneath. Garroway claimed Pamela didn't approve of his friends and had no friends of her own. While Garroway's public pronouncements about his strange schedule, that going to work at 5 a.m. "makes for a better, healthier life," presented a brave front, he never mentioned that the early mornings and late nights were fueled by ever-increasing doses of The Doctor to keep him awake and alert, and Seconal to help him sleep. Though it made him incredibly productive, there was only so long the candle could burn at both ends.[15]

In spite of occasional controversy and changes in format, *Today* still ruled mornings. CBS, calling an end to the *Good Morning!* experiment, took one more chance with a morning program hosted by country music singer Jimmy Dean. For a while it looked like Dean's show was beating *Today* in the ratings, but Jac Hein charged that many of those ratings came in markets where Dean was being shown on kinescope. "In cities where we compete, we beat him all the time," Hein said. CBS finally gave up, canceling the Dean show in December and leaving only *Captain Kangaroo* as its morning offering.[16]

Meanwhile, Jack Lescoulie returned to *Today* in June, let go from the flagging *Tonight! America After Dark*. The intrepid Mary Kelly, after six years of service and tens of thousands of miles of travel, was promoted to associate producer. "Perhaps the wall of resistance against women in TV production has finally started to crumble," Marie Torre wrote, "and maybe the TV men are coming around to the idea that women can contribute a little more to TV than décolleté necklines." And the program continued to pick up sponsors, including ones not normally associated with morning television. The Vermont-based Rock of Ages Corporation, manufacturer of gravestones, began advertising on *Today* in September.[17]

Wide Wide World was picked up for another season, although it would alternate on Sundays with a new series called *Omnibus*. *Wide Wide World* would also feature appearances by a new correspondent, Columbia University instructor Charles Van Doren, whom NBC had signed to a contract after he had rocketed to fame as a contestant on the quiz program *Twenty One*.

The third season of *Wide Wide World* debuted with a presentation on "Man's Challenge of Space." Jack O'Brian praised the program for having "far less of that goshawful arty gadding about just for the sake of screeching 'look where I am!' and settled upon a single, certainly mammoth enough subject to tell a specific TV tale, and it did so, mighty importantly." One change, augmenting David Broekman's majestic theme with a strange, otherworldly tonal sounder accompanied by modernistic animation of a globe, irritated at least one viewer: "It is a woeful, weird, irritating noise that doesn't seem to fit the program. It seems more like a warning of a raid from Mars. Is there any reason why he couldn't have a soft, sweet melody instead? Why have such an incongruous element in such a good program?"[18]

In November, *Wide Wide World* took a look at its own industry, as an episode titled "The Fabulous Infant" looked back at the first decade of big-time television. Kinescoped clips brought back moments that seemed like only yesterday: the big news events such as the Kefauver hearings and the atomic tests, the televised burlesque of Milton Berle, the video vaudeville of Ed Wynn and Jimmy Durante. There were clips from the Chicago School, including *Kukla, Fran and Ollie* and *Garroway at Large*. Once they were pioneers. Now they were museum pieces.[19]

There were occasional glimpses of the old Garroway. On Christmas Eve NBC spent part of the evening with the Garroways, squeezing enough remote unit gear into the townhouse for a half-hour special. Jack Haskell and Barbara Carroll sang a Christmas song that had been written for Garroway's Chicago program. The Garroways reminisced; he remembered a Christmas Eve aboard the minesweeper, while she recalled a Christmas Eve in the Tunisian desert. Garroway read "Yes, Virginia, There Is a Santa Claus," and showed off some Garroway-esque Christmas gifts, such as a silent alarm clock for those who liked to sleep late, a cork anchor meant for drifters, and an eleven-foot pole for use on those one wouldn't touch with a ten-foot pole. John Crosby wrote that the "interesting experiment in Christmas Eve programming" was "the sort of simple show that used to come out of Chicago back in the days when television had no money to speak of but lots of brains and enthusiasm."[20]

Once, Fred Allen had observed, "With Dave Garroway, Burr Tillstrom, and Fran Allison there, Radio City should be torn down and rebuilt in Chicago where it might be rechristened Television Town." Now, Radio City had won out. The innovations of the Chicago School had been absorbed by television as a whole, and what seemed fresh and exciting in 1950 was now commonplace in 1957. Even Garroway said that kinescopes of *Garroway at Large* now seemed "very dated," adding, "In those days, the things we did were fresh, the people were new, the shows were modest. We weren't as worried. Now the spirit is gone. Everything is speeded up. What was fresh then is so old-fashioned now. It is extinct."[21]

Gone, too, was the whimsical Garroway of 1950. In its place was a Garroway who was increasingly concerned about the dangers of the times.

15

Today's fifth year explored concepts in longer form. Some segments explored subjects like drought in the Southwest. Another, about school segregation in New York, showed while so much attention was being paid to schools in the South, injustices were happening in other parts of the country. Other features could take a lighter angle, such as a piece about Russian teenagers' reactions to hearing jazz music played over the Voice of America. John Crosby praised the features, saying they covered important features in an original style, and were just long enough to be effective. This new way of presenting features deserved more notice, Crosby wrote. "*Today* gives a news feature flexibility."[1]

Big topics increasingly came to the fore, and as they did, the program and its network began to make enemies. As political leaders in the South vocally resisted the civil rights movement and the *Brown v. Board of Education* ruling, as Black Southerners fought for equal rights, *Today* paid more attention to what was happening. Garroway, the longtime foe of bigotry, often had to interview politicians who seldom hid their contempt for equal rights. And any question, comment or reaction by a television personality could, and often would, be taken by Southern viewers as contempt for the region, or worse.

In April 1957, Mississippi governor J. P. Coleman appeared on *Today* to talk about the state's attempts to attract industry and improve the state's economy. Coleman denied that segregation was a "waste of manpower" and said that a separate-but-equal doctrine was "the only way we can do it." Garroway asked Coleman about reports that 40,000 people per year were leaving Mississippi. Coleman replied that others were coming to Mississippi, and the exodus meant "we're getting rid of the undesirables." Columnists in Mississippi praised Coleman's appearance and accused Garroway of having "a slight air of holding his nose" and using "outdated figures as well as outdated attitudes toward the state" while asking "loaded questions." One writer, who eventually made needling Garroway a trademark of his columns, wrote that "blasted, bigoted, boorish Garroway" had apparently derived his knowledge of Mississippi "from a 1903 encyclopedia or the Communist *Daily Worker*." The civil rights movement was a subject Garroway felt strongly about, that would figure prominently in coming years. But that autumn, a startling event galvanized his greatest worries.[2]

On October 4, only weeks after *Wide Wide World* had examined the challenges and potential of rockets and satellites, the Soviet Union launched a satellite into orbit. The first man-made object put into space signaled more than just a technological achievement. If Russia could put a little beeping ball into space, it would be only a matter of time before it could fit a nuclear warhead atop a missile, able to threaten the United States. "The Reds have come forward with what might appear today to be a toy or a novel device, but which tomorrow could well be an instrument of destruction," one editorial read. While most commentators treated Sputnik like a local fire, it said, Garroway had been the exception: "From the first hour of Sputnik's launching, Mr. Garroway has seized every opportunity to warn the American people what Sputnik really is and what it can really mean." It was the beginning of the end for a lighthearted *Today* and a lighthearted Garroway. There would still be moments of fun, but *Today* would never stray far from an undercurrent of seriousness. Garroway's greatest fears would never stray far from his thoughts, either on camera or in his mind.[3]

By 1958 there was no doubt *Today* was Dave Garroway's show. He was now a producer, with both on-camera and behind-the-scenes ability to influence the program's direction. It was so much Garroway's program that a rumor circulated the show would formally be renamed what many were already calling it, *The Dave Garroway Show*.[4]

Early that year, Garroway circulated a lengthy memorandum outlining what he felt worked and what needed to be changed. He told Marie Torre that he felt *Today* was "too choppy, too segmented, too formal. The way our features keep coming on, we don't give the people at home a chance to break away and get things done around the house." Garroway worried viewers would tune out. Instead, his memorandum implored, "Let us not be so fascinating." Garroway wanted more audio features, more music, more interludes that didn't require the full attention of the audience. Garroway also wanted to give cast members a chance to sit together at a table and converse about current events. This, he felt, would "inject warmth."[5]

Torre wrote a column about the "let us not be so fascinating" memorandum. A *Today* staffer later told her that the column greatly aggrieved Garroway. He denied using the word "fascinating," although Torre clearly recalled him using it. Torre later wrote that in 1959, after she served ten days in jail for refusing to name a confidential source during a lawsuit, Garroway vetoed a suggestion to interview her on *Today*. When another staffer later proposed Torre for a guest appearance, "Garroway apprised the young woman that I, along with two prominent Americans, would appear on his show over his dead body."[6]

Controversies notwithstanding, the program was tackling hard-hitting topics. "America's television audiences are thirsting for more knowledge of America's critical problems," producer Jac Hein said, explaining that *Today* would spend more time looking at a range of topics that included population growth, geriatrics, housing, science, medicine, missiles, and physical fitness. Some features would last several programs, and there would be more discussions. Garroway would express more of his own opinions on the air, as well. The host said the idea came after a seven-week break the previous summer, when "I did a lot of heavy reading and soul-searching and made myself aware of what's going on in the world. I decided that our show could do some good in helping to mold public opinion…help make it more responsive to leadership."[7]

Those opinions galvanized after Sputnik. Jac Hein noticed. "When Sputnik went up, he was really depressed," he said. "He thought we should spend more money for missile research, and we encouraged him to say so." Garroway himself explained, "For a long time I've had a great fear of Russian actions and attitudes. After the Sputnik, I found a sudden desire on the part of the public to be informed." He denied they had set out to make *Today* "a totally serious, intellectual program. I'm not leading some kind of a one-man crusade to arouse the public." He did, however, want to keep Americans from getting complacent, wanted to provide informed answers to urgent questions. In other venues, Garroway admitted he had received inside information, unclassified but still sobering, from people he had done shows with. The revelations had left him gloomy and pessimistic, and figured into his change in perspective. Garroway maintained the new perspective had struck a chord, saying that letters from viewers had more than doubled from the previous year.[8]

One of the strongest responses came after Garroway interviewed Nelson Rockefeller on *Today* in January 1958. The Rockefeller Brothers Fund had commissioned a study on national preparedness. Its findings, which stated the United States could become a second-rate power within two years, disturbed Garroway. He spent twelve minutes interviewing Rockefeller about the report, then invited viewers to write for a copy. They expected 5,000 requests, but got more than 200,000. The response, Garroway said, showed "that people are not complacent. There has not been any change in the basic audience that watches *Today*. Rather, there's been a basic change in the thinking of many people." At times, Garroway held forth with his editorials for five or seven minutes until realizing the audience would only take so much. "Now I try to do it with short jabs," he said. "We could improve our ratings by sensationalizing the news. But we prefer to keep the ratings where they are and do a meaningful job with the news. I think that, rather than present the news as one crisis after another – people get sated with that – our job should be to present it as the one continuing crisis that it really is."[9]

For some, the new Garroway was heavy viewing, even creeping into the normally easygoing Sunday hours. Harriet Van Horne, watching a *Wide Wide World* installment about rockets and missiles, felt the weight. "Granted, we all feel a new responsibility, born of recent events, to keep abreast of scientific developments," she wrote. "It's all very well to have the nation's experts explain what makes a rocket rise and how the moon got its craters, but isn't there time for a philosopher, or a poet to say a few words some Sunday afternoon? Are we to forget the humanities because Russia got her moons in the sky first?"[10]

The specter was never far. During a March installment of *Wide Wide World* devoted to American military readiness, Garroway asked a Marine rifleman during a live hookup if he thought there would be a war. "Damn, I hope not, Mr. Garroway," the Marine responded. This struck one observer as having "rather graphically expressed the feelings of all of us." Jack O'Brian, a longtime champion of Garroway's style, was getting weary: "You can't watch Dave Garroway's *Today* show without his extreme pessimism (about war, recession, Eisenhower) rubbing off."[11]

But then there was light. Early in the morning of February 9, 1958, at Mount Sinai Hospital in New York, Pamela gave birth to a five-pound, five-ounce baby boy. The child, born two weeks early, was named David

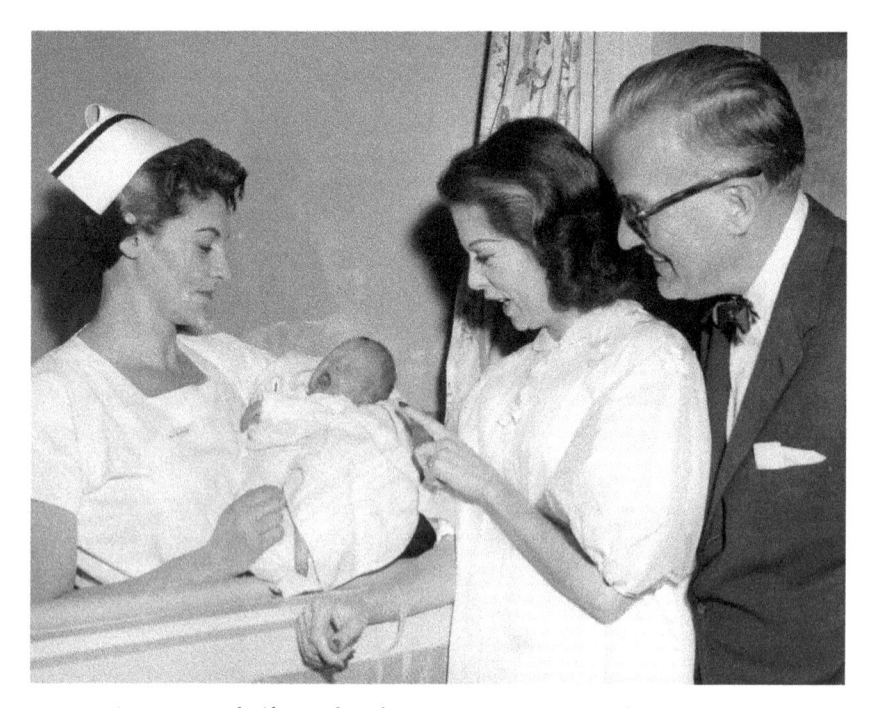

Garroway and wife Pamela welcome Dave Garroway Jr., February 9, 1958. (Paris Day collection)

Cunningham Garroway VIII. Dad, who had spent six restless hours in the waiting room, was overjoyed. A nurse brought baby David out: "My son. Four minutes old. Looking exactly like Mr. Magoo, of cartoon fame." It was something of a relief to have a son, he said: "I am, or was, the last of the Garroways. This might have been the last possibility to carry on the family name. I don't know why that's important. Still, it's rather bleak to be the last of anything."[12]

While Pamela looked after the baby, Garroway felt concerned about Michael, fearing that his expressions of enthusiasm about his new brother might conceal a fear of being forgotten. Garroway made a point of spending time with him after he came home from work, and went to functions with him at school. Michael was a little embarrassed when his classmates asked for autographs. "You never don't give autographs," Garroway replied. "Refuse and you lose five friends. Consent and you gain two."[13]

Garroway confessed he had no preconceived notions about what he wanted his new child to become. "I had no set ideas about what I wanted him to do, or be. And I haven't now," he said. "I only hope to train him to see and hear and think and feel for himself, without imposing my way. To expose him to all the thoughts and ideas there are, to things like wit and humor, as well as music, literature and art...to get him to look through a microscope and telescope for as complete a picture as possible of the world he lives in...and then let him go as and where he wants." He even admitted that more children might be on the way. "I don't know how many children we intend to have," he said. "I expect to have a few more children, at least two within the next ten years, God willing." Since he was in the Navy when Paris was born, he felt he was "experiencing fatherhood for the first time."[14]

The new baby didn't keep Garroway from his demanding schedule, however. "Pamela appreciated having company those early weeks when she was warming the first bottle," he said. After a while, she began sleeping in a little later, usually up around 7 a.m. to watch *Today*. "She's my best critic," he said. "She comments on everything from my crooked necktie to the day's guest, and offers me helpful advice." He credited her with providing suggestions to help the program appeal to women.[15]

After she recovered from giving birth to Dave Jr., Pamela returned to volunteering at a hospital three days a week, and said she planned to take nursing courses to expand her responsibilities. Garroway said he had no objections to the prospect of her going to work someday. "Pamela's only complaint is that she doesn't see enough of me," he said. "I get one day off every two weeks. She complains about that and so do I." Pamela replied, "I would miss not working at all, but my days are full and happy working as a wife and mother and helping others."[16]

In the midst of all this, Garroway found time to opine on less pressing matters. Still in love with jazz, he sounded off on the state of music in America. "America's ear isn't yet tuned to jazz – completely. People who object to jazz do so I think because they don't know what it is. Many think it's interchangeable with rock and roll." He groused that teenagers "buy rock and roll records because they don't know enough to buy anything more worthwhile." He blasted rock and roll as "pap" and "flavorless junk" with inane lyrics: "There's a tune out called 'Short Shorts.' The lyrics consist of four words: 'I like short shorts.' Believe it or not, it took three men to write it."[17]

He sought to help with that, presenting a musical special called *Swing Into Spring* that April, featuring an all-star lineup of his favorites: Benny Goodman, Ella Fitzgerald, Harry James, the McGuire Sisters, Jo Stafford, Ray Eberle, Bambi Linn and Rod Alexander, Red Norvo, and Teddy Wilson. As much as he liked the lineup, Garroway doubted he would add another series to his schedule. "I'm not interested in doing an all-entertainment program." he said. "It's possible that I will be conned into doing one, but I don't see how. I'm not interested in the money." Besides, he said, *Garroway at Large* wouldn't hold up as well as it did in memory. "If you put it on today, people would say 'He's imitating Perry Como.'" Still, he held out hope that live programs would make a comeback, that the networks' attraction to filmed shows from Hollywood would blow over. "I give films a year or two more and then the public will tire of it and advertisers will insist on shows being live. That's when they'll come back."[18]

One casualty of the changing television landscape was *Wide Wide World*, canceled in June 1958. General Motors, its sponsor from the series debut, had considered sponsoring a one-hour version of fifteen shows the following season, but decided against it. The cancellation also threw the future of *Omnibus*, the alternate-Sunday series, into question. Garroway had found out secondhand. "No one ever told me not to come to work, that the show wasn't on anymore," he said. "I had to read it in the newspaper." Despite interest from a potential sponsor, he doubted it would return, "and I'm quite unhappy about it. The reality shows are disappearing from TV, and they're being replaced by quizzes and fantasy." He subsequently speculated that GM's decision was prompted by the economic recession, that the $6 million cost of the series was more than the company wanted to bear. Garroway mourned not only the loss of the program, but what was happening to the medium. "TV is now an art form that is derived from other forms," he complained. "It isn't doing its own job, bringing immediacy to events. These days, TV is presented as yard goods. Films are convenient and residuals are comfortable. You can sell a film series in May and then sit back and not worry for a year."[19]

The cancellation doomed ambitious plans. *Wide Wide World* had planned to venture into Europe, and producers even had begun negotiating to take viewers inside the Kremlin and visit with Soviet premier Nikita Khrushchev. Instead, *Wide Wide World*'s final installment looked at an increasingly popular genre transplanted from movies to the small screen, the Western. After an hour and a half spent with cinematic and television Western stars, including Gary Cooper, James Arness, Gene Autry and James Garner, *Wide Wide World* galloped into the sunset.[20]

It wasn't the only farewell that summer. *Today* had to move. A rival television manufacturer complained that NBC staging a daily network television program from the big, glass-fronted Exhibition Hall, which doubled as a giant showroom for corporate parent RCA, amounted to unfair competition. The studio, with what Garroway had once called "wall-to-wall windows," had become a famous tourist stop and one of the show's signatures. Its fame, however, couldn't overcome its operational limitations: a limited lighting system, a cramped control room nicknamed the Snake Pit, and other factors that kept the program from realizing its full technical potential. The installation of a gigantic Venetian blind several years before had helped reduce glare on sunny mornings, but it could only do so much.[21]

On July 7, the cameras took one last look through the window, slowly panning across the crowd of people who for years had engaged in what Jack O'Brian had once dubbed "that gentle larceny of the expensive NBC air." Garroway, capturing the nostalgia that had gripped cast and crew alike, remembered the many people, names big and small, who had visited the studio the last six years. What mattered most, he said, was people. "People, that's what this show is all about, really. The things people do, the things people think others should and shouldn't be doing...the laws people make, and break...the honors they win...their joys, their sorrows... Yes, it's that simple. *Today* is a show about and for people...and it always will be...How many people, the great and the near-great, and the average Joe have we talked with here?"[22]

When it returned the following Monday, *Today* now originated from Studio 3K inside the RCA Building. It was historic in its own right, created in part from the first television studio in the building. When a wall was taken out to merge two adjoining studios into the present 3K, it became a spacious and comfortable studio. New technologies and capabilities allowed a more sophisticated program to be staged. Since 3K was the first studio inside 30 Rock configured for color broadcasting, it opened up more possibilities down the road. While the Exhibition Hall had no dedicated space for commercials, 3K allowed space to be set aside just for live spots. It seemed like a great new home for an increasingly sophisticated program. Mary Kelly marveled that 3K's control room was as large as the old studio.[23]

The loss of the trademark window, itself as much a part of the show as Garroway, took adjustment. "There were advantages to being 'in the window,'" Fred Lights remembered. "We didn't have any real scenery, but we always had people or the outdoors to shoot if we needed a picture." That compounded an already chaotic first day in the new studio, which Lights compared to the chariot race from *Ben-Hur*. When the two hours of the East Coast feed were complete, there were thirty seconds to fill before the third hour began for the later time zones. In years past, the director could have ordered a shot of the people in the window. Not so in 3K. "No one had thought about a replacement for the window," Lights said. "We had nothing to shoot." After the show, an aquarium was put in the studio, an actual fishbowl taking the place of the fishbowl window.[24]

More changes were coming. Soon after the move, Helen O'Connell, weary of the morning hours and wanting to move on to other things, took her leave. Actress Betsy Palmer was to take on the role now known as the "*Today* Girl." NBC announced that Charles Van Doren, the former quiz show champion who had signed a three-year contract with the network, would become a regular contributor to *Today* in October. Van Doren came to *Today* after an unhappy stint in NBC's Washington bureau, where he never really found where he fit in a hard-news environment. *Today* would let him talk about literature, history, poetry, science, religion, education, or anything in an array of other topics.[25]

Along with new faces, there was a format change. *Today* would abandon its "total newsreel concept" in favor of four separate half-hour segments, with hard news in the first and third half-hours. The second and fourth half-hours would be used for longer features, analysis segments, and the new "column" segments: Jack Lescoulie with sports, Betsy Palmer with a "woman's page," and Charles Van Doren's cultural affairs segment. Instead of top-name celebrities, entertainment would come from talent seeking a break or a comeback, or performers who illustrated the offbeat side of the performing arts. In time, this format would evolve into a more flexible format, and some segments were reworked or eliminated while others, such as an art segment, were added. Not everyone was happy with these format changes. Mary Kelly, who had been with *Today* since before its first broadcast, registered her displeasure by leaving NBC.[26]

There were other warning signs. One morning in October, fifteen minutes before air, Garroway slumped in his chair and blacked out, collapsing in the arms of a startled Betsy Palmer. He was hauled away in an ambulance to Mount Sinai Hospital. The doctors could find nothing amiss with Garroway except fatigue. "He's been doing a lot of extra things lately, running here and running there," an NBC spokesman said. "He's just played out, that's all." Garroway took the next several weeks off to recuperate, swatting down rumors that the collapse meant he was leaving *Today*. When he did return, he gave up his formal producing duties. "It's really more than one man can do," Garroway said, though he continued to exert considerable influence over the program's content. He also pared back his hours. "If I'm not home by noon my wife comes to get me at 12:15." He still enjoyed *Today*, though. "I live it, eat it, breathe it, and – as I found out on my recent enforced vacation from the show – I'm pretty lost without it. So I expect to be around a good, long time. It's a lot more to me than my bread and butter. It's my life."[27]

In the meantime, Betsy Palmer became another casualty of the morning hours. "If I continue with the *Today* show, I will no longer be the gay, bright-eyed Betsy they hired," she told Marie Torre. Garroway and the staff, delighted by her bright and smart personality, wanted her to stay. Palmer, however, didn't like how the strange hours were making her edgy and irritable. "The job's not worth it," she said. Privately, staff members were also concerned about Charles Van Doren. Much as they liked him, they didn't think he fit in on *Today*.[28]

Part of the *Today* format allowed stations to cut away at twenty-five and fifty-five minutes after the hour to insert their own local breaks. This was known as "co-op" time. Not all stations took the cutaway, and for those markets *Today* provided a brief fill period. One morning, writer George Grim watched Garroway during a co-op interview with a beauty firm executive. She handed Garroway two pictures, one a "before" and the other an "after" picture showing a dramatic difference. Garroway examined the photos carefully and showed them on camera. "The after picture has been retouched quite a bit, hasn't it?" he asked. The executive was quiet. "Hasn't it?" Finally, she admitted, "Well, maybe just a little retouched." "Thought so," Garroway said.[29]

To Lou Bradley, who had worked on *Today* for several years, that kind of integrity was one of Garroway's strengths. "Dave always believed the integrity had to be there," he said. Bradley saw it himself when he worked with Garroway on commercials. "If Garroway didn't feel a commercial represented how he felt or how he would do things, he wouldn't do it. If he didn't believe it was the way it should be done, there was no way he would do it."

When Garroway was given that creative freedom, magic could happen. "The way he could say things, the way he could make things happen, always seemed so right," Bradley said. "Whatever it was he was given to do, whether it was from the news department or elsewhere, he would re-weave it." If Garroway was given a good reason why the commercial should be done straight, he would do it, "or he would do an alternate that would be just right for him and make the commercial work right." The result was something far better than Garroway was given. "Very few people could write for him. They couldn't get the color or whatever it was," Bradley said. "He could make things just so right. He could make it believable, make all the shades just right. Because he was terrific."[30]

Bradley believed Garroway's integrity made the commercials stronger, too, and how he did them helped hold the show together. "Dave felt that commercials were an integral part of the show and should be dealt with as a piece of the pie," he said. "He would transit in and out of the commercials as if they were a part of the program." Although Lescoulie or other on-air talent might handle some commercials, "the bulk of the whole show was carried massively by him."[31]

Garroway inspired loyalty in those who worked for him. Prop man Bernie Florman remembered that Garroway had last-minute ideas that challenged him, but "you could never say no to Garroway." Once, returning from a foggy vacation at Westhampton, Garroway told Florman he wanted to open a suitcase and have fog come out. Florman put a smoke candle inside. The effect, with clouds billowing out of the suitcase, delighted Garroway. "He thought it was hard, but it was easy."[32]

They even stuck with him in the harder parts of the job. Since commercials were the first items covered in rehearsals, Bradley had to make sure Garroway was awake and ready for work, whether in New York or out on location. "A lot of times I would have to call him more than once," Bradley remembered. Sometimes he would have to go over to Garroway's townhouse to pick him up; the host, having pulled an all-nighter working on his cars, would be sound asleep. "I wasn't afraid of getting the guy there," Bradley said. "We were there, he had to be there, and he knew. He just needed some prodding." When *Today* did a week in Rome, Bradley went to the Garroways' hotel suite to retrieve the host. Garroway was still in the twilight zone. Pamela, who was already up, whacked her husband across the backside: "Get up, David, honey. Go to work."

On one occasion, Bradley figured in an impromptu on-air prank. He had agreed to buy Pamela's Ford Thunderbird. Before the show, he gave Garroway a sealed envelope; inside was the money for the car. Bradley suggested he count it, but Garroway put the envelope in his pocket and went on. During a segment that day with Milton Berle and Henny Youngman, Berle cracked, "You couldn't pay me to do this interview." Garroway looked over at Bradley "and smiled this big, huge Garroway smile that no other human being ever had." He then pulled the wad of cash from the envelope and started counting the bills off in front of Berle. "It devastated the whole studio," Bradley remembered.[33]

Garroway "always made you feel a part of what was going on," Bradley said. "I just loved working for him. I never got tired. I never lost interest. He seemed to cause you to generate something, something you'd never do for someone else. You certainly wouldn't mind doing anything for him." One year Bradley was invited to a Christmas party at the Garroway townhouse. "Dave had a good time with all the folks who were there," he remembered. The gadgets all through the house never failed to fascinate. Bradley, finding that an old ring-type phone in Garroway's collection didn't work, felt an urge to take it apart and fix it. To be invited, to be on Garroway's "bonbon list," felt like an accomplishment. "I thought I'd come as far as anyone could possibly get close to him," Bradley said, remembering it made him feel important and that "you really mean something on the show besides just being a person on the show that just did a job."[34]

More often, the Garroways had much smaller get togethers. Since Garroway didn't care for the kind of small talk that most dinner parties contained, he and Pamela organized biweekly dinners, invited a few couples, and had an expert in some field give a presentation for a couple of hours. Each couple paid $10 as a token fee for the speaker.[35]

The year 1959 dawned with grand thoughts. The seventh anniversary at hand, *Today* convened a forum of seven thinkers to consider a question: "On the basis of what has happened in the past year, where are we now, and where are we going?" The panel included Iowa physician Dr. Lonnie Coffin, who said transportation now let him help more people in one day than five doctors could before; critic Deems Taylor, who said television "is not the ideal place for serious music"; film producer Samuel Goldwyn, who felt pay television would enhance entertainment; United Nations undersecretary Ralph Bunche, who believed there was "no immediate threat of atomic war"; Frank Lloyd Wright, who diagnosed one modern problem as "too much science and too little art"; cartoonist Al Capp, who believed "the ridiculousness of our situation is much more real than the imminence of our total destruction"; and author Mark Van Doren, who maintained "a great strength of spirit can find hope." A letter blasted *Today* for how it staged the forum, making "the most dedicated and creative people of our time stand for two hours" like "figures in a waxworks" until "the great Garroway conferred life and legitimacy upon them with his magic light." Considering that many of the panelists were of advanced age, the writer asked, "Has Garroway gone mad?"[36]

Garroway himself found a strange upside of the world situation: "People watch fantasy shows these days, I believe, because they want to escape from reality as never before. But as the situation of the world gets worse – which I'm convinced that it will – people are going to want to turn from fantasy to television's reality programs so that they can be informed about the condition of the world, terrible though it may be." (One editor wrote of Garroway's insistence that the worsening world would improve television: "Watch it, Garroway; you make war tempting.")[37]

Today kept trying new ideas, some better than others. The indoor studio had stolen the live audience, so NBC set up bleachers in the studio, hoping to bring back the spontaneity the window had provided. Starting in March, forty visitors per morning were allowed in, but were not provided with coffee. The experiment didn't rekindle the spark, and it was soon discontinued.

A more intriguing experiment came when a new technological advance, videotape, had shown its abilities to present recorded programming with a fidelity kinescopes couldn't offer. As RCA and NBC invested more in videotape capabilities, the network urged its top stars to consider doing shows from Europe via videotape. Garroway and *Tonight* host Jack Paar were among the first to commit, each planning to do two weeks of shows from Paris in the spring of 1959. The prospect excited Garroway. "I want to show Paris to Americans in the way that only television can," he said, hoping to do the show from a different place in Paris each morning. "There won't be any editing or retakes. I'll talk and interview people and generally be a guy showing Paris to friends back home."[38]

Paar's plans to tape in Paris fell through, but the plan to bring *Today* to Paris held up. NBC contracted with a European company, Intercontinental Television, for production services. The *Today* cast and crew headed to Europe for a week's worth of programs, to be recorded on tape and flown to New York for airing. Frank Blair would remain in New York to provide live news breaks.[39]

The first program, on April 27, was meant to make headlines because of an interview with actress Brigitte Bardot. It did make news, but for a more serious reason. That morning, just as the first Paris show was about to air, 1,500 NBC employees, ranging from broadcast engineers and news writers to operations personnel and air conditioning engineers, walked off the job. Officials of the National Association of Broadcast Employees and Technicians, accusing NBC of hiring a European company that paid its employees less for producing the shows, refused to air the videotapes. For more than two hours NBC went dead. Local stations rushed to put on test patterns or old movies until management personnel got the network back on the air. The feud dragged on for two more weeks. As network officials negotiated with union leaders, the hobbled network stayed on the air as staffers were pressed into service as technical personnel.[40]

Meanwhile, *Today* continued to record in Paris, with the disputed Monday show finally aired the following day; the only real casualty was the abandonment of taping the Friday show at Les Halles, the Paris produce market. The Bardot interview, seen at last, prompted Jack Gould to write, "It must be hoped that the Engineers' Union will be a bit more selective in its choice of programs to dispute. Seeing Mademoiselle Bardot walk around at breakfast time is the next best thing to a good cup of coffee." Viewers watched Garroway zoom through the streets of Paris in a Simca sports car, driving with one hand while pointing out landmarks with another. On another installment, Garroway finally made it into the Eiffel Tower without having recording equipment forbidden by the gendarmes, with Bardot confessing she had never been up in the tower. Garroway said he thought Parisians went up there every day. "Only Americans come up here every day," she replied. There was a fashion show, an interview with writer Marcel Pagnol, and other features, particularly many views of the Paris area.[41]

"One can't escape the impression that this is the sort of thing television should have been doing all along," John Crosby wrote. "Perhaps it will bring some new excitement to TV. The possibilities in the news field alone are boundless since tape is faster, more accurate and more flexible and much less bother than film."

Still, the demands of the American broadcasting model could tarnish these beautiful moments. One morning as Garroway and Charles Van Doren stood on the second level of the Eiffel Tower, the camera panned around the Paris skyline as the hosts pointed out landmarks. The camera's gaze came to rest on Napoleon's tomb. "Ah, yes. A magnificent monument," Garroway said, launching into a sales pitch for Rock of Ages cemetery monuments, a *Today* sponsor. In another moment at the Tour d'Argent, Garroway savored a look at an exquisite platter of pressed duck, then strode over to a chafing dish full of boiling water and extracted a sample of du Pont nylon carpet to demonstrate its color-fastness. "It's a good thing the French won't see the commercials," Crosby wrote, "several of which could easily start a war."[42]

16

In July 1959 *Variety* estimated Dave Garroway's value to NBC as a television star was $60 million. Only Perry Como, at $65 million, earned more for NBC. Garroway was the fourth-largest-grossing personality on television, behind Arthur Godfrey, Ed Sullivan and Como.[1]

Aware of his value to his network, and looking out for his personal fortunes, Garroway worked to make sure his image was always out there, and in the best possible light. The public relations firm Lobsenz and Wirsig maintained a busy schedule of publicity opportunities for the Garroways. Some were story ideas planted with feature writers for major national magazines. Sometimes these articles carried the byline of Garroway or his wife, but were really ghostwritten. Topics ranged from an article explaining why Garroway had built a bomb shelter, to another article with his thoughts on spanking children, to another with his thoughts about the future of television. There was a proposal for a story about how Garroway got up in the morning. Other projects involved persuading newspaper columnists to write about him. Even *Alfred Hitchcock's Mystery Magazine* entered the picture, with the firm arranging to have a piece of fiction with Garroway's byline published in the June 1959 issue. The firm kept score, as well, noting that a writer for *Glamour* had written a recent story that was "not entirely favorable toward Mr. Garroway," so contact with her had been held off. Exposure for Pamela was a priority, too. "We feel that it is definitely an advantage for Dave Garroway's wife to receive publicity and whenever possible we do place stories concerning Pamela and her philanthropic activities such as the Metropolitan Hospital," one report read.[2]

Many of these pieces presented the Garroways as a model of domestic bliss, with Garroway the overworked but doting husband and father, and Pamela the understanding and happy housewife. "David's courtesy, I now know, is inbred," went a March 1959 article under Pamela's byline but written by Gladys Hall. "After nearly three years of marriage he never gets up to mix himself a drink without asking if I would care for one; never sees me pick up a cigarette that he doesn't get up and light it for me." Hall painted Pamela's life as one of bliss, in which "my happiest hour of the day is when I'm in the kitchen preparing dinner, while David sits in the living room reading his paper." Another piece, under Dave's byline, made the family's month-long summer getaway to the Westhampton house into the ideal vacation, packed with fun activities: building a garage for the Jaguar, enjoying his twin-Evinrude runabout, tinkering with his telescope. "Take my advice, and discover the secret of a good vacation: doing the things you really like to do, whether it's traveling, or reading or whatever. Do it, pamper yourself and don't be an 'oh, so glad to be back in the office so I can relax' type of man come that certain Monday morning."[3]

Also in the works were a "hard cover travel book" that would be bylined by Garroway, "directed at parents and their children and would include all original photographs of interesting places throughout this country." Freelance writer Loretta Tyson would write the book and Garroway would have approval over the content. The agency also tried to get Garroway involved in introducing, and possibly acting in, a television series about department stores. An effort to get Garroway a syndicated newspaper column went nowhere, but several columns with his byline were prepared for the NBC Press Department to distribute while regular columnists were away during the summer. The agency tried to book Garroway to narrate Joseph Levine's film *Destruction of the World*, based on a Jules Verne story, but could not agree to terms with Garroway's representatives at William Morris. They even tried to get every ounce they could out of Garroway's participation in a Memorial Day race at Bridgehampton, until he told them to dial it back so he could enjoy the race.[4]

The publicity made Garroway out to be, at worst, a harmlessly eccentric but eminently likable neighbor with a wide collection of unusual interests. None of it hinted at the strain in the Garroway marriage, or Dave's continual issues with depression, or that he overworked himself to the point of exhaustion and then stayed up well past midnight working in the garage, sometimes until 3 a.m. Or, for that matter, his substance issues: the Doctor to keep him alert, the Seconal to put him to sleep.[5]

On the *Today* staff, it had been known since the first day that Garroway operated with some extra help. Fred Lights once brought his father, a dentist, to the set. They sometimes saw Garroway take out his little bottle. "My father could see Dave's reaction to it," Lights said. "Then I watched Dave, and it certainly wasn't good for him." Frank Blair recalled Garroway asking co-workers, "Anybody like a sip of The Doctor?" Betsy Palmer remembered that "Dave took some sort of green stuff in the morning. He took things to get him to go to sleep and to wake up."[6]

He was able to hide it around some, like Lou Bradley. "I never saw him drunk, never saw him inebriated in any form at all, never," he remembered. "I saw him a little out of it from fatigue and God knows what else. He'd get mad over technical things in the studio. The anger was there and gone." On other occasions, it was unmistakable. After she became a *Today* Girl in 1959, Florence Henderson saw Garroway apparently floating on a cloud. "I just feel so wonderful today," he told her. "I've been up for three consecutive days and nights, and I'm working on a car." Her astonishment was interrupted when she noticed skin was missing from Garroway's thumb. "I thought I was pulling out glass fibers," he explained. "But I went to the nurse upstairs and she said I was pulling out skin fibers." It was a sign of compulsive skin-picking, one characteristic of amphetamine overuse.[7]

To viewers at home, all seemed well. A Texas columnist wrote that Garroway "is such a placid and easy-going individual that he makes me nervous. I get all tense as I watch him taking everything in such slow, calm strides." No matter what scenes of devastation the columnist saw, "there sits Garroway, waving slowly and calmly, saying 'Peace.' I wish he would explode just once." Another viewer had a different take: "Someday I'd like to see Dave Garroway raise his hand and say 'Peace,' and then get a Mau Mau poison dart right in his forehead."[8]

With his increased editorial freedom, Garroway opined about things that concerned him. He had a longstanding interest in mental health, fueled both by his university studies and his ongoing efforts to understand what was happening in his own mind. In December 1957 he had started a campaign for the Psychiatric Research Fund during a *Today* segment. Garroway promoted it when he could and visited its offices often. The following year *Today* originated from Central Islip State Hospital for a report on mental health problems in the United States. In January 1959 he presented a special report on "Mental Illness in Soviet Russia," part of an ongoing series about psychiatric conditions and treatment.[9]

As the decade ended, his foremost concern was global. Garroway remained determined to make viewers aware of what he called "a national emergency" in which "our heads could be blown off at any time." While concerns about the possibility of nuclear war were common throughout the 1950s, Garroway became outspoken to the point of single-mindedness. He could, for example, spend two days on an examination of the situation in Berlin and whether old prejudices could be put aside to unite against the Soviet Union. Or he could opine about a new obsession, one that he built in his basement.[10]

In September 1959, *Family Weekly* carried a two-page article titled "Your Family Should Have a Fallout Shelter." Complete with photographs and diagrams, Garroway described how he built his own fallout shelter for $700. "The important fact is that it's there – ready for the time it may save the lives of my wife Pamela and my three children." He reassured readers that building a shelter didn't mean living in morbid fear. Instead, he likened it to an insurance policy "so you can feel more secure when you know you've provided for the worst, should it come." He also maintained that if more people built fallout shelters, it might prevent a war. "If Americans would face the fact that nuclear war is possible and prepare for it, there probably would be no war. The preparedness of the people is as great a deterrent to an aggressor as armies." He confessed that he and Pamela didn't talk to the children about the "grim business" behind the shelter. "It's something they wouldn't understand and shouldn't be made to yet. It's enough that they participate in the drills which we have made into family fun."[11]

In addition to segments on *Today* about bomb shelters in general, Garroway was proud of his own shelter and talked about it often. He had *Today* do a feature about it, hoping it would encourage viewers to build their own. Producer Gene Jones went over to the townhouse for a look. Over the big steel vault door at the shelter's entrance, he saw a double-barreled shotgun on pegs. What was it for? "So if necessary, I can kill anyone that tries to come in." On the opposite wall was a bicycle. "After the bomb drops," Garroway said, "I'm going to open the door, get on my bike, and pedal away."[12]

Garroway grew more openly pessimistic. A writer for *Help!*, a magazine created by former *Mad* editor Harvey Kurtzman, asked Garroway if he would want Khrushchev on *Today* for an appearance. Garroway said he had learned during the premier's 1959 visit to the United States that there was little one could discuss with him. Garroway recalled calmly calling Khrushchev a murderer during their short encounter, and the Russian leader merely blinked in acknowledgment. "There's not much more you can say to him," Garroway said, "except that we're here, we're ready and we're strong."[13]

Some interpreted Garroway's stance as needlessly hostile. "Why must we Americans show our worst side to the Russians?" asked a viewer in South Dakota after Garroway's coverage of Khrushchev's visit. "He is the President's guest and the guest of the American people, and should be treated as such with respect. You, who mold American opinion, must bear a great part of the blame for the discourteous treatment given to the Russians. Why can't we meet them half way? Give us intelligent and courageous opinions and attitudes we can respect, that show respect for ourselves and others. Else what are you there for?"[14]

Garroway's deteriorating condition was a factor in the next big change to *Today*. It was encouraged by the success of the Paris adventure, which had even spawned talk of a series from shows from Japan. If a show from abroad could be successfully presented on videotape, so could one from New York. In August, NBC announced that *Today* would move to videotape in September. Each day's program would be recorded, live-to-tape, the afternoon before. Only Frank Blair's news segments at the start of each half-hour would be done live.[15]

Producer Bob Bendick told *TV Guide* that taping in the late afternoon would let the staff be more responsive. "There are more things happening at four in the afternoon than at seven in the morning," he said. For instance, if something happened in Congress they could get responses while the body was still in session. Bendick also said a late-afternoon taping time might allow Garroway to visit a Broadway rehearsal or a television program rehearsal, or Jack Lescoulie could cover a sporting event while it was underway. Videotape also meant they could eliminate the live third hour, and the entire country could see the same two hours of *Today* each day. Behind the scenes, Bendick made the change to help Garroway. After his collapse the previous year, videotape presented a way to relieve some of the demands in his crushing schedule.[16]

The host didn't want to talk about any of it. Was Garroway angry? Bendick denied it. "There's no friction whatever on that score. Dave didn't say anything, one way or the other, about the tape. So I wouldn't try to read anything into that, as far as that goes." The show wouldn't lose spontaneity, the producer maintained. "It'll be purely incidental, a mechanical convenience, that's all." Bendick said *Today* had been presenting filmed features since the beginning with no complaints, and he couldn't understand the brouhaha. "Anyway, our news segments and vital last-minute stuff will be live. Look, the less said about tape, the better." Would any of the changes affect Garroway? "No," Bendick said. "The show is Dave's way of life. He'll be here as long as the show is."[17]

Bendick also hoped the afternoon taping time might help the show's search for a new *Today* Girl. "The fact that we'll be working in the afternoon and not the early morning might make her more available," he told *TV Guide*, although he admitted that no applicant had complained about the show's early start. Florence Henderson remembered that taping the program was never really a topic. "Nobody ever talked about it or tried to hide it," she said, "but it wasn't discussed." Just as it allowed an exhausted Garroway a change of schedule, it was agreeable to her own schedule. "Having started out in the theatre and done so many nightclubs, morning is difficult for me," she said.[18]

The new system meant that on most days, *Today* taped its segments at 4:30 p.m. for next-day airing. Frank Blair would do live news breaks at the usual times in the morning. That was the plan, at least. In practice, Garroway often had to be in the studio for live inserts. "We thought it might make things easier," he said later, "but all it's done has spread the day out from early morning when we do the live portions to 6:30 in the evening when we finish taping for the next day." Nobody was happy, and certainly not the critics. "*Today* becomes yesterday," went a common refrain. One writer grumped, "When you see Dave Garroway on your set, he will be at home and presumably asleep. Whatever news value the program had will be dissipated; you will be reading later developments in your morning paper."[19]

Today's use of videotape would figure in another controversy, this one spawned by a revelation about one of its own.

Rumors that the big-money quiz shows had been rigged gained substance in mid-1958, after a *Dotto* contestant provided evidence that a competitor had been given answers in advance. After stories of similar manipulations on other quiz shows, the Manhattan district attorney's office opened an investigation. Herb Stempel, whom Van Doren had defeated on *Twenty One*, had insisted that he was fed the answers by producers, and that he was instructed to lose. Van Doren had repeatedly denied that *Twenty One* was dishonest. In October 1958, Van Doren was summoned to the Manhattan district attorney's office for questioning. He insisted that luck, not contrivance, had been responsible for his success on *Twenty One*.[20]

The following August, Van Doren was in the *Today* studio reviewing some notes before the daily story conference. Richard Goodwin, a staffer for the House Committee on Interstate and Foreign Commerce, introduced himself and told Van Doren that the committee was to hold hearings on the quiz shows. He produced a copy of the grand jury proceedings, which Van Doren had thought were under seal on orders of a Manhattan judge. Goodwin said Stempel's testimony contradicted Van Doren's, and *Twenty One*'s producers had returned to the grand jury and confirmed Stempel's account. Not only had Van Doren not known he could change his testimony, but Goodwin said the producers wanted to warn him but were told they couldn't. "Goodwin also told me that I wasn't the only one who had lied," Van Doren later wrote. "From all that he said, I realized that the committee wanted my story to come out at hearings in Washington." Goodwin advised Van Doren not to say anything to anybody. Stunned, Van Doren went to the story meeting but couldn't stay focused. He quickly begged out, telling Garroway his daughter wasn't feeling well and his wife needed help with her.[21]

Van Doren had met with NBC officials and provided more details about the doings on *Twenty One*, but had still withheld key information. The result, he said, made his actions "seem even more mystifying" to the network brass. When Van Doren did not respond to an October 8 invitation to testify before the House committee, NBC suspended him. In a panic, he requested a week's leave of absence from Columbia University, and he and his wife drove from one New England town to another. "I simply ran away," he said, not only trying to flee newsmen and photographers, but himself. "I still could not face up to what I had done." Though he had hoped to protect himself and his reputation and the faith others had placed in him, "I was coming closer and closer to a true understanding of my position." The turning point, he later testified, was a letter from a woman who had admired his work on *Today*. The only way he could live with himself, she wrote, was to admit whatever he had done. "Suddenly, I knew she was right." Van Doren phoned his attorney and told him his plan. "God bless you," the lawyer said.[22]

As the controversy unfolded, Blair's newscasts had provided brief updates on the investigation, but no one mentioned it at any other points. It was a sensitive topic, on-camera or off. Writer Earnest Joiner, scheduled to appear on *Today*, needed help finding the studio. "Where does a guy go to get the answers for the Dave Garroway show?" he asked a group in the NBC lobby. "The silence that followed was cathedral, and I doubt if anyone other than myself noticed the chill north wind whipping down my Botany 500."[23]

Now that Van Doren had confessed before the House committee, NBC wasted no time cutting ties. On November 3, Garroway was preparing to tape the Wednesday segments of *Today* when word came of Van Doren's dismissal from NBC. He had kept silent on the controversy, but now felt he had to say something.

"I want to talk for a few moments about Charlie Van Doren, my friend," Garroway began. He said he'd been asked time and again when he would say something about Van Doren's troubles but had not wanted to judge him until he was judged "by my betters, including Charles Van Doren, who has judged himself now." He then read from NBC's statement announcing Van Doren's release. "And I wonder what you want me to say."

Garroway spoke of his friendship with Van Doren. "There is a certain openness about five o'clock in the morning," he said, and their many travels together for *Today* had helped them know one another. "I came to love Charles, to love his inquiring mind, his enthusiasm, his rightness, and I wonder what you want me to say. He wronged himself. Of course he did. I think you agree on that." Garroway recounted Van Doren's statement on *Today* when he pledged *Twenty One* had been played honestly. Then he read from the NBC statement that Van Doren was fired for dishonesty.

"We are a little family on this show, strange as it may seem," Garroway continued, his voice getting husky. "Whatever Charles did was, of course, wrong. I cannot condone it or defend it, and I have no intention of doing so. But we will never forget the non-Euclidean geometry essays, or the poetry of Sir John Suckling which Charles left with us." Garroway remembered having breakfast with Van Doren and his father the day Charles earned his doctorate. Emotion overwhelmed Garroway, his voice breaking. He spoke of how much Van Doren loved to teach, how much he loved his family, of watching their little girl grow up. "What do you want me to say?" He paused, tears welling in his eyes. "I can only say I'm heartsick." There was a station break. Garroway left. Jack Lescoulie took over the remainder of the program, telling viewers, "Dave has gone home."[24]

Garroway's reaction to the controversy spawned a controversy all its own. Garroway later said that he had wanted to talk "not about Charlie in particular, but about the whole race of men who were sort of forced into what happened to him. I never got a chance to say that, though, because I was so emotional I couldn't speak." Some were taken by surprise that it had been pre-recorded. A Shreveport editorial described Garroway's "touching scene," followed by his walk-off. "Now it is revealed that all of this was acting. It was taped the day before and what the public was seeing was just a taped emotion by Garroway. Obviously it was meant to create public sympathy for the 'dear departed.' It was more TV phony business." Even those who knew of *Today*'s recording practices wondered why it was aired, and felt it was a misuse of videotape technology. "One can sympathize with Garroway for his deep emotional involvement in the disgrace of Van Doren," Jack Gould wrote. "But when it was revealed that his collapse in front of the cameras was recorded, kept in the shop overnight, and then put on the air, there can only be one question: Why?" Cleveland Amory said the affair, which "has all the earmarks of one more fraud," was a reflection on "the current overuse of tape." Cynthia Lowry wrote that "while Garroway's emotion undoubtedly was genuine, the fact that it was used as if it were live some sixteen hours later gave the whole thing a phony aspect. Furthermore, it annoyed some viewers when they found it was a taped episode." One writer asked columnist Harry Harris, "Seems there is something new on television, a 'leaky' Paar on the *Tonight* show and a 'leaky' Garroway on the *Today* show. Now wouldn't it be just dandy if they could get a PLUMBER for a sponsor?"[25]

Noel Parmentel in the *National Review* skewered "the American susceptibility to adult bawling," saying that "The spectacle of a congressional committee being had by this maudlin fake wasn't enough; it was followed by the soppiest collection of public tributes since the death of Lou Gehrig. People who ought to know better suckered up like marks on the midway. Dave Garroway broke up in the middle of a Method rendition of 'Friends, Romans, Countrymen,' and had to be helped off the set."[26]

After weeks of this criticism, Garroway provided a lengthy rebuttal on the November 20 *Today* program. Telling viewers that "our integrity has been attacked," Garroway not only reminded the audience that the program was taped, but that the move to videotape had been widely publicized when the decision had been made some months before: a story put out via the major wire services, made available to hundreds of media outlets, and even the subject of a cover story in *TV Guide* that August. Garroway said that when Van Doren was suspended, the reporters knew when to show up at the studio to get comment. "None of them showed up at 7 o'clock in the morning. They all came at 4:30 in the afternoon." Now, Garroway charged, they seemed to have forgotten it when his emotional response was broadcast. After reading an excerpt from a story that claimed the disclosure of videotape was withheld until after the broadcast, Garroway scored the story as "frankly, dishonest." He also claimed that one prominent television critic continued to go after *Today* for its supposed dishonesty even after Bendick wrote him a letter explaining how the program worked.

Garroway took his case to the audience. Explaining a little about how videotape worked, Garroway said their philosophy was to show things as they happened. "We don't believe it's good television if you shoot a program like ours in dozens of pieces and paste them together," he said. "That's the reason why we did not edit out my emotional outburst, or collapse as it's been called, for Charles Van Doren. This is a reason for us which far outweighs the others. When we first decided to tape this program we set a hard and fast rule that we would never change any part of the show once it was recorded. To do otherwise would be, I think, unethical." Although he was "deeply embarrassed" by weeping on camera ("It's kind of an unmanly thing to do, no matter how sincere the emotions expressed are"), he would not apologize for it. "It was an honest expression of my feelings." He also stood by the decision to air it. "What do you suppose the newspapers and magazines would have said when it was learned, had we followed their course of not playing it because it was emotional?" He imagined stories about NBC being accused of more deceit, asking "why has Garroway been muzzled?" In particular, he criticized a piece in *Life* that claimed a "revelation" about the tape delay. Garroway called the *Life* comment "a falsehood. We were exactly what we seemed to be. We are, we believe, the people we are."

Garroway closed with a defense of the taping practice, listing an array of distinguished guests the program likely would not have been able to get except that tape delay made it possible to fit their schedules. "We feel we've done nothing for which we should be ashamed. On the contrary, we are proud of this program, what it has done and what it will do, and I feel it's time somebody stood up and met this underhanded attack squarely. It's time somebody exposed the unconscionable smears for what they are. I'm glad I've had the opportunity to be one of the first to speak up. I feel I owe it to you. It's a part of what we always tried to do, to bring you the truth."[27]

It didn't move the critics. Harry Harris wrote that Garroway's "grousing" about the videotape controversy "kind of loses the point. Presenting an unedited tape is fine. But breaking down and being unable to complete a program makes sense only if you're appearing live. If you're suddenly all choked up during a taping session, what's to prevent you from calling a 10-minute 'break' to regain your composure, and then getting on with it?" Harris later alluded to television's recent controversies: "Garroway suggests that the convenience of West Coast viewers, rather than his own comfort, is the principal reason *Today* shifted to tape. As TV has been constantly demonstrating lately, ANYTHING can be rationalized. But sometimes it requires a lot more 'reaching.'"[28]

John Crosby was saddened by Garroway's snap at the critics. "The terrible thing," he wrote, "is that Garroway is probably sincere in saying it." Crosby stated that it seemed impossible to get people in broadcasting to understand that while they labor under the control of advertisers, newspaper people didn't work that way. He mentioned Jack Paar's recent tirade that newspaper columnists had become "zealots" about the payola scandal and kept being critical of broadcasting. Radio and television, Crosby said, were the topic of Congressional inquiry, hence the focus. Since the newspapers didn't start the scandal or the investigation, "why blame us?" Crosby wrote, "The tradition is freedom to observe and report the facts as they are, not as the business office wishes they were. It's the tradition of freedom that people like Garroway and Paar can't understand because they've never had any." Cynthia Lowry likened the NBC bookends in less flattering terms: Garroway, she wrote, "is turning into a regular daytime Jack Paar with his breakdowns and pop-offs." Walter Winchell, a longtime Garroway booster, warned he "is making a mistake tangling with newspapers. It's the function of a star to make friends – not critics."[29]

Three months later, Jack Paar walked off *Tonight* in mid-taping, upset that the network had cut a joke from his program. NBC aired the program as recorded, complete with Paar's rambling preamble to the walk-off itself, because the network was sensitive about what cutting the incident would mean in the press. No doubt, NBC executives remembered the aftermath of the Garroway incident. In a column, Marie Torre recounted what had happened months before: "Rather than sully the names of these men with charges of 'publicity stunt,' shouldn't we all be feeling a little grateful that there are still people around who are capable of honest emotions?"[30]

17

Dave Garroway rang in 1960 in living color and white tie, presenting a salute to American music as host of "Our Musical Ambassadors," an installment of *The Bell Telephone Hour* on January 1. It was an all-star lineup: Louis Armstrong, Jane Froman, pianist Grant Johannessen, and Shirley Jones and Jack Cassidy. Between segments an upbeat Garroway, channeling the spirit of the Chicago days, presented informative and light-hearted lead-ins that tied in to the theme of music as a way for different cultures to understand each other.[1]

The promotion of understanding was a Garroway mainstay. Only a few days before, he had used a few moments on *Today* to pay tribute to an unsung hero who worked in their midst. Garroway had learned that Eugene Bullard, a Rockefeller Center elevator operator, had been the only Black aviator in the First World War. Wounded six times, Bullard had been awarded fifteen French decorations, including the Legion of Honor. Garroway interviewed Bullard on *Today*, displaying his array of medals to viewers. At the segment's end, the crew spontaneously burst into applause.[2]

Not everyone appreciated Garroway's definition of understanding. As civil rights activists spoke up in more determined voices, and as *Today* gave more coverage to their efforts, defenders of the status quo became increasingly vocal. "There isn't hardly a morning that he doesn't come up with some parcel of news concerning our Southern problem, but it is always one-sided," a Florida viewer wrote, accusing Garroway of a "one-man crusade" and suggesting he pay attention to discrimination in New York, or come to the South to see the situation himself. "This could pay off, unless, of course, Mr. Garroway is out to capture the most valuable player award from the NAACP." A Mississippi editor, citing secondhand evidence, claimed Garroway's comments about Miss Mississippi being named Miss America for two consecutive years were done with "green-eyed fury," and called him "one of those northern bigots who likes to lambast [sic] the South with innuendo." A Mississippi columnist who made a particular hobby of ridiculing Garroway on civil rights, the death penalty and anything and everything else, suggested that the old Ed Wynn nickname of "The Perfect Fool" should be applied to Garroway: "He must receive special coaching in stupidity, for no man could possibly be so muddy-minded without help."[3]

To celebrate its eighth anniversary, *Today* went to Washington, D.C. The idea came from producer Gene Jones, who also suggested that Garroway interview President Eisenhower. Arrangements were made and everything appeared to be in order. It was to be an impressive program: a tour of the Capitol, Florence Henderson singing from the grand staircase of the Library of Congress, even a visit to the Supreme Court's great courtroom.

A few hours before taping was to begin, word came that Eisenhower wouldn't participate in the program. *Today* now had to fill an entire half-hour with little notice. As Robert Metz later wrote, Garroway, who was upset by Eisenhower's refusal, suggested that if he could stand on the White House lawn, he could fill the time telling stories about the building. Writers huddled in the hotel suite with reference material and assembled some facts about the White House. Garroway dictated the notes into a tape recorder, and the results were transcribed and put on a teleprompter. The words on the prompter looked unorganized, but when the tape rolled, Garroway gave a virtuoso presentation that gave no hint of the panic behind its creation.

At the Supreme Court, Garroway stood by in irritation as crew members set up for the shoot. Gene Jones needed to move a table and summoned John Dunn, who was serving as Garroway's assistant, to help. Dunn, who knew Garroway's moods, hinted that he needed to stay near Garroway. Jones didn't know the host was nearby, nor did he care if he was. "Fuck Garroway!" he yelled. Jones was transferred off the *Today* unit soon after.[4]

Garroway's uncanny ability to extemporize, sometimes with the help of crude notes and other times off the top of his head, astounded some and exasperated others. Writer Earnest Joiner had appeared on *Today* a few months before. When the interview began, Joiner noticed that questions had been loaded on the teleprompter, and stole a glance toward the prompter so he might have a second to think of an answer. To Joiner's surprise, the questions Garroway asked bore no resemblance to those on the prompter. In the background, Joiner heard a writer: "On the Dave Garroway show, who needs writers?"[5]

To Betsy Palmer, working with Garroway provided an education that helped her in other roles. "I learned to listen to Garroway on *Today*," she said. "If you listened to him, you could tell where the talk would go. It was his handling that produced the best shows." Florence Henderson said that Garroway was "absolutely the best" as a host. "I think he understood this medium called television incredibly well," she said, even if his "amazingly brilliant" but complicated nature could be unsettling. "You didn't always feel as comfortable as you might," she said. "Sometimes he'd go, 'We have the most *amazing* thing on the show today! It's a scale that's anti-gravity.' And you'd go '...*okay!*'" Although he was consistently kind to her, Henderson remembered Garroway was "very much a control freak."[6]

Nor was Garroway immune to flights of whimsy. One day during a discussion, Garroway mentioned the phrase "more fun than a barrel of monkeys." He wondered aloud, "I'd like to see how much fun that is." A few days later, a barrel was brought into the studio. Out crawled several rhesus monkeys. "They went berserk," Henderson remembered. As the monkeys ran around the studio and climbed up into the lighting grid overhead, a startled Henderson jumped atop the desk to protect herself. "They were pooping everywhere," she recalled. "I never knew how they got them down."[7]

The whimsy went abroad when *Today* visited Rome in April on another videotaped adventure. But while Paris had demonstrated excitement and possibility, the Rome tour left some unimpressed. Harriet Van Horne complained that "the motor scooters and the shape of the Roman girls stirred far more excitement in the smiling Lescoulie than did the monuments to Rome's glory. Garroway, as the senior briefing officer, had apparently read the 'research' prepared by *Today*'s staff, but he fastidiously avoided more historic references than were absolutely necessary." Van Horne criticized Garroway and Lescoulie for their "ho-hum demeanor, the meager background knowledge and utterly banal remarks."[8]

As Robert Metz later chronicled, the Rome trip also led to the end of Bob Bendick's tenure as executive producer. Garroway had been moody at points during the trip, and while performing Marc Antony's funeral oration at Caesar's tomb, he and John Dunn got at loggerheads. Fed up, Bendick reprimanded Garroway in front of the crew; his obstinance, Bendick said, was holding up the taping. Stunned and chastened, Garroway completed the taping session. Later that year, while in Los Angeles for the Democratic convention, Garroway bumped into NBC president Robert Kintner at the airport as they waited on a flight to New York. Garroway told Kintner that Bendick needed to be replaced. Kintner went to a pay phone, called New York, and ordered that Bendick be relieved.[9]

The following month, *Today* did a two-hour boat ride around Manhattan that alternated "a number of breathtaking scenes" with ad-libs and humorous from Garroway that didn't always land, and a few stunts, such as a woman waterskiing around the tour boat in the Harlem River. In a rather puzzling lead-in to an underwear commercial, against a shot of the buildings on Wall Street, Garroway said that all the men who work there wear underwear. One review praised Garroway's candor in admitting New York's shortcomings along with its triumphs. "It was a visually rewarding program and a worthy project. I move that *Today* hit the road. Let's see the U.S.A. with Dave Garroway."[10]

That June, Garroway turned his attention toward freedom of expression. In a *Look* magazine article ghostwritten by Peter Van Slingerland, Garroway opined that Samuel Adams or Thomas Paine would be horrified to see that "Americans have turned into a bunch of verbal Casper Milquetoasts." The article worried that Americans only gave lip service to "freedom of speech," and permitted it only if things weren't said too loudly. Instead, it charged, "we want walking tranquilizers, men who will feed us bland platitudes and happy assurances that all is well with the world," and men who told the public only what it wanted to hear.

The article accused newspapers of not taking strong editorial stances out of fear they will offend readers and advertisers, and worried that special interest groups would hijack what the majority wanted. Making things worse was an attitude by the public of "I'll keep quiet and mind my business, if you'll just leave me alone." The result, the article charged, was the rise of demagogues like Joseph McCarthy. "Unless we want to lose our precious freedoms, we must start rocking the boat. We're letting freedom of speech go by default. The habit we have formed of not speaking up is becoming increasingly more difficult to break. Remember, it's the habit of not exercising freedom that makes a people easy prey for dictators."

The article also reminded the communications industry that it has "more than a responsibility, we have an obligation" to present unpopular views. The public, too, needed to hold networks, stations and newspapers responsible. "Too many of the letters written to legislators, to newspapers and magazines and to television stations, are the work of cranks complaining that they have been abused. The people who want more adult fare sit on their hands." The article closed: "In large part, it's up to you whether we let freedom of speech go by default. The price of liberty is more than eternal vigilance. Freedom, like a muscle, must be exercised, lest it atrophy. Perhaps, if we work together to encourage the free expression of all ideas, good and bad, irritating and tranquilizing, in time we will be able to mean something when we talk about freedom of speech."[11]

Garroway found himself in a hornet's nest. Columnist George Sokolsky disagreed with the article's accusation that the public was being spoon-fed by the Eisenhower White House, claiming that there had been far worse efforts by previous administrations. He challenged Garroway on the claim that it was difficult to find diverse viewpoints, suggesting he read five different New York papers and see the different points of view among them, and sometimes the different points of view within an individual paper. "Garroway's piece reminds me of the conversation between a Russian and an American journalist," Sokolsky wrote. "The American claimed that he was free to say anything he wanted to say. Challenged by the Russian, the American shouted, 'Truman is a so and so.' The Russian said: 'That is no sign of freedom. That is nothing. I can do the same. I can say, 'Truman is a so and so.' Freedom, Indeed!"[12]

Westbrook Pegler skewered Garroway for using a ghostwriter. "I take this to mean that Mr. Garroway, a pundit of the TV, cannot compose his own thoughts in readable prose, but must resort to the services of a ghost," he wrote, adding that he had tried several times to contact Garroway at NBC by telephone, all without success. "So all I have to go by is a photograph of a rather doe-eyed visage, with biscuit-mix features poised on puffy hands, gazing vacantly at, perchance, an idiot-card covered with the text of Mr. Van Slingerman's article 'By Dave Garroway.'" Suggesting Garroway "is so demure that you might say the cat has got his tongue," Pegler said, "I would test whether he really is denied freedom of speech in my forum or is too bashful to exercise the precious heritage which heroes bled and died for at Valley Forge." Pegler came back for Garroway in a later column, writing, "Garroway yearns for truth without the zeal or intelligence to learn it or the conscience to expound it."[13]

Walter Winchell appreciated the *Look* article, seconding its assertion that cranks dominate the commentary while people who want quality programs say nothing. "The above is true," Winchell wrote. "Complacency works on the side of idiocy. Vigilance is not just the price for liberty – it is an eternal debt to those who fought and died for it. It's about time Americans realized this. The ride Paul Revere started must never end." Meanwhile, a Fort Lauderdale television writer was acerbic: "Television takes a few lumps from one of its own in the current (May 28) issue of *Look* Magazine when Dave Garroway rips the medium for unimaginative programming. 'We can watch television day in and day out with little risk of encountering a stimulating or irritating idea – one that might kick us into action,' says Garroway. Well, welcome aboard, Dave."[14]

In a guest column for the vacationing Cynthia Lowry, Garroway returned to the issue of complacency, calling the lack of interest in what's going on in current events "one of the greatest problems facing this country today." He mentioned his disappointment that when *Today* correspondents asked people on the streets what they thought of President Eisenhower's Japan trip being cancelled due to riots in Tokyo, many of them were barely concerned. "It was almost like talking to a baseball fan whose team had just lost. 'It's too bad,' he'd say, 'but there's always tomorrow.'" This worried Garroway, and he returned to a characteristic theme. "Is there always a tomorrow? I hope and fervently pray so, but in the atomic age there's always the threat that one little figure will push one little button, and then there will be no tomorrows. The answer to this threat or to any other threat to peace is not resignation and complacency, and it has never been in this country. The answer is action. We owe it to ourselves and our country to be aware. Our greatest danger is not that the Russians are doing too much, but that we are doing too little."[15]

In September, the imprint Garroway had made on *Today* was made official. NBC renamed the program *The Dave Garroway Today Show*. Despite the confident appearances, there was concern. According to author Robert Metz, Garroway was concerned his tenure on *Today* would soon be in jeopardy and that he should have something new in the works. Garroway was especially concerned after Robert Kintner, a former newsman and ABC executive, had been named president of NBC. Garroway had met Kintner in 1941, when they were covering the Louisiana Maneuvers. In the years since, Garroway had gone on to fame as a disc jockey and television host, while Kintner moved into the executive ranks, becoming a strong advocate of his networks' news divisions.[16]

In August 1959, Gerson Associates had polled the members of Congress about their morning television habits. Of 250 members of the House of Representatives who watched morning television, 184 regularly watched *Today*. Of the fifty-three senators who watched morning television, forty-eight regularly watched *Today*. Of those, nearly eighty-three percent of those senators and nearly sixty-two percent of those congressmen gave *Today* the highest rating in "broadening the public's general knowledge." NBC also promoted to potential sponsors that the show drew more than 16,000 pieces of voluntary mail from viewers during the first three months of 1960, and that a recent program devoted to government matters "attracted letters and wires from thirty-four Senators and Representatives," including House speaker Sam Rayburn and Senate Minority Leader Everett Dirksen.[17]

Garroway wrote years later that he believed this study offended Kintner. *Today*, which was not a production of NBC News, was drawing higher trustworthiness ratings than programs produced by the news division. Garroway believed Kintner was further offended because he did not consider Garroway a real journalist. He also suspected Kintner believed *Today* needed to be headed by a newsman. In Garroway's opinion, Kintner's "ancient Hildy Johnson idea of the reporter" would have reporters trick guests into saying things they'd later regret just so they could get a story. In contrast, Garroway had built *Today*'s style around bringing newsworthy guests into a non-threatening environment where they didn't have to worry about being ambushed. There, "they relaxed, and gave us story after story." Kintner's philosophies, Garroway said in 1977, "began the building of a wall between entertainment and news in an attempt to make NBC a news network. I didn't realize it right off, but I was on my way out from that moment until I left the show in 1961."[18]

In the meantime, there had been talk that Garroway would return to prime time. In January, right after "Our Musical Ambassadors," he discussed the possibility with Marie Torre. "Maybe the time is here," he said, promising that the format of the special he'd just hosted ("So rigid! So fixed!" he complained) would not be the format of any new show of his. To another writer, Garroway said he had turned down twenty offers that would have been moneymakers. His main concern was that he wanted to do a show his way. "I'll admit, I've been very stiff about it. I want the right time on the right night with the right budget. Everything has to be right." In the meantime, he had dabbled as a guest host on other programs, winning praise for a stint guest-hosting *Talent Scouts* while Arthur Godfrey was on a safari. "He exuded the usual Garroway personality, a bit of a familiar touch here, a little warmth there, and a shyness that Godfrey never had," one review said. "Humility, maybe, but never shyness."[19]

Later that year, Garroway had producer Robert "Shad" Northshield work on a concept for a prime-time special that could lead to a new series. Northshield hired Andy Rooney, who had written for Godfrey, to write the special. Garroway didn't like Rooney's script and turned the project over to his favorite writer, I.A. "Bud" Lewis. To help out, Lewis asked Lester Colodny to work on the script with him. Along the way, Garroway fired Northshield from both the special and *Today*. Norman Kahn was now producer of a special that was going over its budget. Only when Garroway agreed to pay for part of the program did the project pass muster with NBC. The result was *Dave's Place*, a November 18 special framed around a lighthearted tour through the RCA Building's studios, punctuated by special features and musical numbers, as Garroway walked the halls and told stories from his twenty-three years with NBC. It would also be a throwback to the Chicago School: the format inspired by *Garroway at Large*, the title a salute to *Studs' Place*.[20]

The program began with Garroway pulling up outside the RCA Building in his Jaguar, greeting the viewer and walking toward the skating rink. Inside the building, Garroway wandered the halls of 30 Rock, showing off a videotape suite and several studios, including the studio where *Today* originated. He told stories from his years at NBC, with special emphasis on his time working in Studio 8H during the Toscanini years. Along the way, there was music from singer Julie London, and comedy from Cliff Norton, Sid Gould, Bernie West, Helen Halpin, and double-talk artist Al Kelly. The Joe Wilder Sextet and the New York Woodwind Quartet provided more music, as well as a joint performance of a new song by Alec Wilder. Some Garroway touches were in the program, too: a "motion sculpture" sequence with stainless steel rods vibrated with electricity; and a sequence with Garroway on the RCA Building's observation deck, gazing at the stars and leading into a sequence discussing the insignificance of humans against the scale of the universe. Commercials were worked inventively into the program, and one strange sequence morphed a photo of Garroway into the face of RCA chairman David Sarnoff. "We've called this *Dave's Place*, and it surely is," said Garroway. "Good night, and thank you, David."[21]

The program left reviewers torn. Harry Harris of the *Philadelphia Inquirer* felt the constant commercials from the program's many underwriters in the first half were a distraction, and that perhaps the program should have been called *Dave's Store*. "As Garroway, using the *Person to Person* amble, strolled up and down corridors of the RCA Building in New York's Rockefeller Center, reminiscing about the twenty-three years since he was first employed there as a pageboy, the ex-*Wide Wide World* host seemed reduced to serving as guide to an extremely narrow world." Another review called it "a stab at re-creating the atmosphere of the old *Garroway at Large* program" that didn't quite fly. "A closing sequence rather oversimplified the theory that man is pretty small potatoes compared to all creation. The show, though pleasant in spots, bore out this viewpoint."[22]

Dave's Place, true to its troubled creation, disappeared as soon as it was done. A decade later Lewis remembered the script as "slap-dash" and the result was "not a particularly good show." Nor, despite Garroway's hopes, did it lead to an offer from NBC.[23]

18

In January 1961, *Today* marked its ninth year with a subdued anniversary show featuring a series of drop-ins by celebrities, including comedians Jan Murray, Morey Amsterdam and Jack E. Leonard. Marie Torre saw something in the moment's downplayed nature. "Where it once crackled with spontaneity, it now moves with organized lethargy," she wrote. "Where the discussions once related to freshly-minted news, the colloquy is now restricted to one or two-day old news." Torre blamed the television industry "using and abusing videotape to a fare-thee-well, with the result that 'live' TV, the lifeblood of the industry, has diminished to an all-time low this season." A spokesman denied anything was amiss. "We're all sold out," he told her. "Ratings are good." He pointed out that *Today* was now doing its Monday shows live, but "the general reaction to this Monday show is no different from the other shows we tape." Torre concluded "that viewers, alas, have been conditioned to imperfection."[1]

Garroway himself said *Today* seemed to be in a "narrow" phase, which he blamed on "too many men in business suits, but we'll soon get out of this and on to something else." Some in the audience were getting impatient, such as a Chicago viewer who called a competing program "a refreshing relief from the trivial drivel heard on the Dave Garroway program. Let's retire Garroway; then, perhaps, the ole bird might be employed as an owl to scare away the starlings who are giving the air lines such a hard time these days."[2]

Six days after the program's anniversary, John F. Kennedy was inaugurated as president. *Today* devoted the entirety of the program to the inaugural, and Garroway took Paris and Michael to Washington for the event, showing them points of interest around the city. At the inaugural ball he stood in a group near the entrance, waiting for the new president and first lady. As they entered, Garroway reached for a small camera in his pocket. A Secret Service agent then reached for his own pocket. Garroway withdrew the camera just in time to avoid an incident.[3]

Kennedy also agreed to sit for an interview with Garroway in connection with the 150th anniversary of the University of Massachusetts General Hospital, a meeting NBC called "the first exclusive interview with a sitting president on a regularly scheduled TV program." The interview touched on a concern Kennedy and Garroway shared: mental health issues. Garroway's own concern had lasted for years, while Kennedy's sister Rosemary had been institutionalized. The interview also examined Kennedy's concern that "a steady decline" in physical fitness standards had jeopardized the nation's survival. "Our society is quite sophisticated and we are in a very dangerous period in our world history," Kennedy said. "We have unrelenting foes who are determined to destroy us," and in such perilous times, "I think we have to be fit."[4]

Inspired by the call to service for the nation's good in Kennedy's inauguration speech, Garroway challenged viewers to describe what they were doing for their country. It drew many responses. A school cafeteria director wrote that she and her staff were working to provide the best possible food they could at the lowest cost to the most students in the shortest time, "and to spread a little good cheer at the same time." A more muscular response from an Amarillo viewer suggested that Americans get involved with government at all levels, from national to local, to fight what the writer called a "psychosis of appeasement" toward the Communist world. "If people would take an active interest in their government and would rid those Reds or 'pinks' from positions of power and influence, then the government might be able to start an offensive in this war that we are losing and thereby keep America from coming under Communistic slavery."[5]

Other messages to *Today* sounded a harsher note. *South* magazine, based in Birmingham, wished Garroway "new gears for his secondhand social conscience." A columnist wanted Garroway to stick to news and features "and leave the editorializing to the later-in-the-day NBC braintrust, Huntley and Brinkley. Your weighty talks at 7 and 8 a.m. can be as unpalatable as pig's hocks and sauerkraut for breakfast."[6]

The intrigue behind the scenes of *Today* had mostly stayed out of the papers. In 1961, it broke into the open. While *Dave's Place* was in development, Shad Northshield was released from both that program and *Today*. Norman Kahn took over as acting producer, only to be replaced in March by Fred Freed. Beryl Pfizer, who served as a writer and on-air talent for

Today, counted four producers that came and went during her time with the program. There were jokes about a revolving door for producers at the show. A common refrain around NBC when *Today* hired a new producer was "When Garroway fires him, we want him."[7]

It led to awkward scenes. An NBC executive complained that while Garroway was telling someone on the show that he liked them, he would then insist the executive fire that person. Garroway would never drop the axe himself. "The first hint you got that you weren't in favor was when somebody called you in to fire you, some poor devil who had been delegated to break the news to spare Dave's feelings," a former press agent said. Beryl Pfizer, who had been given notice that she was being released from her service as a *Today* Girl, recalled a morning when RCA chairman David Sarnoff was to appear on *Today*. "Want to meet the man who fired you?" Garroway asked. As Pfizer met Sarnoff, who cheerily said he and his wife enjoyed her work on *Today*, it quickly became clear the General didn't know what had happened.[8]

It wasn't just producers. Garroway had writers, *Today* Girls, and other staffers let go, sometimes seemingly on a whim. It rattled staff members, who wondered if they could be next. Sports broadcaster Lindsey Nelson watched a *Today* Girl trying to conceal her nervousness as a piece came to a close. After the segment ended, Nelson asked the still-rattled girl what was wrong and told her not to worry if a piece ran long. "That's the luxury of doing a two-hour show," Nelson said. She replied, sweat still glistening on her brow: "If I run over, Dave will blow sky-high, and I need this job." Pfizer, in a 1984 reflection on her time working with Garroway, wrote that after several weeks of staff changes and firings, one writer said, "Well, he's finally done it. Dave fired the audience. There was no one else left!"[9]

Garroway's tendencies could create havoc in a carefully-planned program. "He would arrive in the studio at the last minute and find fault with everything," Pfizer wrote. "The scripts were bad, the props were no good, the set should be rearranged, the lighting needed fixing, the mike didn't sound right, the commercials were all wrong, and he didn't like the guest." Sometimes he rearranged segments on short notice, sending writers and producers scrambling. Other times, he threw out carefully-written questions to follow his own paths, as when he asked Vivien Leigh, "If you lost all your hair, would you wear a wig?" ("I could have died!" Pfizer remembered.)[10]

How could Garroway get away with it? Pfizer felt the fault was NBC's as much as Garroway's, for it had given him so much control over the program. When Garroway was unhappy with the program, or even with his own performance, she believed he took it out on the staff. A network executive felt it was Garroway's personality. "There was never any question of his brilliance," he said. "But nobody could get close to him. The minute you tried, a door closed. He drove me crazy in more than one way." Still, the executive felt for Garroway: "There were such depths of feeling and affection that I felt he was afraid to explore." Longtime associate Ted Mills saw this after he and Garroway got at cross-purposes. It haunted Garroway for years. One evening on a dinner date with Mills' ex-wife, he confessed that the loss of Mills' friendship grieved him, so overcome by tears they had to leave the restaurant. Beryl Pfizer felt a strange sympathy for Garroway. "I felt like he was a little boy who had come from Chicago and was overwhelmed by New York and Rockefeller Center. There was so much pressure on him."[11]

Bud Lewis saw insecurity. "He liked people to think him really deep," he said. Instead, Lewis felt Garroway had "a paper-thin mind" that could ask only about three questions on any given subject. "He wanted to be thought clever, when as a matter of fact he couldn't even manage a joke." Lewis believed this happened because Garroway had become a star in the early days of television, when fame could be found just by doing something different. "Dave didn't know what he had," Lewis said, and couldn't see what others found fascinating about him. Since he had clever people to supply him with material, Lewis felt Garroway became dependent on them, to the point he didn't feel comfortable going to the White House to accept an award from President Kennedy without having Lewis type up a few comments that Garroway could ad-lib. When the presentation happened, Garroway exchanged a handshake and a very brief chat with the President, and the ceremony was over.

At other times, Garroway's tendencies disturbed Lewis. At the theater with his wife one evening, Lewis received an urgent message from an usher. Garroway wanted him immediately. Lewis phoned him. Couldn't this wait until after the theatre? "If you don't come right now, I'll jump out the window," Garroway replied. To his wife's consternation, Lewis went to see Garroway, only to find the matter was "absolutely trivial."[12]

Jack Lescoulie maintained that his relationship with Garroway was strong. "I can tell you this," he said in 1960. "I've worked with him for eight solid years, and I've never had a cross word with him. When you work with a guy at the hours we did and get along with him that well – in show business – you gotta know that the guy lives up to his signature, which is always 'peace.'" Frank Blair, though, cited Garroway as a reason why he was happy not to have all the pressures of being a host. "Over the years, I watched Dave Garroway change until he became a haunted man," he said in 1962.[13]

What redeemed Garroway, Pfizer wrote, was that "he was better at being on television than anyone I ever saw in a studio. The minute the camera's red light went on, he seemed to be able to turn a switch inside himself, brush aside the chaos he had created and become the Garroway everybody knew and watched on the screen." This was the Garroway that prompted Lescoulie, watching Garroway talk with Perry Como one morning, to observe, "Watching you two guys together, I can't help but think what a wonderful spot this would be for a sleeping pill commercial."[14]

The show he was on remained vital. "Night no longer extends from dusk to dawn," one observer wrote. "It is that interval between Jack Paar and Dave Garroway when one escapes from television." Columnist Cecil Smith wrote of a fourteen-year-old friend who watched Garroway each morning. "I can't imagine anyone doing better whether fourteen or forty-one." Praising the show's easy manner and solid content, Smith said, "I can think of nothing better that would prepare a young or old mind for the day."[15]

For as much as Garroway's control over the program could bring chaos, it could also provide opportunity. He had learned about a young performer and writer named Oscar Brown Jr., who had distilled his thoughts about people who prey on others "just for kicks" into a musical called *Kicks & Co.* Garroway had Brown and dancer Zabethe Wilde perform a number from the show on *Today*. The positive reviews and tremendous mail response prompted Garroway, who knew the show needed funds to cover its $400,000 budget, to turn over the entire March 28 edition of *Today* to an on-air audition before 4.7 million viewers. Contributions flooded in: $5,000 from a Colorado military officer and his wife; a $1,000 gift from Miami; a five dollar check from an Indiana music teacher; even a $5,000 donation from a couple who had planned to buy a house but decided to invest in the show. The on-air audition helped put *Kicks & Co.* over the top. Garroway told Brown at the end of the telecast, "I have only one request to make: a ticket to the closing performance, because I want to be sure to live a long life."[16]

During her time on *Today* Beryl Pfizer kept daily notes about the man known by some on the staff as "Big Spooky." Some things she chronicled were goofy, such as the time he insisted that six of his teeth had fallen out and he had put them back into place with tooth glue… and then showed her a can labeled "tooth glue." Some were bizarre, such as his story that he rented a car in Mexico, saw tire tracks on the roof, and concluded an airplane had bounced off. Some were gross, like the day he dipped a comb in his tea, ran it through his hair, then sipped the tea.

Other observations signaled deeper issues. She wrote about him hoarding things that had been featured on the show: a toy car game, an enlargement of the Declaration of Independence done for a set piece, a hoarding tendency so pronounced that comic Jack E. Leonard asked why Garroway didn't take home the ashtrays as well. Paranoia crept in: Garroway's obsession with his bomb shelter; the installation of microphones in the gargoyles in front of his townhouse, so he could listen to people planning to break in. He was convinced that his outspokenness against communism guaranteed he would be one of the first to be liquidated in a Soviet invasion of America.[17]

Others reported strange occurrences when they were with Garroway. One Sunday night, hosting *Monitor*, Garroway insisted that a folding screen be put up so passersby couldn't see him through the large windows that let observers look into Radio Central. On a few occasions, including at least one lunch with an NBC executive, Garroway insisted that mysterious forces had turned his undershorts backwards. So many things – the hoarding, the paranoia, the reports of inexplicable phenomena – were signs that amphetamine psychosis, from years of The Doctor, were affecting his sense of reality.

It wasn't just NBC people who noticed. Mike Cook, who dealt in exotic cars, did some work on a sports car that Garroway received in return for an endorsement. Garroway invited Cook to go with him on a test drive. As they drove, he not only told Cook that he was disappointed in the car, but said he had a private investigator follow his assistant through Europe when she picked up the car from the factory. "As the sun set and the streets darkened," Cook remembered, "Dave's ramblings became like chapters in a Stephen King fantasy." After the test drive, "I never heard from him again, nor did he ever pay the bill for the mods to the Herald."[18]

Underneath Garroway's outward serenity was a deep unhappiness. Lindsey Nelson, doing a guest spot on *Today* one morning, noticed tears streaming down Garroway's face during a commercial break. "I've got to quit crying on the show," he told Nelson. "People can't understand what I'm saying." Every once in a while, the mask slipped on the air. A discussion on communism with a delegate from a Communist-controlled country turned into a strange argument with the man, completely unlike the placid Garroway style. Garroway justified it as the kind of "speaking up" that all anti-Communists should do, but at least one viewer was disturbed by its "disjointed" nature.[19]

A year before, Garroway put together a list of personal "assets and liabilities." He noted his "health, good" and "career, successful," including the high ratings and $11 million in billings *Today* was bringing in; his excellent reputation among viewers, advertisers, and public officials; the thirty-one awards he and the program had won. "Personal outlook – growing awareness of the fantastic time in which I lived, and some deep satisfaction that I seemed able to make some small share in making others aware of the urgency of the times – of the need to distinguish reality from fantasy, to show some of the techniques used by certain groups to distort & confuse reality. No one ever had a job more satisfying to himself, nor looked forward more to each day's work than Dave Garroway did, from 1952 to the fall of 1960."

In the other column he listed foremost the "diminishing" health of Pamela ("extensive therapy, diagnosis uncertain") and his shortage of time ("both my family and *Today* began to need more time for proper maintenance and added responsibilities"). Those responsibilities, he felt, were straining relations with those he worked with. He lamented an "increasing failure to communicate with top NBC management" and with his agent, accountant, his business manager, his own employees, and some staffers on the program. This, he wrote, led to "failure to understand the nature of business ethics and practice in my industry in corporate structure and policy, the handling of money, income tax theory and practice and effective supervision of personnel in my employ – and associates."[20]

19

To the public the Garroways' lives seemed ideal. In 1960 a *Ladies' Home Journal* writer portrayed a busy but happy couple whose only tribulation after four years of marriage was, in Dave's words, "we don't have much time together." With a townhouse in Manhattan and a Long Island beach house; with the arrival of Dave Jr., the finalized adoption of Michael, and Paris coming east to be nearby; with Pamela enrolled in pre-med courses at Columbia University, hoping to specialize in adolescent psychiatry; and with a long-haired dachshund named Joey, all seemed blissful. "My happiest time of the day is the cozy married-feeling hour I spend in the kitchen while David sits in the living room reading his evening paper," Pamela said. "If I could use one word for Dave, it would be 'wise.' His heart is wise."[1]

Garroway portrayed the part of a wise father, urging parents to let their children march to their own drummers. A 1960 article under his byline noted that although eleven-year-old Michael had no interest in his dad's automotive hobby, he "plays football and fences with the gusto of a private taking off on a weekend pass," tinkered in the shop building clocks and radio sets, and built model kits. "He is constantly fashioning new inventions that make me chase after him to find out how he did it." Although Dave Jr. was only two, he had found his own corner of the shop "but, being a properly independent Garroway, David Jr. never lets us know just what it is he's building." While sixteen-year-old Paris enjoyed painting and music, Garroway bragged that he had changed her musical tastes. "At one time, she was a Rock 'n' Roll fiend. I hid my chagrin and let her go her own way. I made sure, however, that plenty of good jazz and classical music was played around the house. In her own good time, Paris found she got more pleasure from good music than bad, and used her Rock 'n' Roll records to line the garbage can."[2]

Reality was different, and Charlie Andrews knew there was a mismatch. "Garroway should have married a milkmaid and she a dentist,"

Pamela speaks with Dave before he heads off in the Jaguar. (Paris Day collection)

he said years later. "Instead, they found each other." Garroway knew his own troubled history with relationships; after a couple of years with a woman, he withdrew, perhaps due to his emotional issues, and lost his fondness for her. His marriage with Pamela not only involved his own issues, but hers as well. Years later, Garroway criticized himself for marrying her. "When I think of how stupid I was to marry my second wife, after a few moments laughter overcomes me and I slump at the typewriter."[3]

It was all falling apart. Dave was overworked, under stress, staying up too late and getting too little sleep, his Dexedrine addiction eating into his mental and physical health. In Pamela, he saw issues. How many were genuine, how many reflected sour grapes, and how many were the result of Dave's drug-induced paranoia will never truly be known, but in his unpublished memoir Garroway claimed she alternated between being "the maddest, most withdrawn" and "the most calculating, violent, shrewd, normal-looking at times." The "mad" and "withdrawn" side of her personality, he wrote, was planning to divorce him, take their children, and move back to France. The "calculating" side, he felt, set out to do it.[4]

Garroway arranged for her to see a prominent Manhattan psychiatrist, Dr. Henry Horn. Getting her to go, he wrote, was its own challenge. "You couldn't have dragged her to a psychiatrist's office with a team of horses," he claimed. Sometimes, "she would agree to go but never arrive at his office." Garroway also learned that if he called the doctor to ask if there was anything he could do to help, the doctor was required to inform her of the call, "whereupon almost invariably the patient misinterprets that call, and quits."[5]

By early 1961, the marriage was effectively over. Garroway claimed months later that Pamela had told friends she was going to leave, but dropped her plans when told she had no grounds for divorce. Instead, he insisted, she "intended to destroy me unless she got what she wanted," and would do so through his money and his children. He charged that she had been plowing through his money, that she had boasted before leaving on a vacation that she intended to be unfaithful while on the trip. Garroway hired attorneys and private investigators, who could find no evidence of infidelity that would hold up in court.[6]

As it became clear the marriage was done, Garroway got his personal attorney to work on a proposed settlement for Pamela. Garroway later wrote that as the attorney met with Pamela, "I saw a most peculiar look on his face." When they talked privately after the meeting, the lawyer shook his head: she wanted, Garroway remembered, "more than you have, plus more than you're making." The Garroways, estranged, spent more time apart. Garroway avoided the townhouse, spending more time at the Westhampton Beach house, often taking Dave Jr. along with him.[7]

On April 25, the phone rang in the FBI's New York office. A famous voice on the other end asked to speak to a special agent at once "about a communist conspiracy." That afternoon an agent drove to Westhampton Beach. For hours Garroway detailed a series of attacks and circumstances that led him to conclude "there is a Communist conspiracy to destroy him," although he just as quickly told the agent that the Communist angle was only a possibility, and that he felt he should notify the FBI so it might be on the record. The agent noted that Garroway acknowledged the information wasn't specific enough to warrant investigating his claims, and that he knew his situation "appears to have developed out of domestic and business problems that only he can solve."[8]

Inevitably, his troubled marriage entered the picture. Garroway told dark tales of Pamela's first husband, claimed Pamela was associated with Communist cells in Paris and had been involved in "marijuana raids" there. He outlined his suspicions about her patriotism and her private life. He claimed that two weeks after they married, her personality turned. He said he had tried to get her psychological help, but was unable to find out how she was doing since she had threatened to bring the doctor up on charges if he told her husband anything.

It didn't stop with Pamela. Garroway said the domestic help she hired for the house seemed disturbing, with one of them being "highly neurotic and uncivil" and "making an occasional pass at him." Furthermore, Garroway claimed that a woman who had been an assistant for him at NBC had "an odd relationship" with his wife, that he had a private detective investigate her, and that she "is in league with his wife."

The FBI agent returned to the office and transcribed his notes into a document for the record. There was no follow-up.[9]

Late on the night of Thursday, April 27, as Garroway and son dozed in the beach house, Pamela placed a phone call to Dr. Horn at his home number. She sounded distressed and nervous. After she hung up, Horn called back. The housekeeper answered. "Go check and see how Mrs. Garroway is," he said. "I'm worried. She just called me and she was upset." The housekeeper hurried toward the bedroom. Paris, awakened by the commotion, joined her. In the bathroom, they found Pamela, in her night clothes, slumped on the floor, unresponsive. The housekeeper felt for a pulse but couldn't detect one. She tried calling Dr. Horn, but he had already left to come over to check on Pamela. After Horn arrived, the police were called. Detectives found large quantities of medications in the bathroom, but all were reported intact.[10]

On Friday morning, *Today* viewers heard Frank Blair deliver a grim announcement at the top of the newscast. "It is with deep regret that we announce the death Friday of Pamela Garroway, wife of Dave Garroway. She was found dead of unknown causes in the couple's midtown home." The remainder of the show, with Paul Cunningham filling in for Garroway alongside Lescoulie and Beryl Pfizer, had been taped the day before, isolated from the overnight tragedy that now bookended each segment.[11]

Garroway, notified by phone of his wife's death, hurried with Dave Jr. back to Manhattan. His attorney took Paris and Michael to a hotel while detectives investigated.[12]

After an autopsy, the medical examiner stated Pamela had likely died from an overdose of barbiturates. Garroway disputed this, saying that those who blamed the overdose "are on very delicate ground. She was very sick," he told an interviewer two months later. "We were trying to get better medicines for her even when it happened." He believed she could have gotten her medications mixed up. In the things he couldn't explain, he saw shades of the sinister. "There were so many...things," he said. The "hysterical" phone call to Dr. Horn concerned him. He also pinned some blame on a watchman he hired after a kidnapping threat. "I asked him afterwards, 'Didn't you hear her call the doctor?' And what did he say? 'No,' he said. 'I had the TV set turned on too loud.'"[13]

Dr. Horn told reporters that Pamela had been distressed by the divorce proceedings, and that marital trouble had been a factor in her recent hospitalization. Months later, a reporter asked Garroway: had his schedule been a factor in her death? "No," he said, holding back anger. "Pamela was sick, quite sick, for two years before she died. The show was not responsible in any way. I was available to her any time she wanted to see me." There was a pause. "So I carry no guilt." Another pause, a shake of the head. "But all this is painful and irrelevant. Because she's gone...."[14]

Garroway took more time off to see after family business. John Charles Daly, the gentlemanly moderator of the panel show *What's My Line?*, substituted as host. Garroway finally returned May 15, briefly pausing to thanking viewers for the thousands of messages he had received after Pamela's death.[15]

He plunged himself into the goings-on of the moment, drawing fire for interviewing civil rights activist James Peck, who had been involved in the Freedom Riders movement. After Garroway called Peck "a hero," the *Jackson Clarion-Ledger* cited an anti-Peck dossier compiled by Senator James Eastland to charge, "TV's Dave Garroway and other South-slappers have odd notions of 'courage.' We are moved to wonder if the old saying about birds of a feather has any possible application with regard to the beautiful friendship apparently existing between Garroway and Peck." Another writer called him a "foremost South-baiter." The *Shreveport Times* shredded Garroway and NBC for not mentioning Peck's record of arrests and allegations of aiding Communist causes: "If they wished to present Peck despite his criminal and anti-American background, that was their privilege. But that criminal and anti-American background should have been made known so that viewers could consider it in evaluating Peck." A Shreveport viewer wrote a bigoted letter that included a boycott of *Today*: "I will never turn it on again or listen to your drivel again or that of the other Rat Pack admirers such as John Daly, Ed Sullivan and Ed Murrow. It is evident from the general tenor of all your programs, the subject matter and guests used, that you hate the South. I hate you and all the others who keep slapping me in the face every opportunity you find." Another Shreveport viewer wrote, "*Captain Kangaroo* is much more educational and entertaining than Garroway."[16]

Garroway was reaching a breaking point, and more than ever, the prospect of a *Today* without Garroway seemed real – to him, to NBC, and to viewers. He complained that his life had become a tunnel between the house and the studio. He was tired, he explained to *TV Guide* writer Richard Gehman, over a drink in Garroway's townhome. "I'll soon be fifty," Garroway said. He felt his attitudes had "standardized themselves into about twenty-five different cliches. I'm tired of them and everybody else must be." He hoped to travel and get new ideas ("I've got to do more listening"). Gehman knew, however, that Garroway differed with NBC on the direction of the program.[17]

It was nothing new. Gehman noted there were tensions between Garroway and NBC that went back at least two years. Garroway, according to "reliable sources," had balked at the network's directive to emphasize entertainment. At the same time, Garroway worried that NBC News wanted to take over *Today*, had Robert Kintner's blessing to do so, and knew the division would install its own personnel as hosts. If Garroway stayed, it would be to play whatever role he was allowed. "They wanted somebody to stand on a platform and shout the news," he said in 1977. Years later, Dave Jr. said, "They just wanted him to be a talking head and read the news and nothing more."[18]

Garroway claimed that Kintner's pressure campaign had been going on for some time, and that he had tried to influence the selection of guests and wanted more Republicans scheduled on the program. Garroway wrote that the final straw, in his view, came on the January 13 program, marking *Today*'s ninth anniversary. An engineering slip-up routed a congratulatory phone call from President-elect John F. Kennedy to Garroway's home instead of NBC, and on the show Garroway mentioned Kennedy calling him at home. According to Garroway, Kintner interpreted it as a personal call instead of an official NBC call, and the host claimed Kintner told a Chicago reporter that Garroway "won't be around here too long anyway."[19]

After that, Garroway said, things changed. His office was moved from a two-room suite to a succession of smaller rooms. His two telephone lines were cut to one, which he had to share with his secretary. The program's budget was cut. Major Dumas, who had served coffee and pastries to the crew and guests since that first morning, was let go. "They did all kinds of things, like taking all the telephones off my desk and making it unbearable to function," he told a reporter in 1971. Dave Jr. claimed, "He wasn't officially fired, but they did everything they could to make him feel unwelcome." In 1975, when a reporter asked why he had to leave *Today*, Garroway complimented the reporter on being the first to ask the right question. "Maybe I can talk about it after two or three people have died," he said.[20]

In Garroway's final weeks on *Today*, Richard Gehman watched a rehearsal in Studio 3B, Garroway with coat off and open collar, reviewing material with a hum of activity around him. He paused only when an assistant brought Dave Jr. in for a visit, the first time Garroway had seen his son in several weeks. Only a few seconds later, he had to take a phone call. Gehman watched Garroway play with a large set of keys with his free hand. "He obviously was tense, holding himself inside the Dave Garroway shell with an immense effort," Gehman wrote. Yet a few minutes later, Garroway sat down at his desk, his coat and tie straight, and on cue looked into the camera as the relaxed and breezy Dave Garroway his viewers loved. "How he's been able to do this for damned near ten years, I'll never tell you," Freed said to Gehman.[21]

Cecil Smith, arriving in a cab at Rockefeller Center on a sunlit morning, saw another scene. The cab driver pointed out a big man, well-dressed, standing on the corner, staring down "with a face that was wreathed in agony, in utter despair." The cabbie said, "You ever see a sad millionaire? That's Dave Garroway." To see the man who made "peace" his trademark, Smith wrote, "as a figure of despair was devastating."[22]

Late on the evening of May 24, Garroway met with his business attorney. After hearing Garroway out and reviewing his contracts, the attorney assured him he could extract Garroway from his contracts with NBC. The next day they composed resignation letters, which were hand-delivered to General Sarnoff, NBC chairman Robert Sarnoff, and Robert Kintner late on the afternoon of Friday, May 26.

In his letter to Kintner, Garroway stated that he was leaving *Today* "for the reasons that my duties on that program are too burdensome to permit my continuing it." Although he was prepared to stay on through the end of his contract on October 31 or until NBC could find a replacement for him, he requested to be released as soon as possible. Garroway stated that he left "with a real sense of regret," and thanked Kintner and NBC for "a unique privilege in being associated with the *Today* program." He stated that neither Kintner nor NBC had tried to censor or restrain his freedom of expression. "This is a privilege and a trust which I will always appreciate and which I hope to make clear in any announcement or statement I may make to explain the reasons for my leaving the program." He hoped to be back. "I am in no sense retiring, just taking a breather and a look around. I feel there is no more important kind of program in the future of television than *Today* and I hope that we will be again operating in this area in the future after this rest."[23]

That evening, Garroway's PR representative sent out a press release. In it Garroway stated that he was terminating his association with *Today* effective October 31 "or before, should we agree to an earlier date." He expressed great regret for leaving, but the grind of working on *Today* for twelve to eighteen hours a day had left him with no time "to stop and do some listening. I want to start looking, thinking and listening to people. If I am to help to make the people who choose to listen to me aware of the facts, good and bad; and the beauties, great and tiny; of the exciting and explosive world we live in, I must become wiser myself." He mentioned the books on his shelves, unread; the telescope and microscope that taught him "more about children, flowers, poems, beauty, truth and life and death from these things than any others." He mentioned that he must be "the best father I can be to three beautiful and exciting children, during a critical period in their lives. Our family needs each other now more than ever." He thanked NBC and its executives, and the *Today* staff, for their assistance over the years. He thanked the *Today* audience for its devotion. He closed with a hope that "this interruption" would help him better prepare "to make what contribution I can to – Peace." Garroway and his attorney also prepared letters to send to *Today* clients to explain Garroway's departure the following week. "In each of these I made no accusations or implications of trouble," Garroway remembered, "but gave other and plausible sounding reasons, so as not to embarrass NBC and to make it possible to eventually return, should management change."[24]

While the wire services ran with the story, there was another issue. Both Kintner and the junior Sarnoff were in Canada on a fishing trip over the Memorial Day weekend. Neither Sarnoff nor Kintner formally replied to Garroway. However, the network's vice president for talent negotiations, James Stabile, paid Garroway a visit. During the meeting, Stabile asked Garroway what he really wanted. Garroway felt "a chill in the air." He told Stabile what he sought: "a clean break of the entire NBC relationship except of course for the payment of deferred income. He quickly agreed and without question said he believed it could be done." Garroway notified his attorney, who promised to work things out with NBC. Since Garroway had said he was willing to abide by a contract that demanded his services on *Today* until the end of October, he asked to be released from the show as soon as possible, and also requested he be allowed to take the two weeks of vacation called for in his contract.[25]

On June 12 Garroway's attorney showed up at the office, saying he was about to make a deal "immediately" with Stabile. Garroway repeated his desire "for a clean break with NBC except for the deferred payments." The attorney said he understood. A couple hours later, the attorney came back "with a document and a smile." The document, he said, was just what Garroway wanted. "Sign it and you're out." Trusting his attorney, and relieved to get away from NBC, Garroway signed the document and gave it back. The attorney took all the copies with him.[26]

In his correspondence both to NBC executives and inquiring viewers, Garroway tried to make his departure from *Today* seem like only a temporary pause. "I have left you for a while, but only for a while," a form letter to concerned viewers read. "I have, despite the press reports, in no sense 'retired' but simply am taking time out to take a kind of mental shower bath." He had made similar pledges to NBC's executives and in a public release.[27]

Regardless, it was difficult news for many. "Dave Garroway's announced resignation from NBC-TV's *Today* show will no doubt sadden a great many viewers," one columnist wrote. "He is a sincere, believable man, who has made a good many friends through the *Today* show in his ten years as its host." Cecil Smith wrote, "While certainly everyone must view with sympathy Garroway's decision to leave his show after nine years – particularly, after the tragic death of his wife – still, he will be sorely missed. He adds an extraordinary element of dignity and stature to the show, even in aimless chitchat and in the peddling of preposterous products. He has warmth and friendliness and an aura of great integrity – qualities not easy to come by in the TV rat race." Fred Remington wrote, "It's hard to think of any other individual television could as ill afford to spare as Garroway. In a medium not noted for an extravagant estimate of audiences' mentality, he paid his audiences the compliment of presuming they could be interested in the things he is interested in. His interests are profound and wide-ranging, and he had the gift of communicating them in a simple, unpretentious, ungimmicky way. There aren't too many like him on TV."[28]

Garroway's foes in the South saw it as a triumph. The departure of "TV Communistator Dave Garroway," wrote one, "will cause no tears to drop in Dixie." Another speculated that pressure from Southern audiences had prompted *Today* "to lose its bigoted star." Some feigned sympathy: "Of course we know of the terrible tragedy in his family and we offer our deepest sympathy," went a Mississippi column, "but we believe that his leaving the air lanes will be one of the greatest aid the South could have had, by his absence. A letter in another Mississippi paper chortled that "poor Dave is leaving in a state of rubber-band limpness, with the whole log on his shoulder, not just a chip – why? Because he knows that he has utterly, hopelessly, dastardly, completely, cowardly, and shamefully failed in the attempt to perpetrate the one desire to cause violence in Mississippi."[29]

The most poignant reactions came from those who knew him best, those who worked with him on *Today*. Lou Bradley "could just feel something ominous" when Garroway asked him into his dressing room. "I wanted to tell him 'you shouldn't do this thing,'" Bradley said. "I felt it meant total devastation."[30]

Garroway's final week was a sentimental one, and in a way it brought his NBC career full circle. While work was being done on Studio 3B, *Today* had temporarily made a home in Studio 8H. As a young NBC guide assigned to 8H a quarter-century before, Garroway had witnessed the artistry of Arturo Toscanini and the comedy of Fred Allen. One day that final week, he donned his old page jacket and took viewers on a televised tour of the studio, telling of historic broadcasts and interesting moments from the studio's decades.[31]

On the June 16 broadcast came his leave-taking. After a recorded report concluded, the final two minutes gave Garroway time for a quick, subdued farewell that he insisted wasn't a farewell. "I'm leaving television very temporarily," he said, "for enough time to find out what's going on, listen to people instead of talk. When you talk a lot, you don't hear much, you know, and you don't read much either when you do the *Today* show." Garroway expressed his desire to learn more about the world so he could come back through television "and do more to preserve that in which I hope you and I believe, this system of government, and the human individual." He thanked viewers for all the letters they had sent and promised to respond to each of them. One final time, Garroway wished the audience "much love...and peace." As "Sentimental Journey" came up behind, he raised his right hand in the familiar gesture. After a few seconds, the picture dissolved to a promotional slide for NBC's coverage of an auto race that weekend.[32]

It was over. Garroway later said walking "slowly and regretfully" from the studio after that segment was a memory that would always stand out. Cynthia Lowry wrote that Garroway "made a sentimental adieu to the *Today* show audience on Friday and almost broke down in tears while doing it." Robert Lewis Shayon wondered if, while Garroway left to seek wisdom, his spirit would remain on *Today*. "To interrupt a successful career for such a quest is an act of integrity. One hopes the medium will do a bit of questing of its own while he takes his hard-earned sabbatical. Yes or no, with or without added wisdom, television will need 'Dave Garroway Tomorrow.'"[33]

Garroway wasn't the only one leaving. Jack Lescoulie, tired of the early-morning schedule and wary of the format change, also quit, soon to co-star in an educational program for children. "For seven years I got up in the dark and touched my feet against the cold of the bedroom floor. Then for a year and a half, the program was taped a day earlier and I began seeing some friends and leading a normal life again." When the show went back to all-live and emphasis switched to live news, "I quit. It was too early. It's that simple." He denied rumors that he was angry at NBC for passing him over as Garroway's replacement. "I love to support," he said. "The guy in charge is the one who gets all the blame if ratings drop or anything goes wrong."[34]

Several names had been discussed as possible Garroway replacements. For a while John Charles Daly, Garroway's recent substitute, was the leading candidate. NBC balked when Daly insisted on naming his own staff and having input on subject matter, the same conditions that led to friction with Garroway. Other prospects included Arlene Francis, as part of a male-female co-hosting team, and Garry Moore, who opted out because he didn't like the early hours.[35]

Instead, NBC looked within its news division, giving weeklong on-air auditions to Edwin Newman, Ray Scherer and Sander Vanocur. The job finally went to John Chancellor, whose NBC career had started in Chicago. Throughout the 1950s Chancellor had built a reputation as a serious correspondent, covering politics and civil rights. He exemplified the harder-news approach NBC sought in the restyled *Today* program. Reluctant to take the job, turned off by the early-morning schedule, Chancellor finally accepted when NBC offered him too much money to pass up. He had first met Garroway in Chicago in 1950. "Everybody knew who he was, and when I'd see him in a corridor I'd say, 'Hello, Dave.' And he said, 'Er...hello, fella.'" The new host admitted he hadn't really watched *Today* in five years. "I like Dave," he said, "but after all, he was of a different generation and he had a different style."[36]

The new era began July 17 with Chancellor as host, Frank Blair taking over Lescoulie's old role of sidekick and announcer, and Edwin Newman as the newscaster. Garroway was present for the handoff, calling Chancellor "the best possible choice" in "this most important time of informing the nation." He asked viewers not to compare Chancellor to him: "It doesn't give John a chance to be himself and do the fresh new things he plans to do. Please forget what has happened up here." Then he smiled at Chancellor. "Good luck, buddy. Make it *your* show."[37]

To viewers, the difference in the new *Today* was jarring. Pittsburgh columnist Fred Remington praised the potential Chancellor brought, but lamented the loss of Garroway and Lescoulie. The program had "a strange and lonely look" that brought to mind "a new family in a house long occupied by familiar and highly regarded neighbors." Another wrote the show had "too many chiefs and not enough for Chancellor to say or do," and believed the older format, with Garroway a strong master of ceremonies, worked better. A viewer wrote, "We are very disappointed in the *Today* show since Dave Garroway left. John Chancellor seems like a good fellow and must have a fine news background but the show is too repetitious." Marie Torre saw promise in Chancellor, but felt *Today* was "now almost all news, and deadly serious, and one dimensional," and even the musical interludes seemed downbeat. One staff member at a television station joked that Chancellor, with his hard-news background, raised up his hand and said "War!"[38]

The style Garroway had perfected for *Today* had become what the public expected. Instead, Chancellor's *Today* was, as one author called it, "the evening news in the morning." Blair's personality was ill-suited for Lescoulie's old role of sidekick and announcer. Chancellor's refusal to do commercials also irritated NBC. Some critics, such as Cecil Smith, saw potential: "This show is not the *Today* that used to be. But in its new guise, it is as expert a two hours as television offers us these days." For others, the new formula didn't work. "Now *Today* is just another cut and dried program, run by the news department," one columnist wrote. "One thing you can always say for television executives – if they have a good thing, they sure don't mind ruining it." Others mourned the loss of people who felt like old friends, Garroway and Lescoulie: "We had our breakfast with these two gentlemen for the past ten years and enjoyed every minute of it. The program is still on, but just doesn't seem the same without our pals." Lou Bradley, who had worked alongside Garroway, felt him irreplaceable. "Nothing for me was ever the same after he left. No other talent that has ever done that show has ever come up to him."[39]

With Pamela's passing, Garroway had hired a housekeeper to look after Dave Jr. One was a German woman. Dave Jr. remembered his dad telling him she had worked as a secretary for a Nazi during World War II. One day, convinced she was going to kidnap Dave Jr., Garroway called the airport reservation desk and learned of a reservation, in her name, for one adult and one infant to fly to Germany that night. It turned out the reservation was for someone else with her last name. Suspicious nonetheless, Garroway let her go a couple of days later. "He felt like he had to dress like an SS commander to get through to her," Dave Jr. said. "He wore a black cap and a black leather coat and ordered her never to see me again. He did this because he was still worried about her becoming too attached to me. He said, 'This was cruel, but I felt it had to be done.'"[40]

After she was dismissed, Garroway hired other housekeepers to look after little Dave. "Most were cool, and some were mean, but they all cleaned up after me, cooked for me, and generally spoiled me," Dave Jr. remembered. When he got out on his own, he found he didn't really know how to look after things for himself after years of having others do it for him, and it caused problems with roommates and with women. "I have made progress over the years," he said, "but still suffer from this syndrome. I'm considering starting a support group for people with Housekeeper Syndrome."[41]

To reporters, Garroway talked of his need to spend more time with the children, to make sure they grew up with the emotional support they needed. It included a spiritual angle. Even though Garroway professed strong personal beliefs, but not an organized religion ("It's a more mystical thing than that"), he planned to raise the children in a formal religion for a while, "and then at some time I'll take over and tell them what I think and feel. Children need a church. It gives a certain solid background that parents cannot instill properly."[42]

He put more time into the issues that concerned him. NBC, he maintained, had only told him once – during the Charles Van Doren affair – not to discuss a topic, and even then just for twenty-four hours. Being free from NBC, however, allowed him to speak more openly. In late June, Garroway testified at a high-profile FCC hearing about program procurement and practices. He was on the docket alongside not only producers Worthington Miner, David Susskind, Mark Goodson and Bill Todman, but producer-entertainers including Ed Sullivan and Perry Como. A New York University professor, scheduled to testify between Garroway and Como, couldn't believe it: "What am I supposed to be, the lettuce between the ham and the mayonnaise?"[43]

Before the commission, Garroway expressed concern that television was being pulled in divergent directions by its various interests: the viewer, the network, the station, the sponsor, and the stockholder. These competing interests had left television "internally tortured by built-in conflict." At the same time, television had to adhere to vaguely-articulated government mandates to serve the public interest. "Congress has never clearly stated who's in charge and what is the purpose of the medium," he charged. "While other competitive media are not regulated, TV functions under regulation. Yet, to the stockholder, it is in the arena of free enterprise competition." He wondered, perhaps rhetorically, why the FCC regulated radio and television, but not other forms of media. "Difficulty occurs because non-regulated media which also depend on advertising for principal revenue rightly consider TV a potent economic enemy," he said. "If TV is to continue without federal subsidy, should it not be placed in a competition with the other media?" Garroway also expressed concern about violence in filmed television programs, "not only for my own three children but for those of others," and spoke of a timer he had installed on his set to ration his children's viewing. Garroway felt one or more broadcast industry officials needed to show some leadership to help solve the problem.[44]

The critics pounced. In particular, newspaper editorials couldn't wait to puncture Garroway's logic. The *Mason City Globe-Gazette* reminded Garroway that since broadcast media relied on limited broadcast spectrum allocation and thus required licensing, the government had an interest in making sure it was used for the public good; meanwhile, other forms of media were open to anyone and didn't need that kind of regulation. "That shouldn't be difficult for as alert a mind as Dave Garroway to comprehend." An Oregon editorial questioned the wisdom of testimony by Garroway, Moore, Como and Sullivan, comparing it to "launching an investigation of delinquency by grilling the local choir boys," and suggested "the FCC is searching more for headline than information."[45]

Garroway continued to worry about the Soviet Union and civil defense. He accused most Americans of "putting their heads in the sand" about the possibility of nuclear war, and spoke again about his well-equipped fallout shelter. He hoped war could be avoided. "My predictions are more hopeful than scientific. I trust we'll never have to use our fallout shelter. I trust we can, with a strong leadership, get at least a working stalemate with the Russians. I don't think we can change Communism, but it has the seeds of self-decay in it. All we need is time, and that's where you can't predict. Time is what we don't have much of." To Val Adams he said, "What I'm most interested in is alerting people to where we stand and how short the fuse is. I feel guilty about not doing anything." His fight against Communism turned into action when, at the suggestion of Attorney General Robert Kennedy, he met with United States Information Agency director Edward R. Murrow and discussed how Garroway could assist the agency in getting some USIA presentations shown on American networks, and how to get some American programs available so USIA could show them overseas. Garroway said that in spite of forty job offers he had, he wanted to help Murrow. "That's a job that needs to be done."[46]

In his own life, he began to share more of what was on his mind. He explained his need to leave *Today* (his children, he said, "need me, and I need to reassess myself") and his lack of a circle of intimates to help bear the burdens ("it takes much time and effort to love somebody"). He talked of being a night person ("always have been," he said) and told of staying up all night once or twice a week, of anonymously walking streets early in the morning and watching the handful of people out and about at that hour. But he brushed off reports that he was a "tormented" man. He said he felt "no burden of guilt" over Pamela's passing, but felt his main responsibility was to see to his children's well-being. He spoke of taking Michael on tours of prep schools and his acceptance to Choate, which "did a lot for his self-confidence"; of feeling an even deeper love for his children than before ("the magnitude of love has no limits"); of spending time with people he found interesting and stimulating; even that "I see the sky more clearly now. I've actually gone to the park and looked at trees. I've met trees again. I hadn't really looked at one in years."[47]

He still wanted to return to commercial television. Careful not to burn bridges with NBC, he attributed his departure to nothing more than exhaustion. "The work load became so great that I didn't have time to prepare things I said. And the load was getting heavier and heavier. I was having to do more and more jobs myself, with less help. But NBC was good. They never told me what to say or what not to say. I don't want to say anything about NBC that would be misconstrued. I may go back to work there." Or somewhere else; he claimed firm offers from two networks, but that on his next project "I will insist on creative control. That's one lesson one learns the hard way. The areas I want to concern myself with are truth and reality. Too much of television is fantasy these days."[48]

He expressed optimism that television would begin to offer better programming, encouraged by the new Kennedy administration and the criticisms of the industry by FCC chairman Newton Minow. "Right now there is great ferment in the TV industry. For the next year the programming is pretty well fouled up, but by the 1962-63 season, I predict, not bashfully, television will be greatly strengthened. And that is the year when I intend to get back into it." An industry insider who knew Garroway said, "From a purely practical point of view, I feel his future in television depends upon how soon he comes back. If he waits too long, he'll find out that, like everybody else, he is replaceable."[49]

20

In early August, Garroway met with Lou Weiss to renew his contract with William Morris. It wouldn't be that easy, Weiss said. The "clean break" his attorney had negotiated with NBC had indeed freed him from *Today*. However, NBC had retained a five-year right of first negotiation and first refusal. If Garroway got an offer, he was required to provide NBC with a detailed description of the proposed program, including format, costs, and a description of the material. He was then obligated to give NBC fourteen days to respond. Since no network or producer would willingly provide so much valuable information to a competitor, the clauses effectively froze Garroway's chances to get lasting work. Garroway investigated. NBC's legal office told him the "first refusal" clause had been included at his attorney's insistence. Garroway suspected NBC had pressured him to agree to the clause. No, his attorney replied; the clause was included in error, and NBC hadn't requested it.[1]

It didn't matter, for the damage was done. In his haste to leave *Today* and NBC, in being overwhelmed with so much after Pamela's sudden death, and in his failure to completely vet the agreements he was signing, Garroway had handed NBC veto power over his television career until 1966. As the years passed, and job after job failed to take hold, he openly lamented how he hadn't handled things correctly. "I realize now how naive I was when I signed that," he said in 1965. "I received nothing in return for it, and managed to give up five years of a $100,000-a-year contract that would have paid me whether I worked or not." The agreement had also destroyed his value as a William Morris client. Jac Hein, looking back years later, said Garroway was "pumped up tremendously" by William Morris, but the agency "dropped him like a hot potato" when he left NBC, hurting his chances for future jobs.[2]

Garroway hired Martin Goodman, who managed his friend Hugh Downs, and filled his hours with odd jobs while waiting for new television offers. For *McCall's* he wrote monthly columns with reflections on everyday life: "I feel sorry for elevator operators – they have a tough life," one went. "Everybody seems to think they are experts on what time it is." As Christmas neared, he urged shoppers to wait until the afternoon of December 24, when "the stores are almost deserted because everybody sensible has already bought his present," and salespeople are "numb with fatigue and will say yes to almost anything, even such questions as 'May I have this one for free, please?'" The result: "a distinctive set of presents – those that have been rejected by the entire population." For Billy Graham, Garroway narrated the documentary *Decade of Decision*, about the evangelist's rise to national prominence.[3]

He tried to put the past behind him, going on a diet and losing twenty pounds. He was seen on the town again with Betty Furness, who denied wedding bells were in the offing ("Oh, please! Whoever said that gets the award for conclusion-jumping. We had dinner once!") He fulfilled a long-held dream on a trip to Flagstaff, looking through the twenty-four-inch telescope at Lowell Observatory. He hired a crew to renovate the townhouse. "I've been redecorating the house and in a way redecorating my life. There are the children, of course, and I'm discovering gradually that I'm alive again." And, having found the Westhampton home unsuitable for star-gazing, and concerned about how the waves pounded closer and closer with each passing year, he considered selling it.[4]

He extended kindnesses, puncturing a long-held perception that he was cheap. With the help of fellow car enthusiast Ken Purdy, Garroway sneaked a friend's beloved nine-year-old Buick to one of New York's finest car shops, spending well into four figures to have the car mechanically rebuilt. He then sent it to a renowned body and upholstery shop, spending another four-figure sum there. Garroway gave the car back to his surprised friend as a gift, "the most expensive Skylark of all time," Purdy wrote.[5]

He thanked those who had stood by him. "When I left the *Today* show after ten years all sorts of stories went around about me," he said. "They had me taking heroin, drinking myself to death and in a mental institution. None of it was true." To Francis Coughlin, he wrote a note thanking him for what a recent article "did for my somewhat shaken morale. After *Life*, *TV Guide*, & the boys got thru, I was quite a weirdy, and not only defunct, but never had done much, anyhow. Thank you for the restoration."[6]

Garroway's name was occasionally connected with various projects and proposals. An item had him in the running, alongside Steve Allen and Johnny Carson, for Jack Paar's recently-vacated *Tonight* seat. Another named him in connection with a proposal for ABC; still another had him anchoring the ABC newscast to counter Chet Huntley and David Brinkley. On *Today*'s tenth anniversary Garroway returned to 30 Rock to appear on the anniversary special, then appeared on the CBS morning show *Calendar* immediately after, in a cross-network tribute to *Today*'s anniversary. He told hosts Harry Reasoner and Mary Fickett about his time away from television, what he had learned about himself and the world, and said he was ready to come back to television "if they'll have me."[7]

His next television role was as an instructor. He fairly leapt at it, for it was on subjects dear to him. The fledgling National Educational Television network announced in early 1962 that it would produce an instructional series, *Exploring the Universe*, for its 161 stations. Garroway eagerly signed as host. "There's no money involved, to speak of," he said. "I have long felt that no one has really lived who has not looked into the eyepiece of a telescope and microscope, and I look forward to trying to convey the reasons for my excitement to television viewers." He called it "a kind of rear-guard action to prove to television programmers" that entertainment, education, news and other aspects of life could be combined. "We hope to present the fellow in the laboratory as a human being working on problems that affect our everyday life. The series will be, in short, a bridge between the world of viewers and that of the scientist." Garroway denied he would be a teacher on the program. "I'm just going to try to bring some of the wonders of science and the universe to people." He connected the program's value to his foremost concern: "Fantasy is fun, but it is time for Americans to get in contact with good, hard reality. Our opponents are the best realists in the world, and if we don't face up to reality soon we may all be eating potatoes and bread under Communist domination."[8]

While *Exploring the Universe* was in production, Garroway conducted two business deals.

One was a stroke of luck. Garroway had put the Westhampton home up for sale after a nasty storm, concerned by how the seas kept pushing the dunes closer and closer. In early March, he sold the house for

$39,000. The day after the sale closed, pounding seas washed the house into the sound, one of forty-three homes destroyed in a storm. Dave Jr. remembered the scene the next day, of wrecked houses floating along the bay, the only traces of their old house a few pieces of furniture that washed ashore.[9]

The other deal left scars that lasted years. As Garroway remembered, it started "almost whimsically."[10]

In 1962, Garroway was persuaded to invest in a magazine called *FM Listeners Guide*. Roughly similar to *TV Guide*, the new magazine would provide listings of what would be on the radio each week, as well as feature articles about topics related to FM radio. Garroway was initially excited about the potential for this magazine, and some other famous people invested in the magazine as well. Elected chairman of the organization that published the magazine, Garroway became a spokesman for the medium's growth. He urged FM broadcasters to broaden their horizons, to "break out of the box that most non-FM listeners have put it in – that of a highbrow classical musical service," he told an industry meeting in April.[11]

The magazine expanded, adding editions in new cities and changing its format. Part of that was from Garroway, who said he invested in the magazine so he could have a platform "to say what I want to say." He no longer wanted to write the sorts of soft pieces he wrote for *McCall's*. "That's pretty interesting to me, but when the world's on fire and burning down, it's nice to mention the temperature once in a while."[12]

By 1964 Garroway was suspicious of the whole enterprise. He put his stock in the magazine up for sale; he wanted, he said, to concentrate on the programming end of the broadcast business. He formed a production company called Once More Inc., with Jeff Kamen of Kamen Associates as production coordinator and longtime assistant Lee Lawrence as head of research and development. Its Shakespearean name, inspired by a line from *Henry V* ("Once more into the breach, dear lads!"), "was sort of Dad's battle cry in fighting the 'bastards,' as he called them," said Dave Jr.[13]

His suspicions about *FM Listeners Guide* proved well-founded, as the enterprise collapsed. Garroway, as the leading officer, valuable because his was a famous name, became the fall guy. "There is a whole group of businessmen out there who really feel that the money a show-business person makes is money that will eventually be theirs after they handle it a while," Garroway said. Worse, after the debacle, the Internal Revenue Service claimed that Garroway owed $7 million. He was worth $3 million. "It's not as though I was one of those people who tried to worm out of paying his taxes," Garroway protested. "I paid them faithfully every year and thought that I had paid the right amounts." He had been caught up in loopholes that could cost him more in interest and penalties than he earned during that period.[14]

Seven years of legal battles ensued, an ordeal compounded by Garroway's tendencies. "Our house was Watergate headquarters before Watergate," Dave Jr. said. "Every phone call was tape-recorded and then painstakingly transcribed by not one, but two full-time secretaries." A storage room in the house filled with boxes of documents and tapes. Dave Jr. watched as his dad had meeting after meeting, stretching into the night, with lawyers. "The thing was, they kept going to work for the other side," Dave Jr. said. "He once said he had twenty-three lawyers in a row stab him in the back and turn his information over to the other side." One of Garroway's secretaries believed he should have just let it go. "It was basically just a bad investment that he lost money on and could have just written off," she told Dave Jr. "Instead he went after them, tooth and nail, hiring lawyer after lawyer, who took his money, to attempt to retrieve his investment." To her, it was a waste of time and money, as Garroway sought personal justice to the point of a vendetta, regardless of costs.[15]

In time Garroway found an attorney he trusted. The attorney "once confided to Dad that he was ashamed of his profession," Dave Jr. said. In his search for trustworthy counsel, the elder Garroway began studying law books. "I read law because I had so much trouble understanding my lawyer. I kept reading until one night my lawyer said he bet I could pass the bar exam." Garroway took the challenge and passed the New York bar exam, but had no interest in a law career. "An honest attorney would either destroy himself or leave the profession," he said. "Once I ran an ad in the *Wall Street Journal* saying: 'Wanted: An honest, ethical, disbarred lawyer.' I got about twenty answers from people in jail."[16]

In the end, with legal representation he trusted, Garroway prevailed. "The whole thing was so bogus," Dave Jr. said, "that a lawyer for the other side did not even show up in court on that final day." With no opposing counsel present, the judge dismissed the case. To Garroway, those were some of the sweetest words he had ever heard. Although the legal risk was gone, so was much of Garroway's fortune. "The IRS didn't get it," Dave Jr. said. "*FM Listeners Guide* made off with some, but the lawyers got most of it. When you're high-profile, you're a very big target."[17]

"It was a very bad time," Garroway said years later. "I found out, very quickly, that I am no businessman. I also found out that a business project isn't like a television show. If a show is bad, you forget about it, there is always the next one. But in a business you don't just take your losses and walk away. It goes on, for years." Again, he saw darker motives. "I believe I was deliberately lured into publishing to keep me out of the entertainment field. I went into business, and I wasn't a businessman." Dave Jr. also wondered if his dad was targeted for his stance on civil rights. "Did the government use the IRS to take Dad down because he told too much of the truth to the American people on live TV?" he mused. "I believe he thought so. Although I have to consider maybe they were just doing their job and they made an honest mistake. I doubt I'll ever know for sure."[18]

Meanwhile, odd jobs appeared, some more dignified than others. He turned down an offer from Ralph Edwards to host a summer replacement program for CBS, likely due to a veto from NBC. He published the ghostwritten *Fun on Wheels*, a book of games to keep children occupied on long car trips. He constantly talked of program ideas that were reportedly ready to go at a moment's notice, of "twenty-one offers upstairs, and I'm working them around." One was a weekly sports roundup, *Dave Garroway's Sports Spectaculars*, that he hoped to sell to NBC for Sunday afternoons.[19]

In spite of his desires, the offers he accepted from those that NBC approved seemed somewhat humiliating. In June 1962 he co-hosted an awards program for *TV Guide*. "They came to me and I was glad to get the job," he said. "I don't know why anyone's picked me lately." He made his peace with the assignment by seeing a chance to "reestablish my image in the industry, not in the public mind. I don't wish it to be a narrow image, someone who's always haranguing about peace, fallout, etc." *The TV Guide Awards* wasn't a memorable return for Garroway, saddled with lame jokes that some critics felt must have been written for someone else. (A typical gag: "There's a panel discussion among Ricky Nelson, Tuesday Weld, Tommy Sands, Sandra Dee and Fabian on medical care for the aged. It's moderated by the AMA. That's Anna Maria Alberghetti.") Others found him "quite ill at ease as the master of ceremonies," or "mostly content to cue the toothpaste, camera and gasoline commercials."[20]

The following month brought an even more incongruous role, in Miami co-hosting the Miss Universe pageant alongside Gene Rayburn and Arlene Francis. Garroway was stationed off-stage, interviewing contestants, sometimes transcending the bubbly format, asking Miss Canada about relations between her country and the United States, or extracting a comment from Miss Brazil about how Americans were perceived in her country. To some he said he accepted the assignments to "erase the impression that I'm a sober old fuddy-duddy concerned only with bomb shelters and peace and the ultimate destiny of mankind." But as he drove in a rented Thunderbird with *Miami Herald* TV columnist Jack Anderson, a forlorn Garroway spoke of a "bleak" future that would keep him off regular network television for three more years, claiming that litigation was keeping him from moving on some show proposals. NBC, through a spokesperson, denied it was holding Garroway back, telling Anderson that all of Garroway's requests to do outside work had been approved.[21]

To another Miami writer, Garroway was blunt. "No one wants to buy what I have to sell. I don't conform enough to the pattern." He split with Martin Goodman, signing with another manager. Within a month, a syndicated television columnist received a question, perhaps the out-of-work performer's ultimate insult: "Is Dave Garroway dead?" Even the Chicago School had become enough of a relic that the Museum of Modern Art included a *Garroway at Large* episode in an exhibit saluting the history of television.[22]

While Garroway couldn't find regular work, he was becoming a go-to guest host. In 1962 Arthur Godfrey, whose once-formidable media empire had receded to a weekday radio program over CBS, scheduled a two-week vacation. Garroway was invited to fill in for him. A young jazz singer named Carol Sloane, with a new album on the Columbia label, received a phone call one day. Would she like to be Garroway's guest vocalist on the Godfrey show? Sloane, who remembered watching *Today*'s debut as a fifteen-year-old at home in Rhode Island, was thankful not only for the chance at a nationwide audience but also for the chance to work with "a living legend and a major hero of mine." Garroway told her that while riding in a cab a few weeks before, he found a magazine someone left behind, and its cover story was about her album. "I listened to it," he said, "and decided I wanted to hear you sing every day."[23]

Sloane remembered the scene in the Godfrey studio: Garroway at a desk, the overhead lights turned down to "a confessional dimness," she and an octet in a corner of the studio. At the desk Garroway had a gooseneck lamp, several daily newspapers, some record albums, a telephone, and his reference books and notebooks. He had created an quiet haven in the studio, turning the normally-extroverted Godfrey show into an intimate and gentle daily visit. The lessons learned from his radio days in Honolulu and Chicago had never left him. Garroway commented about whatever was on his mind, discussed books and records and performers he liked, and had Sloane perform a song each day. "He was an attentive audience, smiling, never taking his eyes off me and the band," she remembered. During the two weeks, she said she grew to adore Garroway as she once adored her high-school English teacher. Garroway liked her, securing her an appearance on the *Talent Scouts* television show.[24]

A few days after Godfrey returned to the show, Garroway phoned again. Would she please visit him at home? She took a cab to the 63rd Street townhouse and met Garroway. Immediately she became acquainted with the gadget-filled nature of Garroway's daily life, as the first thing she noticed was a Norden bombsight. Garroway had called because he needed a dozen copies of *The Cosmic View*, a words-and-picture book by Kees Boeke that demonstrated "the universe in ten jumps." He didn't have time to find the books himself. Could she help? "The research assistant in me responded," Sloane remembered, "and I accepted the assignment."[25]

Before she left, Garroway asked if she wanted to see his bedroom's security system. Sloane wondered if he was trying to seduce her. He halted at the bedroom's threshold; the system was armed, he said. Inside, she could make out through dim lighting a mattress on the floor, with books and papers around it. If they went any further, Garroway said, it would activate lights, sirens and strobe lights, "like an attempted prison break at Sing Sing." Furthermore, he claimed, the system would automatically notify the local police precinct. Impressed by Garroway's thoroughness, she went off to find the books. A few weeks later, she delivered the books to his home, had a cup of tea with him, "and with a firm handshake and huge smile, he saw me to the door."[26]

A year later, Sloane performed at a little country club on Long Island. One evening, she saw a familiar face in the audience. It was Garroway, who seemed "preoccupied, remote and somewhat desolate of spirit."

During a break she went over to thank him for coming. "Oh, I just wanted to hear you sing again," he said. "But I may not be here for the second set." As she went off to start the show, he kissed her on the hand. By the time she left the stage, he was gone. Sloane was "disappointed and a bit broken-hearted."[27]

There were other changes. Garroway replaced his trademark signoff of "peace" with the word "courage." During an appearance on *Talent Scouts* Garroway said "peace" had become overused. He later explained the idea had come from a poem by Amelia Earhart, which included the line "Courage is the price that life exacts for peace." "I became uncomfortable saying 'peace.' It was a supplication, a wishful desire. But there isn't any peace, unless possibly peace of mind for some people...very few." When he discovered the Earhart poem, " I liked that. It's active and affirmative. So I used it."[28]

There was a more personal reason. In 1961, Lee Lawrence, Garroway's researcher and close friend, had been attacked and thrown from her third-floor balcony. Her body badly broken, she was in a coma for six months. Defying doctors' fears she might die, she endured a two-year hospital stay to regain her health. Garroway changed his benediction to "Courage" as quiet encouragement to his friend. Still, as 1962 – a year in which the United States and the Soviet Union came within a hair's breadth of nuclear war, during the Cuban Missile Crisis – came to a close, the change to Garroway's sign-off struck at least one observer as the most "ominous portent of the year."[29]

In his private life, Garroway replaced the sea-threatened Nemo Point with a summer home he leased in Remsenburg, in the Hamptons. Dave and Dave Jr. spent weeks at a time away from Manhattan's hectic ways. While Garroway read and relaxed, Dave Jr. played in the backyard and explored the property's four acres. A big barn near the back of the property beckoned the curious boy, as did a swamp where he fed pieces of banana to an old turtle that showed up at the same time each morning. With all the turtles, deer, birds and other wildlife around, Dave Jr. recalled that it was very noisy in the mornings, "like a zoo." One day as Dave Jr. played in the yard, he threw a knife against a tree. The knife bounced off the tree and hit him in the leg, breaking his kneecap. For the rest of his days Dave Jr. carried wire in his knee, put there by the doctor who reassem-

*Father and son look to the future, 1964.
(Courtesy of the Associated Press)*

bled his broken kneecap. The countryside location, away from the lights of Manhattan, made an excellent spot for an observatory. Garroway set up a telescope with an Alvan Clark lens, and proudly told his son of how the great telescope maker had rubbed rouge on the lens with his thumb to achieve its final polish. Dave Jr. recalled seeing the rings of Saturn through that telescope.[30]

Garroway pondered selling the Manhattan townhouse. "The two of us don't need fourteen rooms," he said. Instead, he wanted to buy land in Riverdale and build a dramatic California-style home overlooking the Hudson, "the kind that look like they're built into the side of a cliff. We'll have a spectacular view and all we need is enough room for the piano and books." He worked on his cars, collected gadgets (the Norden bombsight, purchased as surplus for $29.75, was a particular favorite he loved showing visitors) and worked on a design for a new, more affordable telescope that could be put into mass production. His endless fascinations continued to bring joy. "Is there anything I'm not interested in? I don't know yet," he said. "In a way, this is annoying to me. I get curious about all kinds of things, which means I tend to lose direction and evaluate everything at the same weight. But still, my curiosity doesn't stop."[31]

He spent time with his children. Paris had graduated from Whitfield School, and Garroway had spoken at the graduation ceremony. She and a school friend spent three weeks with him in Remsenburg over the summer. Little David continued to be a source of joy, repeatedly interrupting one interview to ask his dad to stop talking and come play with him. At night, not sleeping much (only three hours, claiming he "wouldn't be fit to live with if I had eight"), the loving father played his piano, softly, so he wouldn't wake his sleeping child.[32]

In February 1963, *Exploring the Universe* made its debut on NET. The series, based on a book by the same name, was a partnership among the American Foundation for Continuing Education, New England Television and McGraw-Hill, and supported by the National Science Foundation. Each episode in the series was based on a chapter from the book, and the consortium planned study and discussion groups in sixty-four cities nationwide. A press release promised that Garroway would take viewers on an informal journey through the world of modern science with distinguished guests including Nobel Prize winners I.I. Rabi and Edward Purcell, Harlow Shapley, Robert Oppenheimer, Walter Roberts, Maurice Goldhaber, Martin Schwarzschild, Philip Morrison, and Margaret Mead. "I hope this series conveys some of the feeling of excitement that science brings to me," Garroway said. To a columnist, he said the series was meant "to bring the citizen into touch with the scientist, so that each will know what the other is up to."[33]

The series premiered to mixed reviews. Percy Shain of the *Boston Globe* said Garroway "seems to revel in his new assignment" and predicted that "before it's over, Dave ought to be as popular with the young, adventurous, eager-to-know set as he was with their mothers just a few short years ago." Harry Harris of the *Philadelphia Inquirer* praised the program as "an outstanding example of how to make a complex subject not only comprehensible but continuously entertaining. Garroway managed this via ingenuity, informality, sincerity and knowledgeability." In Cedar Rapids, Iowa, columnist Alan Gill wrote that Garroway's return "is the nicest, quietest triumph of the year."[34]

Others saw reason for concern. Gee Mitchell thought Garroway was "ill at ease, fumbling most of the time." Jack Gould said Garroway "has accepted a deceptively difficult assignment. He is acting the part of the layman who has a healthy curiosity about the world of science." However, Gould found him "not really too effective" in the premiere episode. "He became rather badly tangled in his own narration, and the questions that he asked of Dr. Margaret Mead, the anthropologist, were very superficial and wanting in some underlying thread of consistency." Gould hoped Garroway would ease into the role in later episodes, "particularly if he does not forget his homework in preparing for each installment." Though Tucson reviewer Tony Fortuno thought Garroway's style was appropriate, "the program fails to arouse or excite any distinct impression for the viewer, except perhaps a gentle awe." Noting that the program spent a lot of time on people talking, Fortuno wrote, "One of the scientists stated at the end of the show, 'Man cannot rest until he finds out where and what kind of life exists in the universe.' But odds are that man will be resting peacefully at the close of *Exploring the Universe*."[35]

For Garroway, enlightenment and ideas were most important. "Television isn't anything in itself," he said. "The ideas that can flow over it are the important things." And he encouraged the propagation of television that provoked thought. He told viewers on the debut telecast of Philadelphia's public TV station that "educational TV" is not as stuffy or as highbrow as the term might make it seem. "Isn't every TV station educational? Educational is too Sunday schoolish. Couldn't we find a better word?" It was a battle he waged on several fronts, not just in broadcast media. His interest in General Semantics, "the science of how we use words," prompted him to write several columns on the subject that were published nationwide, urging readers to learn more about how it could help relations among human beings, in areas as personal as marital relationships and as complicated as dealing with prejudice. Garroway even chaired sessions at a 1963 semantics conference at New York University.[36]

Nor had his concerns subsided about the world situation. The battle of the mind was every bit as important to him as a divided Berlin or a Communist Cuba, another front in a cold war. "I'm still plugging reality over Nowheresville, U.S.A.," he said, "with the general idea that those who live in the latter may be a touch out of touch if they should someday be gently awakened by the soft nudge of a Communist rifle butt." The man who built his own fallout shelter spoke out about civil defense and spoke against those who opposed it. Before a 1963 Congressional hearing, he took apart the arguments of a group called Citizens For a Sane Nuclear Policy, which had argued against fallout shelter programs and civil defense efforts. "By the premise implied in the word 'sane,' if you disagree with the views of this group for 'a sane nuclear policy,' what, by inference, must you be? Insane? Yes." Garroway said the group's argument hadn't been based on logic, and that without adequate fallout shelters, an attack on the nation's fifty largest cities could kill 143 million people.[37]

He further drove home the point in an advertisement for the New York Office of Civil Defense. Not only did he encourage bomb shelter construction, he said, but "I suspect the motives of those who don't." A New York organization, the League Against Obnoxious Television Commercials, protested that the ad represented "the beginning of the use of mass media by the government to create a uniformity in public opinion to government action." The advertisement was pulled, the governor opened an investigation, and the state's civil defense director eventually resigned.[38]

Free agency also meant Garroway could openly be involved in politics. When his friend Nelson Rockefeller sought the Republican presidential nomination in 1964, Garroway hosted a two-hour telethon for him before the Oregon primary. It didn't go well. Of the hundreds of questions that came in from viewers, Rockefeller only got to about thirty. The governor was also on camera only about half of the program. Garroway's time away from regular television was showing: he talked too much, mispronounced Oregon place names, called guests by incorrect names, didn't manage the time wisely as moderator. One viewer gave Garroway credit for providing unintended comedy. Another called the broadcast "a miserable flop."[39]

Alongside Garroway's attempts to be profound were more commercial efforts. Rumors circulated that he might host a new ABC quiz show, but the offer never came to pass. Instead, his next effort literally was commercial, as Ford Motor Company hired him to promote its 1964 models. Ford's marketing manager credited Garroway's longtime interest in cars as one reason he was selected. "You'll dig him everywhere," Herb Lyon wrote, "but what a fate."[40]

The Ford deal brought income, but not satisfaction. He knew it.

From time to time Garroway typed up a list of "assets and liabilities" in his life, his scientific, systematic way of assessing his life's value. In

1964 he revised the list once more. He now claimed "intolerable pressure" had led to his resignation from NBC, that his business attorney had intentionally disregarded the detailed instructions he had given him about getting out of his NBC contract; he again lamented the $500,000 in income, not to mention the control over his own career, that he had signed away in 1961. His career was dead in the water. Since then, he had hired and fired four agents. "Have not been offered, nor has an agent been able to secure any offer to work in any capacity on any regular radio or television show since that time." The liabilities weren't just professional or financial. Within his life, he saw problems. Much of his stepson Michael's family was now gone. He claimed several people close to him were mentally ill. Some of this was, no doubt, paranoia fueled by the Dexedrine he still used.[41]

Frances Murphey of the *Akron Beacon-Journal* tried to make sense of Garroway. He "is searching for something these days," Murphey wrote. "For what, even Garroway isn't sure. Hedging fifty-one, he seems indecisive about what he wants out of life. Fame and money have already come his way. They weren't enough." Murphey noted his "easy friendliness" was "accompanied with a detachment hard to bridge. He peers at you through or over spectacles without seeming to really focus." Murphey remembered seeing Garroway in 1958, at the height of his power, "a more harried man, caught in a weary web of fame. He had contracts through 1965. He had it made – until his private world caved in." Where he did find comfort, as always, was within his forest of fascinations. The man who could be aloof and introverted could open up when he found a kindred spirit. When he learned comedian Jackie Mason was interested in astronomy, Garroway gave him one of his telescopes.[42]

Publicly, he tried to project a sense of having it all together. "At the end of three years I've torn up the instructions, the checklist, and put the machine into gear," he wrote in one column. "I'm running wide open down the right track and let me tell you it's a pretty good feeling. I now think you go out and get things and bring them home. The fuel that I've found to run this machine was suggested to me very casually one day by a friend. 'Dave,' he said, 'remember there is such a thing as courage.'

"I don't know why that sentence worked for me; it just might for you. Try a drop in your tank and see what happens and – courage!"[43]

21

In May 1964, WCBS radio host Jack Sterling was taking two weeks' vacation. The New York station needed someone to fill in. Garroway, who had ably substituted on Arthur Godfrey's radio program not long before, got the call. WCBS made the most of it, with ads showing Garroway in front of a microphone, headphones over his ears, looking right at home. The ads asked, "Did you hear Dave Garroway this morning?"[1]

Enough people did, and on May 18 Dave Garroway joined the WCBS lineup. He had two shows: *Garroway A.M.*, weekday mornings from 11:10 to noon, and *Garroway P.M.*, a free-flowing forty-five minute afternoon show with a "blend of reality and fantasy." The station promoted Garroway in newspaper ads almost daily. "Garroway is back on WCBS! (please don't watch him!)" went the inventive campaign, celebrating the return of "this wonderfully humorous, very human being."[2]

Free-form Garroway could get interesting, but could also veer into rambling to the point of ponderousness. Kay Gardella liked the concept, but grew tired of Garroway's "inverted intellectualism," of trying to find intellectual insight in the insignificant. "That is, pretending that the act of ringing the weather bureau for a report is confusing to a caller, which it isn't. Just to Garroway filling air time." Sometimes Garroway used the show to explore serious topics, as when he interviewed Senator Hubert Humphrey about the value of federally funded medical research. Other times he gave listeners more than they bargained for. A WCBS ad that promised "Garroway'll give you a piece of his mind" came unexpectedly true in September when, irritated about the movie *Fail-Safe*, Garroway blistered it in a commentary that ended in a four-letter word.[3]

In between radio obligations, he worked in other gigs: narrating a Labor Day documentary for the AFL-CIO, hosting a special for the New York Legislature showing how the state's business was conducted, voicing a film that illustrated how the New York Stock Exchange worked, making a quick trip to Chicago to appear on a special. He even appeared on the WCBS float in the Macy's Thanksgiving Day Parade that year.[4]

All seemed well. Then Garroway quit WCBS in early December, citing "pressures of other commitments." After his last show on December 18, he said that despite assurances the WCBS program wouldn't take much preparation, "I found it was a full-time job, and more than full time." He thought about what might happen next. "I want to spend more time with my seven-year-old son," he said. "We might take a long trip together. I've been reading a lot about Australia. It is still kind of a frontier and I've been thinking I might want to give it a try."

As Garroway's career came to another hiatus, Lawrence Laurent lamented, "Probably the saddest commentary on television these days is the simple fact that Dave Garroway is not working in TV."[5]

Four months later, ABC had a problem. A New York television program called *Night Line* had become a sensation. Hosted by disc jockey Les Crane, *Night Line* featured celebrity interviews and a call-in segment for viewers. Crane was young and outspoken, and the show featured controversial discussions and a confrontational tone. It generated buzz – the show "whipped up more talk around New York last year than anything since Jack Paar," one critic noted – and, as a third-place network looking for a breakout hit, ABC put it on nationally as *The Les Crane Show*, weeknights from 11:15 to 1 a.m. "The network is determined to establish itself in the late-evening entertainment field," Richard Doan wrote, "even if it takes, as the saying goes, all day. There are two principal reasons: the money to be made at it and the growing shortage of movies."[6]

What had worked locally didn't catch on nationally. After thirteen weeks, Crane didn't find an audience. ABC retitled the program *Nightlife* and tried an array of guest hosts, trying to find something that might work. Shelley Berman, Pat Boone, Jack Carter and Allan Sherman had each taken a week's turn as host. On April 20, Dave Garroway took the desk for a week. Garroway "brings a low-key change of pace to the ABC night-owl program which will be watched closely for impact," Doan wrote.[7]

It worked. By the second night *Nightlife* had found its sparkle, as Garroway swapped stories with Arthur Godfrey, and Morey Amsterdam performed comedy. The next night was pure Garroway: a locksmith discussing how to prevent locks from being picked, a musical performance from Carol Sloane, and a feature about space exploration told in films and models. The next night, Don Herbert, famous as Mr. Wizard, demonstrated scientific principles.[8]

The Garroway magic was back, and it charmed the critics. Garroway "has given a new aura, a polish and an air of distinction to ABC's dismal flop," Ben Gross wrote in the *New York Daily News*. "Garroway should be made the permanent emcee of this attraction." Donald Freeman of Copley News Service wrote, "The program enjoyed an immediate improvement. Garroway, of course, has style – at any hour. Style, class, the old panache. Listen, Perry Como could take cool lessons from Garroway." Paul Molloy of the *Chicago Sun-Times* urged ABC to "cease its search and sign him up for some sort of duration."[9]

In June, ABC made its decision. The program, reworked by veteran producer Dwight Hemion, would avoid the controversies that led to earlier hot water, and become a more traditional entertainment-oriented show. Crane would get another four-week tryout as host, with comedian Nipsey Russell as his sidekick. Garroway would return in "a special segment of the show that will be his to use as he pleases, discussing or demonstrating anything that captures his highly individual fancy." It was nice, but not enough, wrote columnist Dorothy Stanich: "I wish they'd give him the entire show."[10]

Some found Russell and Garroway the best part of the program. "Crane was lucky to have such a fine pair of bookends," Kay Gardella wrote, "to boost him in his undeveloped areas – comedy and knowledge." Gardella cited a Garroway segment in which he demonstrated how to make a "devastation computer" from a piece of paper, to determine how far back you needed to be to keep a skyscraper from falling on you, as giving the program "just the right slant. Now all he and Nipsey have to do is make sure Crane stays upright until he's back in the ABC saddle for good." Another review thought the program was still trying to find itself, and that neither Russell nor Garroway were being used wisely. Gee Mitchell, a Dayton columnist, thought Garroway's segment "inane."[11]

Crane's lease on the program was extended, as were the services of both sidekicks. Garroway was grateful. "I really needed it," he told Cindy Adams. "Maybe I never knew there was that much ham in me. It's just that when I'm facing a camera I relax. It's the only time I can completely. I feel no more fears of any sort. Nobody can get to me. Nobody can ask me to lend them five dollars. Nobody can hurt me. People say I look like I'm falling asleep on television because I'm so casual. Truth is, I'm all tensed up, I'm working my tail off. But, nonetheless, I'm calm because that camera is my friend," he said. "To me, the impersonal eye of that camera spells home."[12]

Once again, as everything seemed right, something happened. *Hollywood Palace* producers Nick Vanoff and William Harbach, who had championed Crane's return to *Nightlife*, suggested the program move to Hollywood. There, they wouldn't compete with Johnny Carson's *Tonight* or *The Merv Griffin Show* for guests. "When you can pick from people like Burt Lancaster and Kirk Douglas," Crane said, "you aren't losing vitality by moving west."[13]

Nipsey Russell was willing to make the move. Garroway wasn't. "I can't move," he told the press. "I've got too many kids in the fire here, so to speak." Hemion had dangled the prospect of flying him to Hollywood every now and then, "but there's nothing firm yet." A few days later, Garroway unloaded. "I made a promise this morning. I'm not going to tell any more lies," he told writer Barry Robinson. Garroway claimed he had been frozen off the program. "The deal was that I was to be a regular guest on the show for as many as one to five times a week. I was on five times in one week, then three, then two, and finally once a week for the past two weeks. Now? I don't know."[14]

Garroway saw nothing on the horizon. "I guess I came to network television in the morning and I'm going out at night," he said. "I haven't worked on network television for four years, and it doesn't look like I have anything to look forward to." He again bemoaned the terms under which he left NBC, his battles with the IRS, his search for an honest lawyer, all the things that had gone wrong since 1961. "As he sat there on the couch," Robinson wrote, "one couldn't help wondering about his future and that of TV. Is there a place in the medium for the man who symbolizes all that is intelligent and informative, all that for years has been the best of TV? Isn't there still a place for one of the medium's programming pioneers?

"'Apparently not,' answers Dave Garroway.

"Maybe time will prove him wrong."[15]

In 1964 Garroway put the 63rd Street townhouse up for sale. He and Dave Jr. moved into a penthouse apartment on 13th Street with a view of Greenwich Village. It was a good place to start over. He had pared his car collection from six cars to three: an antique model, the Jaguar, and a Chevrolet Greenbrier van. The car collection had become useless, he worried; they were stuck in a garage because "in New York, there's hardly room to back them into the street."[16]

While he still loved his cars, the Jaguar in particular, the Greenbrier provided particular fun. "You wouldn't necessarily picture a television star driving around in a camper van," Dave Jr. said, "but Dad said he enjoyed driving a van because it made him feel above it all and right up front, close to things." The Greenbrier also provided Garroway with another benefit: driving around in a plain van made the famous man inconspicuous. Sometimes he extended that to his personal appearance. Dave Jr. remembered "half a closet full of disguises" his dad kept in New York: all sorts of different clothes, a wig or two, different hats and glasses, wads of cotton he could stuff into his cheeks. The famous man could take on the appearance of a common laborer. To his daughter Paris, the disguises made her dad look scary, and she wouldn't want to go out with him. Garroway once claimed the costumes "made me look mean and feel mean," and that "it got me into two fights."[17]

His son believed his dad just wanted a break from fame. "He just wanted to be part of the crowd and walk around and not be recognized or gawked at," Dave Jr. said. "When Dad was out in public as himself, he never minded giving autographs and was always polite to his fans, and never wanted to be arrogant or rude or disappoint them." Putting on a disguise and blending in allowed him to go back to the days before he was famous, and let him watch people while not drawing attention to himself. Garroway also said that going out in disguise gave him another break: he felt that celebrity made him vulnerable to being gouged when he bought things, and disguises that helped him blend in prevented this.[18]

The van also allowed for father-son bonding in a typically-inventive Garroway method. The two would stock the Greenbrier with some food, grab a telescope, get in the van and drive out of Manhattan. From the driver's seat, Dave Jr. said, his dad would hand him a map and give orders to "get us as thoroughly lost as possible." It was a challenge he always accepted. "I would see a road on the map that looked like it might take us up into the mountains and say 'take a right here,'" he remembered. "Sometimes I would just put the map down and go on instinct. I'd say 'take that second left' or 'follow that truck.'" The night would usually end with the two camping out in the van. "We would heat up some soup and fold out the beds," he recalled, and they'd get out the Questar and shoot stars.

Getting lost in the Greenbrier van. (Paris Day collection)

"Sometimes if it got too late and we still hadn't found a good dead-end we would pull into a motel and spend the night. You'd be surprised how hard it can be to get lost sometimes." Sometimes, though, they found dirt roads that weren't even on the map, forgot how they got in, and ended up more lost than before. "It was fun," Dave Jr. remembered.[19]

The van also figured in another Garroway adventure. As the lease on the Remsenburg house was coming up, Garroway suspected the property owner was about to cheat him out of some money. As he moved everything of his off the property, including the observatory he had set up, Garroway planted listening devices in all the rooms. He parked the van out of sight from the house, then turned on a transmitter and a tape recorder. Garroway and Dave Jr. then listened in on the conversations the owner was having with her business partner, taping the conversations as evidence in a potential lawsuit.[20]

More often than not, their adventures were benign, if a little bizarre. One day Garroway showed Dave Jr. a very nice set of cufflinks. They had a gold-plated square base, on which were two pieces of cut iron meteorite. Their value was likely immense. "I'm getting rid of these today," Garroway announced. Dave Jr. couldn't understand why his father would dispose of something so beautiful. "They were given to me as a birthday present by a woman whose affections I rejected," Garroway said. "I think they might be bringing us bad luck." He explained that while he didn't know if things could be cursed or have a spell inflicted on them, he wasn't sure they couldn't be, either. Quoting a favorite line from Shakespeare, Garroway said to his son, "There are more things between heaven and earth than are dreamt of in your philosophy, Horatio." Dave Jr. figured it was his dad erring on the side of caution. He helped his dad build a small gondola out of cardboard, into which they placed the cufflinks. They inflated three balloons with a helium tank Garroway kept in the apartment, then tied the gondola to the balloons. Garroway said a few solemn words, sprinkled salt on the cufflinks, and they set the balloons adrift, watching them disappear into the sunset over Greenwich Village.

"I thought the whole thing was bit bizarre, even for Dad," Dave Jr. remembered. "To hear him talk of possible unknown energies that meteorite from space might harbor did make me a little uneasy, I suppose." At the same time, Dave Jr. felt reverence and respect toward his father. "Dad was easy to admit that he didn't know everything," he said. "Dad often spoke of how little mankind really did know." This extended to his own life, for Garroway was quick to admit when he was wrong, misinformed, or just didn't know about something. Sometimes he would wonder why people found admitting to being wrong such a hard thing for people to say. While Dave Jr. said that hearing his dad admit to being wrong was a little unnerving, since kids like to think their parents know everything, "it gave me a good feeling knowing he didn't pretend he did."[21]

Sometimes the episodes contained wit that stunned the young boy's mind. One evening in 1965, Garroway was getting ready to go to dinner as his son looked out on the Manhattan skyline. Abruptly Garroway said, "I'm going to think out all the lights in New York." He started to act like he was pushing a great weight through the air, grunting and groaning, twisting his face into agony. "Suddenly I noticed on my right a wave of darkness coming toward me," Dave Jr. remembered, as the lights of the city went out south to north. "The wave of darkness rolled over us and I saw the Empire State Building go black, as our apartment went dark." His son didn't say anything, but just looked at him. "For a couple of days," he said, "I thought he had psychic powers."

A couple of days later, Garroway let his son in on the secret: his electrical engineer father taught him that right before a blackout, the lights dim for a few seconds and then go back to normal. On this evening, Garroway had noticed the lights dimming and guessed that a blackout was about to happen. "He sure had me fooled," Dave Jr. said, "but to this day I still think he had psychic powers."[22]

One night Garroway was working with a paper cutter. Suddenly Dave Jr. heard him howl in pain. In a moment of inattention, Garroway had sliced off the edge of his thumb. Dave Jr. asked his father if he was going to the hospital. "No," his dad said. Instead, Garroway stuck the severed piece of skin back in place with cyanoacrylate glue. "It looked Frankensteinish," Dave Jr. remembered, "but I'll be darned if it didn't take." Within a couple of weeks, the thumb had stitched itself back together. "Dad was always a wonder at improvising," Dave Jr. said. The howl of pain was unusual for Garroway, whose son remembered him as not being a groaner or a whiner. The only other time he heard his dad in agony was about a year later, when he was passing a kidney stone, spending an entire night near the toilet groaning and grunting. "The next day, he told me it was the worst pain he had ever felt in his life," Dave Jr. said. "He looked much relieved and said he hoped he would never have another."[23]

Another form of pain struck Garroway, one that hit especially close. The lifelong lover of music came down with an affliction that, he said, made him "stone deaf for all music. You can hear it, but it has the emotional appeal of pots and pans." The condition robbed him of music's emotional meaning. While the many doctors he consulted knew such a condition existed, they had no treatment for it. The condition stretched on until Garroway attended the 1967 Grammy Awards dinner. As Pat Williams' orchestra burst into song, Garroway found himself again enraptured by music. "I rushed out, bought a record by Pat Williams, put it on my big stereo, and I was alive again."[24]

Garroway was concerned about Dave Jr.'s difficulty with reading. Despite being sent to the best reading teachers in the city, nothing seemed to work. One of his secretaries learned about the Institute for the Advancement of Human Potential in Philadelphia. Two doctors, Glen Doman and Carl Delgado, were working on innovative treatments. Figuring that they had tried everything else, Garroway arranged for a visit. "We didn't feel we had much to lose," Dave Jr. said.

At the institute, nine-year-old Dave Jr. was subjected to all kinds of unorthodox tests: eye tests, reading tests, memory and intelligence tests, coordination tests. One test required Dave Jr. to hold and shoot a .22 rifle. From these tests, the doctors determined Dave Jr. had cross-dominance: despite being right-handed and right-footed, he was left-eye coordinated. "This meant that when I read something, the information went to the less dominant hemisphere of my brain and got processed wrong," Dave Jr. said. For instance, although he was right-handed, he shot the rifle from a left-hand position so he could aim with his left eye. The doctors said it came from Dave Jr. being kept in a crib growing up, not being allowed to crawl around. This, they said, kept him from developing proper neurological connections.

Dave Jr. went home with an unusual set of exercises: crawling on the floor, up and down the hallway on knee pads, staring at the middle knuckle of each hand, for twenty minutes a day. He also did eye exercises. Dave Jr. also had to read for thirty minutes each day while wearing a special eye patch equipped with filters. His left eye would look through a piece of blue plastic film. On the page he was reading, he was required to put a piece of red plastic film. This turned the page black to his left eye. "In this manner, the left eye was not weakened but neither did it pass any information to the brain," Dave Jr. said. "Only my right eye saw the words, which would pass into the dominant hemisphere of the brain."

Within six months, the fifth-grader's reading level went from second grade to ninth grade. Back at the Institute for a follow-up, the doctors were impressed. "They pointed out that without being prompted I was now shooting the .22 rifle right-handed, lining up targets with my right eye," Dave Jr. remembered. "I hadn't even noticed." The treatments had improved his life, too. "The kids at school no longer looked at me like I was a dummy because I couldn't read," he said, "and now I read for pleasure." An elated father became a booster for the Institute, joining its board of directors and singing its praises at every opportunity. "Dad could have just thrown up his hands and given up looking for alternatives," Dave Jr. said. "But he never would have, either. It wasn't his nature. Thanks, Dad."[25]

Dave Jr. had inherited his father's curiosity and fascination with the world's wonders. Whenever a thermometer broke, for instance, he loved to push the spilled mercury around and play with it. This struck a chord within Garroway, who gave the boy a ten-pound bottle of mercury for his tenth birthday. In those days, the toxic effects of mercury were not as well-known. Both father and son were fascinated by the substance, pouring it into a bowl and letting it run through their fingers. "Our favorite thing to do with it," Dave Jr. remembered, "was to put it into a bowl and shine a bright light onto its surface." This reflected light onto an adjacent wall, and any vibration would send ripples spreading across the mercury's surface and reflect them on the wall. "You could see your footsteps as you walked across the room as ripples spreading across the bowl," he remembered. "It really was neat!" The elder Garroway even kept a bowl of mercury by his bedside. "I played with it extensively and Dad inhaled it, because we noticed some of it evaporated over the years, but we never seemed to have been poisoned by it," Dave Jr. said.[26]

Garroway's scientific interests included other exotic metals. One day he brought home some sodium metal packed in oil. Dave Jr. watched him slice off a piece, fascinated as the surface oxidized almost as quickly as it was cut. Father and son walked to the bathroom and filled up the bathtub. Garroway solemnly instructed his son to stand back, then tossed the small piece of metal into the bathtub, where Dave Jr. recalled it "fizzed and sputtered around like mad, as though it was a piece of dry ice in a frying pan," until it gave out with a final pop. "If it had been a large piece, it would have blown up," Garroway told his son.

The breadth of his father's interests fascinated Dave Jr. "Pop just loved to turn me on to neat stuff," he remembered. "He once mentioned to me that he had read the entire *Encyclopaedia Britannica*, all twenty-four volumes, not once but twice." From that, his father had been able to become what his own father advised him to become, a generalist who could know a little about everything but not a whole lot about any particular subject. "He saw the world as becoming overspecialized and thought it gave people a narrow perspective," Dave Jr. said. "So to remain the broad-minded renaissance man he was, Dad dabbled in many areas." He also passed along the same advice to his son, who credited it as a likely reason for his efforts in general unified field theory, which "attempts to pull everything together: the relationships between space, time, energy, and everything else." His father's connections sometimes let him feed his growing interests. After they saw the movie *Goldfinger*, Dave Jr. became fascinated with laser beams. Some time later, his father introduced him to Dr. Charles Townes, whose work on developing the laser beam had led to Nobel honors. "Great job, Doctor," Dave Jr. told the scientist.[27]

Another fascination passed from father to son was drumming. On his seventh Christmas, Dave Jr. got a set of bongos from his dad. He enjoyed them so much that one day, during a visit to Garroway's storage unit in a warehouse on 37th Street, they retrieved the old Ludwig snare drum that Garroway had played back during his days in radio. "We took it home along with a pair of metal brushes," Dave Jr. said. "He never used sticks; he only used brushes. He would put on his favorite records and 'stir soup' to the music." Dad provided some initial instruction in using the brushes and then turned him loose. Later, he gave his son a set of drum sticks. "I'm so grateful he gave me that drum that day," he said. "Drumming has helped keep me in rhythm over the years." Dave Jr. was also glad his dad endured his countless hours of practice, playing the drums in time to records at home. Only once could he recall his dad asking him to stop, when he had a headache. "Just once," he said. "Now, that's love."[28]

Garroway told his son that over the years he had compiled a file on how to do all sorts of things, which he called his "how to do it" file. Some tricks in the file involved revenge: for instance, a method he used when he hid fish in a wall to get back at a mean landlord. Others were more benign, such as how to use three fingers to make an impromptu magnifier. "Dad was very clever at figuring out shortcuts, and if there was an easier way of doing something, he would figure it out," Dave Jr. said. Those better methods extended to the unthinkable, for one day he announced to his son that he had figured out how to commit the perfect murder. "I'm not going to tell you," his dad said. "I'm not going to tell anyone. It's a secret that's going to my grave with me!" Despite Dave Jr.'s continued pleas for details, his dad refused to share. "It doesn't look like a murder," was all that Garroway would tell him.

A few years later, Dave Jr. mentioned "the perfect murder" to his dad. "Oh, so I told you that much?" Garroway replied, still refusing to say any more about the scheme. "It got me steamed for a couple of reasons," Dave Jr. said. "First, he was just smart enough to figure out something like that, and he had made me curious about it – and then snubbed me by telling me it was forbidden in knowledge." The second reason was more personal. "He wouldn't tell me! His own son! I mean, what if I needed to kill someone some day? Would he want me to get caught and go to prison for the rest of my life?" To the best of his knowledge, it was the only secret his dad took to the grave.[29]

Dave Jr. found it "a most interesting experience" to be out and about with his famous dad. "You're not in the spotlight," he said, "so you can get a side view and see the audience more clearly than the person actually in the spotlight." When they went out to eat, for example, young Dave would wait for the laughter and conversation in the restaurant to subside as heads started to turn. "It usually took about thirty to sixty seconds, would last about fifteen seconds, and then the conversations would pick back up again." Some people would point. Someone would quietly say, "Hey, look, that looks like Dave Garroway. What do you think?"

"Gee, I don't know. Why don't you go ask him?"

Sometimes they'd follow through. Sometimes they'd ask for an autograph, which Garroway happily obliged. Other times, a starstruck onlooker might say, "Excuse us. We hope we're not interrupting you. Are you Dave Garroway?"

"Why, yes I am," Garroway would reply with a smile.

"Well, we just wanted to say that we've watched your show for years and have really enjoyed your work."

"Thank you very much," Garroway would reply. "I appreciate it."

Sometimes Garroway would hear an admirer speak of watching *Garroway at Large*. Or, once in a while, "I used to listen to you on *The 11:60 Club*." Which would bring a surprised response: "Wow, that was a while ago. I had fun doing that show." Then, as Dave Jr. remembered, the happy fan would stroll off, pleased to have met "the Dave Garroway."[30]

The respect people showed to his dad seemed funny to Dave Jr., who never really got to see his father's work on television. "To me he was just plain old dad, a great guy but nobody special," he said. "How was it all of these strangers treated him like an old friend? I guess it made me understand both Dad's talent, and the power of television in an indirect way." That power rubbed off on Dave Jr. as well, who admitted feeling proud when people treated his father so special. "After all, you are his kid, and you must be sort of special, too." When Dave Jr. was out with his dad, people would often rub his hair and ask Garroway if that was his good-looking son. While Dave Jr. didn't mind the attention, "I hated the hair rubs." Once a fan who asked the elder Garroway for an autograph then asked Dave Jr. for his. "What a thrill!" he remembered. "I signed happily and was giddy for the rest of the day, even though it felt a bit odd."

In his unpublished memoir, Garroway wrote that he didn't think he spoiled his son. Dave Jr. often smiled when he read that, because he didn't think it was true. "Although I think he was careful not to spoil me rotten," he said, "I feel like, at least in some ways, he spoiled me." It wasn't being spoiled with material things, but with experiences. When Dave Jr. was ten, his dad booked a helicopter ride around New York City. The rush and chills Dave Jr. felt when they lifted off were still palpable to him fifty years later. Garroway persuaded the pilot to take them close up to the face of the Statue of Liberty before taking them upstate to see the colors of the autumn leaves from above.[31]

Dave Jr. remembered that his dad loved all kinds of science. Although astronomy was his favorite, he subscribed to all sorts of scientific magazines "and read them all, cover to cover, every month." At dinner Garroway gave his son a summary of what he had been reading. "It was wonderful, like having my own Internet search engine reporting back to me all the interesting, recent developments and research going on in science." Dave Jr. credited this with why he pursued his own love for physics and developed theories of his own. While Garroway had a voracious appetite for science, he maintained a healthy skepticism and often quoted a line he attributed to Shakespeare: "Nothing in science, religion or philosophy is more than a passing garb, worn for a while and then discarded." He often reminded his son, "Don't believe everything you read."[32]

Dave Jr. said his dad often went along with conventional thinking, but once said he didn't think Darwin's theory of evolution could apply to humans. A surprised son pressed for details. Garroway said he didn't think there had been enough time for it to apply to human evolution. "There are too many variations of *homo sapiens* to have evolved over just one million years," he said. "Everybody from a Pygmy Eskimo to a Zulu warrior evolved."

"Well, what do you think happened?" Dave Jr. asked.

"I don't know."

The admission of uncertainty left Dave Jr. troubled. "Not because Darwin might be wrong," he remembered, but because his dad, who usually had an observation or theory on just about anything, didn't have anything else to offer on the subject.[33]

Sometimes Garroway would read a book or a theory and become a champion of it, spreading the theory to his friends. If he read it in a book, for instance, his friends might receive a copy at Christmas. When he read *African Genesis* by Robert Audrey, which proposed humans were the result of a mutation of a vegetarian ancestral primate, Garroway was taken by it. Another of Garroway's favorites was *The Cosmic View* by Kees Boeke, which looked at the world in a series of ten "jumps." Beginning with a picture of a girl sitting and holding a cat, it moved outward by powers of ten to show her town, her country, her continent, her planet, and on out to the edge of the universe. It then moved inward by powers of ten, ending at the atomic level. He even took the lesson to his son's sixth-grade class. "Pop was so impressed with this book, he once had it made into a slideshow at his own expense and showed it at my school at a presentation in the auditorium," Dave Jr. said. At the end, there was a surprise. A week before, Dave Jr. had drawn his dad a cartoon of an intercontinental ballistic missile about to be intercepted by an anti-ballistic missile. That missile was about to be hit by an anti-anti-ballistic missile, and that missile was about to be hit by an anti-anti-anti-ballistic missile, and so forth. "It got a moderate laugh," Dave Jr. remembered.

One evening a ten-year-old Dave Jr. watched his dad adjust his bow tie before going out to a function. "Where are you going tonight, pop?" he asked. "I'm going to an honorary dinner to introduce Dr. Jonas Salk," Garroway replied.

"What's his bag?"

"Why, he was the inventor of the polio vaccine."

"What's polio, Daddy?"

The question stopped Garroway cold. "You mean, you've never heard of polio?"

"No."

Garroway paused for a moment, looked at his son and told him of the terror the crippling disease poliomyelitis had once been, of the thousands it had crippled and disfigured for life, of the parents who lived in terror that their children might be stricken, of kids forbidden from swimming in local pools or swimming holes on sweltering summer days because of their parents' fear they might contract the terrible scourge – and of the miraculous discovery that put an end to that era of fear. "And the kids of today have never heard of it?" Garroway said as he headed for the door. "Wow, what a wonderful thing Dr. Salk did for the world by inventing the polio vaccine." The next day, Garroway told his son that when he went to the podium to introduce Dr. Salk, he began his introduction with that story. "There wasn't a dry eye in the house!" he said. "Thank you, son. You don't know how beautiful what you said was, and what a marvelous story it provided me."[34]

Word got around. Columnist Earl Wilson quoted the Salk story in his column, and for some time the anecdote received play, sometimes from Garroway's frequent retellings. "Sometimes it made me feel a little embarrassed and stupid that my ignorance was the source of his story," Dave Jr. remembered, "but no one ever made fun of me, and I was glad to provide Dad with such evidently good material."[35]

The public Garroway continued to alternate between sunny optimism about projects in the offing – programs always just around the corner, books to be published soon – and frustration about the things that were holding him back. In the meantime, he filled his time with commercials and promotional projects: films for Chrysler and General Electric, radio commercials for an insurance company, guest appearances on others' talk shows, personal appearances at conferences and industrial events. One day he might be upbeat, clowning his way through an interview with a non-stop string of jokes and anecdotes and non-sequiturs; the next, he might be questioning the nature of television, lamenting, "There are only so many television shows which can use guys like me." Or he might be pondering a run for Congress from New York: "I may get licked, but I'm going to make a run for it," he said in 1965. He even did a favor for his estranged *alma mater*, joining two other distinguished alums in winning $15,000 for Washington University in St. Louis on the quiz show *Alumni Fun*.[36]

As 1967 dawned, Garroway looked forward to his release from the NBC agreement, tired of being what one writer called "television's equivalent of the old tramp journalist." He hoped for another talk show. "There's room for a great many people to do some talking, people who will stick their necks out. I would like to irritate the population," he said. When an interviewer suggested the style of H.L. Mencken, Garroway agreed. "Yes, that's a good example. Radio used to be courageous. Lowell Thomas, Gabriel Heatter said what they wanted to. They weren't necessarily controversial." Garroway now felt television was "full of cliches," saying that John Chancellor had "read what he was told." Though he had praise for his old Chicago friend Hugh Downs, Garroway felt "the more you're off camera, the better you are. It's best when the camera focuses on the guest."[37]

The new year would be a quiet one, with more of the same. His closest brush with the limelight was his appearance on the fifteenth anniversary show of *Today*, where he said, "There have been a lot of changes. As a friend of mine said, the OLD Dave Garroway was younger." But most of the year was busy work: a film on behalf of the IRS, a fundraiser to help the New Jersey Astronomical Association build an observatory, moderating a forum in Virginia on the history of American comedy. There was time for a trip to Hawaii, where he reunited with some old friends from KGU.[38]

There was one personal triumph. The devoted amateur astronomer acquired an Alvan Clark Refractor telescope that had been built for Beloit College in 1882. "Stradivarius made 600 fiddles; Alvan Clark built only 139 lenses," the proud owner, who carried a picture of the telescope in his wallet, later said. "The Smithsonian wants me to will it to them, but I think Clark would prefer to have it used!" Garroway never missed an opportunity to promote astronomy, wishing more people would look through a telescope, believing it would not only expand knowledge but lead people to a realization about life. "Most people suffer from what I call 'The Illusion of Central Position,' meaning they think nothing exists but themselves. A telescope proves that isn't so. But then today, most people don't know the difference between astronomy and astrology."[39]

Loring Mandel, who had visited Garroway in the *11:60 Club* studio two decades before, was now an award-winning screenwriter for film and television. Over the years, he had occasion to cross paths with Garroway, and with each passing year Mandel noted Garroway acting differently. On one visit to Garroway's apartment in the 1960s, to persuade Garroway to appear in a sesquicentennial tribute to Illinois, Mandel noted his obsession with his Questar telescope, and listened as Garroway described evenings of looking through the telescope into apartment windows from Central Park. Two decades before, Garroway had revealed to Mandel that his on-air persona was an invention. Now, Mandel saw no animation in him, and felt "his personality had congealed into eccentricity."[40]

Persuaded to join other Illinois-related luminaries as part of the program, Garroway arrived at the Merchandise Mart in Chicago. It was a homecoming after nearly fifteen years. "Where you been, Dave?" asked an elevator operator. "Oh, on vacation," he happily replied. Garroway visited Studio A, where his Chicago School career had taken off two decades before. While the crew prepared to shoot the segment, Garroway told Mandel that he had a new project: setting up high-quality tape recorders in all the rooms in his apartment, keeping them running all the time to capture the messages he was getting from space. From there, Garroway started describing conspiracies on Earth. "His mind seemed blasted," Mandel wrote years later. When the cameras were on, Garroway became the cool, whimsical personality the public knew and loved. After it was done, Mandel never saw him again. Years later he concluded that Garroway, as had happened with other celebrities "trapped by a public persona which proved stronger than the inner self which created it," had turned into "his own fabrication." Mandel wrote, "The inauthentic quality of his life was destructive."[41]

There was a sort of desperation in Garroway's infrequent national media appearances: the paneling ads offering a free set of wildlife prints, the radio commercials for auto insurance, a once-familiar face looking slightly plump and worn, a once-familiar voice now sounding tired and reedy. More often he found himself playing to local audiences, such as taping a local program in Pennsylvania, narrating as Jerry Orbach manipulated the puppets he used in *Carnival* in a lighthearted dramatization of how a television station functioned.[42]

There were those who still wanted him, but their efforts were stymied. A couple of young ABC correspondents, Charles Osgood and Ted Koppel, had worked in radio on the innovative series *Flair Reports*, little five-minute features about interesting or unusual items in the news. As Koppel later remembered, he and Osgood "decided to get into television and have influence. We were young and iconoclastic, doing things our own way." The two had an idea for an ABC morning show and contacted Garroway about anchoring it. He was interested. Osgood and Koppel met with ABC's vice president of programming and presented their idea, believing that having the host already lined up would win the day. "So what?" the executive replied, shooting the idea down. "I'll get anyone I want."[43]

Garroway was on the path of following many a former star put out to pasture. Paul Harvey lamented that "often the Red Buttons or George Gobel or Dave Garroway or Garry Moore was just chewed up and spit out by the insatiable public appetite for something different." Garroway was in the strange limbo of the one-time star, the subject of "is he still alive?" letters to television editors, of rumors that he was in seclusion, in poor health, or had suffered a nervous breakdown. To make matters worse, a former personal manager was arrested after forging $20,000 in checks from Garroway's accounts.[44]

As the summer of 1968 brought unrest, exemplified by the televised riots outside the Democratic National Convention in Chicago, Garroway took a pessimistic view of television's influence on young people. "The riots and unrest by the young which seems to frighten so many adults out of their wits is a natural outgrowth of a TV-weaned generation," he worried. "Violence as the natural order of things has been the message of too much television. Why then should the youth choose any other course? Perhaps if we could give our children microscopes or telescopes and ask them to compare the wonders of those worlds with what is offered on TV, we'd be able to stimulate their minds instead of arousing their imaginations." He didn't see things getting better. "If violence succeeds then the natural reaction is to copy violence, not create something new and untried. Granted, audiences remain constant and, therefore, the executives reason the public is satisfied. But there should be choice and variety. People simply do not go into a book store and simply ask for a book. Nor do they ask for just a record at a record store. Why then must we assume that they simply want any TV program?"[45]

22

In fall 1968 Dave Garroway, more than fifty pounds lighter after four months on a rice diet at Duke University's Kempner Institute, proclaimed himself "full of the old zip and altogether ready to return to the television wars." A broadcast group had named him "man of the year," an honor at least one critic thought "about ten years late." He had recently impressed critics and viewers by filling in on Dick Cavett's interview program, showing flashes of his old magic. In January, he had filled in for a week on a Cincinnati talk show. He was hungry for opportunities. "I figured I had used up enough of my life doing nothing," he said. "I wanted to be doing something myself. For the last two or three years I have been consciously looking for a job." When an offer came to host a daily program in Boston, "I jumped at it."[1]

That April, RKO announced the new Garroway series, *Tempo Boston*. It pleased him not only to be back on television, but to come back to Boston. "I like Boston more than any other city in the country," he said at the press conference announcing the show. Recounting his boyhood years in the city and his experiences at Harvard before the war, he said he knew the city well. "I never expected to be back but now that I am, I'm most pleased." The move satisfied another desire, for he had fallen out of love with New York and wanted out. The decision to leave had been made firm after Dave Jr. was held up and mugged three times within a year. "Twice he had his bicycle stolen out from under him, once his watch was taken. I decided to leave New York. Not just the city – the same kind of thing happens in Westchester. I had to get out of the entire area."[2]

The new Boston show, ninety minutes long, aired in the late morning. Garroway told *Time* that *Tempo*'s premise was "the desk and sofa concept." With a staff of six, they put on a daily program that covered anything and everything. From the very first show, *Tempo* made headlines. Lieutenant Steven Harris, a crew member of the Navy spy ship *Pueblo*, spoke of the ship's capture and the crew's imprisonment by North Korea the previous year. "There is a great deal more to be told" about what happened, Harris said, saying the North Korean system was "a hundred times worse" than most Americans realized. Responding to charges that the ship's captain surrendered the ship without a fight, Harris said, "I don't think anyone can be considered delinquent." His comments on Garroway's program were picked up by the Associated Press and carried nationwide.[3]

Most editions of *Tempo Boston* were a mix of the controversial, the scientific, the whimsical, the literary and the musical. A group of MIT scientists might demonstrate laser beams. Priests arrested for burning draft cards might talk about their cause. An author would be interviewed. A musical guest would perform. On one episode, a segment discussed hair weaving, and Bud Collins consented to having a hair weave performed on stage while the amused host watched safely from the sidelines. "Garroway kept saying, 'Well, it's interesting,'" Collins wrote of the surreal experience. "I thought he sounded snobbish – probably because he has lots of hair."[4]

Anything and everything was fair game. It was a mix similar to *Today*, but adapted for the sensibilities of a new era. *Time* said Garroway's "often waggish" taste "brings in such atypical guests as the proprietor of an ant colony, the mother of twenty-three children, a pewtersmith, a psychiatrist discussing transvestites, and an eighty-eight-year-old barbell buff." One program featured Garroway's interview with a wax dummy of Albert Einstein, borrowed from a local museum. More monologue than anything else, Garroway "conversed" with Einstein about the famous $E=mc^2$ equation, and about science and religion. Garroway sought to be interesting and relevant. "This is the way to feel young again," he said. "I want contact with youth. I sympathize with their aims. I want to be in touch with what they're doing. I approve of their activism, although I don't know whether I like it or not. I won't say I don't trust anyone over thirty, but it gets close to that sometimes. I'd like to try to bridge the generation gap." Nor was he afraid of stirring things up. "I won't carry a torch, but I won't shrink from controversy or opinion."[5]

The show demonstrated as much. Atheist Madalyn Murray O'Hair, whose appearances on other programs had drawn protest, had a surprisingly muted appearance on *Tempo Boston*. The interview prompted only two angry phone calls, a sign Garroway believed represented changing times. During the Vietnam Moratorium that October, the program went to two hours and provided extensive coverage of the protests. People were watching *Tempo* and engaging with it, so much that WBZ distilled highlights into a weekly program aired on Saturday evenings. This, wrote Percy Shain, "indicates how well his new show has taken hold here." *Time* praised Garroway's show for being done live, an antidote to "the prefabricated world of television." Though Garroway's show faced competition from reruns and game shows, *Time* called it "far more interesting than most of Boston's local programs – and, for that matter, the network competition as well."[6]

For the first six months or so, Garroway and son lived in the Somerset Hotel on Boston's Commonwealth Avenue. They then moved into a beach house in Scituate, about an hour from Boston. Perhaps remembering the sad fate of Nemo Point, Garroway purchased a home made of poured concrete, with a roof of barreled vaults also cast in concrete, atop a sturdy sea well. "It could have withstood a nuclear blast, no less a howling Nor'easter," Dave Jr. remembered. "In a big storm, waves would come pummeling in, hit the sea wall, and go straight up and then back down." During one such storm, Garroway thought it would be neat to go out on the sea wall as the waves crashed in, so he bought a couple of wet suits. Safely clad, the Garroway men went out and watched the water smash against the sea wall in front of them, "toasty warm" in their wet suits. "The one-hour drive to Boston every day was a grind," Dave Jr. recalled, "but the serenity of the ocean made it worthwhile." Fifty years later, he still missed that house.[7]

Garroway's beloved telescope was set up beneath an aluminum dome, and Dave Jr. sometimes joined his dad there. "Once he showed me the rice-like clouds which are constantly railing up on the surface of the Sun," he said. "He said each one was half the size of the Earth." One day they watched Mercury transit the front of the Sun. They built a two-stage rocket, sending a white mouse on a wild ride skyward. During the summer Dave Jr. caddied at the nearby golf club that his dad belonged to. Though Dave Jr. said he wasn't the best caddy, he enjoyed occasions when he could play a round with his dad.[8]

Garroway didn't get out very much. "I don't care much for social life," he said. He rarely dated and seldom went to the theater. "My chief enjoyment is in playing with little David. He can make me laugh." While his relationship with Dave Jr. was close, those with his other children were distant. Paris was now twenty-six, living in Hawaii and working as an interior decorator. "I guess she spends most of her time surfing," Garroway said. Of Michael, now twenty and attending university in Paris, he said "We're not very close, but we're not estranged, either."[9]

Tempo Boston's success persuaded RKO that there was a wider audience for Garroway's program. In November 1969 it was retooled into an hour-long program with a studio audience and a call-in segment. The program, retitled *Garroway*, would also have a segment called "Garroway at Large," where Dave could speak his mind on any topic. It would debut November 24 in Boston, Philadelphia and New York, while work began to get the show aired in Providence, Hartford, Washington, Baltimore and Los Angeles.[10]

The new program started strong. Garroway started off quietly reading Joyce Kilmer's poem "Trees," only to be interrupted by cheerleaders, a marching band, and Professor Irwin Corey carrying a potted tree. Before the hour was up, the audience had been treated to a song from Anna Maria Alberghetti, a conversation with former presidential aide Ted Sorensen, a discussion on Vice President Agnew's comments about bias in television news, and more comedy from Irwin Corey.

Garroway "is back in top form, visually and verbally, his face and figure streamlined again to match his spare, but astute conversation," Harry Harris wrote in the *Philadelphia Inquirer*. Praising the crackle of the live format, Harris wrote, "Garroway's great – a shrewd interviewer, a show-wise emcee and a classy and charismatic human being." The program "represents a welcome upgrading of morning air fare." Kay Gardella liked it, too. "Like everything else he has undertaken," Gardella wrote, Garroway "brings a unique, searching point of view to the contemporary scene."[11]

Garroway tried to be easy in how he drew people out, feeling people were primed for attacks. "I want them to say what they think without fear of criticism," he said. "I want a guest to give his entire views on an issue. An attack stymies the flow of information." Guests, he said, "come in low-key and don't pressure until I tell them we're doing the show live. And then everything changes. They go right to work." The location in Boston also helped. "When people travel that distance to be on TV they make an effort to do something." He also felt his job as host was to moderate, not pontificate. "When people call up and ask questions I'll let the experts answer. I don't want to play God."

Yet for all his charm and easy-going nature, Garroway could be a penetrating interviewer. Journalist Joe McGinniss found himself in a televised hot seat while promoting his book *The Selling of the President 1968*. "Dave Garroway does an interview that makes Barbara Walters look like my three-year-old daughter," he later wrote. As an example, he quoted an on-air inquiry from the genial host: "Now I'm going to quote a line of your book out of context, Mr. McGinniss, which you may say is unfair, but it's not nearly as unfair as what you did to Mr. Nixon."[12]

As tended to happen, the luck ran out. Metromedia, which had purchased RKO Television, wanted out of live television. "They went back to movies and the show came off," Garroway said. Affiliates began to drop the show in mid-February. WOR, which had carried *Garroway* in New York, replaced it with *The Joe Franklin Show*. *Garroway* aired for the last time on February 27. Viewers complained. "What is wrong with Boston?" one asked. "I think the type of show Mr. Garroway conducted was too rich for its blood. This talented and humble man added to the pleasure of daytime viewing immeasurably. How could the television moguls be so short-sighted?" Another wrote that Garroway "is an outstanding performer and person and has always presented entertaining and thoughtful programs. WNAC-TV will be much poorer without him."[13]

Garroway, who decided to remain in the Boston area for the time being, picked up a consolation prize of sorts. WGBH, the Public Broadcasting Service affiliate in Boston, hired him for an informational show about the station. Airing on Thursdays beginning in July, *2's Company with Dave Garroway* took a look behind the scenes at Channel 2, talked with the station's personalities, and showed short films.[14]

Though Garroway was glad to help promote an educational channel, he hoped for another commercial opportunity. Nothing was in the immediate offing, though, and he was soon back to taping promotional pitches. "I miss television sometimes," he said while in Charlotte on behalf of a furniture company. "I miss the joys and the agonies. But I've found things to keep me busy." He didn't care for much modern television, anyway. "Ratings for such shows are not high enough and the ratings game runs the business," he said. "Television is an economically-controlled business. It's there to make money. Networks don't worry about the fairness of news. They worry about getting ratings." The one hope he had was for public television. "The networks give to public TV money. It's conscience money. They do this to get the people off their backs. I guess this is the nature of the communications business."[15]

In the meantime, Garroway's manager Al Bruno moved to Los Angeles. His move made Garroway wonder if the West Coast might be fertile ground for a comeback. When Bruno told him of an opportunity at Los Angeles radio station KFI, Garroway leapt. His son took the relocation well. "I was sad because I was just getting used to Massachusetts," Dave Jr. remembered, but when he learned his dad's new job meant moving to Los Angeles, suddenly "it didn't seem so awful."[16]

23

Once more Garroway pulled up stakes, crating up his collection of artifacts and miscellany for the move west. He leased a house in Studio City with a layout suitable for using his telescope, and enrolled Dave Jr. in a private school. The Scituate house went up for sale. The Alvan Clark telescope didn't make the trip, and Garroway eventually abandoned hopes of bringing it to California. The Smithsonian pleaded for it, but Garroway refused. "People are to look through it, not at it," he insisted. Garroway eventually sold it at a deep discount to a small college in Pennsylvania, which used it as the basis of a working observatory.[1]

The telescope didn't make it, but the Jaguar did. Garroway didn't drive it much, though. "He got too many jealous looks," Dave Jr. recalled. "In New York, back in the day, people would give you the thumbs-up if they saw you driving a nice car. But in the '70s in Los Angeles, it didn't go over as big, because everybody wants to be that guy driving the Jag." More often, Garroway drove a Camaro. When his first one overheated and blew up, Chevrolet gave him a new one with a special engine built for law enforcement. According to Dave Jr., the car could "haul ass." One night, trying to pass a car on a slick Mulholland Drive, Dave Jr. accelerated and the Camaro fishtailed, nearly sending him over a cliff. The brush with disaster made him a cautious driver the rest of his life. "Just the thought of flooring a car makes me queasy," he said. He never emulated his father's racing adventures, preferring to stay with drums. "They are much safer to drive."[2]

The new KFI program began late in August. Garroway described the three-hour show as "a few records, a lot of talk and a few commercials." He hoped for a few guests and a chance for some monologues. "It will be a show about things that concern people today. There'll be some elements of education, some elements of entertainment. And, I hope, there will be at least one element of surprise." Reviewer Don Page called it "an alternate route to the yak and the musical flack." Although Garroway was often "interesting, bracing, whimsical," he could also drone on, talking himself into traps. "When Garroway is good, he's excellent. When he's off his game (unprepared?), he's pretty dull." Even with the off days, Page wrote, "You keep going back to it, because you want to hear him when he's good."[3]

Cecil Smith was driving home from a speech CBS executive Mike Dann gave about the state of television. Dann, a onetime NBC executive, cited *Wide Wide World* as an example of the adventurous and imaginative programming television needed to do in hard times. The reference prompted Smith to think about Garroway and "that effortless, relaxed style." When Smith turned on the car radio and heard Garroway's program, "it was almost like a legend coming to life," as he heard the veteran broadcaster "treating the listener as an intelligent and informed human being, talking to him as he would a friend over a drink." Smith said, "His wit is as quick and agile as ever." One interviewer compared Garroway's free-associative rambles, which were new to the Los Angeles radio audience, with the sometimes nostalgic monologues Jean Shepherd had made famous on New York radio. "Sort of," Garroway replied. "I'm not that good, though. I don't have that many memories, but I do have some, and more today than in the past."[4]

Garroway adjusted well to Los Angeles. "I was a little worried," he said, "but nothing about it is as bad as an Easterner hears it is. The smog is not nearly as bad as in New York. I was surprised. It's really quite a pleasant place." His views about New York had only hardened since leaving. "Don't ask me about that wonderful girl I loved so much who has become a vicious painted slut! I miss the New York that was." Nor did he miss the people: "Nobody looks at you or speaks to you there. They're all angry."[5]

But California could be vicious in its own way. In February 1971, Dave Jr. was one day away from his thirteenth birthday. His father told him he would go to bed a boy and wake up a teenager. The next morning, the new teenager was rudely awakened as the house violently shook. It was an earthquake. Terrified, he ran into his dad's bedroom. "First I saw the waves sloshing out of our pool onto our patio through the glass doors in Dad's bedroom," he remembered. Out in the valley beyond, he saw transformers exploding in bright flashes as they fell from utility poles. While catastrophe unfolded, while the house shook, the senior Garroway stayed in bed, smiling. "See what being a teenager is like?" he yelled over the racket.

The ground settled. Dave Jr. looked at his dad. "Weren't you scared?"

"Nope. I just enjoyed it."[6]

Garroway insisted the move to California and the shift to radio was a conscious decision "not to fight the past. I decided to walk away from it." He wanted to look toward the future, citing the words of Harold Russell, the double amputee who won two Academy Awards for his role in *The Best Years of Our Lives*: "It isn't what you've lost. It's what you've got left." Leonard Laurent, calling Garroway "an old tiger whose hide is full of scars and whose mind is full of battles lost," wrote, "He has been away for a long time, much of that time unemployed, but Garroway is not the kind of man who can be idle for very long."[7]

Garroway admitted he took the KFI job because it was the only one available. He still yearned to get back into television, and insisted projects were in the works. He had been trying to get a new version of *Information Please* on the air, but balked at the restrictions placed on the revival by the program's rights holder. He would, he said, even go back on *Today* if he could: in spite of his differences with the show's direction, "I'd grab it in a minute." It was better than not working, which ate at him. "The only thing I never want to do again is not work," he said. "When a man stops working, he stops functioning. He needs to work." He had even started taking acting lessons. "I'm available for anything," he said. "Who knows what I might get a chance to do next? After all, here I am on the West Coast...it would be handy to know a little bit about the trade."[8]

CBS, meanwhile, was looking at summer replacement series for the *Carol Burnett* timeslot. Producer Robert Tamplin and producer/director Bill Hobin were developing a series that would give up-and-coming performers a chance for national stardom. Instead of a *Talent Scouts* contest, *The CBS Newcomers* would feature an ensemble. There would be comedians, musical groups, singers – but no rock groups, for those represented an audience they weren't seeking. Tamplin visited fifty-six cities and auditioned hundreds of young performers for the show. The idea, he said, "is to find people whom the networks would like to develop for future CBS series and variety shows. We want to build talent for television."[9]

The CBS Newcomers featured a number of industry veterans: head writer Charlie Isaacs, musical director Nelson Riddle, and Chicago

School veteran Bill Hobin. What they didn't have was a familiar face to welcome the audience, introduce the acts and bridge segments. CBS president Robert Wood asked Hobin, "What's the glue to hold it together?" Hobin thought back to Chicago, where he had directed *Garroway at Large*, whose format was an inspiration for the new show. "I'd like to get somebody like Garroway," Hobin said. Wood replied, "Why not get Garroway?"[10]

It was a shot of life for Garroway, and he was grateful someone remembered. "Suddenly, there was this call – and the whole world changes its complexion," Garroway said. "When you're off television this long, the networks think you've passed into another world," he added. "I've missed a place to sound off. I'm a ham." He was happy to be back with his old colleague Hobin, who praised Garroway as "one of the best television salesmen we have." Tamplin said they chose Garroway "because he is excellent at holding a show together; a host with a soft style. He'll coordinate it beautifully."[11]

Garroway threw himself into the new job, working hard in rehearsals, getting to know his new writers and staff, as well as the young performers in the cast. He had a five-person writing staff to feed him material, but "I don't know if that's a luxury or a handicap," he said. "In the past, I had only one, an idea man." He hoped the fact CBS produced the program, and was putting a lot of resources into it, would help it become a regular series. As *The CBS Newcomers* came closer to air, Garroway announced his plans to leave KFI at the end of his contract year. Part of it, he said, was his hope the new show would become a regular program. "Work leads to work," he told a reporter.[12]

The second chance at a network television career excited him. Driving in to the lot at Television City, seeing his name on a reserved parking space, "was like being reborn. It was something I never again expected to do, a good moment. I'll be talking to almost a new set of listeners, like a new generation." Walking before the cameras, he said, "I felt it again – the old ham bone in me. It felt good. Almost like not having ever been away." He hoped to bring back his low-pressure style that was born in a low-budget format, but didn't know how well it would work in a big-budget era. Still, he hoped "to make real people out of these young singers, dancers and comedians, usually through little, light conversations." Garroway thought highly of the young performers. Watching a rehearsal one day with Hobin, Garroway commented on their youth and energy, how eager they were on stage. "They remind me of the way we were. Remember, Bill?" Hobin nodded. "They have some precedent," he said. Garroway softly replied, "Yeah. We didn't know what we were doing."[13]

On the evening of July 18, CBS viewers saw a familiar smiling at them through the screen once again. "My name is Dave Garroway. Do you remember?" he said. "I did my first show in 1948 and here I am tonight, a newcomer...But it's a kick being here even if some of the newcomers weren't even born when I was doing TV in Chicago. That was a long time ago, back when Ed Sullivan was just one of the kids on *Juvenile Jury*." From there, Garroway introduced acts from the ensemble of young performers: singers Paul Perez, Gay Perkins, Cynthia Clawson, Peggy Sears and David Arlen. The Californians, a vocal group from a nearby church, provided more music. A five-person comedy troupe called the Good Humor Company performed physical comedy. Also in the cast were singer Rex Allen Jr., and comedians Joe Garzia and Rodney Winfield.[14]

Much as he had on *Garroway at Large*, Garroway wandered between acts, this time conducting little interviews with the performers, helping viewers get to know them, serving as the youngsters' avuncular guide to the world of television. And time was left at the end for Garroway to deliver a philosophical aside. On the first show, he lamented the modern disposable culture: people drinking from disposable cups and glasses, wiping their faces with disposable napkins. From his pocket, he pulled out a fountain pen. "It saddens me to think there are those watching this show who have never owned one of these," he said. "It didn't write under water, and it didn't write upside down, but it wrote beautifully. And then – get this now! – when it ran dry, you didn't throw it away. You filled it again, and again, and soon it fit your hand. It got to be your pen."[15]

Reviews were mixed. A Fort Lauderdale reviewer said that Garroway's return brought nostalgia, but after that, "the action was 1971," and in spite of hit-or-miss acts, the program showed promise as "good escape from regular blah summer programming." Kay Gardella credited Garroway's experience with salvaging a show full of talent on a tryout. "That's all it was, really, a tryout. All need a little seasoning before they're ready for the big league. All, that is, except Garroway. Peace." San Francisco reviewer Dwight Newton said *Newcomers* "ranged from quite good to really bad. Don't knock it," but hoped Garroway, who "looked good, slim and radiant," would get better lines than "the terribly stilted generation gap lines he struggled with last night." Don Freeman praised Garroway as "the epitome of easygoing professionalism, a sure-handed master of the subtle intricacies of the medium," and hoped *The CBS Newcomers* would "wear well. We shall see. One might also hope that the writing on the show will gain in sharpness and believability." Dick Shippy, though he lamented the program's rough edges and Garroway's "idle and too often, inane" conversation with the performers, singled out the fountain pen monologue as reminiscent of Garroway's Chicago days. "It wasn't cute, it wasn't folksy; it was just whimsical...and it was Garroway." Another writer called it "a moment to savor – a sweet observation to carry home like Mrs. Miniver's 'pebbles' and share with someone you know will understand and be as delighted as you were." Clarence Petersen of the *Chicago Tribune* said the commentary was "a small golden moment" that "said as much about our disposable culture as any ten volumes of protest literature."[16]

Those who didn't like *Newcomers* held nothing back. "Sitting outside watching fireflies do their thing might prove to be more interesting than watching the Newcomers do theirs," wrote Joyce Wagner in the *Kansas City Star*. Orlando reviewer Colby Sinclair felt Garroway was a poor choice: "Garroway's generation gap with these youngsters was canyon wide." Emery Wister of the *Charlotte News* wrote, "You could almost smell the moth balls," calling Garroway "a little out of place. You can say that again for his feeble attempts at humor. The emcee style he displayed last night was over the hill ten years ago and the show's writers did him no favor with the dialogue they gave him."[17]

UPI writer Rick Dubrow called *Newcomers* "a visualized generation gap," believing Garroway was "victimized by the foolish and self-consciously cute dialogue" that he engaged in with "several disastrous acts." The fountain pen monologue, he wrote, let Garroway "exhibit some of the special charm that has made him a unique stylist in the art of communications" and "was miles ahead of the rest of the hour." The rest of the program, however, was a "dousing of new talent by old devices."[18]

A few were downright savage. Judy Bachrach of the *Baltimore Sun* eviscerated the "stuffed turkey" that CBS had aired. "Words fail me," she wrote. She couldn't believe Garroway's "achingly predictable" jokes about being a newcomer, or "the lyrics to 'We've Only Just Begun' chanted in Garroway alexandrines," which "take second place in meaning, depth and scope only to 'love means not ever having to say you're sorry.'" Referring to a segment when Garroway folded a $20 bill into an isosceles triangle, Bachrach wrote, "My Uncle Paul used to do similar things with nickels at cocktail parties. Generally he was never invited again. Definitely nobody paid him for it." One critic later went so far as to say Garroway "looks these days as if he had been coated with shellac."[19]

Calgary columnist Bob Shiels wrote that Garroway didn't fit the program. "Garroway may have been a gas two decades ago, but he's over the hill now. He blows lines, misses camera cues, and generally acts as though he's been away from TV for so long he's forgotten what it's about." he wrote. "The Newcomers weren't particularly impressive last Sunday. They're supposed to be professionals, but they don't act like it. Old Dave's attempts to laugh it up with them are downright pathetic." Tom Hopkins of the *Dayton Daily News*, though far less scathing, captured the mood of several critics: "Let's hope this isn't where Dave finishes."[20]

Subsequent episodes, and adjustments to the series (including a new "street people" comedy segment, featuring the Good Humor Company in a segment modeled after Allen's Alley), didn't improve prospects. "They have the help of the pros at CBS, but even old hand Dave Garroway, who is host, seems to be doing it with one hand tied behind his back and someone else's toupee on his head," Detroit critic Bettelou Peterson wrote. The show "just didn't have the polish and the material was obviously second layer." Percy Shain of the *Boston Globe* wrote "There was so little to salvage in this hour-long stanza that it has to be set down as a waste of time" and suggested "someone (probably the writers) should be sued for perpetuating such a mis-mash."[21]

As the show's brief run concluded, Garroway had no illusions. "The television show was too good to be true," he told Cynthia Lowry. "It was so much fun for me it was almost indecent, like doing *Garroway at Large* again." He tried to see hope in knowing the network was keeping the costumes and scenery in storage, and in rumors the show could come back as a replacement series, but he had to be realistic. "There are so many TV things in the wind, I am feeling confused." He spoke again of prospects: one special about to move, another two under discussion, some commercials, and even some acting lessons. "I want to be ready for anything."[22]

The end of *The CBS Newcomers* coincided with his departure from KFI. Publicly, Garroway said the radio series had become a grind, that eighteen hours a week on the air required "an awful lot of things to talk about." Garroway's secretary at KFI, Sylvia O'Gilvie, saw something else at work. "He was frustrated and misunderstood the whole time," she remembered. The station's middle-of-the-road music format frustrated him, and didn't let him play enough jazz to satisfy him, or conduct enough long-form interviews. "He was marvelous to work with," she remembered, "kind, compassionate and bright, witty, but very shy." The end of his KFI stint left him "relieved," she recalled. "I left, too. I couldn't stay there without him."[23]

Again a free agent, Garroway took a rafting trip down the Colorado River rapids with Dave Jr., and worked on the golf game he had resumed after moving to California. Although some projects were in the works, Garroway said what he really wanted was his own talk show, but one that had an entertainment aspect as well. He liked David Frost's interviewing style and had become fond of Dick Cavett's work, seeing in him "a certain irreverence that darts in and out. He asks hard questions and smiles but sticks to his guns. It's easy to get cowardly and make your guests all love you. But that's not what this business should be." Garroway felt he would be especially good as a host because he felt closer to people than he had before. "I have more empathy for other people's problems, I guess, because I've had a few problems myself."[24]

For as much as he disliked its present format, *Today* provoked an ache in his heart. A few years before, while in New York, he had walked past the old RCA Exhibition Hall. "I have no regrets about leaving *Today*," he said, "but I sometimes do have a nostalgic twinge when I watch it." What did he miss most? "Being a part of a show where we could put people on the TV who had something to say. When that happened, it all seemed worthwhile, even that getting up in the morning. Other times, it wouldn't work." His old Chicago colleague Hugh Downs was about to step down from *Today*, with Frank McGee about to replace him. Garroway wasn't concerned. "Frank will play it straight. He'll be fine."[25]

Garroway came back to *Today* in October for Downs' last day as host. Jack E. Anderson, television critic for the *Miami Herald*, found himself as nostalgic as Garroway for a time long gone. "Seeing the bespectacled Garroway on the screen evoked memories of the old format of the show, a format which has changed considerably, and I'm not so sure for the better." Anderson yearned for the fun the show had in the Garroway days, "those days when the show was not so studio-bound, so remote from those people who used to press their noses to the windows in the old ground floor location."[26]

24

With *The CBS Newcomers* and his KFI show now history, Garroway was again an itinerant performer, nibbling the edges of a business that had little use for him. There was the obligatory appearance on the *Today* anniversary special in 1972. Now that eighteen-year-olds could vote, Garroway enlisted Pat Weaver to help with a concept on a series to help educate young voters. He hosted a syndicated special, the *National Automotive Trouble Quiz*, featuring Peggy Cass, Louis Nye and racer Peter Revson in a lighthearted effort to educate drivers on car trouble, how to fix it and how to prevent it. His investment in acting lessons paid off with a guest role as a cantankerous judge on an episode of *Alias Smith and Jones*. Almost unrecognizable without his glasses, with hairstyle and muttonchops out of the 1870s, Garroway's character seemed symbolic of the man himself, a man at odds with times that had left him behind. "I worked hard at it," Garroway said, though he didn't see himself getting into stage work. "So much trouble remembering the lines. That's how I had to do the TV role, a line at a time." On the set, he befriended actor Peter Duel. "We had a casual half-hour talk of spider webs and stuff and I thought 'What a nice easy guy for this business.'"[1]

More frequently, when Garroway surfaced in the media, it was as a spokesman. A chain of regional banks hired him for a series of ads. It was jarring to see Garroway in large-rimmed glasses, looking thinner, wearing a necktie instead of a bowtie, plugging passbook savings accounts or cookbook giveaways. Or it was as a special celebrity marshal or attendee at some charity event, or as a guest on an anniversary special or nostalgia program alongside people like Gisele Mackenzie and Sid Caesar, fellow prisoners of an unofficial nostalgia circuit, onetime pioneers left behind by changing tastes.[2]

Garroway knew the medium had changed, and he became increasingly outspoken. He criticized the programs (of *The CBS Newcomers*, he said, "If that was the caliber of people found after a year of expensive auditions, the future of show business is very bleak") and the decisions of those who ran the networks. "Television is worse now than ten or fifteen years ago," he complained, bemoaning the lack of real people on television, people the audience knew for distinctive personalities. "I mean real people, that people watched, that they knew – Sid Caesar, Milton Berle, Garroway, perhaps – they were strong personalities that the audience knew, and reacted to. It seems so bland and prepared now." Recalling the "fly on the nose" incident from *Garroway at Large*, he lamented the loss of spontaneity, the kind of inventiveness and lack of pretense he now could see only on low-power Spanish-language stations. "You'll never see anything like that on TV today. But, then, I don't know...maybe I'm the only one around who misses that kind of television. Maybe I belong in another, long-gone era when people had time for nonsense." He remembered Fred Allen, so eager to appear on *Garroway at Large* that he paid his own way to Chicago and refused a salary, and mourned "that kind doesn't exist any more." He even lamented what television had done to people: "I brought them together in little rooms to gather around a tube and not say anything to each other, just look. That's the saddest part."[3]

Sometimes Garroway didn't realize how out of step he was with the times, and it led to embarrassing moments. In 1974, hosting a salute to jazz at the Newport Jazz Festival at Lincoln Center, Garroway was in the company of an all-star lineup that included old friends such as Jackie Cain and Roy Kral. He seemed shaky as he took the microphone, and his rambling commentary prompted an audience member to shout, "Shut up and let 'em play!" Though one review noted that Garroway's style improved as the show went on, another implied his time had passed: "His mind seems elsewhere these days, and his remarks and jokes are neither tasteful nor pertinent."[4]

There were occasional rumors, such as a Washington-based television show. More often what he got was small projects, like a *Bicentennial Minute* segment for CBS during the run-up to the Bicentennial, or a series of public service announcements as a favor for his old friend Lee Lawrence, now working for a presidential commission to help the disabled. It was busy work, just enough for a taste, but never enough to quench the thirst. The attempts he initiated, such as a weekly syndicated radio series called *Dave's Place*, a revival of sorts of *The 11:60 Club*, didn't take hold.[5]

He even tried the networks once more. He approached ABC president Fred Silverman with an idea for a program about retirement planning.

The network wasn't interested. "Dave, four or five or six years from now, this show will be a standard feature," Silverman told him. "But if I took it into the program board today, I would be kicked out. You're ahead of your time." Garroway said the program was "of interest to everybody, directed to everybody. But twenty percent is directed to those over forty-five, who should be learning to retire." Spurned by the networks, he tried to syndicate it. Garroway even went under the knife, letting a manager talk him into a facelift that had little effect on his appearance.[6]

The longer he went on, the more dejected he felt, and the more he complained. "There haven't been any offers," he confessed to Tom Shales. He second-guessed his move to California. "If you're from the East, it's awfully hard to break in out here. I haven't said a word in public in two and a half years." A piece in the *National Enquirer* hinted at darker forces at work. "I've been blacklisted because of my conservative views," Garroway was quoted. "Right wing opinions – like the fact that America still is in danger from Russia – just aren't very welcome on network TV." He continued, "Even though I'm sixty-two, I have things to say that are important to the American people. We're falling behind in the arms race with Russia – and, to put it simply, Russia could beat us in a war. Something like that scares hell out of me. But, as I said, my opinions aren't popular. People say that I'm a has-been. But I'll be back one day."[7]

The industry had left him behind and didn't care to look back. Sometimes, that was literally so. At the 1975 Emmy awards, a reporter noted a bespectacled man standing in the back of the vast room at the Hollywood Palladium, "a former giant of the early TV industry, unnoticed and ignored. Dave Garroway was either looked through or never even recognized by present-day luminaries during the two-hour show." Visiting Garroway at home, writer Leonard Feather watched the former host look through his telescope and thought about how the only stars he saw now were those in the heavens. "One wonders how, in Minow's name, there cannot be an air space for Dave Garroway in the age of Wolfman Jack."[8]

He was tired and wounded. Reporter Bill Granger interviewed him in 1976, noting that "the chuckle that had been a million-dollar asset for NBC for nearly two decades" was a dry ghost of what it once had been. Garroway was slumped in the chair, looking "ill and tired and you had to strain to hear him. His voice was the unflected shadow of the voice that had talked soothingly to a generation." The voice came alive only when he was remembering the Chicago days or criticizing what had been done to *Today* ("There's no structure to it. It's so cut up. There's no humanity, there's no empathy"). He was still looking for work. "We're working on an interview show now. I think they've got five stations who will take it. I don't know...."[9]

For as frustrating as his professional life was, Dave Garroway still found great happiness in his collection of interests, and in his relationship with his son. Perhaps becoming a father later in life had an effect, or perhaps suddenly becoming a single parent had promoted their closeness, but Dave Jr. was treasured by his father, who saw wisdom in the boy. "He is fourteen, although he may be 412. I'm not sure," he told an interviewer in 1972.[10]

That year, after looking at what he estimated were "two hundred houses," Garroway and son moved into a ranch house on a cul-de-sac in the Santa Monica mountains, with a view of the San Fernando Valley below. The home had many windows, giving a sense of openness that Garroway liked. It also had no swimming pool, which had been a constant headache at the rental house. Mulholland Drive ran behind the house, and the Garroways frequently heard the squeal of tires as late-night car races played out.[11]

Garroway soon filled the home's sunken living room with an array of his collected curiosities: a framed collection of butterflies, another framed collection of exotic insects, the Norden bombsight, an abacus, a small liquid wave machine, a gyroscopic gimbal. On a table sat a piece of the original Mount Palomar mirror that had shattered while cooling. Garroway saw art in these inventions, and loved having them on display. Sometimes they satisfied his curiosity. "One of his favorite pastimes was to take a piece of surplus apart to see how it worked, and study the design and functions within," Dave Jr. remembered. "Sometimes he would call me over and say, 'Look at this! Isn't that a beautiful design?' Or 'Whaddya think this does?'" They also fueled conversation. The piece of the Mount Palomar telescope, for instance, inevitably drew questions from visitors who couldn't figure out what it was. "Dad always delighted in giving his little run-through about each item," Dave Jr. remembered. "It seemed like the discussion of their design and utility would always lead to other topics."[12]

Garroway outfitted the house with a quadraphonic sound system. The two rear speakers sat in the corners, on the carpet. Garroway mount-

With Dave Jr., Paris and Michael. (Paris Day collection)

ed the two front speakers on the wall with pipe fittings. The result, Dave Jr. said, was incredible. "It sounded great, as the sound boomed down on you," he said. "The pipes didn't soak up as much vibration as the carpet, so the sound was crisper also."

Garroway's love of telescopes necessitated one modification: replacing the regular glass in the large living room windows with glass that was optically flat. This allowed him to look out on the world with his beloved Questar telescope, getting a distortion-free view while sitting in his living room. "I'm sure it cost him a pretty penny, but it was worth it to him," Dave Jr. said. "With the new glass, we could sit on the couch, put the scope on the table and see the world. I still remember seeing the water in the aqueduct cascade down the mountain across the valley in Sylmar."[13]

Just as he had in New York, the tireless tinkerer set up a workshop at his new home in California. "He had a full shop," Dave Jr. remembered, "complete with a lathe, acetylene blowtorch, air compressor, and basically every tool known to mankind, and a few that weren't." There, he could do virtually anything, from common household repairs to manufacturing parts to keep his beloved Jaguar in fine working condition.

Most often, he would go to the shop to "putz around," as he called it. For the first couple of years, the shop was very disorganized. "It took him a good six months," Dave Jr. remembered, "but organize he did." Into the garage came many drawers and cabinets. He put them in the center of the garage, where they supported a work table. Inside the cabinets were all kinds of parts, alphabetically labeled and organized. No potential storage space was wasted, as Garroway measured the spaces between the rafters and had cardboard boxes custom made to fit between them. Metal strips fastened to the rafters held the boxes in place, and an index taped to the wall identified what was in each box. When Garroway needed something, he'd consult the list and haul the appropriate box down from the rafters.[14]

Garroway collected not only objects, but reading material. He maintained subscriptions to 150 trade publications, ranging from a beekeepers' magazine to *Jewelers' Journal*. He also read the *Encyclopaedia Britannica* religiously. He read anything and everything. Once, after reading a book titled *How to Profit From the Coming Depression* ("a thick paperback," Dave Jr. recalled, with "a very serious cover on it with green pyramids and eyes of gods"), Garroway absorbed the author's warning to invest in gold, which would hold its value in times of economic peril, and bought several bags of gold coins.[15]

Now he had to figure out how to get the coins from the point of purchase to his safe deposit box, several miles away. Instead of hiring an armored car service, Garroway called a taxi. "Sometimes I think Dad might have been just a little too thrifty," Dave Jr. said, "as the good Scot that he was." Garroway promised he would pay the driver extra because it was a special trip. Garroway sat in the back seat with the gold, a shotgun across his lap, as the taxi took him and his fortune from the gold dealer in Hollywood to the bank in Studio City.

Along the route, the taxi was rear-ended. In the accident, the bags containing Garroway's gold broke. In the middle of it all he sat, surrounded by gold coins, holding a shotgun. The car couldn't move. Garroway handed the shotgun to the cabbie with instructions to guard the gold, then found a phone, called a tow truck for the stranded cab, and called the taxi service for another cab. Back he went to the stranded taxi and its nervous cabbie. The tow truck and the replacement taxi arrived. Garroway gave the original cabbie a generous tip, loaded his gold into the new taxi, and everything finally arrived at the bank. All the gold was counted; none of it was missing. For years Garroway relished telling the story, praising the cabbie as a hero. "He could have done anything," Garroway would say, "but he stayed and risked his well-being to guard my investment. What a man!"

Over time, the gold lost its appeal to Garroway. After reading more investment advice, he decided to sell all his gold and invest in the stock market. Years later, visiting his dad in Pennsylvania, Dave Jr. remembered the story of the taxicab fiasco. They had a good chuckle about it, then his dad looked away, shaking his head. "Do you know if I'd held on to that gold, we'd be millionaires today?" Garroway's reverse-Midas touch revealed itself again when he invested in a tomato farm in the San Joaquin Valley. He happened to buy in during a drought year. "Father was never that great with money. He once described himself to me as 'just this country boy in the tanks surrounded by sharks.'"[16]

Sometimes his eccentricities became amusement. He had long been known for unusual and humorous holiday greetings. In his later years, Garroway sent form letters to his friends at Christmas. In them, he detailed some complicated mathematical formula he had devised for determining the size of that year's gifts to friends. The 1974 letter, for example, read: "I would like to call your attention to a recent synthesis of mine in magneto-yulo-thermohydrodynamics. With the Garroway QUARK equation, I have freed Christmas! The QUARK can be computed by the simple equation % CA divided by TCB, where CA is the percentage of individual Christmas affection and TCB the total Christmas budget...A very merry Christmas. Peace, David." Enclosed would be a check. Clark Dennis, who had worked with Garroway in the Chicago days, told Charlie Andrews that his check was in the amount of $2.69. "Why, that son of a gun!" Andrews replied. "He only sent me eighty-four cents."[17]

Other adventures took the Garroways to new and exotic places, to see unbelievable sights and make unforgettable memories. A lover of all things celestial, Garroway chased solar eclipses when he could. "It's as indescribable as sex," he said. "It's as mystical an experience as I know. I don't know why. It's just a shadow." It mystified him regardless, and he had shared it with Dave Jr. when he could. He had taken him to the outer islands of Virginia to view an eclipse, making a trip of it in the Greenbrier van.[18]

In July 1973, when a solar eclipse would be visible at Lake Rudolf in Kenya, Garroway decided to make a grand tour of it. He booked a trip through Ker and Downey, a famous English safari agency, then took his son to Abercrombie and Fitch, then a premier safari outfitter, to get clothing and boots for the trip. Once in Africa, the Garroways visited several game preserves and shot countless pictures of all the wildlife they saw. Then it was on to northern Kenya, where they viewed the total eclipse from the edge of Lake Rudolf. "It was quite a show," Dave Jr. remembered. "The stars came out, and all the local birds freaked and took to the air, squawking madly."[19]

On the way back they toured Europe. In Paris, they stayed at Garroway's favorite hotel on the banks of the Seine, north of Notre Dame Cathedral. Garroway told his son that it was much busier now than it was when he visited back in the day, and lamented that by talking about it on *Today* he had ruined it by increasing its business too much, turning it "upscale and pretentious." He also didn't like that tourist boats would go by at night, when they would shine spotlights on the hotel and other landmarks. One night, he used those lights to play a practical joke. The next time a boat shined its light on the hotel, Dave Jr. pretended to wrestle his dad to the floor and choke him. As they laughed their way through the pantomime, they realized the boat had stopped, backed up, and continued shining its light in their window. "We stayed crouched down in the corner and wondered if the police were coming soon," Dave Jr. remembered. After a while, the boat moved on. No police came.

Bad weather in Paris meant they had to do most of their sightseeing indoors. After several days touring the Louvre, they drove a rental car to the countryside and Chartres Cathedral. Dave Jr. was overwhelmed by this "huge, awesome" place. On the way back, they stopped by the side of the road, set out a white blanket by the forest and enjoyed a picnic lunch of bread, wine and cheese.[20]

Then it was on to Greece. Garroway, who always seemed to be reading two or three books at once, condensed the most interesting information about their tour stops and shared it with Dave Jr. through the day. On the day they visited the Acropolis, it was 110 degrees. Garroway lined his day bag with a plastic bag, then filled that bag with ice and bottles of Coca-Cola. From the hotel, they took a cab. It had no air conditioning. The cab driver, making small talk with his passengers, said he'd heard on the radio that it was one of the hottest days in the recorded history of Athens. He seemed ready to faint. Garroway gave his son a wink as he reached for the day bag. "Would you like a cold Coca-Cola?" The amazed cabbie stared at the bottle in disbelief, and, as Dave Jr. remembered, "gave Dad a look like he wanted to marry him." Garroway took out two more bottles for himself and Dave Jr., and the ride suddenly got happier. In those moments, Dave Jr. aid, his dad was "a combination of MacGyver and Felix the Cat. He always had something in his bag of tricks to save the day."[21]

When Dave Jr. was seventeen, they went to the Far East. At a hotel restaurant in Tokyo, a local band was playing covers of current American hits. Dave Jr. remarked to his dad that the band was playing really well. Garroway suggested they stand and bow to the band as they left. When they did, the band members smiled and bowed with their heads. The saxophone player lit up his solo as the Garroways left. "He was really jazzed by our gesture," Dave Jr. said. His dad agreed. "You could hear the happiness in his music." Little things like that, Dave Jr. felt, made his dad a special guy.

The Garroways went from Tokyo to Hong Kong and Taiwan, visiting museums and seeing natural wonders. The Taiwan visit did not start out well, as Garroway was not reunited with his Questar telescope after landing. An airport official told Garroway they couldn't find it. "This was the first time I ever saw Dad get really mad," Dave Jr. said, remembering that seeing his father so angry "had me shaking in my shoes." Garroway believed the airport officials were trying to rip him off. The outburst worked and Garroway got back his beloved telescope. For the rest of the day, however, Dave Jr. thought about his father's display of temper; thankful his dad had never gotten that angry with him, he resolved never to do anything that would incur similar wrath.[22]

The Garroway temper was sometimes deployed in the name of liberty. Garroway believed too many Americans took their basic liberties for granted. He was fond of a quote, often attributed to Thomas Jefferson, that "the price of freedom is eternal vigilance." He got involved in causes to preserve freedoms, even if they seemed unusual causes. When adult film star Harry Reems faced federal prosecution over his film roles, Garroway joined Warren Beatty, Lorne Greene, Jack Nicholson and others in a fundraiser to help Reems with his legal fees.[23]

Garroway believed citizens were allowing their constitutional rights and freedoms to be eroded day by day. It disturbed him. On the day a young Dave Jr. passed his driving exam, father and son waited at the counter for the clerk to issue Dave Jr. a temporary license. Casually, the clerk grabbed Dave Jr.'s hand, pressed his thumb into an ink pad, and took his thumbprint.

"Hey!" Garroway said. "What did you just do?"

"Why, I just took your son's thumbprint. That's all."

"Did you ask my son if you could take his thumbprint?"

"Why, no," the man replied. "It's just customary to take someone's thumb-"

"Customary?" Garroway's voice had gotten louder. People started to stare. "Oh, really? Is it mandatory?"

"Well, no. There's a sign over there that states it's not." The clerk pointed to a tiny sign hanging in the office reading "Thumbprint Not Required." It didn't mollify Garroway. "How's anybody supposed to read that?" he replied.

"Look, mister, I'm just trying to do my job," the clerk said. "If you want, I'll tear up this thumbprint right now."

Garroway wasn't satisfied. "Oh, no. You took it and you got it now. You might as well keep it! I just think it was very wrong for you to take it from him without first informing him of his rights!" As they headed for the door, Dave Jr. felt the stares of onlookers. Outside, Garroway apologized to him. He didn't mean to embarrass him, he said, but he shouldn't be embarrassed because it was every citizen's duty to look out and stand up for their rights, no matter how small those rights were. "Those people in there staring at us like we were out of line should have been applauding us," Garroway said.

To Dave Jr., the truth of his father's words became apparent when thumbprints became mandatory for the issuance of driver licenses. "He was right on the money," his son reflected. "I think Dad took a golden opportunity to teach both myself and the public that day that, indeed, eternal vigilance is the price of freedom." His father would not have liked post-9/11 America, Dave Jr. believed. "Dad would roll over in his grave if he knew about the PATRIOT Act."[24]

Garroway continued to read anything he could get his hands on. Clark Dennis, who had sung on *Garroway at Large* in the Chicago days, now owned a bookstore in Studio City. One day Garroway stopped in. "I'm going to a hospital," he told Dennis. "What are the biggest books you've got?" Dennis sold him the *Random House Encyclopedia*, the *Complete Shakespeare*, and *Webster's International Dictionary*.[25]

Other Garroway pastimes included birdwatching, projects around the house, and stargazing. His social life was quiet, and only occasionally did he make the celebrity columns. "I'm not exactly in the movie star set," he said. His sojourns into Beverly Hills were to visit "a great little hardware store" there, not to see celebrities. "I've lived here now for three years and I've never seen a movie star walking around, or riding his bike in Beverly Hills, those things you're supposed to see here." The writer couldn't tell if Garroway's tone, and his look of mild amazement as he said it, were an act.[26]

Although Garroway was philosophical about being famous, he impressed upon Dave Jr. the importance of keeping a decent reputation. In particular, he warned his son against getting busted for drugs. That, he worried, could become a scandal with career-damaging implications. "I was only twelve or so when he mentioned it, so I took it pretty seriously." As he grew older, Dave Jr. did try some drugs, but was very cautious ("paranoid, some of my friends claimed") in how he did it.

Only once was Dave Jr. caught in a bust. He was with his girlfriend at a cast party for his eleventh grade class's school play, at the Bel Air home of producer Burt Schneider, who had just released *Hearts and Minds*. That night, Schneider's home was raided. Dave Jr. was in the living room when the cops busted in. One stood in the middle of the room and pointed at people, calling them out as "present" or "under the influence." That would determine the offense with which a person would be booked later on.

A few at the party escaped over a fence, but about thirty young people were hauled away in handcuffs to a station in west Los Angeles. Dave Jr., who had just arrived and was not stoned, was charged with being present in the area where marijuana was being smoked. An attorney arrived to advocate for the teenagers. All of them were fingerprinted and formally charged, then released to their parents.

As parents arrived, Dave Jr. looked for his dad and grew concerned. Finally, Garroway arrived, one of the last to get there. "I thought maybe he was just letting me sit there to teach me a lesson," Dave Jr. remembered. "I figured he would be at least a little mad. Dad didn't get mad very often, so when he did, it was a big deal." Instead, Dave Jr. watched his father walk up to the cop at the window, getting as close as he could to the officer's face.

"What's my son charged with?" Garroway demanded.

"Being present in the area in which marijuana is being smoked."

"Is it illegal to be present in the area in which murder is being committed?" Garroway roared back.

"Well, smoking marijuana is illegal," the cop replied.

"So is murder!"

The officer, startled by Garroway's fury, gave him the paperwork and turned away. Garroway looked at Dave Jr. "Come on, son." As they headed out, Dave Jr. realized not only that his father wasn't angry with him, but that he had figured out what had really happened. "He realized it was a politically-motivated bust right away," Dave Jr. said. Garroway fumed at the police's rationale for all the arrests. "Just being present where a crime happens to occur is a crime?" he said. "That's unconstitutional!" In the end, all charges against those at the party were dropped.[27]

Dave Jr. had another brush with the law one evening, while with his girlfriend at an overlook off Mulholland. They were approached by policemen who wanted to see what was going on. In the process, they discovered a couple of joints in Dave Jr's pocket. It was a small amount, but enough for them to arrest him. Garroway came to the station, retrieved his son, and punished him by selling the Honda automobile he had given him for his 16th birthday. "That hurt," Dave Jr. recalled. "A little too much discipline, I thought!" No charges were filed, and the incident never made the papers. "Maybe the cops dropped the charges when Dad told them he sold my car," Dave Jr. said.[28]

The senior Garroway's own interactions with the authorities were more civic-minded. Once, learning the police wanted to start a community watch group, he offered his house as a venue for an interest meeting. It would also give the Garroways a chance to meet their neighbors, whom they seldom got to see living up in the hills. The police happily accepted Garroway's offer, but, as the host, he would have to inform the neighborhood about the time and location of the meeting. Garroway decided that instead of putting flyers inside neighbors' mailboxes, he would tape them to the mailboxes with fluorescent tape. The bold tape would grab the neighbors' attention – plus, Dave Jr. remembered, Garroway loved using that bright tape anyway.

All went well at the meeting. The police gave their presentation, the neighbors mingled, and it seemed like a great success. The next morning, however, one of the neighbors reported that his house had been robbed. The burglar had left a copy of the meeting announcement by the door, along with a wall clock that had been unplugged at the moment the meeting had begun. Garroway's bright tape had not only alerted the neighbors to the meeting, but it was a tip-off to burglars. "Dad did not feel too good about this," Dave Jr. said. "I think he felt like he was responsible." There were no further community watch meetings at the Garroway house.[29]

A lingering sadness emerged every now and again. Writer Leonard Feather and his wife lived not far from Garroway and had known him for years. One evening, they saw the local PBS affiliate was showing *The Blue Angel*. Knowing Garroway was a fan of Marlene Dietrich, and knowing he was sitting at home alone, they invited him over. "He sat in front of the set, uttering hardly a word, for the duration of the movie," Feather remembered. "When it ended he rose, thanked us and left. David was never a man for small talk."[30]

Other instances were more frightening. Back home from a day at the US Festival, tired after fighting traffic on the drive home, Dave Jr. crept inside. His eyes were red from smoking marijuana, and he didn't want to catch grief from his dad about it, so he quietly closed the front door and didn't turn on any lights, hoping to avoid waking him up. Something wasn't right, though. There was dirt and pieces of clay on the floor. A couple of plants that had lived in clay pots by the door were now in the middle of the hallway. Suddenly Dave Jr. felt an adrenaline rush, wondering if a burglar was in the house, wondering if his dad was okay. Slowly, he crept toward his father's bedroom. There were two large holes in the ceiling, made by a couple of shotgun blasts. Dave Jr. wondered if his dad had been murdered, or if he'd taken his own life. "Dad told me over the years that I should not be surprised if he did some day, because he suffered from depression so badly," Dave Jr. said.

As he rounded the corner and braced for the worst, Dave Jr. saw his dad lying on his back, eyes closed. "It's okay," went the familiar voice. "Go to bed now. I'm almost asleep." Dave Jr. obeyed. Or he tried to, at least. All night he wrestled with his emotions: relief that his dad was okay, but anger because his dad had obviously shot the holes in the ceiling and made a mess in the floor. He wondered if his dad's rampage was his fault for coming home so late, and spent the hours worried and upset.

The next morning Dave Jr. went in the living room, fully prepared for his dad's wrath. Instead, his dad shuffled into the room, the rough night written on his face. "He'd had a bad reaction to a new drug his doctor had prescribed," Dave Jr. said. "He said it made him feel like he wanted to tear his skin off, and that was why he flew into such a rage." Dave Jr. confessed his fear he'd done something that upset his dad. "No, no, no," Garroway replied. "I was just letting off some steam. I didn't think I've ever felt so awful." Then Garroway looked around at the mess he'd made. "But you'll notice I didn't break anything expensive." Dave Jr. breathed a sigh of relief. "Dad was back!" he said. "Even in times of trouble he always managed to keep his sense of humor."[31]

Dave Jr. did know about his dad's Dexedrine use. "He never mentioned the downside," Dave Jr. noted, although his dad kept a hardbound book titled *Amphetamine Psychosis* in his library and had scribbled occasional notes in the margins. Most of the time, Garroway's Dexedrine use didn't really interfere with his demeanor. Even at the height of his drug use, he was "normally so sane and patient and well-controlled in every situation," Dave Jr. remembered.

Still, his dad's paranoia could come to the surface. One Friday evening Garroway heard loud screaming and yelling from a house next door, which belonged to an actor well known for his work in westerns. Dave Jr., who was in the garage loading the trunk of the Camaro with garbage bags for a run to the dump, didn't hear anything. Suddenly his dad closed the garage door. "Quick! Get inside!" Garroway whispered. "I think I just heard a murder." The two fled into the house, locking all the doors and windows. Garroway ran to his room to call the police while Dave Jr. looked out to make sure no one tried to break in. Garroway soon joined him.

After several moments, nothing had happened. Garroway phoned the cops twice more. Suddenly a helicopter hovered overhead, shining a bright light on the driveway. A group of officers, guns drawn, slowly made their way along the driveway. The spotlight from above abruptly stopped, glaring down on a garbage bag sticking out of the Camaro's trunk. The helicopter's loudspeaker blared, "Come out with your hands in the air!" Garroway and son slowly walked out the front door. "We live here!" Garroway yelled over the blast of the rotors. "We live here!"

The cops, guns still drawn, guided the two over to the car. Hands on its hood, the two were frisked. Garroway then spoke to the officers, one of whom spoke into a radio. The helicopter flew off. After more discussion with the sergeant, the officers put their guns away. A few moments later, they left, looking relieved. "Let's go inside," Garroway told his son. He explained that the police, seeing the Camaro stuffed with garbage bags, thought a burglary was in progress. Garroway laughed at the idea of the garbage being loot.

"What about the murder?" Dave Jr. asked.

"Oh, they went next door," Garroway said, "and it turned out just to be some rambunctious partier hooting and howling."[32]

Another episode wasn't funny at all, and decades later, Dave Jr. still couldn't bear to talk about it: a devastating scene of watching his dad acting "downright delusional." A shocked Dave Jr. retreated, overcome by tears. "Here was a man I loved more than anyone in the world, slowly coming unhinged before me. How bad was it going to get? What could I do?"[33]

Garroway's thirty-year use of Dexedrine had taken its toll. Over the years, he had tried higher and higher doses. At the height of his *Today* duties, he was using up to a thousand milligrams a day. Gradually he weaned himself down. By the time Dave Jr. became aware of his dad's drug use, Garroway was down to forty milligrams per day, which was still at the level of overdose. Garroway insisted he wasn't addicted since he had stopped using it several times, and wouldn't use it if he got sick. One day, Dave Jr. watched his dad loading capsules with Dexedrine powder. "I've been using it for thirty years and I can't say anything bad about it," Garroway said. He looked up and thought for a few seconds. "It gave me a career." Dave Jr. thought this was odd. "I thought he got his career despite his drug use," he said.[34]

His dad didn't hide the habit. "Dexedrine was not a source of shame for Dave Garroway," his son said. "He hid his drug use from no one. This included the Seconal he took at night to get to sleep." Furthermore, Garroway prided himself on his restraint in drinking. "Have you ever seen me drunk?" he would ask Dave Jr., knowing that the answer would always be "no." Somehow, he hadn't killed himself, but the damage to his body was apparent, even if he hadn't noticed. During a check-up, a doctor told Garroway that he'd had two minor heart attacks, and showed him an electrocardiogram readout attesting as much. Garroway hadn't even noticed when they happened. But that news is what Dave Jr. believed made his dad get serious about quitting for good.

It wasn't the first time Garroway had tried to quit. Once, his manager suggested he see how he would do without it. For days Garroway lay in bed in his pajamas, hardly ever getting up, instead spending most of his time reading. "He would speak when spoken to, but didn't have a whole lot to say," Dave Jr. said. "Nor would he do his usual tinkering in his workshop." One day two weeks later, Dave Jr. saw his dad in the hallway, a smile on his face, the obvious result of Dexedrine. "I'm not much fun without it, am I?" he asked. Dave Jr. said that his dad "felt he was better with it than without it and was definitely a lot more fun to be around, although there were other family who would dispute this."

So did his secretary, who sometimes considered him his own worst enemy. The paranoia induced by the drug made him suspicious. "He would insult and alienate even his closest friends by thinking they were out to get him, or get something out of him," Dave Jr. said. His secretary watched friends, horrified at Garroway's disintegration through drug and alcohol use, distance themselves from him. Once, Garroway reunited with a couple of old show business friends, who had gone on to great fame in acting, at a dinner at Chasen's. The secretary remembered seeing one of those friends, shocked by how much Garroway had deteriorated, looking on in obvious distress.[35]

Only years later could Dave Jr. realize just what this meant. Although his dad could often conceal the effects of his drug use, he still knew it took a toll. "I guess you just don't see it as much when you're growing up with someone like that, because to you that's just normal old Dad. A child doesn't have anyone else to compare him with," Dave Jr. said. "Most kids just sort of view their Dad as a superhero, and I was no different."

One day when Garroway was near sixty, he sat down at the kitchen table. "I can't take it any more," he told his son. "It just makes me nervous now. It no longer makes me feel good any more." Garroway sought professional treatment, first at Cedars-Sinai and then at Calabasas Hospital. With their help, the addiction was broken. "He was his same kind of self without the Dexedrine, but not as animated or talkative," Dave Jr. said. This took some adjustment for Dave Jr., who was so accustomed to the "on" version of his dad. He never imagined his dad, usually a fountain of information, could actually be boring. Dave Jr. found something pleasant in it. In those final years, the drug habit broken, "Dad was relaxed, and I think happier than he had ever been."[36]

The contentment extended into the spiritual. He befriended Dr. Robert Schuller, pastor of the Crystal Cathedral in Garden Grove. Moved by the spirit, he accepted Schuller's invitation to speak at Sunday services in November 1976. "You can't believe the miracles that have happened in my life," he told the congregation in a guest sermon that was later aired on Schuller's *Hour of Power* telecast.[37]

In early 1977, the show that critics once called "Weaver's Folly" was celebrating a quarter-century on the air. NBC devoted the entirety of the January 14 *Today* to a celebration. Frank Blair and Jack Lescoulie joined the program, and Dave Garroway returned once more. A replica of the original *Today* anchor desk, with monitors and a projection map, was constructed in the studio. For one morning, the prospect of recapturing the magic on national television too good to pass up, Garroway put aside his feelings about what had become of his old program.

"Hello, old friend, and good morning, too!" Garroway cheerily announced as the program began, the picture temporarily black-and-white to simulate an early *Today* broadcast. "As I was saying when I was so rudely interrupted myself, seventeen years and thirty-eight days ago, we're about to give you the news of the morning." Frank Blair broke the spell, referring to the present moment, before the picture's color returned and Tom Brokaw, Jane Pauley and Gene Shalit introduced the day's proceedings. Brokaw said that when *Today* debuted, his family was living in a place where they could barely get television. Pauley said she was learning how to walk. It was a measure of how long *Today* had been around: the show was now co-hosted by someone who could not remember a world without *Today*.

It was a fun, breezy reunion. Brokaw – who had, days before, compared the experience with "being at Old-Timers' Day at Yankee Stadium, standing in center field with Joe DiMaggio" – talked with Garroway, Lescoulie and Blair. The three men joshed about the old days, telling stories about embarrassing moments, about incidents with J. Fred Muggs, talking about their current doings, discussing their memoir projects. Later, Brokaw talked with Garroway and Pat Weaver, with Weaver remembering the process by which Garroway was named host, and how Weaver realized Garroway would be an excellent host. Neither thought highly of modern television (What would you change? Brokaw asked. "Oh, you'll need an *hour* for that," Weaver said, rolling his eyes). Brokaw thanked Weaver and Garroway for what they have done to make *Today* last. "See you on the fiftieth!" Weaver said. "Amen!" Garroway added.[38]

"Peace." Garroway returns for the 25th anniversary of Today, 1977, along with Jack Lescoulie (center) and Frank Blair (right). (© The Estate of Raimondo Borea, courtesy of Gartenberg Media Enterprises)

In a corner of the studio, *Washington Post* television writer Tom Shales watched as Brokaw moderated a discussion among three eminent thinkers, including historian Daniel Boorstin. While others in the cast yawned or talked among themselves, Garroway stood in front of a monitor, intently watching the discussion. "How lucky are the people who can sustain that kind of passion for experience," Shales wrote. "These are the kind of people who ought to be on television."[39]

As the program concluded, all the on-air personalities, past and present, gathered around a large birthday cake. Garroway held up his hand and gave his benediction of peace, and the program concluded. William Henry of the *Boston Globe*, watching Garroway, Blair and Lescoulie "back, for one morning, to nibble at the edges of a business they once mastered," chronicled the sad scene that followed: Frank Blair, complaining about the small size of his pension check, insulting friends, and asking a producer if he could fill in as the newscaster sometime; Jack Lescoulie's doleful proclamation to a companion that coming back had made retirement seem worse. Henry saw Garroway, "once the biggest star at NBC," standing "all but alone. His suit bagged at the waist, and he had unknowingly smeared his coat with pink icing from *Today*'s birthday cake."[40]

Garroway had again been forgotten. Meanwhile, J. Fred Muggs, now living in Florida, continued to perform in thirty-minute shows before audiences. The comparison between the stardom of the simian and the disappearance of Garroway, wrote a columnist, "is living proof that the only American equivalent of a Soviet non-person is a former television star."[41]

The medium no longer had a place for him. Even his old show seemed alien to him. He didn't watch it much, he said, because he now slept late in the mornings. Although he liked both Brokaw and Pauley ("a winner," he called her), he didn't like what had happened to *Today*. "They're compartmented into little boxes," he said. "They never move around. They don't talk to people out there in the audience as we did." Nor did he like the perpetual hard-news approach, which helped run him off a decade and a half before. "I suppose it was inevitable that it should have a more hard news approach, given the times. But I think at that hour they could be a little more relaxed, do some moving about the studio, not be so relentlessly anchored in their chairs." He blamed the "straight-laced" policies of NBC News for making the show "very tight and formal and rigid to me now. There's no joy."[42]

The medium he helped shape now left him cold. "I don't even watch it very much at all," he confessed to an interviewer. Although he would glance at listings and make a note to tune in to anything that seemed interesting, he wasn't a regular viewer. "Why watch one police story when I've seen five thousand by accident when I turn the set on?" he said. He felt there was a sort of Gresham's Law – the bad driving out the good – in television programming. "I don't put television down entirely," he said, "but it is far from what it could be. It could be such a thing. It could be a fairyland of delight going all over and doing all kinds of things that are not being done here. British television is much more advanced in that way than we are. They take chances."[43]

A year earlier, he had compared modern television to Pavlov's experiments. "We have gone through the apathy phase, the don't-give-a-damn phase and are now in the reversal phase," he told Cleveland Amory. "We're giving our people twenty bowls of food – i.e. news – a night, telling them this is hot or cold, good or bad, bitter or sweet, tasty or rotten, sexy or boring. We get furious over some little personality item of total idiocy but don't give a damn about the United Nations or some country being taken over or war starting." He paused. "The next phase will be the paradoxical – the brainwashing – and finally the coma." Garroway added he had found the movie *Network*, Paddy Chayefsky's satire about amoral television executives who swap a network's integrity for trashy, violent shows that get high ratings and make a handsome profit, all while disregarding the hefty human cost of these moves, "amazingly accurate." He insisted he had seen many of the "dirty tricks" it dramatized.[44]

Radio did not cheer him much, either. "There's just nothing of worth on the radio," he said. Conditions out near his home meant he had difficulty picking up signals from the two jazz stations in the Los Angeles area, and he could only listen to them while in his car. "Radio out there is all mishmashed, country-western hash, that stuff – I don't even know how to describe it." Instead, Garroway listened to his record collection.[45]

As much as he detested what had happened to broadcasting, he yearned to get back in the business on a regular basis. Retirement "means death to me," he said in 1977. "I'll never retire. When you get the point of retirement, you're dead or might as well be." For all his yearning and all his efforts, the results were few; the most high-profile of them was providing the voice for a stop-motion figure of himself in the 1979 Rankin/Bass holiday special *Jack Frost*. In the meantime he worked on other projects, helping the National Retirement Council with outreach to help people plan for their retirements. He lent a fourteen-inch telescope to NASA so the agency could observe the occultation of Uranus in March 1977.

And, as his old colleague Frank Blair had done, Garroway had begun work on a memoir, which he dictated on a series of tapes for later transcription. He maintained the title would be *Garroway at Length*. "It gets longer every time I write," he said. "It doesn't have an end." Garroway signed a contract with the Bobbs-Merrill publishing house, with the book slated for a fall 1978 release.[46]

Bobbs-Merrill paid Garroway a hefty advance for the book and Garroway dictated a first draft. It was pure Garroway, the manuscript wandering in a stream-of-consciousness style, jumping from topic to topic. A biographical vignette might be interrupted with a description of a scientific principle, or a lengthy discourse on something else. At other times, Garroway's recollection of events varied from what had actually happened. Bobbs-Merrill planned to fix this in the editing process, a ghostwriter steering the narrative back on course. When Garroway learned his memoir would not be published unaltered, he returned the advance and canceled the deal. The draft, never finished, was filed away.[47]

25

Dave Garroway's love of astronomy had led him all over the world. In 1975, it took him to a country he had long viewed as America's chief adversary. He and other astronomy buffs had gathered on a hot day in August at New York's John F. Kennedy International Airport, bound for three weeks of visiting Russia's largest telescopes, which included the largest telescope in the world.

The tour had been organized by Sarah Lee Lippincott, a Swarthmore College astronomer and president of the International Astronomical Union. She had worked at Swarthmore since 1942, eventually becoming director of the Sproul Observatory. With her mentor Peter van der Kamp, Lippincott had conducted extensive research in the field of astrometry, which studied the positions and motions of celestial bodies. A brilliant scientist who had been a pioneer for other women in the field of astronomy, Lippincott had also studied on a Fulbright fellowship and co-authored a book. A journalist described her as "a sturdy, cheerful woman" who lived near the college and rode her bicycle back and forth to work. "Swarthmore is her home and her life." She confessed that after decades in astronomy, it was her instinct to look up when she went outside at night. "I looked up as I walked down my back stairs the other night and almost fell and broke my neck," she said.[1]

Garroway and Lippincott knew of one another, but had never met in person. "I hate to say it," she said in 1983, "but I only knew him by hearsay. I didn't look at the *Today* show in the early days." For years Lippincott's friends had urged her to watch Garroway's programs, mentioning his interest in astronomy and his pleasant on-camera demeanor, but she never had. Knowing him only by reputation, she wasn't surprised by what she found when they finally met, neither by his love of astronomy nor by a demeanor she called "so gracious, so charming, so quiet and low-key," reflecting an "extremely high-class man of great quality."[2]

When they finally met at the airport, the two struck it off instantly.

They sat together on the airport bus and on the plane, and their bond strengthened throughout the trip. They vowed to keep in touch. In Garroway, Sarah found "a very gentle person, a person of high intelligence" and noted his "encyclopedic mind, but one who can put it all together and think it through and deliver it in an original manner." She considered him "a charming person, a warm person, a person who knew how to use his many, many talents," and "a man of very high quality."[3]

With him in California and her in Swarthmore, there was a distance issue. However, they traveled back and forth to see each other. Gossip columnists picked up that Garroway had a love interest. Some mistook her name with that of a current pop sensation, saying "Dave Garroway has fallen in love with a Farrah."[4]

As togetherness became inevitable, they had to determine where to live. At first they considered Garroway's adopted California, but Garroway grew fond of Swarthmore and the life and friendships Sarah had built there. It offered him a place to feel settled after a lifetime of moving around. "He told me he had forty addresses during his life, and he had a running list of the places he had lived," Sarah told Terry Gross in 1983. Swarthmore was close to Philadelphia, and from there New York was not far at all.[5]

Leaving California meant liquidating much of his collection of gadgets and curiosities. In the past, it had emotionally overwhelmed him. "His solution was just to pack the most precious items and move away from the rest, give it to Goodwill, the movers, whatever, just leave it," Dave Jr. remembered. "It cost him money but saved him mental anguish." This time, Garroway held a big yard sale, advertised in the *Los Angeles Times*. The two-day sale drew a crowd, the famous and unknown alike. Among the shoppers were Irving Wallace and his son, who had written *The People's Almanac*, one of Garroway's favorite books. They were smitten by a console from an early computer, one of Garroway's favorite pieces, full of lights and knobs and dials. As the Wallaces carted off the piece of computing history, Dave Jr. saw his dad "congratulate the Wallaces on their similar taste and eye for beauty."[6]

An earlier parting had been especially painful. In 1977, Garroway put his beloved Jaguar up for sale. Car collector Jackson Brooks had seen Garroway's advertisement in *Road and Track* and arranged to see it. He found Garroway to be a pleasant man who seemed "despondent and down on his luck." After a careful examination of the car, Brooks bought it for Garroway's asking price of $18,000. Brooks later recalled the thick glasses Garroway was wearing. "He told me he was going blind," Brooks wrote, recalling that "he could hardly see to sign the title." As Brooks drove away with the Jaguar, bound for his Colorado home, he caught a last glimpse of Garroway. "I could see that it was a sad parting with an old friend for him."[7]

Soon the home in Swarthmore was "full of all kinds of gadgets, astronomy gadgets and all sorts of things," Sarah remembered. Garroway brought his record collection, and often played the music he loved by the people he had known through the decades. Sarah remembered jazz often being in the air in their home, among all different kinds of music. They seldom watched television and didn't watch *Today*. "It just did not have the appeal for either of us," she said. "I was usually getting up and trying to get off to do some astronomy, and he was thinking his own thoughts or doing something else or reading. He was an avid reader. And we just did other things." She also sensed his frustration about his stalled broadcasting career. "I think he felt he was not being used," she said, "and that it was a bit of a waste. And I agree. He had so much to offer, and it is too bad that it was stifled at some stage."[8]

To anyone who asked, Garroway continued to criticize what had become of the medium. "It's workmanlike," he said in 1979. "When you consider the amount of time the networks have to fill in a day, it's amazing. It's as if you took four New York theaters and had them present new shows all day and all evening, seven days a week. How good would they be?" He missed the excitement and innovation of the Chicago days. "Being live is being alive. Taped shows are like canned food." He doubted new technological advances, such as smaller portable cameras and microwave relays that allowed instant live coverage of news events, would be used effectively. "I doubt if it's what TV news needs a lot more of: fires, murders, accidents, more fires."[9]

Instead, what made him satisfied was the intellectual stimulation of a college town, making new friends among Sarah's circles, enjoying discussions in small groups. "He was not a gregarious person," Sarah remembered. "He was a very private person and I think our friends respected this. He was not one for being gregarious or being a party-goer. He was absorbed in a small group of friends, but not as a celebrity." Those he befriended enjoyed his company. "Dave was one of the most interesting men I ever met," said neighbor Helen North, who chaired Swarthmore's classics department. "I was always impressed by the tremendously wide range of his interests and his knowledge. He could talk intelligently about almost anything. He had a way of talking, not just parroting something he had read. He was always a great joy."[10]

Age and wear, accelerated by years of his now-gone Dexedrine habit, were catching up with him. The drug posed enough problems for people with healthy hearts, but Garroway had a congenital heart defect that put him at additional risk. During a checkup a doctor told him he'd already had two heart attacks, so minor that Garroway hadn't really noticed them. Now he endured more serious symptoms, notably low energy and depleted physical endurance. He couldn't muster the strength to wash his car or do any other physical tasks. He now had to keep a tank of oxygen by his bedside. A doctor diagnosed him with a faulty heart valve, and on October 10, 1979, Garroway had double-bypass surgery at a hospital in Houston. Initially, everything looked good. Garroway hoped he could resume a full-time career soon. Sometime during the recovery, though, he contracted a staph infection. Despite repeated and increasingly aggressive treatments, the infection would not go away.[11]

It's common for heart patients to encounter depression after a procedure, even if the person in question has no history of depression or mental health issues. In Garroway's case, his existing issues with depression, coupled with an infection that wouldn't clear up, made things worse. Lee Lawrence, who talked to Garroway twice a week as she worked on a book about the early years of *Today*, explained in a letter to Pat Weaver: "Sometimes he's 'up' and sometimes 'down' and sometimes, Glory Hallelujah he's that guy – Dave Garroway." Though she hadn't been with him since he got out of the hospital, her conversations with nurses and with Sarah indicated he was feeling better. "I can tell he's coming up on the scale of attitude from the expected depression post-surgery to a more positive frame of mind," Lawrence wrote.[12]

Sometimes Garroway was still social. Helen North was glad to see him show up for a lecture she gave at the college library in 1980. When Garroway heard somebody say there weren't enough seats, he went off to find more chairs for her. "I had admired him for many years and never thought I'd see him setting up folding chairs for me," she said. Sometimes there was joy, as when Dave and Sarah were formally married at

Trinity Episcopal Church in Swarthmore.[13]

At other times, Garroway's mood was down, and his reclusiveness had an edge. When a *Philadelphia Inquirer* reporter requested an interview in 1981, his response was uncharacteristically sharp. He had refused interview requests from people he had worked with on *Today*, he said, and "If I turned them down, I'm certainly going to turn you down." Sarah tried softening the blow. "He is not the man you remember on TV," she explained. "He's a totally different person."[14]

Those closer to him saw a change, both in his mood and his appearance. The man who once strolled the neighborhood and chatted with neighbors now seemed frail and withdrawn. A next-door neighbor remembered how vigorous he was when he moved in, and that he had still shown the charisma that made him such a beloved television presence. As Garroway's infirmities took hold, something changed. "That light diminished," she said. "He looked so fragile. He was not well."[15]

26

In January 1982 the old gang assembled once more for *Today*'s thirtieth anniversary, and NBC gave over its morning show for two hours of reminiscing. All the names were there, including the original host. Executive producer Steve Friedman noted the concern among show staff about if the sixty-eight-year-old Garroway could carry the show. To his relief, Friedman found him up to the challenge. "He set a tone for the whole broadcast that day," Friedman later said. "We built it around him."[1]

The anniversary show was a sentimental journey that seemed right in line with Garroway's sensitivities, lighthearted yet nostalgic and occasionally profound. All the great moments were replayed, starting with Garroway's very first "good morning" from 1952. The Garroway of 1982, his longish silver hair combed back, looking handsome and distinguished in a dark suit, his glasses thicker to cope with failing eyesight, horsed around once more with Jack Lescoulie and Frank Blair, the years not having diminished their rapport. Blair knew of Garroway's health issues, but thought his old colleague seemed bright and happy. "He looked just like the Garroway of old," Blair recalled.[2]

The haunted Garroway, who remembered what nine years of late nights and early mornings did to his life, was never far away. Co-host Bryant Gumbel, who had just joined *Today* after years as a sportscaster and was three years younger than the program itself, asked him about those early days. Garroway paused for a moment. "You are now in the first phases of the beginning of your real life, Bryant," he said, sounding like a father giving hard-earned advice to a son. "You'll find that out in years to come. At least I did. It changes you from one man into another. And you will feel differently about the world, very much so, if you're on three or four or five years." Jane Pauley, picking up on Garroway's initial hope that the program would discuss the news without being "stuffy" about it, asked him why he didn't like stuffy things. "I don't like stuffy things or people very much, I guess. There was so much to talk about and

Garroway with Jane Pauley and longtime friend Hugh Downs, celebrating the 30th anniversary of Today *in January 1982. (American Heritage Center, University of Wyoming)*

do, and there still is in this world, that I don't find it a very stuffy world even today."[3]

The morning went on, hitting the usual touchstones: clips of J. Fred Muggs, an interview with Pat Weaver, John Chancellor remembering how difficult it was to be Garroway's replacement in 1961. Barbara Walters, who parlayed her early role in Garroway's time into a co-hosting job and eventually went on to stardom at ABC, came back to spend several segments reminiscing. Lee Meriwether, who went on to a successful career in acting after leaving *Today*, came back to help Willard Scott with the weather, telling of how Garroway's weather maps had been pre-filled in red chalk that was invisible on black-and-white television. Even Estelle Parsons, for whom *Today* had been a waypoint on the path to a career as an Oscar-winning actress, came back to join the party.

Willard Scott stepped outside 30 Rock for a live shot with the old RCA Exhibition Hall in the background, chatting with passersby about the anniversary. One "just happened" to be David Letterman, who joked about his late night talk show, set to begin February 1 – a program whose irreverent, break-the-fourth-wall nature made it a spiritual grandchild of *Garroway at Large*. The joyous mood was broken only by a tribute to the late Frank McGee and by regular updates about the deadly crash of an Air Florida passenger jet in a Washington snowstorm the previous afternoon.

As the morning's festivities ended, the current hosts and their distinguished guests formed a half-circle on the studio floor, flanking a five-tiered birthday cake at center stage. The camera panned around as each person smiled and said good morning to the audience. All except one. Jane Pauley suggested they start slicing the giant cake. Gumbel replied that there was one more special goodbye from a special man. The strains of "Sentimental Journey" came up in the background. The director cued a shot of Garroway, a quiet smile on his face. Not able to take the stage manager's cue with his poor eyesight, several around him gently said "Dave?"

Instantly, Garroway's face lit up. He looked to the camera, held his head high, raised his right hand once more in the familiar gesture.

"I'm Dave Garroway...and peace."

In an echo of the final moment from that first morning in 1952, all those around him started to applaud. As the camera slowly zoomed out, Garroway and Gumbel shook hands. Gumbel handed the first slice of cake to Garroway. Helen O'Connell beamed at Dave as Betsy Palmer, Florence Henderson and Lee Meriwether gathered around him. Garroway gestured toward the plate in his hand. "I said 'peace' and I got one!" he said, to peals of laughter from the women. Over a wide shot of the on-set celebration, the tune concluded, the program logo came up, and the screen went to black.[4]

The anniversary show, the moment back in the spotlight, the reunion with old friends and colleagues, the light atmosphere, all left Garroway feeling happy and grateful. Back home, he wrote a letter to Friedman. "I really had more pleasure and joy being on *Today* last week than I can easily tell you," he began, thanking the producer for "the deft way" the staff handled him and his wife, for the souvenirs they'd been given, for the whole experience. "I really do thank you for a great morning," the letter ended. "Now, let's talk about 1987."[5]

After Garroway returned home from the anniversary program, the infection that had plagued him flared back up. In March he was back in the hospital, and the next several months brought a series of hospital stays. He approached his sixty-ninth year with lingering physical pain, failing eyesight, depression holding as firmly as ever. His medical insurance was being depleted by the hospital stays, and by procedures that offered little hope of avoiding a slow, painful demise. In June he was in the hospital yet again, staying for six weeks. When he came home on July 16, friends thought he looked fragile and depressed.[6]

Four nights later, Dave and Sarah attended a dinner party at the home of a Swarthmore professor. The evening drew Dave from his gloom, and he spent the evening in delightful conversations with his host, who had long been impressed by his broad range of interests and his down-to-earth demeanor. That evening, she found him "relaxed, charming and witty." The Garroways returned home and retired for the night.[7]

On the morning of July 21, Dave and Sarah awakened and shared breakfast. About a quarter to nine, Sarah went out to keep an appointment.

They don't want to die, he had once said of those who end their own lives. *They just can't take the pain for that much longer.*

At twenty minutes past nine, the houseman arrived for his daily shift. He found Dave Garroway on the floor between the study and the kitchen, still in his bedclothes, a discharged 12-gauge shotgun next to him.[8]

The next morning, the same studio that had hosted a joyous gala anniversary six months before, the same studio where Garroway had wished viewers "peace" one more time, was somber. A stunned *Today* staff presented a tribute to the original master communicator. Frank Blair, hastily summoned from his home on the South Carolina coast, Jack Lescoulie and Betty Furness returned to remember their fallen friend. Tom Brokaw, now co-anchoring NBC's nightly newscast, lauded Garroway and his "extraordinary ability to look right through the lens and talk directly to you." Barbara Walters, who started writing for *Today* shortly before Garroway's departure and eventually became co-host before departing for ABC, acknowledged his post-*Today* difficulties, both in his career and his life.

Steve Friedman remembered the letter Garroway had written six months before, and reflected on Garroway's personal torment. "You never know what demons work," Friedman said. "The thing that makes these people so special may be the very thing that destroys them." A few days after Garroway's death, Sarah remembered the day of the anniversary show. "He was in very good shape for that show," she told a reporter, but about a month later his health began to let go. "Because of the unsuccessful surgery and his generally bad physical condition, he felt there was just no future."[9]

Over the years, in conversations with Dave Jr., Garroway had explored the idea of euthanasia. When one's quality of life was completely gone, Garroway believed, there was no point in sticking around. Instead, there was something to be said for the word that, in Greek, meant "a good death." On occasion, he had told Dave Jr. not to be surprised if he came home one day to find he had taken his own life. There had been instances – for instance, the night Garroway, seized by a reaction to a new drug, had shot the house up – when Dave Jr. thought his dad had committed suicide. Those had been earlier times, though, before his dad's body began to break down. The persistent staph infection was "when I believe he finally decided to check out," Dave Jr. said. "Rather than go slowly and painfully and have all of his savings depleted, he decided euthanasia was the best route."

After word of his father's death, Dave Jr. took a day off from work to mourn. The next morning, he walked to the bus stop. In a newspaper machine he saw that day's *Los Angeles Times*, and on the front page was a picture of his father. "It was a bit surreal to share my father's passing with the world," he said. "I guess when someone dies, it's sort of personal and you want to keep it in the family." Instead, Dave Jr. felt for perhaps the first time the love and respect the public held for his dad. When he got to work, his colleagues offered condolences and sympathy. "It was very comforting, and my tears of grief were replaced by tears of pride."[10]

More tributes came. Former NBC board chairman Julian Goodman praised Garroway as "a wonderful broadcaster – intelligent, talented and extremely hardworking," but "he seemed to be pursued by some kind of demons that none of us ever quite understood." Goodman added, "You know, anybody who can make things look so easy, like Dave did, always is working tremendously hard to foster that illusion. All I can say is that the man's life was filled with a great deal of stress. He was a great broadcaster and I was very fond of him." NBC News president Reuven Frank said, "He became a household word simply by being himself. No acts, no routines – just Dave Garroway." John Chancellor said, "Dave took great care and great pride in letting all of his personal characteristics out onto the air. He let people see him, but he wasn't a showoff. He was no hot dog."[11]

Those who worked closely with him were saddened, but not shocked. "It was really not surprising," said Bill Healion, who had worked on *Garroway at Large*. "He was, at times, quite moody, a very deep man, also very intelligent." Healion mused that "sometimes there is a fine line" between sanity and going over the edge. Jac Hein called Garroway "a hurt man" who had suffered not only Pamela's death but "the industry turning a cold shoulder on him. He often made that comment to me and my wife, 'They don't want me any more.' Networks and talent agencies can be cruel." Hein pointed out that Garroway had tried everything to find work. "He loved entertaining. He wanted to do that until the day he died. Instead, he did a lot of suffering.[12]

Tom Shales mourned not only Garroway's passing but "how much of value has been lost forever and, as far as television goes, how sadly distant and remote the bright beginnings seem now." Shales wrote, "Everyone who's come after him has owed him something. He wasn't just the born 'communicator' – the title originally given him as *Today* host – he was an inventor. Inventing TV-the-machine was not that hard. Dave Garroway helped invent what you put on it once you've got it."[13]

Leonard Feather of the *Los Angeles Times* criticized how the television industry had thrown away "this gentle, honest soul who had given TV more than it could ever repay him," writing that "the same executives who piously lamented his passing could surely have restored in him some measure of self-confidence with an assignment at least lightly comparable to the one he lost in 1961, when his wife's suicide was followed by his departure from the *Today* show. Television has desperately needed someone of his unique eloquence and erudition, but the vast wasteland has simply grown vaster than ever."[14]

At the end of that night's *NBC News Overnight* – a late-night news broadcast whose intelligent, low-key, slightly irreverent demeanor would have fit neatly within the Chicago School aesthetic – co-anchor Linda Ellerbee spoke of what Dave Garroway had meant. In place of her usual benediction of "and so it goes," Ellerbee raised her right hand, as Garroway had, and said "peace."[15]

In September, at the Primetime Emmy Awards ceremony, Barbara

Walters, now one of the most well-known television journalists in America, stood on stage before hundreds in the Pasadena auditorium and millions in a nationwide television audience and narrated a brief tribute to Dave Garroway. As clips of Garroway's years on *Today* and *Wide Wide World* played, the orchestra struck up an appropriately relaxed version of "Sentimental Journey." Walters spoke of the charm and style he had brought, and the gratitude the television industry owed him.

"And, in particular, there's at least one person tonight who owes a career to Dave Garroway," she added, mentioning a young writer whom he hired three months before leaving *Today*. "'You'll like it here,' he said, and he was right." Then she added: "I was that writer, and I liked it there for fifteen years. So from that fortunate writer, Dave, and from all of us here, we wish you, as you always wished us – peace."[16]

The Garroway family organized a private graveside service one week after his death. Sarah worried the curious would overrun the service. Paris, Dave Jr., and Michael and his wife attended, and the service was conducted by a Swarthmore religion professor.[17]

When Garroway's many friends requested a way to gather and remember, a memorial concert was arranged at Swarthmore. At first the family wanted an intimate gathering and placed small notices in local papers inviting friends and fans to write for tickets. Instead, thousands of requests poured in, far beyond what the 520-seat hall could handle. The family postponed the event for a few months, as Michael later explained, so the focus could be on their dad's life "rather than the spectacular aspect of the way he died."[18]

Michael, now executive director of the Community Music Center of Boston, arranged the performers, who donated their time. Sarah worked with Swarthmore to arrange the facilities. Everything came together, with one exception: Peggy Lee, who had been scheduled to appear, had a prior commitment on Broadway. To a reporter, she remembered the good old days: "I remember walking across the street with him in Chicago, holding his big hand, and I felt like I was walking with a giant."[19]

On a snowy Sunday afternoon the fortunate hundreds came to Swarthmore's Lang Concert Hall for a program Michael hoped would lift the spirits of those who loved his stepfather, to present music he loved and memories of the man. Leonard Feather contributed notes for the program. "This evening, some of Dave's friends are gathering to remember him, to tell one another how much he is missed, and to sing and play his praise. This is a sentimental journey for which we regret the necessity, while admiring the spirit in which the participants embark in it. Peace."[20]

Those whose lives he had touched, whose lives had touched his, shared their music. A broken kneecap couldn't keep Marian McPartland from coming on stage to play "There Is No Greater Love," followed by "Emily," which she had performed on *Today* for Garroway long ago. She told stories of running out to her car to catch segments of *The 11:60 Club* between her performances long ago. She recalled that when she'd last played at Swarthmore nearly two years before, Dave and Sarah had been in the audience. "I have a feeling he's still here," she said. Jackie Cain and Roy Kral, discovered by Dave at Chicago's Jumptown, played and sang some of his favorites, including "You Smell So Good," which Kral said Garroway always got "a kick out of." Kral recalled him as "warm, very bright, eloquent, elegant, tweedy, homespun." Cain called him "warm, intelligent, with a very special vision of the world."

Sarah Vaughan, whom Garroway had anointed the Divine One long ago, shared "I've Got The World On A String," then a Gershwin medley that closed with "Someone To Watch Over Me." As the extended applause subsided, she said she felt Dave "sitting here peeking out at us." She told stories of her time with Garroway: the speedy car rides around Chicago, the car she was able to buy when his constant mentions of her over the radio tripled her salary. Once more, for him, she sang "If You Could See Me Now," the song that had sent Dave tripping down the stairs in ecstasy when he first heard it, the song that prompted him to boost her career. A heartfelt rendition of "Send In The Clowns," her voice taking off as the piano went silent, brought the crowd to its feet. One more time, she sang Dave's favorite song, "Tenderly," the song she had crooned over the phone when he couldn't make it to her club. The crowd applauded. Sarah Garroway went to the stage and embraced Sarah Vaughan. The performers took a curtain call, and the Garroway children joined in thanking each performer, giving each female performer a bouquet of pink flowers.[21]

Audience member Rev. Hooker D. Davis of Chester, Pa., who braved the snowstorm, had been a Garroway fan in the 1950s. "It was a grand evening for a grand man," Davis said, "a beautiful benediction for a man who spent his life giving others a chance." NBC aired a brief segment about the concert the following morning on *Today*; a Philadelphia public radio station recorded the concert and aired it in April.[22]

The concert drew an audience that included many of Garroway's old friends. Some, like Lee Lawrence, were almost like family. Dave's longtime favorite writer and friend, Charlie Andrews, told Dave Jr. the story of how Garroway, not feeling well one day in Paris, had recorded a report from Notre Dame Cathedral inside the bathtub in his hotel bathroom, the echo simulating the acoustics inside the cathedral. To Dave Jr., who had heard many stories from his dad about Andrews but had never met him, it was a wonderful moment that brought evocative memories.

During the concert, Dave Jr. listened to Sarah Vaughan, whom his father had championed in an era when it wasn't easy to champion a Black performer. Dave Jr. remembered that Marian McPartland had persuaded his dad to buy him a piano. While Dave Jr. only got a few lessons into piano playing, it helped him learn to play drums a little better. "It was indeed an honor to see my father so honored and revered," Dave Jr. said. "It made me feel I have some big shoes to fill." For the rest of his life, Dave Jr. felt that responsibility.[23]

Dave Garroway's legacy lived on in another way. With the family's help, the Institute of Pennsylvania Hospital in Philadelphia opened the Dave Garroway Laboratory for the Study of Depression in 1985, named in honor of his "concern with mental health and depression...which added much to public awareness of this illness." The first edition of *The Garroway Report*, the institute newsletter, featured a pair of eyeglasses as its logo. "This work will be done in the name of Dave Garroway in recognition of his efforts to further public understanding of mental illness and for greater public acceptance of treatment. We hope that through this program that bears his name, will come the answers that eluded him."[24]

As the Internet age dawned, new opportunities emerged for the Garroway children to discover aspects of their dad they had been unable to see. "I am one lucky kid," Dave Jr. said. "How many people get to go back in time and see their father doing his thing on television fifty years later?" A quick search of YouTube could yield clips of Garroway on *Today* or appearing on any number of programs, such as *What's My Line?* Dave Jr. recalled that when his dad tried to get copies of some of his own programs, he was told they had been destroyed. "I am getting to view stuff that Dad did that I am pretty sure he never got to see," he said.

While the Internet allows people to view vintage clips of Garroway at work, it is also a breeding ground for rumors and misinformation. For example, an article on the crowdsourced Wikipedia repeated an old tale that "The Doctor" consisted of Vitamin B and codeine, when Dave Jr. knew it was vitamin E and Dexedrine. Dave Jr. also took exception to a claim that his dad was fired from *Today*, when in truth he resigned. Dave Jr. notified the Wikipedia editors, who corrected the error about "the Doctor" but let stand the tale about being fired. While disappointed, he was philosophical, "Oh, well," he said. "I suppose Wikipedia is entitled to choose whatever version of Dad's end at NBC they wish."[25]

Other interactions were happier. A man in Los Angeles was going through some papers after his father, a CBS executive, passed away. He found a collection of photographs taken while *Today* was doing remotes from Europe. The man contacted Sarah, who put him in touch with Dave Jr. "How a bunch of NBC photos wound up with the head of CBS I cannot guess and will probably never know," Dave Jr. wrote. "That is because I figure never look a gift memory in the mouth." When they met at the CBS studios in Burbank, the two shared tales of what it was like to grow up with high-powered fathers. As they looked through the photos, a lot of memories came back.

The passage of time never diminished a son's pride. To his own last days, Dave Jr. would be asked, "'Oh, any relation to *the* Dave Garroway?'" When Dave Jr. replied that he was, he frequently heard things like "Gee, your dad was great. I used to watch him all the time!" Dave Jr. would then share that his dad "was just as cool off-camera as he was on."

Other responses stirred emotion. "Sometimes people would say, 'You sure were lucky to have such a great dad. I bet you miss him.' This is when pride wells up inside me, and my eyes get damp.

"'Yes, indeed,' I would say."[26]

EPILOGUE
Remembering my brother, Dave Garroway Jr.
by Paris Day

What an interesting human being and character my brother David Garroway Jr. was. He was as inquisitive, unconventional, genius, laid-back and full of knowledge as his dad had been. He was also humorous, witty and playful.

I was his older sister, by fourteen years, and grew up in St. Louis with my mother, Adele. Many of our childhood experiences and memories of our father therefore differed. It was only later in my adult life, after our father's passing, when my brother and I came together, that I realized the impact Dad had on both of us. David's intention, as an adult, was to honor and memorialize our father, but with David's untimely passing, the opportunity to honor my brother is now mine.

David came into this world with curiosity and intelligence which was rivaled only by his dad's. David grew up in New York with his brother Michael, Dad, and many housekeepers. It was not until David was a young man in his teens, while visiting me in Hawaii and later at my hand-built log home in Colorado, that our adventures and relationship truly began. These visits not only allowed me to get to know my younger brother, but also gave me the opportunity to learn more about the father he knew.

Dad loved teaching David about science, astronomy, mechanical and electrical engineering, art and music. By traveling with Dad, David was able to explore many cultures of the world, different geographies and natural wonders. Dad also taught him how different forms of government and economies functioned, and included many controversial theories about our own government. David would say that Dad had spoiled him with experiences. As David grew older he became more and more fascinated by conspiracy theories and enjoyed researching these theories, as well as sharing them with friends and family, whenever he could. He also wanted to make others aware of the urgency of the times, as Dad had done.

Growing up in the shadow of his father's spotlight, he witnessed not only the glory of fame but also the darker side, including his father's struggles with depression and addiction. Witnessing this two-sided coin, young David was making decisions about his own future. He knew he wanted to be a good communicator of truth and knowledge as his father was. His first step was attending the Columbia School of Broadcasting. David's first job was being a disc jockey at a country music station, which seems to be the deciding force in him realizing that broadcasting was not for him. He realized that he did not have the same passion or drive that his dad had. Growing up, he witnessed firsthand that happiness is not synonymous with fame and fortune.

David's passions were playing the drums and sharing his truth and knowledge with individual people as they crossed his path, whether it be on a beach, amongst the redwoods or on the streets. David was friendly and easily engaged with people. Some considered him a genius and some enjoyed his quirkiness. Some were less like-minded, but many became wonderful lifelong friends whom he routinely called or visited with. They supported him in many ways, but were skeptical about some of his theories, which sometimes were pretty wild. They loved his sense of humor, his easy-going manner and his knowledge about so many unusual things.

David was a free spirit and lived his life in the moment as much as he could. He was uninterested in a lot of material possessions, following conventional norms, or practicing social graces. He had a kind of a "take me or leave me" attitude, with a smile on his face. David did not lead a particularly easy life, but no matter what happened he could put some kind of positive spin on it and go forward.

As I recall, sometime in his mid-life, David was diagnosed with and treated for heart disease. Its severity led him to make serious changes in his lifestyle. He began studying alternative healing, natural medicine, and nutritional supplements including nootropics. He began limiting his exposure to harmful energies from electronics, the sun, and toxins in food and water. He ate organic whenever possible.

As an adult, David became more serious about studying science, particularly quantum physics and quantum mechanics. He was particularly interested in alternative energy sources and vibrational energies from tensor coils and crystals that were in harmony with nature's core energies. He augmented his knowledge of science with Western religious teaching, Eastern spirituality and the wisdom of old masters and philosophers.

At this point, David began doing experiments and formulating new theories, while working with other physicists and inventors. He hoped to contribute to these fields of science and began publishing his new ideas on the Internet, including his antigravity theory, ether dynamics, zero-point energy and the aspects of right- and left-handed energies. Eventually his love of science took him to the annual Tesla Tech Conferences in New Mexico, which brought together scientists from around the world who were exploring extraordinary new technology. These conferences offered a forum for presentations and discussions of new scientific ideas and philosophies that are not commonly accepted by mainstream science. David made several presentations at Tesla Tech during the 2000s. In 2017, he presented his theory, "Implosion of Aether and Universal Energy," and introduced the model of his 3D Garroway Tensor Coil, which produces right- and left-handed spiraling energy. Initial experiments had shown that this energy from the coils would help seeds germinate faster and grow stronger. It was theorized that this energy could be used to benefit food production for the future, as well as possibly being used in wound healing.

After our Dad's passing, David's main intention was to finish our dad's autobiography. He began writing short stories about his life and adventures with Dad that were eye-opening, insightful and charming. David made many trips to visit me and we would work on writing and editing his stories. Eventually we made two trips together to research and gather more information on our father's radio and television history. We visited the broadcasting archives at the University of Wyoming and the University of Maryland. To our delight, in addition to the many articles and documents, we found we were also able to view short segments of his TV shows and listen to tapes from his early radio shows. We gathered so much interesting information about our father's career that David became somewhat overwhelmed, and decided to put aside the project for a few years. Although he was not actively working on the biography, he was gathering additional information by watching old TV clips of our Dad. I think this was David's way of staying close to our father and visiting with him.

In 2017 David and I decided to be roommates. He moved in with me in a little town in western Colorado. In addition to taking a break from our father's biography, David had also decided that he needed a break from all the challenges of city living. He wanted to rest and focus on getting healthier. The transition to quiet country living was not as easy as he had expected. At first, it was too quiet and peaceful for him. He stayed home most of the time and spent most of his time playing on the drum set he kept in our garage, or working on his studies and scientific experiments.

David had always been a social person, unlike Dad, but when he lived with me wanted to stay close to home. When he did go out, he would go to a weekly jam with local musicians or travel to "open mike" venues, with different musicians, in the nearest big city. He eventually came to appreciate his new surroundings and did start to relax, and took time to really smell the roses and get to know the birds that nested on our front porch.

In contrast, I had taken a different path by studying art and psychology. I realized that my interest in psychology was influenced by my Dad's psychiatric struggles and I wanted to understand them. I loved the outdoors and all things nature. Dad's love of art had also rubbed off on me, and I was passionate about creating many different kinds of art throughout my life.

David and I had such different perspectives on life that our days were filled with very interesting discussions, healthy or sometimes heated arguments, and the occasional dollar bets on factual disagreements. When we went outside in the morning I loved to look at the blue skies and billowy clouds, while David was counting the chemtrails and telling me what was raining down on us. Slowly we became able to appreciate each other's point of view, which led us to joking about our differences. Basically, we really did enjoy each other's company but we did have struggles that mostly revolved around David's "Housekeeper Syndrome," which followed him into adulthood.

We eventually got very good at compromising. We learned from each other and shared experiences. David took me camping in Wyoming to see a total solar eclipse and I took him to bluegrass festivals in sunny Colorado. We spent a lot of time talking about Dad's depression and how it had impacted our lives. We assumed that we were genetically disposed to depression, but dealt with it in different ways. In summer vacations and my junior year of high school living with my David, our brother Michael, Pamela and Dad, I saw how depression could destroy people. I made the decision then, at seventeen, that I was not going to let depression get a grip on me. Occasionally, bouts of depression come my way but I was always able to get through it with counseling and a forward-thinking, positive outlook on life. David had grown up with depression all around him, in pretty stark terms, and living in that environment was normal for him. He decided just to accept depression as part of life and not fight it in the way that I had.

We enjoyed identifying parts of Dad's personality and behaviors that we had both taken on. For example, we were both generally laid back and loved to communicate with others. We both stacked half of our beds with books and magazines to satisfy our curiosity, our thirst for knowledge and our love of reading. We both loved music, but we loved all kinds of music Dad never would have tolerated.

Just as David was getting ready to start working on Dad's biography again, out of the blue we were contacted by Jodie Peeler, who was in the process of writing a biography about Dad. David and I were thrilled to collaborate with her. It started to look like a book about Dave Garroway's life would actually get written. David's dream of memorializing and honoring his father was possibly coming true. We were already planning a trip back east that fall, and going to meet Jodie in South Carolina would work perfectly. We took all of our research papers. David took his stories and I took my photographs of Dad. We stayed for the weekend and had great fun getting to know each other, telling stories, laughing and discovering we were on the same page about the intent of the biography. The pandemic came shortly after, so the rest of our collaborating and updating was done over the phone. David called Jodie regularly, sometimes just to visit and tell her about his latest scientific discoveries or to talk about progress on the book, or share more stories about Dad.

On Christmas night of 2020, Jodie sent David the first draft of the Dave Garroway biography, which we couldn't wait to read. We were still in the process of reading through it when David suddenly passed away, only a month later. David hadn't finished reading the draft, but he had seen his dream come true.

This book is part of their legacy. I will also be working on extending the Garroway legacy by having their prized Questar telescope repaired, and then passing it on to my children and grandchildren so they can learn more about the vast universe that my father and brother loved so much.

To my brother, who lived with zest and courage, may you now rest in peace. Although you are no longer with us, may your memory be forever held in the pages of this book, and in the hearts of those who knew and loved you.

Paris Day
March 2022

Notes

CHAPTER 1

1. Dave Garroway, draft of uncompleted memoir, Lee Lawrence Papers, Special Collections, University of Maryland Libraries, 4.

2. Garroway, Maryland draft, 3-8; Garroway, revised draft of uncompleted memoir, Dave Garroway Papers, Collection 10344, American Heritage Center, University of Wyoming, 9.

3. Garroway, Maryland draft, 1-2; Garroway, Wyoming draft, 8

4. Garroway, Maryland draft, 7.

5. Garroway, Maryland draft, 9-10; Garroway, Wyoming draft, 18.

6. Garroway, Wyoming draft, 8, 10-11.

7. Garroway, Wyoming draft, 13.

8. Garroway, Maryland draft, 2-3, 12.

9. Garroway, Wyoming draft, 11-12; "My First Car," *Parade*, October 14, 1962, 20.

10. Garroway, Maryland draft, 10; Garroway, Wyoming draft, 13.

11. Garroway, Maryland draft, 10; Garroway, Wyoming draft, 5-7, 20.

12. Garroway, Wyoming draft, 20-21.

13. Garroway, Wyoming draft, 18-19.

14. Garroway, Wyoming draft, 9.

15. Garroway, Wyoming draft, 21-22.

16. Garroway, Wyoming draft, 11-14; "Get the Facts Before You Judge," *Clarion-Ledger* (Jackson, Miss.), August 18, 1957, 47.

17. Garroway, Wyoming draft, 13.

18. Garroway, Wyoming draft, 14; *Mark Trail*, Summer 1951, p. 62, clipping in Dave Garroway Papers.

19. Garroway, Wyoming draft, 16-17.

20. Garroway, Wyoming draft, 22-23.

21. Garroway, Wyoming draft, 23-24.

22. "You Can't Go Home Again, Confused Garroway Notes," *Greenville News* (Greenville, S.C.), August 28, 1955, 33.

23. Garroway, Wyoming draft, 24-25.

24. Garroway, Wyoming draft, 27.

25. Garroway, Wyoming draft, 30.

26. Garroway, Wyoming draft, 32, 28-29.

27. Garroway, Wyoming draft, 29-30, 38.

28. Garroway, Wyoming draft, 31-32.

29. Garroway, Wyoming draft, 25.

30. Garroway, Wyoming draft, 25.

31. Garroway, Wyoming draft, 26.

CHAPTER 2

1. Garroway, Wyoming draft, 34.

2. Garroway, Wyoming draft, 35.

3. Garroway, Wyoming draft, 35-36.

4. Garroway, Wyoming draft, 36.

5. Garroway, Wyoming draft, 39.

6. Garroway, Wyoming draft, 41-42.

7. Richard Gehman, "Today With Garroway," *Coronet*, March 1954, 104; Dave Garroway with Martin Abramson, "Dave Garroway Says Give Your Children Love – and Liberty!" *This Week*, August 28, 1960, 10.

8. Garroway, Wyoming draft, 14-15; "Three-Time Winners," *St. Louis Globe-Democrat*, December 11, 1932, 51.

9. Garroway, Wyoming draft, 44-45.

10. Garroway, Wyoming draft, 42-44.

11. Dave Garroway Jr., written recollections, undated.

12. Garroway, Wyoming draft, 47; Al Weisman, "From U. City High to Radio Stardom," *St. Louis Post-Dispatch*, December 23, 1949, 3C.

13. Garroway, Wyoming draft, 47-48.

14. Garroway, Wyoming draft, 48.

15. "A High Winner," *St. Louis Globe-Democrat*, January 15, 1928, 84; "Mrs. Charles Eaton Takes Sweepstakes in Lighting Contest," *St. Louis Globe-Democrat*, January 3, 1928, 1; "Winners of Prizes in Xmas Lighting Contest Announced," *St. Louis Globe-Democrat*, January 3, 1930, 8.

16. Garroway with Abramson, "Give Your Children Love – and Liberty!"

17. Garroway, Wyoming draft, 57.

18. Photograph in *St. Louis Post-Dispatch* April 23, 1931, 35; Garroway, Wyoming draft, 32.

19. Garroway, Wyoming draft, 50-51. Weisman, "From U. City High to Radio Stardom"; Phyllis Battelle, "What's Troubling Garroway? Rolls-Royces and Bomb Shelters," *Philadelphia Daily News*, August 2, 1961, 36.

20. Garroway, Wyoming draft, 50-51.

21. Garroway, Wyoming draft, 57-58.

22. "Three-Time Winners."

23. W.J. McGoogan, "Father and Son Golf Event is Again Won By the Garroways," *St. Louis Post-Dispatch*, September 21, 1931, 14; Maurice O. Shevlin, "Garroways Retain City Title in Father-and-Son Golf Meet at Normandie," *St. Louis Post-Dispatch*, September 12, 1932, 9; W.H. James, "Reflections from the Sidelines," *St. Louis Globe-Democrat* September 19, 1933, 7; "Garroways Win Father and Son Golf Tourney," *St. Louis Post-Dispatch*, October 1, 1934, 14; "Father Defeats Son, 1 Up, for Normandie Title," *St. Louis Globe-Democrat*, October 16, 1933, 11; "Bridge-Golf Game Originated Here By Local Player," *St. Louis Star and Times*, January 4, 1932, 15.

24. Garroway, Wyoming draft, 54-56; "Golf Made Minor Sport By Athletic Council of Washington U.," *St. Louis Post-Dispatch*, May 26, 1934, 11; "St. Louis C.C. Women Take Golf Honors," *St. Louis Globe-Democrat*, June 5, 1934, 10.

25. Garroway, Wyoming draft, 51-53;

26. "Recovers $100 Bill Through 'Hypnosis,'" *St. Louis Star and Times*, May 11, 1933, 2; Frank Edwards, "The Missing Money Mystery," *Orlando Sentinel*, February 26, 1967, 125.

27. Garroway, Wyoming draft, 53.

28. Garroway, Wyoming draft, 53-54.

29. Weisman, "From U. City High to Radio Stardom"; "Washington U. Golfers Off for College Meet," *St. Louis Star and Times*, June 20, 1935, 22; "Bear Squad Tapers Off For College Golf Event," *St. Louis Globe-Democrat*, June 22, 1936, 13.

30. "Comment: Mr. Garroway and the Unconstructive Critic," clipping from Washington University alumni magazine, undated; Dickson Terry, "They Didn't Let the Old School Down," *St. Louis Post-Dispatch*, May 10, 1966, 49.

31. Garroway, Wyoming draft, 58-59; "Sales Convention of Chance Company Here This Week," *Centralia Fireside Guard*, January 8, 1937, 1.

32. Garroway, Wyoming draft, 59-60.

33. Garroway, Wyoming draft, 60-61.

CHAPTER 3

1. Garroway, Wyoming draft, 62-63.

2. Garroway, Wyoming draft, 62-63. DeVere "Dee" Engelbach went on to become a producer and director in radio, with one of his most notable production credits being NBC's *The Big Show* in 1950-51. He later became a television production company executive.

3. Garroway, Wyoming draft, 63.

4. Garroway, Wyoming draft, 64-66.

5. Garroway, Wyoming draft, 64.

6. Garroway, Wyoming draft, 64-66.

7. Garroway, Wyoming draft, 67-68.

8. Garroway, Wyoming draft, 68.

9. Garroway, Wyoming draft, 69.

10. Garroway, Wyoming draft, 72-74; Gehman, "Today With Garroway," 105; "Guide Garroway Wins Golf Tournament," NBC Transmitter, June 1937, 1.

11. Garroway, Wyoming draft, 65.

12. "Former Radio City Guide Shows KDKA Some Speed," *Pittsburgh Press*, March 4, 1938, 33.

13. Garroway, Wyoming draft, 70; Margaret McManus, "Dave Garroway Has Spent Year Doing a Great Deal of Thinking," *The Post-Standard* (Syracuse, N.Y.), July 8, 1962, 73.

14. Garroway, Wyoming draft, 71-72, 70.

15. Garroway, Wyoming draft, 70-72; Kay Barr, "KDKA Pittsburgh," *NBC Transmitter*, April 1938, 6.

16. Garroway, Wyoming draft, 72-76; "Former Radio City Guide Shows KDKA Some Speed"; Jane Hamilton, "Phone Girls Thrilled By 'Answers' Program," *Pittsburgh Sun-Telegraph*, March 4, 1938, 38. Garroway's recollections while writing his memoirs three decades later were of being asked during his audition to imagine describing the last hole of the U.S. Open, but contemporary accounts state Garroway was asked to imagine describing a parade.

17. Garroway, Wyoming draft, 87.

20. Fred Remington, "Four Faces of Dave," *Pittsburgh Press* TV section, February 26, 1961, 4-5; Garroway, Wyoming draft, 83.

CHAPTER 4

1. Barr, "KDKA Pittsburgh."

2. "'Press Parade' Launched With Two Programs," *Pittsburgh Press*, March 21, 1938, 1; "12 Press Programs Begin New Service Over KDKA," *Pittsburgh Press*, March 20, 1938, 1; "'Press Parade' Again on Radio," *Pittsburgh Press*, March 23, 1938, 36; "Press and KDKA Studio Opened By News, Music," *Pittsburgh Press*, March 27, 1938, 2.

3. Jane Hamilton, "Two 13-Year-Olds In Air Finals," *Pittsburgh Sun-Telegraph*, April 10, 1938, 46; "Sunday On Your Radio," *Pittsburgh Press*, April 24, 1938, 52; Si Steinhauser, "Motor Square Garden Broadcast To Launch Electric League Show," *Pittsburgh Press*, April 15, 1938, 29; Si Steinhauser, "Historic Clock Broadcast Star On Radio Salute to Harmonites," *Pittsburgh Press*, August 9, 1938, 11; "Zelienople: Clock Rededicated," *New Castle News*, Au-

gust 13, 1938, 16.

4. Darrell Martin, "Hoover Talks; Mickey Rooney Cantor's Guest," *Pittsburgh Post-Gazette*, October 17, 1938, 11; "Etiquette, Social Culture Problems," *The Tribune* (Scranton, Pa.), May 4, 1939, 7.

5. Garroway, Wyoming draft, 85-86.

6. Darrell Martin, "CBS Mikes to Explore Scranton Mine," *Pittsburgh Post-Gazette*, November 3, 1938, 19; "Milk Fund Donations Lag; Drive Still $52,000 Short," *Pittsburgh Press*, December 12, 1938, 2; "'Press Parade' Again on Radio," *Pittsburgh Press*, March 23, 1938, 36.

7. Garroway, Wyoming draft, 76; Si Steinhauser, "Tell Stars Leave Air or Screen," *Pittsburgh Press*, June 19, 1939, 12; George A. Zerr, "Work in Local Boat Yards Is At Standstill," *Pittsburgh Post-Gazette*, July 8, 1939, 14; Darrell V. Martin, "County Fair on Farm and Home Hour," *Pittsburgh Post-Gazette*, August 30, 1939, 12.

8. Si Steinhauser, "No Special Event!" *Pittsburgh Press*, July 14, 1939, 16.

9. Garroway, Wyoming draft, 77.

10. Garroway, Wyoming draft, 78-79; "Announcer Plans to Ascend Tower," *Pittsburgh Press*, September 7, 1939, 32; Darrell V. Martin, "Rita Rhey Auditions With Whiteman," *Pittsburgh Post-Gazette*, September 8, 1939, 24.

11. Darrell V. Martin, "Jane Cowl in Star Theater Drama," *Pittsburgh Post-Gazette*, September 27, 1939, 16; "'Aerial' View of Span Broadcast by KDKA," *Pittsburgh Press*, September 28, 1939, 28; Charles F. Danver, "Pittsburghesque: Page from a Scribbler's Journal," *Pittsburgh Post-Gazette*, November 17, 1939, 12; "KDKA Broadcasts Bridge Interview," *Pittsburgh Press*, December 4, 1939, 2.

12. "Martinets," *Pittsburgh Post-Gazette*, November 3, 1939, 18.

13. "David Garroway Wins Radio Prize," *Pittsburgh Post-Gazette*, November 3, 1939, 4; Jim Luntzel, "KDKA Pittsburgh," *NBC Transmitter*, December 1939, 10.

14. Darrell V. Martin, "WWSW Swingsters Ready To Do Battle," *Pittsburgh Post-Gazette*, December 28, 1939, 14; Vincent Johnson, "KDKA Brings Question Bee With Experts," *Pittsburgh Post-Gazette*, March 18, 1940, 14; Jim Luntzel, "KDKA Pittsburgh," *NBC Transmitter*, March 1940, 9.

15. Si Steinhauser, "Scientists to Describe Eclipse In Radio Plane-to-Ground Talks," *Pittsburgh Press*, April 7, 1940, 57; Margaret Carlin, "Never Far From Radio," *Pittsburgh Press*, September 4, 1966, 75.

16. Garroway, Wyoming draft, 79-83; "Off the Dial," *Pittsburgh Post-Gazette*, May 7, 1940, 9.

17. Garroway, Wyoming draft, 84-85; "Ethel Clark's Radio Flashes," *Ogden Standard-Examiner* (Ogden, Utah), February 11, 1940, 13; Carl Apone, "Maurice the Music Man," *Pittsburgh Press Sunday Magazine*, December 2, 1962, 4.

18. Garroway, Wyoming draft, 83-84; Vincent Johnson, "Hoover Talks on 'National Defense,'" *Pittsburgh Post-Gazette*, May 27, 1940, 19.

19. Tom Birks, "Favorites Defeated In West Penn Golf," *Pittsburgh Sun-Telegraph*, August

22, 1940, 17; Claire M. Burcky, "Young Eliminated In West Penn Golf," *Pittsburgh Press*, August 22, 1940, 21; "Surprises In Golf Tourney," *The Record-Argus* (Greenville, Pa.), August 23, 1940, 28.

20. Garroway, Wyoming draft, p. 86.1-86.5.

21. Patrick J. Kelly, "Mikemen Are Like Salesmen," *Pittsburgh Press*, August 27, 1940, 8.

22. Garroway, Wyoming draft, 93-94.

23. William S. Robbins, "Daily Dialings," *Latrobe Bulletin* (Latrobe, Pa.), September 10, 1940, 4; Vincent Johnson, "President On Air Again Tonight," *Pittsburgh Post-Gazette*, September 11, 1940, 6.

24. Garroway, Wyoming draft, 95.

25. Edward R. Rothhaar, "An Evaluation and Historical Survey of the Television Program Series *Garroway at Large*" (M.A. thesis, Ohio State University, 1959), 10.

26. Garroway, Wyoming draft, 98-100.

27. Garroway, Wyoming draft, 104-105; Edith Virginia Young, "Society in St. Louis," *St. Louis Star-Times*, January 13, 1941, 16; "Miss Adele Dwyer, D.C. Garroway Jr., Married at Church," *St. Louis Post-Dispatch*, February 16, 1941, 48.

28. Garroway, Wyoming draft, 102-106.

29. "News, Radio and Movie Men To 'Cover' Battle of Bangboards," *The Daily Times* (Davenport, Iowa), October 29, 1940, 35; "War Games To Be On WMRC," *The Greenville News* (Greenville, S.C.), September 15, 1941, 10; "Today's Radio: Bazooka Burns Returns to Air Tonight at 7:30," *Atlanta Constitution*, September 16, 1941, 19; Garroway, Wyoming draft, 95.

30. Garroway, Wyoming draft, 95-96.

31. Ed Meyerson, "Man of Today," *TV Radio-Mirror*, June 1954, 92.

32. Garroway, Wyoming draft, 97. Garroway shared the recipe in the July 5, 1959 edition of *This Week* Magazine, a weekly supplement in newspapers nationwide.

33. Garroway, Wyoming draft, 97.

34. Vincent Johnson, "'Buff' Donelli on Prevue Tonight, With Dukes' Game Aired Tomorrow," *Pittsburgh Post-Gazette*, November 14, 1941, 30; "Daily Programs Will Cover Army Maneuvers," *The Gazette* (Cedar Rapids, Iowa), November 16, 1941, 29; "This War," *The Daily Record* (Long Branch, N.J.), November 26, 1941, 8.

35. "Radio Star Parade," *Sioux City Journal*, November 2, 1941, 13.

36. Paul K. Damai, "Radio Short Circuits," *The Times* (Munster, Indiana), January 21, 1942, 15.

37. "Butterfield's Stag Golf Meet Brings Out 200," *Chicago Tribune*, May 10, 1942, 30; Ben Gross, "Listening In," *New York Daily News*, June 21, 1942, 345; E. Bowden Curtiss, "Rev. Arthur G. Adams Will Speak On 'Worship and War' Broadcast," *The Capital Times* (Madison, Wis.), July 22, 1942, 11; Charles Chamberlain, "Lawson Little, Byron Nelson Tied For Lead At End of First Round In Tournament," *Owensboro Messenger*, July 24, 1942, 8; "Radio Dial

– Today On Air," *Arizona Daily Star* (Tucson, Ariz.), July 25, 1942, 13; J.B. "Buck" Woods, "J-G Sports Dope," *Journal Gazette* (Mattoon, Ill.), July 29, 1942, 5; "Three Tie For Medal in Chicago Amateur On 71s," *Chicago Tribune*, August 18, 1942, 20.

38. Larry Wolters, "W-G-N To Give Full Election Report Tuesday," *Chicago Tribune*, November 1, 1942, 159; Vincent Johnson, "No New Songs About Victories Due to Disc Ban, NAB Asserts," *Pittsburgh Post-Gazette*, December 23, 1942, 28.

CHAPTER 5

1. Dave Garroway Jr., written recollections, undated. The story of the Navy's V-12 program, which trained young men to become Navy officers, is ably told in *The Navy V-12 Program: Leadership For A Lifetime* by James G. Schneider (Boston: Houghton Mifflin, 1987).

2. Garroway, Wyoming draft, 31-32.

3. "Notice of Separation from U.S. Naval Service," document in Garroway family papers; Garroway, Wyoming draft, 108-109; James Abbe, "New Bob Hope Show Will Premiere On KRON Tonight," *Oakland Tribune*, October 12, 1954, 16-17.

4. Garroway, Wyoming draft, 111.

5. "Sudden Success? My Foot!," undated article in Wyoming papers.

6. Garroway, Wyoming draft, 113.

7. Garroway, Wyoming draft, 112-114.

8. Robert Messenger, "Last Days of Speed Typing Glory," on the ozTypewriter site, accessed June 14, 2021, https://oztypewriter.blogspot.com/2014/11/last-days-of-speed-typing-glory.html; Garroway, Wyoming draft, 114.

9. Garroway, Wyoming draft, 116.

10. Garroway, Wyoming draft, 117; Ed Sheehan, "We Didn't Make Much Money, But We Sure Had Fun," *Honolulu Advertiser*, November 28, 1965, 12.

11. Garroway, Wyoming draft, 118.

12. Garroway, Wyoming draft, 119.

13. Garroway, Wyoming draft, 119.

15. Garroway, Wyoming draft, 119-120.

16. "Sudden Success? My Foot!"; Ed Sheehan, "Radio Voices Not Heard On The Air," *Honolulu Star-Bulletin*, July 24, 1966, 16.

17. Garroway, Wyoming draft, 119-121.

18. Dave Garroway Jr., written recollections, undated; Garroway, Wyoming draft, 121; Harold Smith, "This Admiral a Gold Bricker and Glad of It," *Chicago Tribune*, February 3, 1945, 2.

19. Garroway, Wyoming draft, 121.

CHAPTER 6

1. Garroway, Wyoming draft, 122; Garroway, Wyoming draft, section 2, 4.

2. Garroway, Wyoming draft, 122.

3. Examples of these classified ads appear in the *Chicago Tribune*, November 10, 1945, 25, and November 18, 1945, 23; Garroway, Wyoming draft, section 2, 4; Garroway, Wyoming draft, 123.

4. Garroway, Wyoming draft, section 2, 4; Garroway, Wyoming draft, 124.

5. Garroway, Wyoming draft, 123-24; "Mrs. Adele Garroway Gets Divorce and Child's Custody," *St. Louis Post-Dispatch*, September 27, 1946, 23; Garroway, Wyoming draft, section 2, 4; Garroway, Wyoming draft, 125-126.

6. "Radio to Carry Special Army Day Programs," *Chicago Tribune*, April 6, 1946, 4; Si Steinhauser, "Pitt-Illinois Grid Game Heads Radio List," *Pittsburgh Press*, August 26, 1946, 25; Doc Johnston, "Today on WCOA," *Pensacola News Journal*, September 7, 1946, 4; Marvel Ings, "Evening With Romberg to Replace Red Skelton Show," *The Capital Times* (Madison, Wis.), May 21, 1946, 14.

7. Garroway, Wyoming draft, 101-102; Dave Garroway Jr., written recollections, undated; Rich Samuels, "Studio A," on the "Broadcasting in Chicago, 1921-1989" website, accessed September 13, 2021, www.richsamuels.com/nbcmm/studioa.html. Over the years there has been considerable disagreement about what Garroway took, what it consisted of, and how he took it. While the author acknowledges the various stories, the accounts in this book are based on the best available and most verifiable information, as well as information supplied by Dave Garroway Jr., who in written recollections and in several conversations with the author was *very* open and candid about his father's habit.

8. Garroway, Wyoming draft, 125-27.

9. Charlie Andrews, oral history, Television Academy Foundation, accessed September 13, 2021, https://interviews.televisionacademy.com/interviews/charlie-andrews.

10. Garroway, Wyoming draft, 128.

11. Weisman, "From U. City High to Radio Stardom"; "Rites to Be Held Today for Noted Jazz Writer," *Asbury Park Press* (Asbury Park, N.J.), November 22, 1967, 2; Dave Garroway, addendum in Wyoming draft, undated, 3; Joan King Flynn, "How Dave Garroway Got Into Television," *San Francisco Examiner*, June 17, 1951, 104.

12. Loring Mandel, "Remembering Dave Garroway," *Television Quarterly*, Winter 2004, 13-15; Rees Lloyd, "Mike Rapchak and His Sound," *The Times* (Munster, Indiana), January 29, 1967, 62-63.

13. Weisman, "From U. City High to Radio Stardom"; "Disc Jockey is Gabby Guy," *Lancaster New Era* (Lancaster, Pa.), June 13, 1947, 5; "After 30 Years as a Musician, Red Coty Knows the Score," *Reno Gazette-Journal*, November 30, 1973, 41; Martin Hogan Jr., "It's an Intimate Thing – Garroway," *Cincinnati Enquirer*, September 20, 1968, 27; Clarissa Start, "Patti Page – Still Just a Girl From Tulsa," *St. Louis Post-Dispatch*, February 3, 1953, 26.

14. Charlie Andrews, oral history; Hogan, "It's an Intimate Thing – Garroway"; "When Dave Garroway Says Peace – He Means Peace," *The Morning Call* (Allentown, Pa.), August

10, 1958, 55.

15. Mandel, "Remembering Dave Garroway," 14-15.

16. Garroway, Wyoming draft, 136-137; Si Steinhauser, "Dumonts to Have First Television Here," *Pittsburgh Press*, December 19, 1946, 47; Carlton H. Ihde, "Dave Garroway: Cited Nation's No. 1 Disc Jockey Despite Barefooted Technique," *Valparaiso Torch*, August 13, 1950, clipping in Dave Garroway Papers; Anton Remenih, "Autos Soothe Disk Jockey's Ruffled Spirits," *Chicago Sunday Tribune*, June 26, 1949, sect. 3, p. 12;

16. Weisman, "From U. City High to Radio Stardom"; Leonard Feather, "Garroway – The Rest Has Been Silence," *Los Angeles Times Calendar*, January 19, 1975, 26.

17. Garroway, Wyoming draft, 139-140; Feather, "Garroway – The Rest Has Been Silence."

18. Peg Bolger, "Dave Garroway Show on WIBA to Guest June Christy Today," *The Capital Times* (Madison, Wis.), June 22, 1947, 8; Dave Garroway, letter to Toni, 7 Jan 1947, in author's collection; 11:60 Club membership card, author's collection; Feather, "Garroway – The Rest Has Been Silence."

19. "Disc Jockey is Gabby Guy"; Nadine Subotnik, "Radio Notes and Comment," *Cedar Rapids Gazette* July 8, 1947, 14. Despite many stories that claimed he taught astronomy at Harvard, Garroway denied he was an instructor there. See, for instance, Anton Remenih, "Autos Soothe Disk Jockey's Ruffled Spirits."

20. Don Freeman, "Downs Views the TV Scene," *Miami Herald TV Preview*, April 30, 1967, 3; Gary Deeb, "Peace – A Final Farewell to Dave Garroway," *Hawaii Tribune-Herald* (Hilo, Hawaii), July 29, 1982, 20; "Wins Prize," *The Newark Advocate* (Newark, Ohio), May 27, 1947, 7.

21. "Chicago Hot Club to Hear Krupa and Band," *Chicago Tribune*, October 20, 1946, 93; Hudson-Ross ads in *Chicago Tribune*, February 21, 1947, 12, and April 16, 1947, 8; "11:60 Club" ads in *Chicago Tribune*, April 27, 1947, 150, and 29 April 1947, 19; Feather, "Garroway – The Rest Has Been Silence."

22. Garroway, Wyoming draft, 137-38.

23. Ann Kolson and Francis Davis, "At Swarthmore, Jazz Greats Pay Tribute to Dave," *Philadelphia Inquirer*, February 7, 1983, 1C and 4C; David Bittan, "Singers' Sentimental Journey," *Philadelphia Daily News*, February 7, 1983, 32; Will Leonard, "...And Sarah Just Improves with Time," *Chicago Tribune*, April 12, 1974, 30; Will Davidson, "Angelic Tenor and Musical Merlin: That's Downey," *Chicago Tribune*, March 30, 1947, 94.

CHAPTER 7

1. "Midwest Disc Jockey Becomes Title Player in Dave Garroway Show," *Greenville News* (Greenville, S.C.), June 22, 1947, 2B; Rothhaar, "Garroway at Large," 14, 23-24.

2. Marguerite Ratty, "Dave Garroway Rides High; Does It With Disks!" *Chicago Tribune*, July 13, 1947, 81; Remenih, "Autos Soothe Disk Jockey's Ruffled Spirits"; Cy Wagner, review of "The Dave Garroway Show," *Billboard*, June 28, 1947, 15.

3. John Crosby, "Radio In Review: A Low-Pressure Thing," *The Evening Review* (East Liver-

pool, Ohio), June 26, 1947, 18.

4. "Why Bring That Up?" *Chicago Tribune*, April 28, 1950, 20.

5. Nadine Subotnik, "Radio Notes and Comment," *The Cedar Rapids Gazette*, August 3, 1947, 27; C.E. Butterfield, "Radio Column," *Green Bay Press-Gazette*, August 25, 1947, 17; "Notes From Bill Doudna," *Wisconsin State Journal* (Madison, Wis.), March 12, 1948, 16.

6. Will Davidson, "College Inn to Present Ventura Sextet Friday," *Chicago Tribune*, July 20, 1947, 147; "Notes From Bill Doudna," *Wisconsin State Journal* (Madison, Wis.), June 24, 1947, 24; Larry Wolters, "Disc Jockeys Are Galloping to New Records," *Chicago Tribune*, September 15, 1946, 8.

7. Will Leonard, "The Jazz and the Glory," *Chicago Tribune Magazine*, December 15, 1974, 43; Feather, "Garroway – The Rest Has Been Silence"; "C&NW Clerk Impresario of Jazz Now," *Ames Daily Tribune* (Ames, Iowa), January 27, 1956, 12.

8. Lois Guthmann, "Garroway, Disc Jockey, Views Prejudices; Reveals His Hobbies, Special Interests," undated clipping in Dave Garroway Papers.

9. "Garroway at Large," *Radio Mirror*, September 1949, 50-51; Ed Meyerson, "Man of Today," *TV-Radio Mirror*, June 1954, 92.

10. Dave Garroway Jr., written recollections, undated.

11. "Hold American Music Saturday Night," *Chicago Tribune*, July 11, 1948, 28; "Top Negro Musicians to Join in Festival in Sox Park Tonight," *Chicago Tribune* July 17, 1948, 16; "Mrs. Davis Heads Fund Campaign of Brotherhood," *Chicago Tribune*, March 14, 1948, 102; "20 Groups Hold Party Today As League Benefit," *Chicago Tribune*, October 17, 1948, 7.

12. Harold E. Mason, "Foe of Racism Returns to Air," *Milwaukee Journal*, July 25, 1971, clipping in Dave Garroway Papers.

13. Si Steinhauser, "KQV Lands City's First Television Order," *Pittsburgh Press*, January 29, 1948, 42; "Notes From Bill Doudna," *Wisconsin State Journal* (Madison, Wis.), January 30, 1948, 8; "Disk Jockey Signed," *Los Angeles Times*, February 20, 1948, 17; Ihde, "Garroway: Cited Nation's No. 1 Disc Jockey"; Rothhaar, "Garroway at Large," 15; Frank Blair and Jack Smith, *Let's Be Frank About It* (New York: Doubleday, 1979), 263; Joanne Koch, "Studs," *Chicago Tribune Magazine*, December 6, 1970, 85.

14. Weisman, "From U. City High to Radio Stardom"; Ihde, "Garroway: Cited Nation's No. 1 Disc Jockey"; Remenih, "Autos Soothe Disk Jockey's Ruffled Spirits"; Edan Wright, "Casual Comedian With the Bebop Specs," *Philadelphia Inquirer Magazine*, September 25, 1949, 13; Alan Gill, "Television Today: A Coper," *Cedar Rapids Gazette*, July 20, 1962, 9.

15. "Magnificently Outrageous: The Portrayal of an SS-100 Jaguar," undated article in Dave Garroway Papers.

16. Dorothy Kilgallen, "Voice of Broadway," *Ottawa Journal*, October 4, 1956, 30; Dave Garroway Jr., written recollections, undated.

17. "Disc Jockeys Pick Favorite Colleagues," *St. Petersburg Times*, November 3, 1949; Will Jones, "Lazy Pastors Get a Break," *Minneapolis Star Tribune*, January 17, 1948, 18; "New Screen Find to be Presented," *Greenville News* (Greenville, S.C.), July 11, 1948, 30; Sheila John Daly, "Pick Favorite Disk Jockey in Teen-Age Poll," *Chicago Tribune*, July 27, 1948, 16;

Raney Stanford, "On The Side of the Angels," *The Daily Tar Heel* (Chapel Hill, N.C.), May 18, 1948, 2; Jeanne Remus, "Don Ameche Bids Farewell to Friends Edgar Bergen, Charlie," *Capital Times* (Madison, Wis.), May 9, 1948, 14; Will Davidson, "Recordially Yours," *Chicago Tribune*, June 6, 1948, 118; ad for Thomas hair treatments, *Chicago Tribune*, August 17, 1948, 12.

18. "Dale Harrison's Column," *Chicago Tribune*, May 27, 1948, 32; "Dale Harrison's Column," *Chicago Tribune*, April 17, 1948, 23; "Dale Harrison's Column," *Chicago Tribune*, June 11, 1948, 30.

19. "Tower Ticker," *Chicago Tribune*, January 1, 1949, 9.

20. Garroway, Wyoming draft, 141-145.

21. Garroway, Wyoming draft, 145-146; Garroway, memoir outline in Wyoming papers, 3.

22. Dorothy Kilgallen, "Voice of Broadway," *Scranton Times-Tribune*, September 18, 1947, 5; Dorothy Kilgallen, "Voice of Broadway," *Scranton Times-Tribune*, December 13, 1947, 5; Louella Parsons, "Keeping Up With Hollywood," *Cumberland News* (Cumberland, Md.), January 19, 1948, 5; Cedric Adams, "In This Corner," *Minneapolis Star*, January 26, 1948, 26.

23. Garroway, Wyoming draft, 146-47.

24. Garroway, Wyoming draft, 147-148; Garroway, memoir outline in Dave Garroway Papers, 3.

CHAPTER 8

1. Rothhaar, "Garroway at Large," 29-30. For an overview of Chicago in mid-century, few sources capture the *gestalt* better than Thomas Dyja's *The Third Coast: When Chicago Built the American Dream* (New York: Penguin, 2013), which includes a section on the Chicago School and some of its notables, including Garroway and Burr Tillstrom.

2. Rothhaar, "Garroway at Large," 31-33.

3. "Toynbee, TV and Chicago," *Christian Science Monitor*, June 3, 1950; John Crosby, "For Chicago School of TV, It's Got to Be Authentic," *Detroit Free Press*, September 17, 1953, 37.

4. Ben Gross, "Trouble with TV: Too Many Copycats," *Chicago Tribune*, January 27, 1962, 56; Joanne Koch, "Studs," *Chicago Tribune Magazine*, December 6, 1970, 86.

5. Koch, "Studs."

6. Charlie Andrews, oral history.

7. Battelle, "What's Troubling Garroway?"; Tom Shales, "Coolest TV Host Can't Find a Job," *Florida Today* (Cocoa, Fla.), September 2, 1975, 1D; "Garroway Explains Why He Wants No Studio Audience," *Boston Sunday Globe*, June 4, 1950, A-8.

8. Shales, "Coolest TV Host Can't Find a Job."

9. John Caldwell, "Radio and Television: Television Keeps Up With Scurrying Sam; Good, Says Caldwell," *Cincinnati Enquirer*, April 26, 1949, 21; Wright, "Casual Comedian With the Bebop Specs"; Rothhaar, "Garroway at Large," 34.

10. "NBC Has a Clever Dolly in the TV Studio – Unseen, Though, to Viewers," *Boston Globe*, December 24, 1950, 28; undated clipping, Dave Garroway Papers. Michael Lowenstein shared with the author his memories of sneaking into the clients' booth to watch *Garroway At Large* as it was being produced. "I was knocked out by the design I saw on *Garroway*," he remembered, "the inspired television design of the incomparable Jan Scott." Loewenstein went on to a 41-year career in television and designed sets for many programs, including *Siskel and Ebert* and a Super Bowl pre-game show for Fox. He credited Jan Scott and her work on Garroway's program as a key inspiration. "I know my design and my understanding of what could be done with this new medium was enormously influenced by her work." Michael Loewenstein, e-mail to author, March 11, 2021.

11. John Crosby, "Garroway and Friends," *The Daily Times* (Salisbury, Md.), September 1, 1949, 18; Rothhaar, "Garroway at Large," 40-41.

12. Crosby, "Garroway and Friends"; Undated clipping, Dave Garroway Papers.

13. Wright, "Casual Comedian With the Bebop Specs"; Jenne Strezlecki, "Garroway – Nonchalance and Humor," *The Daily Times* (Davenport, Iowa), May 10, 1951, 37; Dick Kleiner, "Entertainment World: Two Pinch-Hitters Slated to Replace Robert Q.," *The Daily Sun* (San Bernardino, Calif.), June 1, 1954, 6.

14. Dick Adler, "Can Dave Come Back?" July 1971 clipping in Garroway papers, University of Wyoming; undated magazine review in Garroway papers, University of Wyoming.

15. Wright, "Casual Comedian With the Bebop Specs"; Merrill Panitt, "Garroway Gets Award, Unaffected by TV Fame," *Philadelphia Inquirer*, December 18, 1949, 83; "Looking and Listening with Kay Gardella," *New York Daily News*, October 11, 1949, 84; Larry Wolters, "Garroway Has What It Takes For Television," *Chicago Tribune*, October 9, 1949, section 3, 10.

16. Wolters, "Garroway Has What It Takes"; Jeff Kisseloff, *The Box: An Oral History of Television*, 1920-1961 (New York: Viking, 1995), 191; Will Jones, "TV Outpinches Penny-Pinchers," *Minneapolis Morning Tribune*, July 12, 1950, 29.

17. Anton Remenih, "Video Pulls Wool Over Eyes in Many Ways," *Chicago Tribune*, March 23, 1952, 149; Kisseloff, *The Box*, 192-93.

18. "Sudden Success? My Foot!"; Anthony Monahan, "Maybe I Belong in a Long-Gone Era," *Pittsburgh Press*, May 27, 1973, 162.

19. Martin Hogan, "It's An Intimate Thing – Garroway," *Cincinnati Enquirer*, September 20, 1968, 27; Rothhaar, "Garroway at Large," 41-42.

20. Hogan, "It's An Intimate Thing"; Kisseloff, The Box, 191; Wolters, "Garroway Has What It Takes"; Rothhaar, "Garroway at Large," 51-52; "Garroway Gets Award, Unaffected by TV Fame," *Philadelphia Inquirer*, December 18, 1949, 83, 86; Ben Gross, "Looking and Listening," *New York Daily News*, February 6, 1950.

21. Walter Winchell, "Gossip of the Nation," *Philadelphia Inquirer*, September 16, 1949, 31; undated clipping, Wyoming papers; Crosby, "Garroway and Friends"; Wolters, "Garroway Has What It Takes."; "The Garroway Idea," *New Yorker*, January 25, 1950, 63-64.

22. John Crosby, "Price of Coffee Keeps Idle Fred Allen Awake," *Arizona Republic* (Phoenix,

Ariz.), December 6, 1949, 10; Clarke Thomas, "Allen From Radio to TV?" *The Hutchinson News* (Hutchinson, Kan.), January 29, 1950, 19.

23. Wright, "Casual Comedian With the Bebop Specs."

24. "Garroway Video Seg Eyed By GF," *Billboard*, July 2, 1949, 11; "Admiral May B.R. Garroway TV Show," *Billboard*, September 3, 1949, 9; Harold V. Cohen, "The Drama Desk," *Pittsburgh Post-Gazette*, November 4, 1949, 21; Earl Wilson, "Simplicity Called Sex Appeal Secret," *Dayton Daily News* (Dayton, Ohio), December 20, 1949, 18; Rothhaar, "Garroway at Large," 41.

25. Undated magazine review in Garroway papers, University of Wyoming. Nine months later, *Reserved For Garroway* was picked up by Armour, and the program was retitled *Dial Dave Garroway* to reflect sponsorship by Armour's soap brand. Bee Offineer, "Garroway Replaces Dr. Paul," *Akron Beacon Journal*, November 30, 1949, 11; David Westheimer, "Dave Garroway in New Series," *Houston Post*, April 5, 1950, A-28; John Crosby, "Radio in Review," *South Bend Tribune* (South Bend, Ind.), January 6, 1950, 37.

26. Rothhaar, "Garroway at Large," 58; John Crosby, "Radio in Review," *South Bend Tribune* (South Bend, Ind.), January 6, 1950, 37; "What's This? Is Radio Doing Away With Laughter?" *Boston Globe*, November 5, 1950, 84.

27. "Disc Jockeys Pick Favorite Colleagues," *Tampa Bay Times* (St. Petersburg, Fla.), November 3, 1949, 24; "Benny Again Tops in Poll," *Clarion-Ledger* (Jackson, Miss.), December 22, 1949, 13; Ben Gross, "Looking and Listening," *New York Daily News*, February 5, 1950, 103.

28. Bob Goddard, "Dial-Side Seat," *St. Louis Globe-Democrat*, May 20, 1950, 7; Val Adams, undated column, Garroway papers, University of Wyoming.

29. Offineer, "Garroway Replaces Dr. Paul"; Edith Gwynn, "Jane Pickens To Do Night Club Act," *Cincinnati Enquirer*, January 5, 1950, 15; John Crosby, "Radio in Review," *South Bend Tribune*, January 6, 1950, 37; Layah Riggs, "Let's Talk It Over," *Decatur Herald* (Decatur, Ill.), March 28, 1950, 10.

30. Memorandum from Special Agent Guy Hottel to FBI Director J. Edgar Hoover, July 10, 1949. Federal Bureau of Investigation, Garroway FBI file.

31. Memorandum from L.B. Nichols to FBI Assistant Director Clyde Tolson, July 11, 1949. Federal Bureau of Investigation, Garroway FBI file; memorandum from SAC, Chicago to FBI Director J. Edgar Hoover, July 12, 1949. Federal Bureau of Investigation, Garroway FBI file; W. Lloyd Williams, letter to Federal Bureau of Investigation, July 10, 1949. Federal Bureau of Investigation, Garroway FBI file.

32. Memorandum from I.E. Showerman to Frank M. Russell, reproduced in memorandum from Special Agent Guy Hottel to FBI Director J. Edgar Hoover, August 10, 1949. Federal Bureau of Investigation, Garroway FBI file; Ben Gross, "Looking and Listening," *New York Daily News*, July 15, 1949.

33. Memorandum from A.H. Belmont to D.M. Ladd, June 11, 1951, FBI file; memorandum from L.B. Nichols to Clyde Tolson, January 31, 1952, FBI file.

34. Betty Prosser, "Garroway, Relaxed Master of Purple Prose, Blazes TV Trail," *Terre*

Haute Tribune, January 15, 1950, 53; Ihde, "Dave Garroway: Cited Nation's No. 1 Disc Jockey"; Weisman, "From U. City High to Radio Stardom"; Frances B. Murphey, "Garrulous Garroway," undated clipping, Dave Garroway Papers; Val Adams, undated clipping, Dave Garroway Papers.

35. Betty Betz, "The Teen Set," *Johnson City Press* (Johnson City, Tenn.), May 31, 1950, 14.

36. Ira Morton, "$444 Per Minute To Be Paid Hope," *Deseret News* (Salt Lake City, Utah), February 26, 1950, 31; Rothhaar, "Garroway at Large," 86.

37. Keith Wheeler, "Garroway – A Melancholy Mystic: TV Just Another Stop In Dave's Flight From Sadness," *Chicago Sun-Times*, March 8, 1950, clipping in Dave Garroway Papers; Phyllis Battelle, "What's Troubling Retired Star of Today TV Show?" *Lansing State Journal*, July 30, 1961, 4.

38. "Broadway By Mark Barron," *Evening Sun* (Hanover, Pa.), June 3, 1950, 4; "Program Notes," *Evening Sun* (Baltimore, Md.), June 8, 1950, 38.

39. Bob Houser, "Sports Car Racers Go Round and Round in Speed-Filled Day at Proving Ground," *South Bend Tribune*, June 18, 1950, 19.

40. C. E. Butterfield, "Comedian Fred Allen May Be Seen on Video," *Beacon News* (Aurora, Ill.), May 21, 1950, in Dave Garroway Papers; John Caldwell, "Fred Allen Talks," *Cincinnati Enquirer*, October 22, 1950, 61.

41. Robert C. Ruark, "Chicago Wins Honors in TV Charm," *Berkshire County Eagle* (Pittsfield, Mass.), November 1, 1950, 3; Jack O'Brian, "Radio-Video," *Scranton Times-Tribune*, June 22, 1950, 21; Ben Gross, "Garroway Denies Rumor That He Is A Comedian, But Public Disagrees," *New York Daily News*, July 9, 1950, Sect. 2, 18.

42. Kisseloff, *The Box*, 204-205.

43. Brainard Platt, "Tops in Television," *Journal Herald* (Dayton, Ohio), November 28, 1950, 27; Will Jones, "Show Good Despite Turkey," *Star Tribune* (Minneapolis, Minn.), November 21, 1950, 29; Sidney Eiges, "True Story of Garroway and the TV Turkey," *Boston Globe*, December 23, 1950, 10.

44. Doris Lockerman, "Unfair to Home Listeners," *Atlanta Constitution* January 21, 1951, 21; Cameron Day, "TV Revolution!" *Pittsburgh Press*, July 22, 1950, 9; Paul Gallico, "Commercials He Resents," *Tampa Tribune*, June 24, 1951, 20.

45. Rothhaar, "Garroway at Large," 88; Robert W. McFayden, memorandum to Ted Mills, Jan. 11, 1951, National Broadcasting Company Records, Wisconsin Historical Society.

46. Herbert W. Hobler, memorandum to Thomas Lane, Jan. 22, 1951, National Broadcasting Company Records, Wisconsin Historical Society.

47. Paul Cotton, "On Television," *Des Moines Register*, April 10, 1951, 19; Paul Cotton, "TV Audience is Quick to Assert Its Rights," *Des Moines Register*, February 25, 1951, 30.

48. Lon Lorenzen, "Garroway, Pride of Chicago, May Move Show to New York," *Daily Times* (Davenport, Iowa), April 11, 1951, 36; "Rocky Clark's Tele-News," *Bridgeport Telegram* (Bridgeport. Mass.), April 15, 1951, 30; Art Cullison, "Ted Collins Pulls No Punches," *Akron Beacon-Journal*, April 13, 1951, 38; Rocky Clark, "Channel 4 Blackout Hits the South End," *Bridgeport Telegram* (Bridgeport, Conn.), April 13, 1951, 92; Sid Shalit, "Looking and

Listening," *New York Daily News*, April 17, 1951, 4; Walter Winchell, "Gossip of the Nation," *Philadelphia Inquirer*, April 20, 1951, 47; John Caldwell, "New Sponsor Anticipated," *Cincinnati Enquirer*, April 29, 1951, 127; Jenne Strezlecki, "Garroway – Nonchalance and Humor," *The Daily Times* (Davenport, Iowa), May 10, 1951, 37.

49. Rothhaar, "Garroway at Large," 89-90.

50. R. F. McPartlin, "TV Diary: Westward Ho," *Boston Globe*, April 16 1951, 15; R. F. McPartlin, "TV Diary: Season in the Sun," *Boston Globe*, June 25, 1951, 25.

51. Lawrence Witte, "Static," *The Pointer* (Riverdale, Ill.), July 5, 1951, 7; Larry Wolters, "Radio-TV Stars Off To Europe, But Not For Rest," *Chicago Tribune*, July 1, 1951, 174.

52. Anton Remenih, "Touring Europe a la Garroway Is Daily Laugh," *Chicago Tribune*, July 29, 1951, 8.

53. "No Eiffel Tower Tape for Dave," *Tampa Tribune*, July 22, 1951, 47; "Garroway Has More Troubles in France," *Tampa Tribune*, August 12, 1951, 49.

54. Charlie Andrews, oral history.

55. Remenih, "Touring Europe a la Garroway Is Daily Laugh."

56. Elizabeth Rannels, "Have You Heard?" *Chicago Tribune*, August 26, 1951, 159; Robert Metz, *The Today Show* (Chicago: Playboy Press, 1977), 16-17.

57. Rothhaar, "Garroway at Large," 90; "Armour Eyes Daytime Tele of Garroway," *Billboard*, May 19, 1951, 7; Max Wilk, *The Golden Age of Television: Notes From the Survivors* (New York: Dell, 1976), 196; Lucia Perrigo, "Garroway – More at Large Than On TV," *The Daily American* (Somerset, Pa.), November 10, 1951, 3; Art Cullison, "Take Choice, Smith or Godfrey," *Akron Beacon Journal*, May 21, 1951, 8; Walter Winchell, "Gossip of the Nation," *Philadelphia Inquirer*, May 25, 1951, 3.

58. Brainard Platt, "Tops in Televiewing," *Journal Herald* (Dayton, Ohio), August 27, 1951, 23; Kay Gardella, "Televiewing and Listening," *New York Daily News*, August 14, 1951, 178.

CHAPTER 9

1. Gerry Davis, *The Today Show, An Anecdotal History: The First Thirty-Five Years* (New York: Quill, 1987), 12. Also see "The Communicator, Part I: Athens Starts Pouring In," *New Yorker* October 16, 1954, 37-64 and "The Communicator, Part II: What About The Gratitude Factor?" *New Yorker*, October 23, 1954, 43-76. Weaver's memoir *The Best Seat in the House: The Golden Years of Radio and Television*, co-authored with Thomas M. Coffey (New York: Knopf, 1993), is an excellent overview of his career from his own perspective, although it isn't as in-depth as one would hope about Garroway, *Today* or *Monitor*. Regardless, it is valuable for its insight into Weaver's philosophy and how it formed as he progressed through the advertising and programming ranks.

2. Sylvester L. Weaver, Jr., "TV Will Be Chief Source of Entertainment For 95 Pct. Of People, Says Radio Executive," *Albany Democrat-Herald* (Albany, Oregon), January 30, 1951, 3.

3. Metz, *The Today Show*, 24.

4. Sylvester L. Weaver, Jr., memorandum to NBC personnel, July 19, 1951, National Broad-

casting Company Records, Wisconsin Historical Society.

5. "Today," program proposal by Charles Speer for Davidson Taylor, undated (1951), National Broadcasting Company Records, Wisconsin Historical Society; Davidson Taylor, memorandum to Rud Lawrence, July 10, 1951, National Broadcasting Company Records, Wisconsin Historical Society.

6. Mort Werner, memorandum to Sylvester L. Weaver Jr., July 25, 1951, National Broadcasting Company Records, Wisconsin Historical Society; Today, NBC Television, January 14, 1977; Kisseloff, *The Box*, 369.

7. Rud Lawrence, memorandum to network salesmen, August 2, 1951, National Broadcasting Company Records, Wisconsin Historical Society.

8. Lucy Key Miller, "Front Views and Profiles," *Chicago Tribune*, September 28, 1951, 35; Nick Thimmesch, "Islands Call to This Quartet," *The Daily Times* (Davenport, Iowa), September 27, 1951, 37; "Walter Winchell," *Philadelphia Inquirer*, October 1, 1951, 15; Jimmie Fidler, "Views of Hollywood," *Valley Times*, November 7, 1951, 20; Will Leonard, "Tower Ticker," *Chicago Tribune*, October 31, 1951, 31; "Broadway by Dorothy Kilgallen," *Times Tribune* (Scranton, Pa.), December 6, 1951, 5. Rosemary Clooney wrote that she and Garroway, "one of the most interesting guys I'd ever met," went out when she played in the Midwest, but one weekend when she and a friend went to Fire Island, "Dave had told me he'd be out of town, but there he was with another girl." That was it. Rosemary Clooney with Joan Barthel, *Girl Singer: An Autobiography* (New York: Doubleday, 1999), 60.

9. "NBC-TV's 'Get Hep' Formula," *Variety*, September 8, 1951, 31.

10. *Today*, Jan. 14, 1977; Metz, *The Today Show*, 17.

11. Wilk, *The Golden Age of Television*, 197.

12. Metz, The Today Show, 17-18; Wilk, *The Golden Age of Television*, 197.

13. Wilk, *The Golden Age of Television*, 197; Metz, *The Today Show*, 18; Mort Werner, memorandum to Fred Wile, October 15, 1951, National Broadcasting Company Records, Wisconsin Historical Society.

14. Weaver and Coffey, *The Best Seat in the House*, 232; Kisseloff, *The Box*, 369; *Today*, January 14, 1977; Richard A.R. Pinkham, memorandum of October 15, 1951, National Broadcasting Company Records, Wisconsin Historical Society.

15. Thomas McAvity, memorandum to Sylvester L. Weaver Jr., November 7, 1951, National Broadcasting Company Records, Wisconsin Historical Society; "Thomas M'Avity, N.B.C. Executive," *New York Times*, October 24, 1972, 46; Anton Remenih, "Television News and Views," *Chicago Tribune*, November 13, 1951, 16.

16. Larry Wolters, "Television News and Views," *Chicago Tribune*, November 15, 1951, 109; Jack Marley, "Kukla's Video Time Cut as NBC Sells Time," *Press and Sun-Bulletin* (Binghamton, N.Y.), November 10, 1951, 16; Lucia Perrigo, "Garroway – More at Large Than On TV," *The Daily American* (Somerset, Pa.), November 10, 1951, 3.

17. Truman Twill, "Last Right of Refusal," *Marion Star* (Marion, Ohio), November 17, 1951, 6; John Crosby, "The Sad Story of 'The Chicago Touch,'" *Evening Review* (East Liverpool, Ohio), March 20, 1952, 46.

18. Lucy Key Miller, "Front Views and Profiles," *Chicago Tribune*, October 18, 1951, 63.

19. Walter Winchell, "Gossip of the Nation," *Philadelphia Inquirer*, October 5, 1951, 25; "Walter Winchell on Broadway," *Courier-Post* (Camden, N.J.), December 7, 1951, 24; Jack O'Brian, "O'Brien Slated For T.V. Show," *The Record* (Hackensack, N.J.), December 5, 1951, 51; "TV By Norman," *The Paterson Morning Call* (Paterson, N.J.), December 15, 1951, 9.

20. "Television Early Bird," *Pittsburgh Press*, December 16, 1951, 66; Will Jones, "Garroway – Plus the Kitchen Sink," *Star Tribune* (Minneapolis, Minn.), December 18, 1951, 25.

21. Bill Ladd, "Mama Said Not To Speak To Strangers!" *Courier-Journal* (Louisville, Ky.), November 13, 1951, 7.

22. Merrill Panitt, "Pickup in Sale of Sets Cutting Away Backlog," *Philadelphia Inquirer*, November 12, 1951, 24; Davidson Taylor, memorandum to Rud Lawrence, July 10, 1951, National Broadcasting Company Records, Wisconsin Historical Society. Jim Fleming's struggles with the Russian authorities are detailed in Harrison Salisbury's *Russia On The Way* (New York: MacMillan, 1946), 84-90. The author thanks Jeff Fleming for providing additional information about his father during a most enjoyable telephone conversation in July 2020.

23. "Jack Lescoulie, Today Show Pioneer, Dies," *Los Angeles Times*, July 23, 1987, 3; Jimmy Jemail, "The Inquiring Fotographer," *New York Daily News*, April 7, 1963, 17; Cynthia Lowry, "Television Week," *Beckley Post-Herald* (Beckley, W.V.), April 6, 1963, 19.

24. Fred H. Russell, "Telecast Topics," *Bridgeport Telegram* (Bridgeport, Conn.), September 26, 1954, 33; *RCA Victor Family News*, July 1947, 1-2.

25. Metz, *The Today Show*, 26; Weaver and Coffey, *The Best Seat in the House*, 235; Pat Weaver, telegram of December 10, 1951, National Broadcasting Company Records, Wisconsin Historical Society; "Walter Winchell," *Cincinnati Enquirer*, January 1, 1952, 27.

26. "Today," program proposal by Charles Speer for Davidson Taylor, undated (1951). National Broadcasting Company Records, Wisconsin Historical Society; Russell, "Telecast Topics."

27. "Fans in East To See TV's First Don Juan," *Evening Sun* (Baltimore, Md.), December 13, 1951, 40; Frank Merklein, interview with author, Boca Raton, Fla., July 11, 2016.

28. "Broadway by Mark Barron," *Greeley Daily Tribune* (Greeley, Colo.), January 7, 1952, 11.

29. Ron Lorenzen, "TV's Problem: Will Garroway (Yawn) Morning Program Click?" *Daily Times* (Davenport, Iowa), January 9, 1952, 22.

30. Jack O'Brian, "For Jerry Lester as Yuletide Gift: Dagmar Complete With Topography," *Press and Sun-Bulletin* (Binghamton, N.Y.), December 20, 1951, 34; Lorenzen, "TV's Problem"; John Crosby, "TV Plays Early Bird in New Morning Show," *Lincoln Sunday Journal and Star* (Lincoln, Neb.), January 13, 1952, 10D; "By the Way With Bill Henry," *Los Angeles Times*, January 14, 1952, 31.

CHAPTER 10

1. Kisseloff, *The Box*, 368-372.

2. Kisseloff, *The Box*, 368-372; Dave Garroway, undated notes, Lee Lawrence Papers.

3. *Today*, NBC Television, January 14, 1952, kinescope recording. Much of the description of that morning's broadcast comes from a viewing of this kinescope.

4. Will Jones, "Whatever It Is, Garroway Has It," *Star Tribune* (Minneapolis, Minn.), January 15, 1952, 23. Jones tells the story of how that morning's Minneapolis paper got to the Exhibition Hall for the inaugural broadcast.

5. Civil Aeronautics Board, "Accident Investigation Report: Northeast Airlines, Inc. - Near La Guardia Field, New York, January 14, 1952," adopted November 14, 1952.

6. Tom Shales, "Garroway's Great Gift," *Washington Post*, July 22, 1982.

7. "In Review," *Broadcasting-Telecasting*, January 21, 1952, 26.

8. Janet Kern, "Garroway's New Show Is Imitation of News Program," *Chicago Herald-American*, January 28, 1952; Si Steinhauser, "Something May Be Wrong But Not Your TV Set," *Pittsburgh Press*, January 15, 1952, 35; John Caldwell, "No Need to Watch, TV Show Suggests; Tip To Be Followed," *Cincinnati Enquirer*, January 15, 1952, 14; Art Cullison, "Dave Won't Get 'Em Out of Bed," *Akron Beacon Journal*, January 15, 1952, 26.

9. Jack O'Brian, "Television News Program Is Confusing In Premiere," *Philadelphia Inquirer*, January 16, 1952, 36.

10. Bob Lanigan, "Garroway's Today a Good Show – But It's So Early in the Morning!" *Brooklyn Daily Eagle*, January 20, 1952, 24.

11. John Crosby, "Dave Garroway Trims The Day To Two Minutes," *Evening Review* (East Liverpool, Ohio), January 17, 1952, 50; John Crosby, "First Taste Of 'Big' Television Is Little Sour," *Evening Review* (East Liverpool, Ohio), January 18, 1952, 14.

12. Anton Remenih, "Television News and Views," undated clipping in Dave Garroway Papers; Larry Wolters, "Television News and Views," *Chicago Tribune* 1 February 1952, 41.

13. Nancy Anderson, "Garroway Looks Back at Today," *Green Bay Press-Gazette*, March 19, 1972, 95; Betty Utterback, "Today Celebrates a Silver Anniversary," *Democrat and Chronicle* (Rochester, N.Y.), January 13, 1977, 18.

14. Sylvester L. Weaver Jr., memorandum to *Today* staff, Jan. 22, 1952, National Broadcasting Company Records, Wisconsin Historical Society. In another memo Weaver lamented that in the hectic preparations for the first day, he forgot to order a kinescope. Only about 45 minutes of the very first *Today* program - approximately the first half-hour and the last 15 minutes of the East Coast feed - were preserved.

15. Art Cullison, "Obituaries Read On Radio Show," *Akron Beacon Journal*, January 18, 1952, 36; "Radio-TV News," *The Plain Speaker* (Hazleton, Penn.), January 21, 1952, 15; Bill Henry, "By The Way," *Los Angeles Times*, January 21, 1952, 27; Walter Winchell, "Just In Case You Are Going to the Big City," *The High Point Enterprise* (High Point, N.C.), January 21, 1952, 2.

16. Brandon Hollingsworth, "The King Is Dead," blog entry on Garroway at Large website, February 6, 2018, https://garrowayatlarge.com/index.php/2018/02/06/the-king-is-dead/; Si Steinhauser, "Television Will Be There and So Will Speaker Sam," *Pittsburgh Press*, March 30, 1952, Section 5, 8; Si Steinhauser, "Forums Debate Worker," *Pittsburgh Press*, February 15, 1952, 45.

17. Frank McMahon, memorandum to Sylvester L. Weaver Jr., February 5, 1952, National Broadcasting Company Records, Wisconsin Historical Society; John Caldwell, "It's Woman's Right! WSAI Says Goodby, Then Hello To Peggy," *Cincinnati Enquirer*, March 29, 1952, 4.

18. Merrill Panitt, "Ernie Kovacs' Fans Deliver Protests As Show Bows Out For Dave Garroway," *Philadelphia Inquirer*, March 23, 1952, 109; Danton Walker, "Broadway," *New York Daily News*, May 5, 1952, 42; Frank Brookhouser, "It's Happening Here," *Philadelphia Inquirer*, May 20, 1952, 23.

19. "Television Show Boosting Citrus Will Begin Monday," *Tampa Tribune*, February 10, 1952; Bob Lanigan, "Assorted Notes and Comments About TV, Its Stars and Programs – Current and Due," *Brooklyn Eagle*, March 19, 1952, 19; Will Jones, "Dr. I.Q. Gets Ready for TV," *Star Tribune* (Minneapolis, Minn.), March 3, 1952, 31; "Notice To Brand Name Executives," advertisement in *Chicago Tribune*, February 14, 1952, 57; Larry Wolters, "Pittsburgh Soprano to Star On TV Mother's Day Show," *Pittsburgh Press*, May 11, 1952, 80.

20. Wayne Oliver, "Performers Double As TV Sales Artists," *Arizona Republic* (Phoenix, Ariz.), March 2, 1952, 54; Rud Lawrence, memorandum of February 12, 1952, National Broadcasting Company Records, Wisconsin Historical Society.

21. Brainard Platt, "Tops in Televiewing," *Journal Herald* (Dayton, Ohio), March 7, 1952, 55; Si Steinhauser, "Radio and Television News and Views," *Pittsburgh Press*, May 11, 1952, Sect. 5, 8; John Crosby, "Another Peek At The Dave Garroway Show," *The Evening Review* (East Liverpool, Ohio), April 3, 1952, 16.

22. "Radio and Television," *The Journal Times* (Racine, Wis.), February 1, 1952, 16; Anton Remenih, "Television News and Views," *Chicago Tribune*, March 25, 1952, 27.

23. "Such Noive!" *Cincinnati Enquirer*, January 25, 1952, 4.

24. "They Pass By My Window For All Sorts Of Reasons," *Boston Globe*, August 3, 1952, 71; Sandy Oppenheimer, "Miss Truman Proves a Real Pro," *Bristol Daily Courier* (Bristol, Pa.), August 29, 1959, 3; Tom O'Malley and Bob Cunniff, "Ralph Edwards Is Not Needed," *Akron Beacon-Journal*, September 10, 1954, 36.

25. Kenneth Nichols, "The Town Crier," *Akron Beacon-Journal*, June 25, 1952, 22; John Cameron Swayze, "New York," *Anderson Daily Bulletin* (Anderson, Ind.), January 22, 1953, 4; "They Pass By My Window For All Sorts Of Reasons," *Boston Globe*, August 3, 1952, 71; "A Pause to See Garroway Show Shaped Her Future," *St. Louis Post-Dispatch*, February 23, 1958, 168.

26. Peggy McKinnie, "Air Lines," *Jackson Sun* (Jackson, Tenn.), May 18, 1952, 34; Dorothy Dix, "Begin at Home," *Hope Star* (Hope, Ark.), February 8, 1952, 3.

27. "Skitch Henderson Is On Garroway Show," *Greenville News* (Greenville, S.C.), February 7, 1952, 22; "Dave Garroway, NBC Star, Gives Life's Problems a Twist," *Paducah Sun* (Paducah, Ky.), February 14, 1952, 13.

28. Brainard Platt, "Tops in Televiewing," *Journal Herald* (Dayton, Ohio), March 7, 1952, 55; Larry Wolters, "Television News and Views," *Chicago Tribune*, February 15, 1952, 24; "Easter Parade Set For TV," *Detroit Free Press*, February 18, 1952, 29.

29. "It Must Pay To Rise Early," *Pittsburgh Post-Gazette*, January 22, 1954, 29; Hy Gardner, "Major's Mystery Murder Returns to Headlines," *Oakland Tribune*, March 3, 1952, 13; Ed Meyerson, "Man of Today," *TV Radio Mirror*, June 1954, 92; "Dinner With Dave," *Pittsburgh Press*, TV Magazine, April 29, 1956, 8.

30. Mary Frazer, "Garrulous Garroway, TV High-Jinkser," *Pittsburgh Press Magazine*, June 22, 1952, 26; "Hy Gardner," *Philadelphia Inquirer*, February 23, 1959, 17; John Cameron Swayze, "New York," *Lansing State Journal* (Lansing, Mich.), February 21, 1952, 8.

31. Nancy Anderson, "Garroway Looks Back at Today," *Green Bay Press-Gazette*, March 19, 1972, 95; Frazer, "Garrulous Garroway"; "Garroway Has Relaxed Show, Hard Schedule," *Tucson Daily Citizen*, January 12, 1953, 69; "Today Show," *Democrat and Chronicle* (Rochester, N.Y.), January 13, 1977, 19.

32. "Radio Star Arrested," *Hartford Courant*, April 22, 1952, 3; Rosemarie, "Table Hopping Food and Fun Guide," *Daily News-Post* (Monrovia, Calif.), August 14, 1970, 2; James Tuite, "One Spinning Jaguar Put Garroway at Large," *New York Times*, December 22, 1968, clipping in Dave Garroway Papers.

33. Kisseloff, *The Box*, 369.

34. Dorothy Kilgallen, "Voice of Broadway," *Montreal Gazette*, January 9, 1952, 8; Harold V. Cohen, "The Drama Desk," *Pittsburgh Post-Gazette*, March 22, 1952, 20; "Walter Winchell On Broadway," *Courier Post* (Camden, N.J.), January 21, 1952, 21; Dorothy Kilgallen, "Voice of Broadway," *Montreal Gazette*, June 24, 1952, 10.

35. Ted Ashby, "Sitting In On TV: The Floor Manager," *Boston Globe*, April 2, 1952, 19; Si Steinhauser, "Fred Allen Gets Up Before Breakfast, Tells Why," *Pittsburgh Press*, April 6, 1952, 72.

36. Richard Kleiner, "Dance Rehearsal Is Ho-Hum Affair," *Anderson Daily Bulletin* (Anderson, Ind.), April 5, 1952, 9; Larry Wolters, "Television News and Views," *Chicago Tribune*, June 19, 1952, 20.

37. John Crosby, "Another Look at the Dave Garroway Show," *Evening Review* (East Liverpool, Ohio), April 3, 1952, 48; C.E. Butterfield, "Early Morning Telecast To Be Permanent, MC'd by Garroway," *The Bee* (Danville, Va.), May 22, 1952, 14; Steinhauser, "Television Will Be There and So Will Speaker Sam"; "Radio and Television," *Journal Times* (Racine, Wis.), January 23, 1952, 19.

38. Steinhauser, "Television Will Be There and So Will Speaker Sam"; "Garroway Directors Live Busy Lives," *Evening Sun* (Baltimore, Md.), December 2, 1952, 28.

39. Ben Gross, "Televiewing and Listening In," *New York Daily News*, September 13, 1952, 251; Kisseloff, *The Box*, 370.

40. "Today Camera Tube Much-Desired Souvenir," *Charleston Daily Mail* (Charleston, W. Va.), October 4, 1953, 6.

41. Charles P. Wallace, "Today Show Pioneer Dave Garroway Dies," *Los Angeles Times*, July 22, 1982, 24; Cynthia Lowry, "Television Week," *Beckley Post-Herald* (Beckley, W. Va.), April 6, 1963, 19; Al Morton, "TV Roundup," *Delaware County Times* (Chester, Pa.), September 4, 1952, 19. Lescoulie talked about the ring on the anniversary program *Today at*

35, which aired on NBC on January 31, 1987.

42. Jack Gaver, "Stage Actress Fears Television Medium," *St. Louis Post-Dispatch*, February 3, 1970, 6D; "Televiewing: The Art of Non-Irritation," *New York Daily News*, May 25, 1952.

43. Richard A.R. Pinkham, memorandum to Charles Barry, December. 2, 1952, National Broadcasting Company Records, Wisconsin Historical Society; Jeff Fleming, telephone interview with author, July 10, 2020; Les Ledbetter, "Merrill Mueller, 64, Reported Three Wars and First Space Shots," *New York Times*, December 2, 1980, B-23. Frank Blair wrote at length of his days on *Today* in his memoir *Let's Be Frank About It*, co-authored with Jack Smith.

44. Richard A.R. Pinkham, memorandum to Charles Barry, December. 2, 1952, National Broadcasting Company Records, Wisconsin Historical Society.

45. Richard Gehman, "The Man Who Came To Breakfast," *Esquire*, June 1953, 70-71+.

46. Estelle Parsons, oral history, Television Academy Foundation, accessed September 13, 2021, https://interviews.televisionacademy.com/interviews/estelle-parsons; Anderson, "Garroway Looks Back at Today."

47. Bill Ladd, "Weather Girl Is Quite a Lassie, Despite Her Comparative Anonymity," *Courier-Journal* (Louisville, Ky.), December 3, 1954, 9.

48. Barbara Flanagan, "She's On The Go to Set Up Today Show," *Minneapolis Star*, July 3, 1958, 16; Hal Boyle, "Guest Finder Discovers Job Full of Strange Adventures," *Alamogordo Daily News*, June 1, 1955, 4.

49. Earl Wilson, "Get Up Early and Meet Crazy People," *The Republican-Herald* (Winona, Minn.), January 18, 1954, 4; Hal Boyle, "Guest Finder Discovers Job Full of Strange Adventures," *Alamogordo Daily News*, June 1, 1955, 4.

50. Davis, *The Today Show*, 24-25; "NY TV Biggie Visits Here," *California Eagle*, July 30, 1964, 6.

51. Faye Emerson, "Today Has World's Best Coffee," *Pittsburgh Press*, March 13, 1955, 87.

52. Merrill Panitt, "Current U.S. Scene Mirrored By Today," *Philadelphia Inquirer*, December 21, 1952, 52; Dave Garroway with Joe Alex Morris, "I Lead a Goofy Life," *Saturday Evening Post*, February 25, 1956, 17-19+.

53. Jack Gaver, "Up and Down Broadway," *Panama City News-Herald*, February 19, 1953, 2; Jack Mabley, "Top TV Shows Too Costly For Lone-Wolf Sponsors," *Corpus Christi Caller-Times*, January 30, 1953, 17.

CHAPTER 11

1. Betty Hamilton, "From Pet Shop Chimp to Show Business Star," *The Progress* (Clearfield, Pa.), August 5, 1965, 1 and 13.

2. Kisseloff, *The Box*, 371; Hamilton, "From Pet Shop Chimp to Show Business Star," 13; Earl Wilson, "Gags, Gossip on Broadway," *Miami News* (Miami, Fla.), February 3, 1953, 14; C.E. Butterfield, "On The Air Tonight," *Indiana Gazette* (Indiana, Pa.), February 23, 1953, 12; Jack Gaver, "Promote J. Fred Muggs as Outstanding TV Personality," *Logansport Pharos-*

Tribune (Logansport, Indiana), April 13, 1953, 16.

3. Kisseloff, *The Box*, 371.

4. Hal Boyle, "J.F. Muggs Finds TV His Dish," *Press and Sun-Bulletin* (Binghamton, N.Y.), April 11, 1953, 10; "Semple School Puts TV Show to Work," *Courier-Journal* (Louisville, Ky.), February 22, 1953, 83; "J. Fred Muggs, Esq.", *The Pittsburgh Press Magazine*, May 24, 1953, 10.

5. John Crosby, "About a Chimp and Some Unsponsored Shows," *The Evening Review* (East Liverpool, Ohio), March 17, 1953, 10; John Crosby, "The Veep and the Creep," *Marion Star* (Marion, Ohio), February 6, 1953, 13; Gaver, "Promote J. Fred Muggs as Outstanding TV Personality."

6. Boyle, "J.F. Muggs Finds TV His Dish"; Hamilton, "From Pet Shop Chimp to Show Business Star," 13; Gaver, "Promote J. Fred Muggs as Outstanding TV Personality."

7. Frank Langley, "Behind the Scenes of TV," *Hartford Courant*, July 15, 1962, 114.

8. "The Watchman," *Battle Creek Enquirer*, April 18, 1953, 4.

9. Kisseloff, *The Box*, 371-372.

10. Dick Kleiner, "The Marquee," *Akron Beacon Journal*, March 8, 1954, 3.

11. Kisseloff, *The Box*, 372.

12. "All Things Can Happen On Today," *Miami News*, March 14, 1954, 80.

13. The struggle to sell *Today* and the triumph of Matthew Culligan is told ably in Metz, *The Today Show*, 55-67.

14. Kisseloff, *The Box*, 371.

15. Metz, *The Today Show*, 59-60; Si Steinhauser, "Child Born Blind Composes Song For TV," *Pittsburgh Press*, May 27, 1953, 59; Garroway with Morris, "I Lead a Goofy Life."

16. Richard Kleiner, "East Coast: TV Sales Pitch Is Natural For Gals," *Anderson Daily Bulletin* (Anderson, Ind.), April 12, 1952, 9; "Theaters Seek Own Exclusive Video Channels," *Chicago Tribune*, February 7, 1953, 38; "Gossip From The Studios," *St. Louis Post-Dispatch*, February 15, 1953, 69; Leo Mishkin, "From News to the Music, It's a Peculiar Business," *Philadelphia Inquirer*, February 27, 1953, 38.

17. Art Cullison, "A-Blast Was Dud on Television," *Akron Beacon Journal*, March 18, 1953, 18.

18. C.E. Butterfield, "TV to Rush Coronation Films To U.S.; Radio Will Be There," *Asbury Park Press* (Asbury Park, N.J.), May 19, 1953, 21.

19. "Many St. Louisans Rise Early To View Coronation Telecast," *St. Louis Post-Dispatch*, June 2, 1953, 3.

20. Will Jones, "Coronation? It's a Double Feature," *Star Tribune* (Minneapolis, Minn.), June 3, 1953, 37; James Devane, "Coronation Is Given Big Treatment," *Cincinnati Enquirer*, June 3, 1953, 20. At the time it was said NBC's "secret weapon" Canberra turned back because of a mechanical issue, but later an NBC executive learned that the BBC had the plane's pilot, a member of the Royal Air Force reserve, turn around in order to prevent

American television from showing the coronation before Canadian audiences could see it. See Reuven Frank, "The Great Coronation War," in *American Heritage*, December 1993, available online at https://www.americanheritage.com/great-coronation-war.

21. Bob Considine, "British Critical of U.S. Telecasts," *Cincinnati Enquirer*, June 12, 1953, 7; "The BBC Protests Are In Order," *The Daily Times* (Davenport, Iowa), June 9, 1953, 10; "The Time Is Twenty-One After," *New Yorker*, September 1959, 39-75.

22. "Truman Credits Health To Early-Morning Walks," *North Adams Transcript* (North Adams, Mass.), July 1, 1953, 1; Si Steinhauser, "Time Was When KQV Spurned CBS Network," *Pittsburgh Press*, July 2, 1953, 29.

23. Si Steinhauser, "Politics Endless Pain in Neck to Radio and TV," *Pittsburgh Press*, May 28, 1953, 35; "Garroway Knows Value of American Passport," *Pittsburgh Press*, August 30, 1953, 70.

24. "TV Threat To Books Overrated," *The Daily Times* (Salisbury, Md.), October 29, 1953, 25; Si Steinhauser, "Theme Song Trend Surprises Radio, TV," *Pittsburgh Press*, October 29, 1953, 55; Dick Kleiner, "The Marquee," *Kingston Daily Freeman* (Kingston, N.Y.), March 20, 1954, 3; "Janie Workman Leaves Air To Care For Child; Fred Waring Coming For Personal Appearance," *Courier-Journal* (Louisville, Ky.), November 1, 1953, 94.

25. Bob Lanigan, "Color TV Again Takes Spotlight in Industry," *Brooklyn Daily Eagle*, September 2, 1953, 13; C.E. Butterfield, "Antenna Advance," *Journal Gazette* (Mattoon, Ill.), September 2, 1953, 2. A black-and-white kinescope of this presentation still exists and was included in a commercially-available DVD collection of *Kukla, Fran and Ollie* episodes.

26. Will Jones, "Garroway of Old Coming Saturday," *Star Tribune* (Minneapolis, Minn.), December 4, 1952, 37; James Abbe, "See It Now Gives First Newsreel of Ike in Korea," *Oakland Tribune*, December 8, 1952, 40; "Walter Winchell on Broadway," *Courier-Post* (Camden, N.J.), March 12, 1953, 14; Leo Mishkin, "Fresh Approach Gives New Sparkle to Stars," *Philadelphia Inquirer*, March 10, 1953, 28.

27. Si Steinhauser, "Death of Radio Is Greatly Exaggerated," *Pittsburgh Press*, May 7, 1953, 63; Jack Gaver, "Dave Garroway Is One Of Busiest NBC Stars," *Logansport Pharos-Tribune* (Logansport, Ind.), September 28, 1953, 3; James Devane, "CBS-TV Pats Self On Back For Jackie Gleason Rating," *Cincinnati Enquirer*, May 10, 1953, 102; "Phantom to Return; Stu's Family In Stew," *Minneapolis Star*, May 29, 1953, 27.

28. Larry Wolters, "Television News and Views," *Chicago Tribune*, July 24, 1953, 16; Ken Wallace, "Jill Corey Again Seeks the Spotlight," *The Record* (Hackensack, N.J.), February 7, 1971, 43.

29. Phyllis Battelle, "The Dream Became a Nightmare," *Evening Herald* (Shenandoah, Pa.), December 18, 1972, 4.

30. "Radio-TV-Chatter," *Tipton Daily Tribune* (Tipton, Ind.), October 3, 1953, 2; Art Cullison, "Hartman Makes Scripts Funny," *Akron Beacon Journal*, October 5, 1953, 8; Jack O'Brian, "Radio-TV-Chatter," *Tipton Daily Tribune* (Tipton, Ind.) , October 13, 1953, 5. Frank Merklein, who was a cameraman on the first *Dave Garroway Show*, remembered Garroway giving each crewmember a $10 tip after the program's conclusion; for the time,

this was a substantial sum, defying the rumor that Garroway was a cheapskate. Frank Merklein, interview with author.

31. Anton Remenih, "Critic Levels Sights At New TV Programs," *Chicago Tribune*, November 22, 1953, part 3, 14; John Crosby, "The Old Garroway," *Pittsburgh Post-Gazette*, December 25, 1953, 42.

32. Richard Kleiner, "TV Coast to Coast," *Portsmouth Herald* (Portsmouth, N.H.), October 21, 1953, 6; R.F. McPartlin, "TV Diary – Ups and Downs," *Boston Globe*, April 25, 1951, 41; Wayne Oliver, "Linkletter Meets Match in Quizzing Young Set," *Philadelphia Inquirer*, January 3, 1954, 92.

33. "Garroway Sporting Mysterious Shiner," *Akron Beacon Journal*, November 2, 1953, 2; Walter Winchell, "Gossip Of The Nation," *Philadelphia Inquirer*, November 5, 1953, 19.

34. "Truman Jaywalks To Get View Of Garroway's Show," *Moberly Monitor-Index* (Moberly, Mo.), November 13, 1953, 8; "Truman Says...." *The Daily Clintonian* (Clinton, Ind.), November 13, 1953, 2; Kisseloff, *The Box*, 391.

35. Gehman, "Today With Garroway," 105-106.

36. "Television Letter Box," *St. Louis Post-Dispatch*, December 13, 1953, 38.

37. John Crosby, "Radio and Television," *Daily Press* (Newport News, Va.), January 25, 1954, 10; "Dave and the Chickens," *Newsweek*, January 25, 1954, 56-7.

38. Jack Gaver, "Garroway Gets Credit-Blame On Television," *Alexandria Times-Tribune* (Alexandria, Ind.), November 18, 1953, 2.

39. "TV Star Rams Car as Picture Is Being Taken," *Panama City News*, February 16, 1954, 3; "Garroway Injured in Dade Crash," *Fort Lauderdale News*, February 15, 1954, 1; "Dave Garroway Injured Here in Auto Crash," *Miami News*, February 15, 1954, 36; "TV Star Garroway Injured in Car Mishap During Filming," *Long Beach Independent*, February 16, 1954, 8; "Garroway Resting Comfortably," *Fort Lauderdale News*, February 16, 1954, 4; "Garroway Set To Quit Bed, Rest At Beach," *Miami News*, February 18, 1954, 35; C.E. Butterfield, "Ad Injury Keeps Garroway Off Show," *Evening Sun* (Hanover, Pa.), February 19, 1954, 17; Art Cullison, "Today Needs Dave," *Akron Beacon Journal*, February 25, 1954, 21.

40. Art Cullison, "CBS To Try Early TV, Too," *Akron Beacon Journal*, December 11, 1953, 51; Dick Kleiner, "The Marquee," *Akron Beacon Journal*, February 10, 1954, 26; Jack Gaver, "Television Theater," *The Daily Notes* (Canonsburg, Pa.), March 12, 1954, 9.

41. John Crosby, "Sincere Flattery," *Warren County Observer* (Warren, Pa.), March 18, 1954, 8; Anton Remenih, "Morning Show Rivals Battle For Top Rating," *Chicago Tribune*, March 20, 1954, 33.

42. Crosby, "Sincere Flattery"; Dick Kleiner, "The Marquee," *La Crosse Tribune* (La Crosse, Wis.), March 27, 1954, 7.

43. "Chimp of Distinction," *Altoona Tribune* (Altoona, Pa.), April 20, 1954, 15; "Mr. Muggs... His Mark," *Los Angeles Times Sunday Magazine*, June 6, 1954; "Chimp Is Champ," *Greenville News* (Greenville, S.C.), May 16, 1956, 4.

44. Dick Kleiner, "Fred Muggs – The Chimp," *Monroe Morning World* (Monroe, La.), June 12, 1954, 9; Garroway and Morris, "I Lead a Goofy Life"; "Chimp Takes Bite of Martha

Raye," *Detroit Free Press*, April 19, 1954, 12; Faye Emerson, "Lillian Gish Great In 'Waterfront' Film," *Pittsburgh Press*, July 21, 1954, 37; James Abbe, "Student Night – Tech High, U.C. Share Television Screen," *Oakland Tribune*, November 11, 1954, 22; Steven Battaglio, *From Yesterday To Today* (Philadelphia: Running Press, 2011), 36-37; "Radio and TV," *The Gazette and Daily* (York, Pa.), September 1, 1956, 13; "Plans," *Asbury Park Press* (Asbury Park, N.J.), August 12, 1956, 2.

45. Davis, *The Today Show*, 30; Hal Boyle, "Guest Finder Discovers Job Full Of Strange Adventures," *Alamogordo Daily News*, June 1, 1955, 4; Battaglio, *From Yesterday To Today*, 37.

46. Fred Remington, "J. Fred Muggs Publicity Becoming Painful," *Pittsburgh Press*, July 29, 1954, 45.

47. C.E. Butterfield, "Canadian Football Is New To Viewers," *Miami News*, August 27, 1954, 8.

48. "Look and Listen with Donald Kirkley," *The Sun* (Baltimore, Md.), January 14, 1955, 8; "Phoebe B. Beebe," *Cincinnati Enquirer*, January 16, 1955, Sect. 3, 10; Phyllis Battelle, "Assignment America," *Franklin Evening Star* (Franklin, Ind.), February 2, 1955, 4.

49. Metz, *The Today Show*, 68-69.

50. Metz, *The Today Show*, 107; "Muggs Petting Parties Denounced By ASPCA," *Philadelphia Inquirer*, July 18, 1956, 28.

51. "Garroway Show On Radio Prepared At His Leisure," *Indianapolis Star*, May 30, 1954, 10.

52. Bob Foster, "Hollywood Stunt Man TV Success Story," *Press Democrat* (Santa Rosa, Ca.), April 8, 1954, 9; "Garroway Show On Radio Prepared At His Leisure"; "Bertrand Russell Asserts Hatred is the Road to Death," *St. Louis Post-Dispatch*, April 26, 1954, 13; "Garroway To Re-Enact First Audition At NBC on WFBC," *Greenville News* (Greenville, S.C.), May 9, 1954, 40.

53. Magee Adams, "Look And Listen: New WSAI Forum Notable Fare," *Cincinnati Enquirer*, April 23, 1954, 35; Magee Adams, "Music Listing Shocked Into Popular Classics," *Cincinnati Enquirer*, May 9, 1954, 32.

54. Magee Adams, "Look And Listen: Texans Anger A Shriner Fan," *Cincinnati Enquirer*, May 1, 1954, 30; Kisseloff, *The Box*, 103.

55. Rothhaar, "Garroway at Large," 95-96; Kisseloff, *The Box*, 103.

56. Rothhaar, "Garroway at Large," 96-97; Dorothy Kilgallen, "The Voice of Broadway," Pottstown (Pa.) *Mercury* 8 Mar 1954, 4.

57. Rothhaar, "Garroway at Large," 96; Dick Kleiner, "The Marquee," *Pittsburgh Press*, June 27, 1954, 81; Lawrence Witte, "Impressive Star List For TV Musical," *Newport Daily News* (Newport, R.I.), February 28, 1959, 9; Peg Simpson, "Garroway Series On Friday Nights Good Listening," *The Post-Standard* (Syracuse, N.Y.), January 14, 1955, 30.

58. "Skylarking With James Copp," *Los Angeles Times*, March 27, 1955, 97; Garroway and Morris, "I Lead A Goofy Life," 62.

59. Meyerson, "Man of Today," 68; Faye Emerson, "TV Stars Seek Obscurity In European

Vacations," *El Paso Herald-Post*, July 5, 1954, 22.

60. Garroway, Maryland draft, 81-82.

61. Isabella Taves, "Dave Garroway's Search For Himself," *Redbook*, October 1961, 45+.

62. Si Steinhauser, "Outlook For More TV Dark," *Pittsburgh Press*, April 11, 1952, 33; excerpt from "Dial Dave Garroway" radio program, July 14, 1953, recording in author's collection.

63. "Morse Code with Jim Morse," *Star-Gazette* (Elmira, N.Y.), May 1, 1954, 5; "Bob Foster," *The Times* (San Mateo, Calif.), January 31, 1959, 28; Dave Garroway, "It's A Crazy Day Any Today On TV," *Star Tribune* (Minneapolis, Minn.), July 7, 1954, 36; "What's In A Name?" *Fort Lauderdale News*, August 15, 1954, 16.

64. Garroway and Morris, "I Lead A Goofy Life"; Joan Crosby, "Meet Dave Garroway: Exploring Universe Without Any Misses," *Philadelphia Daily News*, July 11, 1962, 34.

65. Luke Feck, "Non-Sticky Kid Show," *Cincinnati Enquirer*, January 4, 1962, 10; "Radio-TV Notebook," Kingsport Times (Kingsport, Tenn.), September 21, 1956, 6.

66. Garroway and Morris, "I Lead a Goofy Life"; Charlie Andrews, oral history.

67. John Crosby, "Radio and Television," *Lansing State Journal* (Lansing, Mich.), August 27, 1954, 26; "J. LaRosa Premier with Jack Paar Provides Contrast with Garroway," *Marysville Journal-Tribune* (Marysville, Ohio), November 26, 1954, 7.

68. "Network Notes," *Anniston Star* (Anniston, Ala.), December 11, 1954, 23; Kenneth Nichols, "Town Crier," *Akron Beacon Journal*, December 27, 1954, 11. Dorothy Kilgallen, "Voice of Broadway," *Anderson Daily Bulletin*, December 29, 1954, 4.

CHAPTER 12

1. Terry Vernon, "TV Tele-Vues," *Long Beach Independent*, February 28, 1955, 19; "Today - $11,000,000 Baby," *St. Louis Post-Dispatch*, January 16, 1955, 68; Faye Emerson, "Dunking of TV Stars Gives Zip to Life in Deep South," *El Paso Herald-Post*, January 17, 1955, 19.

2. Faye Emerson, "Hazards of Alligator-Wrestling," *Pittsburgh Press*, January 19, 1955, 41.

3. Faye Emerson, "Gobel Leads Comedians As Most Widely Quoted," *El Paso Herald-Post*, February 7, 1955, 15; Herb Lyon, "Tower Ticker," *Chicago Tribune*, February 2, 1955, Part 2, 6; Herb Lyon, "Tower Ticker," *Chicago Tribune*, March 16, 1955, 28; Dorothy Kilgallen, "The Voice of Broadway," *The Times* (Shreveport, La.), February 22, 1955, 9.

4. P.L. Prattis, "Horizon: Are We Americans Chumps Also?" *Pittsburgh Courier*, February 26, 1955, 6.

5. Maggie Wilson, "Tune In: Rise And Shine At 5 April 27 For TV's Super Spectacular," *Arizona Republic* (Phoenix, Ariz.), April 15, 1955, 23; "Hollywood Schedules A-Bomb On Newest TV Spectacular," *Daily Herald* (Provo, Utah), April 21, 1955, 34; "Big Atomic 'Show' Is Delayed," *The Republic* (Columbus, Ind.), April 26, 1955, 15.

6. Walter Ames, "Las Vegas Center of TV Over Week End; Bomb Makes Garroway Wreck," *Los Angeles Times*, May 3, 1955, 30.

7. Dick Kleiner, "The Marquee," *Elmira Advertiser* (Elmira, N.Y.), June 18, 1955, 8; "Fitting

Change," *Post-Standard* (Syracuse, N.Y.), November 21, 1955, 6.

8. "Today Promotes Americanism," *The Call-Leader* (Elwood, Ind.), March 29, 1955, 6; Virginia Irwin, "Help for Widow of a 'Good Samaritan,'" *St. Louis Post-Dispatch*, May 17, 1955, 41.

9. Dennis Hart, *Monitor (Take 2): The Revised, Expanded Inside Story of Network Radio's Greatest Program* (iUniverse, 2003), 29-34. The author also highly recommends Hart's website, The *Monitor* Tribute Pages, at http://monitorbeacon.net/.

10. "NBC Plans 40-Hour Show," *Oakland Tribune*, April 24, 1955, 71.

11. Hart, *Monitor*, 21-22; Jack O'Brian, "Radio-TV Notebook," *Kingsport Times* (Kingsport, Tenn.), June 13, 1955, 9; Jack Gould, "40-Hr. Radio Grab Bag - 'Monitor,'" *Des Moines Register*, June 14, 1955, 11; John Crosby, "Television and Radio," *Daily Press* (Newport News, Va.), June 19, 1955, 8D; Will Jones, "No Beaten Path For This Show," *Minneapolis Star Tribune*, June 22, 1955, 35.

12. Hurley E. Badders, "Tuning In," *The Greenville News* (Greenville, S.C.), June 26, 1955, 30.

13. Eve Starr, "Video Comes of Age In 'Wide, Wide World,'" *Democrat and Chronicle* (Rochester, N.Y.), June 5, 1955, 14.

14. J.P. Shanley, "'Wide World' Shows Broad Scope of TV," *Des Moines Register*, June 28, 1955, 15; "Look and Listen with Donald Kirkley," *Baltimore Sun*, June 29, 1955, 12; Will Jones, "How Old Can New TV Ideas Get?" *Star Tribune* (Minneapolis, Minn.), June 30, 1955, 35; John Crosby, "Television and Radio: Great Big Stage," *Lansing State Journal* (Lansing, Mich.), July 4, 1955, 31.

15. Phyllis Battelle, "Dave Garroway of TV Fame Admits Only One Real Distinction," *Mount Pleasant News* (Mount Pleasant, Iowa), September 14, 1955, 6; "Oil Industry to Sponsor Show," *Press-Gazette* (Hillsboro, Ohio), October 4, 1955, 6; Fred Remington, "'1976' to Get Re-Run 20 Years from Now," *Pittsburgh Press*, October 10, 1955, 35; "Look and Listen with Donald Kirkley," *Baltimore Sun*, October 12, 1955, 12; William Ewald, "NBC-TV Picks Garroway To Emcee 'Wide Wide World,'" The Times (San Mateo, Calif.), August 24, 1955, 22.

16. Kinescope of *Wide Wide World* debut; partial digital copy in author's collection.

17. Dickson Terry, "Four and One-Half Minutes of Television," *St. Louis Post-Dispatch*, October 23, 1955, 76 and 89.

18. Bob Foster, "Wide Wide World Proves Just That," *The Times* (San Mateo, Calif.), October 18, 1955, 15; Paul Cotton, "On Television," *Des Moines Register*, October 18, 1955, 11; Will Jones, "Lecture on Jazz Deserves Encore," *Star-Tribune* (Minneapolis, Minn.), October 19, 1955, 39.

19. Ann and Bill Rabe, "Spectacular, Now Pinpoint," *Polish Daily News* (Detroit, Mich.), December 31, 1955, 6.

20. Jack Gaver, "'Babes in Toyland' Changed Little," *Courier-Journal* (Louisville, Ky.), December 19, 1955, 15; William Ewald, "Christmas on TV Row Backbreaker For Santa Claus," *Brownwood Bulletin* (Brownwood, Tex.), December 15, 1955, 2; William Ewald, "Actors, Actresses Report Resolutions For New Year," *Odessa American* (Odessa, Tex.), January 1, 1956, 11.

CHAPTER 13

1. Jack O'Brian, "Radio-TV News," *Daily Times* (New Philadelphia, Ohio), March 3, 1956, 2.

2. Robert Smith, "An Aptly Named Miss America Shows Some Confidence in Her Country," *Berkshire Eagle* (Pittsfield, Mass.), May 21, 1956, 17.

3. Julia Daugherty, "Video Takes On 'Taming' Of Sanders," *Indianapolis Star*, August 2, 1956, 17; Jack O'Brian, "On The Air," *Sandusky Register* (Sandusky, Ohio), July 27, 1956, 2.

4. Will Jones, "A Plug For Richard III," *Star Tribune* (Minneapolis, Minn.), March 13, 1956, 30; James Devane, "Cornell Fine In Television Debut," *Cincinnati Enquirer*, April 3, 1956, 17.

5. Stanley Frank, "Super-Blooper TV Show," *The Saturday Evening Post*, October 13, 1956, 46+; Steven R. Scheuer, "TV Drama Viewers To Miss Alcoa Hour," *Troy Record* (Troy, N.Y.), September 27, 1957, 8.

6. Jack Gould, "Striking Look Into World of Armed Might," *Des Moines Register*, May 14, 1956, 10; Fred Remington, "Allen Does Nifty Garroway Imitation," *Pittsburgh Press*, August 7, 1956, 39; "Viewing TV With Hal Humphrey," *Honolulu Star-Bulletin*, May 19, 1958, 17.

7. "As We See It," *Press and Sun-Bulletin* (Binghamton, N.Y.), May 15, 1956, 10; Hart, *Monitor*, 67.

8. "Dave Garroway Signs New NBC Contract," *Hartford Courant*, March 18, 1956, 130; Jack O'Brian, "One Hour Not Long Enough For Louella's Life Story," *Cumberland Evening Times* (Cumberland, Md.), March 9, 1956, 19; Charles Mercer, "Garroway's Early Show Has Forced Him Into Isolation," *Argus-Leader* (Sioux Falls, S.D.), February 12, 1956, 35; Dick Kleiner, "The Marquee," *The News* (Frederick, Md.), May 6, 1955, 13; Bob Foster, "Garroway Lives With Many Gadgets," *The Times* (San Mateo, Calif.), August 7, 1956, 15.

9. "Three Toots on Trumpet Belie Jack Lescoulie's Second Talent," *Kansas City Times*, February 27, 1956, 14; Lawrence Witte, "TV-Radio News Bits," *The Evening Independent* (Massillon, Oh.), October 24, 1956, 5.

10. Walter Ames, "Poll Shows Lanza Won New Friends From Tver; Garroway Near Tragedy," *Los Angeles Times*, October 2, 1954, 25; J.T. Matthews, "TV Newsreel," *Daily Republican* (Monongahela, Pa.), October 25, 1954, 3; John Moss, "Playboy on Poker," *Playboy*, November 1957, 24.

11. "Ex-Official Of Columbia Films, Dies," *Hartford Courant*, January 6, 1963, 41; "Ex Movie Head Dies In Westport," *Bridgeport Post*, January 5, 1963, 23; "Drug Overdose Fatal To Wife Of Garroway," *Chicago Tribune*, April 29, 1961, 68; Pamela Garroway with Gladys Hall, "I Married Dave Garroway," *American Weekly*, March 8, 1959, 5-6.

12. Garroway with Hall, "I Married Dave Garroway."

13. Garroway with Hall, "I Married Dave Garroway"; Dave Garroway, Wyoming draft, appendix pages 4-5; Larry Wolters, "Vic & Sade Sought For TV Series," *Chicago Tribune*, September 1, 1955, 30; "Dave Garroway To Marry Film Worker Pamela Wilde," *St. Louis Post-Dispatch*, March 23, 1956, 35; Walter Winchell, "On Broadway," *Lebanon Daily News* (Lebanon, Pa.), April 4, 1956, 13; "Breakfast at 4 A.M. Vowed By Bride of Dave Garroway," *Kansas City Times*, August 8, 1956, 12; Garroway with Hall, "I Married Dave Garroway";

Judith Cass, "Recorded at Random," *Chicago Tribune*, August 18, 1956, 20.

14. Dave Garroway, Wyoming draft, appendix pages 4-5; Gladys Hall, "Little Boy Wanted," *TV-Radio Mirror*, July 1958, 29+; Geraldine Small, "Garroway Summer Station – LI," *Newsday*, June 29, 1959, 31. "Nemo Point" was a reference to the broadcasting term NEMO for remote broadcasts, meaning "Not Emanating from Main Office."

15. Dave Garroway, Wyoming draft, appendix page 5.

16. Frank, "Super-Blooper TV Show."

17. Jack Gould, "Gimmicks on Como Show 'Sophomoric,'" *Des Moines Register*, September 17, 1956, 20; John Crosby, "Television and Radio," *Lansing State Journal* (Lansing, Mich.), September 19, 1956, 41; Peg Simpson, "Wide Wide World Impressive But Getting Pompous," *Post-Standard* (Syracuse, N.Y.), September 19, 1956, 21; Jack Gould, "Garroway Feature Called 'Superficial and Foolish,'" *Courier-Journal* (Louisville, Ky.), December 10, 1956, 14; James Devane, "Wide Wide World Can Learn," *Cincinnati Enquirer*, January 8, 1957, 31.

18. "Television Notes and Gossip," *St. Louis Post-Dispatch*, October 23, 1956, 42; Lawrence Witte, "TV-Radio News Bits," *Evening Independent* (Massillon, Oh.), October 24, 1956, 5; "Ex-Singer Helen O'Connell Likes New Talking Career," *Asbury Park Press* (Asbury Park, N.J.), January 12, 1957, 9; "New Records: Some Words of Hope," *Des Moines Sunday Register TV Magazine*, November 11, 1956, 4; "Today" game advertisement, *Bridgeport Telegram* (Bridgeport, Conn.), December 1, 1956, 19; "Garroway Idled By Old Injury," *Lansing State Journal* (Lansing, Mich.), January 1, 1957, 1.

CHAPTER 14

1. Bob De Piante, "Viewing and Listening," *Oneonta Star* (Oneonta, N.Y.), January 9, 1957, 16; "Just Call Colonel, Ford Will Answer," *Minneapolis Star*, January 8, 1957, 15; Jack O'Brian, "Dinah Shore Show Breezy But Gimmicky," *Courier-Post* (Camden, N.J.), January 14, 1957, 5; Marie Torre, "Elvis Presley May Get His Price," *Democrat and Chronicle* (Rochester, N.Y.), January 9, 1957, 15. The *Mad* parody *The Dave Garrowunway Show* originally ran in the November 1955 issue, but the author's initial discovery of this incredible piece came from its inclusion in the paperback compilation *The Brothers Mad* (Ballantine, 1958).

2. "Jack Lescoulie Leaves 'Today' For 'Tonight,'" *Pittsburgh Press*, January 11, 1957, 39; Lawrence Witte, "TV-Radio News Bits," *The Evening Independent* (Massillon, Ohio), January 23, 1957, 5.

3. "Television Notes and Gossip," *St. Louis Post-Dispatch*, January 29, 1957, 38; Bob De Piante, "Viewing and Listening," *Oneonta Star* (Oneonta, N.Y.), January 29, 1957, 14.

4. "From Pet," *The Progress* (Clearfield, Pa.), August 5, 1965, 13; W. Pinkerton Jr., "Was Muggs Really Mean?" *Quad-City Times* (Davenport, Iowa), April 27, 1971, 18.

5. Marie Torre, "Dave Says 'Goodby, Mr. Chimp,'" *Democrat and Chronicle* (Rochester, N.Y.), January 24, 1957, 16; Julia Daugherty, "Hiram Holliday Is TV's 'Walter Mitty,'" *Indianapolis Star*, January 16, 1957, 13; Donald Kirkley, "Look and Listen," *Baltimore Sun*, January 30, 1957, 10; Pinkerton, "Was Muggs Really Mean?"

6. "David Felts' Column," *Decatur Herald* (Decatur, Ill.), February 23, 1957, 6; Julia Daugh-

erty, "Kokomo Jr. Will Take Muggs' Place," *Indianapolis Star*, March 1, 1957, 19; Hurley E. Badders, "Tuning In," *Greenville News* (Greenville, S.C.), March 10, 1957, 6; Dorothy Kilgallen, "Will Porfirio Go Like Alfonso Did?" *The Tennessean* (Nashville), May 23, 1957, 15.

7. "Chimp Sues Dave Garroway, Associates in Contract Row," *The Town Talk* (Alexandria, La.), September 11, 1957, 13; editorial comment, *Orlando Sentinel*, September 12, 1957, 6.

8. Pinkerton, "Was Muggs Really Mean?" A clip of Muggs attacking Lescoulie's desk was aired on *Today*'s 25th anniversary program in 1977.

9. Don Dornbrook, "Off-Screen Picture of Garroway at Home," *St. Louis Post-Dispatch*, October 26, 1959, 39; Dave Garroway, Wyoming draft, appendix page 6.

10. Dave Garroway, Wyoming draft, appendix page 7.

11. Hall, "Little Boy Wanted"; Dornbrook, "Off-Screen Picture of Garroway at Home."

12. Dave Garroway Jr., written recollections, undated.

13. "Dave Garroway's Steps for Waking Are Well Planned," *Lake Charles American-Press*, October 7, 1960, 33; "Auto Relaxation Of 80-Hour Man," *Cincinnati Enquirer*, May 5, 1957, 74; "They Said He'd Change...But Pam Fits Dave's Mad Life," *Detroit Free Press*, May 12, 1957, 6-TV; "Walter Winchell of New York," *Terre Haute Tribune*, March 18, 1957, 4.

14. "Murrow to Interview Garroway, Blackstone," *Marshfield News-Herald* (Marshfield, Wis.), October 6, 1956, 11; Garroway with Hall, "I Married Dave Garroway"; Walter Ames, "Early Birds Can See Stork Shower On Today Program," *Los Angeles Times*, November 6, 1957, Section 2, 8.

15. Dave Garroway, Wyoming draft, appendix page 6; "June Havoc May Get Series," *Fort Lauderdale News*, May 25, 1957, 11.

16. Grem V. Octapoda, "Rogers Couldn't Make The Grade," *Salina Journal*, April 7, 1957, 26; "New Dean to Bow With 'Smilin' Music," *Minneapolis Star*, April 3, 1957, 37; Marie Torre, "Today Show Miffed At Ratings," *Democrat and Chronicle* (Rochester, N.Y.), July 22, 1957, 8; Will Jones, "TV Goes Thataway," *Star Tribune* (Minneapolis, Minn.), November 27, 1957, 28.

17. "Lescoulie Quits Job On Tonight," *Des Moines Register*, May 22, 1957, 4; Marie Torre, "Pioneer Shorn Of All Video Ties," *Democrat and Chronicle* (Rochester, N.Y.), November 14, 1957, 43; "Vermont Firm Begins New Advertising," *Burlington Free Press* (Burlington, Vt.), August 15, 1957, 14.

18. "Dave Garroway's 'World' Renewed," *Des Moines Register*, May 24, 1957, 14; Jack O'Brian, "Wide, Wide World Changes For Better," *Muncie Evening Press*, September 16, 1957, 5; Donald Kirkley, "Look and Listen," *The Sun* (Baltimore, Md.), September 17, 1957, 10.

19. Ogden Dwight, "On Television," *Des Moines Register*, November 11, 1957, 22.

20. John Crosby, "Television and Radio," *Lansing State Journal* (Lansing, Mich.), December 30, 1957, 9.

21. Larry Wolters, "Radio, TV Still Need The Help Of Fred Allen," *Chicago Tribune*, July 14, 1957.

CHAPTER 15

1. John Crosby, "Television and Radio: News On The Off-Beat," *Lansing State Journal* (Lansing, Mich.), March 4, 1957, 4.

2. "Coleman Denies Segregation Slows Industrialization," *Delta Democrat-Times* (Greenville, Miss.), April 18, 1957, 13; "Interesting Interviews," *Delta Democrat-Times* (Greenville, Miss.), April 21, 1957, 4; Tom Ethridge, "Mississippi Notebook," *Clarion-Ledger* (Jackson, Miss.), April 29, 1957, 8.

3. "Sputnik Is Not A Joke," *The Call-Leader* (Elwood, Ind.), October 28, 1957, 6.

4. William Ewald, "Television Review," *Shamokin News-Dispatch* (Shamokin, Pa.), January 30, 1958, 7.

5. Marie Torre, "Garroway to Curb 'Fascination,'" *Democrat and Chronicle* (Rochester, N.Y.), January 22, 1958, 12.

6. Marie Torre, *Don't Quote Me* (Garden City, N.Y.: Doubleday, 1965), 30-31.

7. Bill Ladd, "Today To Deepen Shows," *Courier-Journal* (Louisville, Ky.), February 15, 1958, 10; "Mail Mountain Gives Notice John Q Is Curious On Defense," *Idaho State Journal* (Pocatello, Idaho), January 22, 1958, 10.

8. Will Jones, "It May Be Today in City For 6 Days During Aqua and Centennial Week," *Star Tribune* (Minneapolis, Minn.), March 2, 1958, 52; Charlie Wadsworth, "Garroway Treated as VIP," *Orlando Sentinel*, March 18, 1958, 4; Charles Mercer, "Dave Garroway Convinced New Seriousness Favored," *The Morning Call* (Allentown, Penn.), February 23, 1958, 32.

9. Jack Gould, "Crises Having Impact on TV News," *Courier-Journal* (Louisville, Ky.), January 10, 1958, 18; Charles Mercer, "Dave Garroway Convinced New Seriousness Favored"; Will Jones, "World Isn't So Wide Now," *Star Tribune* (Minneapolis, Minn.), July 23, 1958, 30.

10. Harriet Van Horne, "Heavy Industry Makes Sunday TV Too Heavy," *El Paso Herald-Post*, January 20, 1958, 17.

11. Charlie Wadsworth, "Daytime TV Shakeup Due," *Orlando Sentinel*, March 4, 1958, 7; Jack O'Brian, "Garroway's Extreme Pessimism Rubs Off," *Muncie Evening Press*, March 13, 1958, 9.

12. "Dave Garroway Becomes Papa," *Pittsburgh Press*, February 10, 1958, 1; Hall, "Little Boy Wanted."

13. Hall, "Little Boy Wanted."

14. Hall, "Little Boy Wanted"; Vivian Brown, "No Secrets For TV Husband," *Austin Daily Herald* (Austin, Minn.), August 16, 1958, 12.

15. Brown, "No Secrets For TV Husband."

16. Brown, "No Secrets For TV Husband"; Helena Kane, "Mrs. Garroway's Wide World: Home, Hearth and Helping Others," *The Daily Oklahoman*, July 17, 1958, 11.

17. Dave Garroway, "Teens Love Musical Junk, Can't Recognize Good Jazz," *Detroit Free Press*, April 6, 1958, 12-TV.

18. Advertisement for "Swing Into Spring," *The Eagle* (Bryan, Tex.), April 8, 1958, 6; Jones, "World Isn't So Wide Now."; "Dave Garroway Takes Dim View Of Westward-Ho," *Daily Herald* (Provo, Utah), April 7, 1958, 18.

19. "Wide World To Stop Revolving," *Detroit Free Press*, June 22, 1958, 59; Bill Ladd, "Director of Six-Show Series To Do 4 on One Network, 2 on Another," *Courier-Journal* (Louisville, Ky.), June 20, 1958, 18; Jones, "World Isn't So Wide Now"; Bettelou Peterson, "Dave Was Surprised By Wide World Death," *Detroit Free Press*, January 4, 1959, 6-TV.

20. "Wide Wide World Dies While Producer Plans," *Independent Star-News* (Pasadena, Calif.), August 24, 1958, 70; "Wide World To Explore Wide West," *Reno Gazette-Journal*, June 6, 1958, 30; Hal Humphrey, "Garroway Western Show Almost Headed Off At Pass," *Detroit Free Press*, June 8, 1958, 63.

21. Earl Wilson, "That's Earl For Today," *Evening Standard* (Uniontown, Pa.), March 18, 1957, 2; "World's Largest Venetian Blind Put Into Use By NBC," *Brooklyn Daily Eagle*, September 3, 1953, 22.

22. Jack O'Brian, "On the Air," *Sandusky Register* (Sandusky, Ohio), February 1, 1955, 3; Otto R. Kyle, "By The Way," *Decatur Daily Review* (Decatur, Ill.), July 2, 1958, 8; Marie Torre, "Today Moving Brings Regrets," *Akron Beacon Journal*, July 10, 1958, 8.

23. Torre, "Today Moving Brings Regrets."

24. Davis, *The Today Show*, 34.

25. Marie Torre, "Comedian Likes TV, Hates Clubs," *Democrat and Chronicle* (Rochester, N.Y.), August 5, 1958, 17; "Today Adds Van Doren To TV Family," *San Antonio Express*, September 6, 1958, 21; Charles Van Doren, "All The Answers," *New Yorker*, July 28, 2008, https://www.newyorker.com/magazine/2008/07/28/all-the-answers, retrieved September 19, 2021.

26. "TV Notes and Gossip," *St. Louis Post-Dispatch*, September 23, 1958, 38; "Today Format To Be Altered, Columns Added," *Courier-Journal* (Louisville, Ky.), September 28, 1958, 96; Dave Garroway, undated notes for autobiography, in Lee Lawrence Papers; Ben Gross, "Donna Reed Makes Bow, Patti Page Comes Back," *New York Daily News*, September 25, 1958, 90. Mary Kelly moved to the Bahamas, where she built a new career creating and hosting radio programs. "Mary Kelly Papers," University of Maryland University Libraries, https://archives.lib.umd.edu/repositories/2/resources/1563.

27. "Tired Dave Garroway Collapses At Studio," *Newport Daily News* (Newport, R.I.), October 23, 1958, 3; "Garroway Will Be Laid Up For While," *Miami Daily News-Record* (Miami, Okla.), October 26, 1958, 11; Marie Torre, "Two Comics Have 'Single' Minds," *Democrat and Chronicle* (Rochester, N.Y.), November 21, 1958, 17; Peterson, "Dave Was Surprised By Wide World Death"; "Reality: That's Next TV Goal of Garroway," *Chicago Tribune* December 28, 1958, 114.

28. Marie Torre, "Actress Wants Out On $100,000 Role," *Democrat and Chronicle* (Rochester, N.Y.), October 21, 1958, 4; Earl Wilson, "It Happened Last Night," *Daily Press* (Newport News, Va.), November 6, 1958, 38.

29. George Grim, "I Like It Here," *Star Tribune* (Minneapolis, Minn.), July 21, 1958, 13.

30. Lou Bradley, notes from taped conversation with Lee Lawrence, June 12, 1979, Lee Lawrence Papers; Garroway, notes in Lee Lawrence Papers.

31. Bradley, notes in Lee Lawrence Papers.

32. "TV Prop Man Says People, Not Objects, Must Be Considered," *Anderson Herald* (Anderson, Ind.), November 19, 1970, 26.

33. Bradley, notes in Lee Lawrence Papers.

34. Bradley, notes in Lee Lawrence Papers.

35. Garroway with Hall, "I Married Dave Garroway."

36. "TV Notes and Gossip," *St. Louis Post-Dispatch*, January 8, 1959, 8D; Ogden Dwight, "On Television," *Des Moines Register*, January 15, 1959, 11; Donald Kirkley, "Look and Listen," *The Sun* (Baltimore, Md.), January 21, 1959, 12; Charles Mercer, "TV's Fantasy Phase Will Pass, Garroway Believes," *Independent Star-News* (Pasadena, Calif.), January 11, 1959, 104; "War And TV," *Montgomery Advertiser* (Montgomery, Ala.), January 13, 1959, 4.

37. Otto R. Kyle, "By The Way," *Decatur Daily Review*, January 2, 1959, 6; Harold A. Nichols, "Omnibus Presents Saroyan Play Today," *Democrat and Chronicle* (Rochester, N.Y.), March 1, 1959, 84.

38. Marie Torre, "TV Personalities Head For Europe," *Democrat and Chronicle* (Rochester, N.Y.), December 24, 1958, 3; Mercer, "TV's Fantasy Phase Will Pass, Garroway Believes."

39. Marie Torre, "Maverick Garner to Gambol," *Democrat and Chronicle* (Rochester, N.Y.), February 26, 1959, 40.

40. "Strike Hits NBC," *Southern Illinoisan* (Carbondale, Ill.), April 27, 1959, 1; E.B. Radcliffe, "Monty Sounds Off," *Cincinnati Enquirer*, April 28, 1959, 22; "Bardot TV Tape Starts Strike On NBC Network," *Philadelphia Inquirer*, April 28, 1959, 3; "U.S. Mediators Try To Settle Strike Of Technicians At NBC," *St. Louis Post-Dispatch*, April 28, 1959, 2; "TV Technicians Strike On Technicality of Tape," *Florence Morning News* (Florence, S.C.), April 28, 1959, 3; "NBC Files $500,000 Suit Against Striking Union," *Philadelphia Inquirer*, April 29, 1959, 26; "Deadlock Unbroken in NBC Strike," *Titusville Herald* (Titusville, Pa.), April 29, 1959, 1; "NBC Rescinds Union Contract," *Corpus Christi Times*, May 6, 1959, 33; "NBC Pickets Observe Formal Dress At Show," *Anderson Daily Bulletin* (Anderson, Ind.), May 7, 1959, 33; Marie Torre, "Video Strike Yields Laughs Too," *Democrat and Chronicle* (Rochester, N.Y.), May 15, 1959, 8; "NBC Technicians, Engineers Vote To End Work Stoppage," *Galesburg Register-Mail* (Galesburg, Ill.), May 16, 1959, 9. A recording of Frank Bourgholtzer anchoring a glitch-filled *News on the Hour* radio broadcast from that morning was featured in somewhat embellished form on one of Kermit Schafer's "Blooper" compilation LPs.

41. "Bardot Tape Brings TV Strike," *Cincinnati Enquirer*, April 28, 1959, 2; Jack Gould, "Brigitte Seen A Day Late In Strike-Delay Interview," *Courier-Journal* (Louisville, Ky.), April 29, 1959, 14; "What Everyone Missed On Today," *Philadelphia Inquirer*, April 28, 1959, 3.

42. John Crosby, "Television and Radio: Whole New Vistas," *Lansing State Journal* (Lansing, Mich.), April 29, 1959, 11; John Crosby, "Tape Crews, Crowds Raise Issue Of Reality," *Hartford Courant*, May 4, 1959, 17; "The Time Is Twenty-One After."

CHAPTER 16

1. Jay Fredericks, "TV's Top Grossers," *Sunday Gazette-Mail* (Charleston, W. Va.), July 19, 1959, 62.

2. Lobsenz and Wirsig Inc., "Activity Report to Dave Garroway As Of May 22, 1959," Dave Garroway Papers.

3. Garroway with Hall, "I Married Dave Garroway"; Dave Garroway, "Dave Garroway's Vacation Is Over," *Daily Reporter* (Dover, Oh.), August 15, 1959, 19.

4. Lobsenz and Wirsig, "Activity Report."

5. Taves, "Dave Garroway's Search For Himself."

6. Davis, *The Today Show*, 35.

7. Bradley, notes in Lawrence papers; Florence Henderson, Archive of American Television oral history, https://interviews.televisionacademy.com/interviews/florence-henderson.

8. Mary Hevenor, "Asides on Rosie, Henny, Daly, Etc.," *Grand Prairie Daily News* (Grand Prairie, Tex.), August 10, 1958, 7; "Like Crazy," *Monroe County News* (Albia, Iowa), October 19, 1959, 2.

9. Bob Williams, "On The Air," *New York Post*, December 13, 1957, 63; "TV Notes and Gossip," *St. Louis Post-Dispatch*, September 26, 1958, 49; Dick Kleiner, "TV And Radio Personalities," *Shamokin News-Dispatch* (Shamokin, Pa.), January 9, 1959, 4.

10. Peterson, "Dave Was Surprised By Wide World Death"; Gunter Knackstedt, "Today Overreaches Itself In Berlin Show," *Cincinnati Enquirer*, April 4, 1959, 9A.

11. Dave Garroway, "Your Family Should Have A Fallout Shelter," *Family Weekly*, September 6, 1959, 4-5.

12. Kisseloff, *The Box*, 393.

13. *Harvey Kurtzman's Help!* December 1960, 4. Garroway is also featured on the cover.

14. Margaret Ratliff, "For Co-Existence," *Argus-Leader* (Sioux Falls, S.D.), September 24, 1959, 4.

15. Val Adams, "Pat Hingle To Star In Television Drama," *Courier-Journal* (Louisville, Ky.), September 30, 1959, 26; Ralf Hardester, "TV Today and Tomorrow," *The Kane Republican* (Kane, Pa.), August 22, 1959, 9.

16. "Garroway No Longer Will Work By The Dawn's Early Light," *TV Guide*, August 1-7, 1959, 20-23; Garroway, undated notes in Lawrence papers.

17. Bob Salmaggi, "Garroway: Playing Hard To Get," *Corpus Christi Caller-Times*, August 16, 1959, 90.

18. "Garroway No Longer Will Work By The Dawn's Early Light"; Florence Henderson, oral history.

19. Fred Remington, "Four Faces Of Dave," *Pittsburgh Press TV Graphic*, February 26, 1961, 4-5; Donald Kirkley, "Bewildering Changes In TV Programs," *The Sun* (Baltimore, Md.), August 2, 1959, 35.

20. Van Doren, "All The Answers."

21. Van Doren, "All The Answers."

22. "NBC Suspends Van Doren In TV Quiz Inquiry," *St. Louis Post-Dispatch*, October 9, 1959, 1; "Van Doren Text," *St. Louis Post-Dispatch*, November 2, 1959, 6.

23. "Scissor Snippings," *The Canyon News* (Canyon, Tex.), October 28, 1959, 4.

24. Garroway's videotaped reaction to Van Doren's suspension was included on a DVD that was included in the 50th anniversary book *This Is Today: A Window On Our Times* by Erik Mink (New York: Andrews McMeel Publishing, 2003); Charles Denton, "Freedom Precious To Dave Garroway," *Cincinnati Enquirer*, July 4, 1960, C-14; "Upset Garroway Unable To Finish TV Show," *Star Tribune* (Minneapolis, Minn.), November 5, 1959, 36; "Van Doren Disclosures Leave Garroway 'Sick,'" *Great Falls Tribune* (Great Falls, Mont.), November 5, 1959.

25. "The Fixed TV Shows In Retrospect," *The Times* (Shreveport, La.), November 16, 1959, 6; Jack Gould, "Contempt For Law Is Most Sickening Part Of Scandal," *Corpus Christi Caller-Times*, November 8, 1959, 8F; "TV Digest: Critics Declared As Confused As Their Medium," *Philadelphia Inquirer*, November 9, 1959, 26; Cynthia Lowry, "'I, Don Quixote' An Earnest, Windy Bore," *La Crosse Tribune* (La Crosse, Wis.), November 10, 1959, 8; Harry Harris, "Quiz Rigging Spurs Viewers' Demands For All-Out Cleanup Drive," *Philadelphia Inquirer*, November 13, 1959, 20.

26. L.T. Anderson, "Susceptibility to Adult Bawling Bemoaned In Van Doren Case," *Sunday Gazette-Mail* (Charleston, W. Va.), November 29, 1959, 32.

27. Transcript of Garroway's remarks in Dave Garroway Papers, University of Wyoming.

28. Harry Harris, "Everyone's Doing It – So Critic Offers Ideas For Improving Video," *Philadelphia Inquirer*, November 24, 1959, 26; Harry Harris, "Merman Shows Top Form," *Philadelphia Inquirer*, November 25, 1959, 16.

29. John Crosby, "TV Can't Understand Free Press Concept," *Hartford Courant*, November 27, 1959, 27; Cynthia Lowry, "From 2 to 13 On TV," *Courier-News* (Bridgewater, N.J.), November 25, 1959, 25; Walter Winchell, "In New York," *Greenville News* (Greenville, S.C.), December 8, 1959, 4.

30. Marie Torre, "Jack Paar Reacted With Honest Emotion," *Democrat and Chronicle* (Rochester, N.Y.), February 15, 1960, 9.

CHAPTER 17

1. "Year's Top News Reviewed In 'Eyewitness To History,'" *The Tennessean* (Nashville, Tenn.), January 1, 1960, 26; Harry Harris, "'Chevy Show' Version Of 'Around The World' Proves Wacky Musical," *Philadelphia Inquirer*, January 4, 1960, 16.

2. "Playhouse 90 To Become Roaming Nighttime Special," *Green Bay Press-Gazette*, January 2, 1960, 20.

3. Robert Lee, "One-Sided," *Fort Lauderdale News*, August 30, 1959, 6; "Random Thoughts By The Editor," *Yazoo Herald* (Yazoo City, Miss.), September 17, 1959, 1; Tom Ethridge,

"Mississippi Notebook," *Clarion-Ledger* (Jackson, Miss.), May 6, 1960, 6. Although the column was about the Caryl Chessman case, the noxious and notoriously bigoted Ethridge seldom passed up an opportunity to take gratuitous swipes at Garroway.

4. Metz, *The Today Show*, 125-26; recording of Jan. 13, 1960 *Today* program, author's collection.

5. "Scissor Snippings," *The Canyon News* (Canyon, Tex.), October 28, 1959, 4.

6. Cynthia Lowry, "Betsy Palmer Just Loves Her New 'Girl Talk' Show," *Standard-Speaker* (Hazleton, Pa.), June 26, 1970, 7; Florence Henderson, oral history.

7. Battaglio, *From Yesterday To Today*, 49.

8. Harriet Van Horne, "Meager Background Work Shows Through On 'Today,'" *El Paso Herald-Post*, April 12, 1960, 22.

9. Metz, *The Today Show*, 126-27.

10. Fred Danzig, "Television In Review," *Traverse City Record-Eagle*, May 31, 1960, 15.

11. Dave Garroway as told to Peter Van Slingerland, "What Ever Happened To Freedom Of Speech?" *Look*, June 7, 1960.

12. George E. Sokolsky, "Freedom of Speech," *The Star Press* (Muncie, Ind.), June 1, 1960, 6.

13. Westbrook Pegler, "Refinement's Public Less Than Vulgarity's," *Pampa Daily News* (Pampa, Tex.), June 10, 1960, 10; Westbrook Pegler, "As Pegler Sees It," *Kingston Daily Freeman* (Kingston, N.Y.), July 8, 1960, 4.

14. Walter Winchell, "Show Biz Memos," *Shreveport Times*, July 10, 1960, 9F.; Joe Bryant, "Summer Jumps The Gun On Television," *Fort Lauderdale News*, June 3, 1960, 7E.

15. Dave Garroway, "Dave Garroway Slaps 'Uninformed' Citizens," *Daily Reporter* (Dover, Ohio), July 13, 1960, 3.

16. Connie O'Connor, "Tickertape," *Palm Beach Post*, September 11, 1960, 65.

17. *Today*, promotional booklet produced by NBC, 1959, in Dave Garroway Papers.

18. Garroway, Wyoming draft, 175-76; Sam Taylor, "TV's Future 'Glum,' Says Garroway," *New Era* (Lancaster, Pa.), March 8, 1977, 11.

19. "Garroway Sets Special Report On Anniversary," *Philadelphia Inquirer*, January 12, 1960, 11; Charles Denton, "Freedom Precious To Dave Garroway," *Cincinnati Enquirer*, July 4, 1960, C-14; Charlie Wadsworth, "Talent Scouts – Now, Do You Want More?" *Orlando Sentinel*, February 24, 1960, 26.

20. Metz, *The Today Show*, 132-133.

21. "Dave's Place Opens Doors," *Fort Lauderdale News*, November 18, 1960, 53.

22. Harry Harris, "Hallmark's 'Macbeth' Is Excellently Filmed But Not Top Video," *Philadelphia Inquirer*, November 21, 1960, 14; "N.B.C. Tries To Re-create Old Garroway Program," *Courier-Journal* (Louisville, Ky.), November 19, 1960, 16.

23. Metz, *The Today Show*, 132-133.

CHAPTER 18

1. Fred H. Russell, "'Girls and Gangs' Set Saturday On Channel 9," *Bridgeport Post* (Bridgeport, Conn.), January 12, 1961, 32; Marie Torre, "Forgotten Anniversary," *Democrat and Chronicle* (Rochester, N.Y.), January 12, 1961, 34.

2. "Garroway Today Show Passes 10th Milestone," *Press and Sun-Bulletin* (Binghamton, N.Y.), January 14, 1961, 24; "TV Mailbag," *Chicago Tribune TV Week*, January 28, 1961, 2. The "starlings" comment was in reference to a series of aviation accidents involving planes hitting birds; one such accident in October 1960, when a Lockheed Electra turboprop operated by Eastern Air Lines hit a flock of birds and crashed after taking off from Boston, killed 62 of the 72 people on board. See Macarthur Job, *Air Disaster, Volume 4: The Propeller Era* (Fyshwick, Australia: Aerospace Publications, 2001), 122-127.

3. "TV Notes and Gossip," *St. Louis Post-Dispatch*, January 18, 1961, 50; Remington, "Four Faces Of Dave."

4. "3 VHF Stations To Carry 2d Press Parley," *Philadelphia Inquirer*, February 1, 1961, 27; "Kennedy, on Garroway TV Show, Laments Physical Fitness Decline," *Daily World* (Opelousas, La.), January 31, 1961, 2.

5. "OCS Cafeteria Head Replies To Dave Garroway," *Kingston Daily Freeman* (Kingston, N.Y.), March 14, 1961, 15; Glyn M. Spearman Jr., "Individual's Job," *Amarillo Globe-Times*, March 6, 1961, 21.

6. "South, A Good Magazine," *Scott County Times* (Forest, Miss.), January 4, 1961, 4; Harold A. Nichols, "Nick's '61 Specials," *Rochester Democrat and Chronicle*, January 1, 1961, 6D.

7. Earl Wilson, "TV, Stage, Movie, And She Types Too," *Philadelphia Daily News*, April 14, 1961, 48; Dorothy Kilgallen, "Red Skelton Tapes Two Things At One Session," *Asbury Park Press* (Asbury Park, N.J.), April 20, 1961, 14; Dorothy Kilgallen, "Perle Mesta Planning TV Celebrity Chatter Show," *Asbury Park Press* (Asbury Park, N.J.), April 6, 1961, 15; "Littlejohn Of A.B.C. Resigns Post," *Courier-Journal* (Louisville, Ky.), January 4, 1961, 10; Fred Danzig, "Tee Vee," *The Daily Times* (New Philadelphia, Ohio), January 5, 1961, 2; Fred H. Russell, "Wayne, Shuster To Have Own Show," *Bridgeport Post* (Bridgeport, Conn.), March 9, 1961, 16; Beryl Pfizer, "Dave Garroway Inspired Loyalty – And Rage," *TV Guide*, July 21, 1984, 29; Battaglio, *From Yesterday To Today*, 56; Taves, "Dave Garroway's Search For Himself."

8. Taves, "Dave Garroway's Search For Himself"; Pfizer, "Dave Garroway Inspired Loyalty – And Rage," 30.

9. Lindsey Nelson, "Tyrant? Driven Man? Garroway Complex," *The Knoxville News-Sentinel*, July 27, 1982, 12; Pfizer, "Dave Garroway Inspired Loyalty – And Rage," 31.

10. Pfizer, "Dave Garroway Inspired Loyalty – And Rage," 28-29.

11. Pfizer, "Dave Garroway Inspired Loyalty – And Rage," 29; Taves, "Dave Garroway's Search For Himself"; Battaglio, *From Yesterday To Today*, 40.

12. Metz, *The Today Show*, 130-132.

13. Doc Quigg, "Early Yesterdays On Today Show," *Chicago Tribune*, January 17, 1960; Don Royal, "Frank Blair: Rather Be One Of Bunch," *Fort Lauderdale News*, July 19, 1962, 38.

14. Pfizer, "Dave Garroway Inspired Loyalty – And Rage," 28-29; Larry Wolters, "Radio-TV

Gag Bag," *Chicago Tribune*, April 16, 1961.

15. "This and That By J.P.H.," *Salina Journal* (Salina, Kan.), April 5, 1961, 4; Cecil Smith, "Garroway Starts Day Off Right," *Los Angeles Times*, March 8, 1961, Section 2, 8.

16. "Early Risers Will Find Garroway Worth While," *Arizona Republic* (Phoenix, Ariz.), March 16, 1961, 52; Harry Harris, "WCAU Production Of 'World Of Sound' Charms And Delights," *Philadelphia Inquirer*, March 29, 1961, 23; Bob Queen, "Oscar Brown, Jr., The Name That Will Make Them Almost Forget That Other 'Junior,'" *Pittsburgh Courier*, April 1, 1961, Sec. 2, 20; Burt Charles D'Lugoff, "'Kicks and Company' Has A Say," *Pittsburgh Courier*, August 26, 1961, 31.

17. Pfizer, "Dave Garroway Inspired Loyalty – And Rage," 31; Richard Gehman, "Dave Garroway: Portrait Of A Tormented Man," *TV Guide* 22 July 1961, 26.

18. Pfizer, "Dave Garroway Inspired Loyalty – And Rage," 31; Hart, *Monitor*, 93; Mike Cook, "Cars for the Stars," *Hemmings Sports & Exotic Car*, June, 2009.

19. Nelson, "Tyrant? Driven Man? Garroway Complex"; Gehman, "Portrait Of A Tormented Man," 26.

20. "Assets and Liabilities," 1960, document in Dave Garroway Papers.

CHAPTER 19

1. "Dave Garroway Thinks That He Is Paid Too Much," *The Daily Herald* (Provo, Utah), June 27, 1960, 21; Gladys Hall, "Mr. and Mrs. Dave Garroway," *Ladies Home Journal*, July 1960, 54.

2. Dave Garroway, "Give Your Kids Love – And Liberty!" *This Week*. August 28, 1960, 17.

3. Metz, *The Today Show*, 134; Garroway, Wyoming draft, 176-177.

4. Garroway, Wyoming draft, 177.

5. Garroway, Wyoming draft, 176.

6. Garroway, Wyoming draft, 177.

7. Federal Bureau of Investigation, "Dave Garroway, Miscellaneous Information Concerning," April 26, 1961. Obtained by author under Freedom of Information Act, 2018.

8. "Dave Garroway, Miscellaneous Information Concerning."

9. "Dave Garroway, Miscellaneous Information Concerning."

10. "Dave Garroway's Wife Dies Of Sleeping Pill Overdose," *Montgomery Advertiser* (Montgomery, Ala.), April 29, 1961, 1; "Wife Of TV Star Dead; Autopsy Due," *Biddeford-Saco Journal* (Biddeford, Maine), April 28, 1961, 1-2.

11. "Sleeping Pills Given Blame For Mrs. Garroway's Death," *Daily Press* (Newport News, Va.), April 29, 1961, 8.

12. "Drug Overdose Fatal To Wife Of Garroway," *Chicago Tribune* 29 Apr 1961, 68.

13. "Drug Overdose Fatal To Wife Of Garroway"; "Sleeping Pills Given Blame For Mrs. Garroway's Death"; Phyllis Battelle, "What's Troubling Retired Star of 'Today' TV Show?"

Lansing State Journal (Lansing, Mich.), July 30, 1961, 4.

14. "Mrs. Garroway's Death Linked With Divorce," *El Paso Herald-Post*, April 29, 1961, 6; Battelle, "What's Troubling Retired Star?"

15. "Daly To Substitute For Dave Garroway," *Abilene Reporter-News* (Abilene, Tex.), May 1, 1961, 28; Fred Danzig, "Television in Review," *Simpson's Leader-Times* (Kittanning, Pa.), May 5, 1961, 19; Cynthia Lowry, "Good Video Shows Lacking Sponsors," *Indiana Gazette* (Indiana, Pa.), May 16, 1961, 32.

16. "Senator Eastland Gives Rundown On Dave Garroway's New 'Hero,'" *Clarion-Ledger* (Jackson, Miss.), May 29, 1961, 6; Charles M. Hills, "Affairs Of State," *Clarion-Ledger* (Jackson, Miss.), May 30, 1961, 2; "The Kennedys, TV and James Peck," *The Times* (Shreveport, La.), May 31, 1961, 6; Byron R. Pipes, "Has Had Enough Of Garroway Show," *The Times* (Shreveport, La.), May 30, 1961, 6; James B. Childs, "Suggests Boycott Of South's Foes," *The Times* (Shreveport, La.), June 25, 1961, 15.

17. Jerry Gaghan, "Garroway Getting Feet Wet – Again," *Philadelphia Daily News*, September 29, 1965, 39; Gehman, "Portrait Of A Tormented Man," 26-27.

18. Gehman, "Portrait Of A Tormented Man," 27; Jack E. Anderson, "Garroway Recalls Yesterday's Today," *Miami Herald*, January 12, 1977, 20; Battaglio, *From Yesterday To Today*, 56.

19. Garroway, Wyoming draft, 175-176.

20. Garroway, Wyoming draft, 176; "Dave Garroway Back On Radio," *The Messenger* (Madisonville, Ky.), January 19, 1971, 2; Battaglio, *From Yesterday To Today*, 56; Judy Flander, "Garroway Seems Too Yesterday For Today," *Washington Star* August 27, 1975.

21. Gehman, "Portrait Of A Tormented Man," 27.

22. Cecil Smith, "Garroway: He Gave Us A Peace He Didn't Find," undated clipping, Dave Garroway Papers.

23. Dave Garroway, letter to Robert Kintner, May 26, 1961; Dave Garroway, letter to David Sarnoff, May 26, 1961. Dave Garroway Papers.

24. Dave Garroway, "Statement From Dave Garroway," May 26, 1961; "Dickler A: NBC Termination," memorandum of January 22, 1963. Dave Garroway Papers.

25. "Today Headliner Quitting NBC Show," *The Tennessean* (Nashville, Tenn.) 27 May 1961, 7; Cynthia Lowry, "Faithful Viewer Gets Last Word," *Corpus Christi Caller-Times*, 30 May 1961, 21; Richard Shepard, "Garroway: 'I Want To Look, Think And Listen," *Los Angeles Times* 30 May 1961, 30.

26. "Dickler A: NBC Termination."

27. "Statement From Dave Garroway," May 26, 1961.

28. Richard O. Martin, "'Expedition To Study Life In Stone Age," *Salt Lake Tribune*, May 29, 1961, 22; Cecil Smith, "Tractor Pitch Is Paar's Best," *Los Angeles Times*, June 1, 1961, Sect. 2, 10; Fred Remington, "Today Has Forlorn And Deserted Look," *Pittsburgh Press*, July 17, 1961, 36.

29. "Editor's Notebook," *Scott County Times* (Forest, Miss.), May 31, 1961, 1; Tom Ethridge, "Mississippi Notebook," *Clarion-Ledger* (Jackson, Miss.), June 27, 1961, 6; "City Notes,"

The Enterprise-Tocsin (Indianola, Miss.), June 1, 1961, 1; Zulah Purvis, letter in *Clarion-Ledger* (Jackson, Miss.), June 28, 1961, 8.

30. Bradley, notes in Lawrence papers.

31. Harold A. Nichols, "Boone's 'Have Gun' Busy Now Filming Fifth Season Shows," *Rochester Democrat and Chronicle*, June 18, 1961, 2H.

32. Video recording of segment, author's collection.

33. Video recording of *Today*, January 14, 1977, author's collection; Cynthia Lowry, "Garroway Says Adieu To Today," *Escanaba Daily Press* (Escanaba, Mich.), June 19, 1961, 10; Robert Lewis Shayon, "Television's 'Tomorrow,'" *Milwaukee Journal*, July 23, 1961.

34. Luke Feck, "Non-Sticky Kid Show," *Cincinnati Enquirer*, January 4, 1962, 10; Richard F. Shepard, "Ambassador Stevenson To Start His Own TV Show," *Warren County Observer* (Warren, Pa.), July 1, 1961, 15; Marie Torre, "Fiction Loses To Fact," *Decatur Herald* (Decatur, Ill.), June 30, 1961, 26.

35. Bettelou Peterson, "Today Put Daly Back Inside," *Detroit Free Press*, May 8, 1961, 30; Marie Torre, "But Who'll Replace Paar?" *Democrat and Chronicle* (Rochester, N.Y.), June 2, 1961, 8; Marie Torre, "Daly Insists On Control," *Evening Review* (East Liverpool, Ohio), June 15, 1961, 16; Bob Thomas, "Arlene Francis' Film Role Is Result Of Sudden Logic," *Miami Daily News-Record* (Miami, Ohio), July 3, 1961, 2; "TV Roundup: 2 Displaced Belles May Be Costarred In Gold Rush Special," *Philadelphia Inquirer*, July 27, 1961, 20; "Chancellor Will Replace Garroway On Today," *Courier-Journal* (Louisville, Ky.), July 5, 1961, 14.

36. Cynthia Lowry, "Action-Adventure Shows Attract Top Audiences," *Times-Mirror* (Warren, Pa.), June 20, 1961, 2; "New Boss Of Today Changes Show Pattern," *Lincoln Star* (Lincoln, Neb.), July 30, 1961, 22.

37. Harry Harris, "All Together: 'We Like Spike!'" *Philadelphia Inquirer*, July 18, 1961, 30.

38. Fred Remington, "Today Has Forlorn And Deserted Look," *Pittsburgh Press*, July 17, 1961, 36; Lyn Connelly, "The TV Corner," *The Indian Journal* (Eufaula, Okla.), October 5, 1961, 6; "TV Mailbag," *Orlando Sentinel*, August 5, 1961, 17; Marie Torre, "New Today Too Drab." *Decatur Herald* (Decatur, Ill.), July 20, 1961, 28; John Moore, "Rome TV Puts On The Dog – An Old Dog," *Press and Sun-Bulletin* (Binghamton, N.Y.), August 6, 1961, 22.

39. Cecil Smith, "Video Does Stuff In Reporter's Role," *Los Angeles Times*, July 25, 1961, 30; "The Watching Post: TV Has Enough In Way Of Ailments," *Journal News* (White Plains, N.Y.), July 19, 1961, 18; Bradley, notes in Lawrence papers.

40. Dave Garroway Jr., written recollections, undated.

41. Dave Garroway Jr., written recollections, undated.

42. Battelle, "What's Troubling Garroway?"

43. Taves, "Dave Garroway's Search For Himself"; "Stars Called To Testify On TV Policy," *Arizona Daily Star* (Phoenix, Ariz.), June 17 1961, 10; Leonard Lyons, "Learns English, A Little By Little," *Evening Standard* (Uniontown, Pa.), June 28, 1961, 8.

44. "TV Defended Against Critics By Perry Como," *Los Angeles Times*, June 29, 1961, 4; "Garroway Says TV Tortured By Conflict," *Press and Sun-Bulletin* (Binghamton, N.Y.), June

28, 1961, 4.

45. "Accountability For Favored Few," *Mason City Globe-Gazette* (Mason City, Iowa), July 10, 1961, 4; "Memo to Garroway On Press Freedom," *Abilene Reporter-News*, June 30, 1961, 20; "Wrong Witnesses," *Statesman Journal* (Salem, Oregon), July 1, 1961, 4.

46. Battelle, "What's Troubling Garroway?"; Val Adams, "Dave Garroway May Return To Television Early In 1962," *Warren County Observer* (Warren, Pa.), September 1, 1961, 15; "Garroway Says TV Tortured By Conflict"; "Dave Garroway May Take Job Under Murrow," *Corpus Christi Caller-Times*, August 2, 1961, 13.

47. Battelle, "What's Troubling Retired Star?"; Rebecca Franklin, "A Quiet Time," *Pittsburgh Press TV Graphic*, November 26, 1961.

48. Battelle, "What's Troubling Garroway?"; Franklin, "A Quiet Time."

49. Battelle, "What's Troubling Garroway?"; Taves, "Dave Garroway's Search For Himself."

CHAPTER 20

1. "Dickler A: NBC Termination."

2. Percy Shain, "Garroway Returns To Be 'Young Again,'" *Boston Globe*, April 17, 1969, 44; Barry Robinson, "Show Notes: Not A Good Time," *Asbury Park Press* (Asbury Park, N.J.) August 10, 1965, 22; Bud Wilkinson, "Friends Of TV Pioneer Say He Was Victimized," *Arizona Republic* (Phoenix, Ariz.), July 28, 1982, 61.

3. Earl Wilson, "Rodgers Drums Up A Premiere Party," *Philadelphia Daily News*, November 11, 1961, 15; *McCall's* advertisement in *Courier-Journal* (Louisville, Ky.), August 25, 1961, 13; "Trying To Avoid Rush? Shop Late?" *Abilene Reporter-News* (Abilene, Tex., November 23, 1961, 59; "Billy Graham Film To Be Shown Here," *Millville Daily* (Millville, N.J.), January 2, 1962, 5.

4. Earl Wilson, "Morey Gives Gags Away," *Philadelphia Daily News*, September 29, 1961, 56; William Hoyt, "TV's Garroway Visits Lowell," *Arizona Daily Sun* (Flagstaff, Ariz.), November 30, 1961, 1-2; Franklin, "A Quiet Time."

5. Isabella Taves, "Rumors 'Explain' Why Garroway Quit," *Philadelphia Inquirer*, October 23, 1961, 28; Ken Purdy, "Automobiles Are People!" *Kokomo Tribune* (Kokomo, Ind.), October 22, 1961, 32.

6. "Dave Garroway Back On Radio," *The Messenger* (Madisonville, Ky.), January 19, 1971, 2; Francis Coughlin, "A Morale Booster For A Man Of Peace," *Chicago Tribune*, October 3, 1961, 22.

7. Herb Lyon, "Tower Ticker," *Chicago Tribune*, December 1, 1961, 16; Dorothy Kilgallen, "Garroway Ponders Television Return," *Asbury Park Press* (Asbury Park, N.J.), December 11, 1961, 8; Hy Gardner, "Peter Fonda Ideal To Play Role of JFK," *Birmingham News* (Birmingham, Ala.), February 1, 1962, 9; "CBS Show To Salute NBC's Today," *Corpus Christi Caller-Times*, January 9, 1962, 19; Cecil Smith, "The TV Scene: The Wasted 'Good Years,'" *Los Angeles Times*, January 15, 1962, Sect. 2, 10.

8. "Garroway Signed By NET," *Fort Worth Star-Telegram*, March 4, 1962; "Garroway Returning To TV With Educational Series," *Arizona Republic* (Phoenix, Ariz.), February 23, 1962, 18; Joan Crosby, "Meet Dave Garroway: Exploring Universe Without Any Misses," *Philadelphia Daily News*, July 11, 1962, 34.

9. Dave Garroway, quoted in undated clipping in Dave Garroway Papers; "Garroway Sells House Day Before Sea Claims It," *Decatur Daily Review* (Decatur, Ill.), March 8, 1962, 1; Dave Garroway Jr., written recollections, undated.

10. Monahan, "Maybe I Belong In A Long-Gone Era."

11. Larry Wolters, "TV Ticker," *Chicago Tribune*, February 17, 1962, 50; "Broadcasters Meet; Collins Defends Them," *Chicago Tribune*, April 2, 1962, 48.

12. Jerry Gaghan, "Carson Steers Cover Show," *Philadelphia Daily News*, May 2, 1962, 41; Dick Nolan, "The City," *San Francisco Examiner*, November 12, 1962, 39; Ena Naunton, "Garroway's Future: 'I Just Don't Know,'" *Miami Herald*, July 13, 1962, 59.

13. "Garroway Sells Mag Interest," clipping of December 21, 1964 in Lee Lawrence papers.

14. Dick Adler, "Can Dave Come Back?" July 1971 clipping in Dave Garroway Papers; Robinson, "Show Notes: Not A Good Time."

15. Dave Garroway Jr., written recollections, undated.

16. Anderson, "Garroway Looks Back At Today."

17. Dave Garroway Jr., written recollections, undated.

18. Monahan, "Maybe I Belong In A Long-Gone Era"; Anderson, "Garroway Looks Back At Today"; Dave Garroway Jr., written recollections, undated.

19. Gee Mitchell, "Who Will Take Perry's Place?" *Dayton Daily News* (Dayton, Ohio), May 10, 1962, 63; "Motoring Diary," *The Guardian* (London, England), April 9, 1962, 6; Harry Harris, "Garroway Spends Time Off The Air Tuning In The Real World," *Philadelphia Inquirer TV Magazine*, June 24, 1962, 2; Ralf Hardester, "TV Today And Tomorrow," *Greene County Democrat* (Eutaw, Ala.), June 28, 1962, 3.

20. Harris, "Garroway Spends Time Off The Air Tuning In The Real World"; Dick Shippy, "Improvement On Awards Show," *Akron Beacon Journal*, June 25, 1962, 12; Fran Conklin, "Fran's Back And Reviewing Summer Repeats," *Orlando Sentinel*, June 26, 1962, 20; Cynthia Lowry, "Sullivan, TV Guide Keep Television Busy," *Evening Independent* (Massillon, Ohio), June 25, 1962, 8; Ogden Dwight, "On Television," *Des Moines Register*, June 26, 1962, 14; Carl Hooper, "Views On Television," *Victoria Advocate* (Victoria, Tex.), July 1, 1962, 32.

21. Rick DuBrow, "Television In Review," *The Daily Register* (Harrisburg, Ill.), July 16, 1962, 8; McManus, "Dave Garroway Has Spent Year Doing A Great Deal Of Thinking"; Jack E. Anderson, "Britain's Commercial TV Getting A Pasting," *Miami Herald* 16 Jul 1962, 11.

22. Naunton, "Garroway's Future: 'I Just Don't Know'"; Dorothy Kilgallen, "Voice of Broadway," *The Times* (Shreveport, La.), July 16, 1962, 17; "Ask TV Scout," *Abilene Reporter-News* (Abilene, Tex.), August 31, 1962, 38; Cynthia Lowry, "Television," *Nashua Telegraph* (Nashua, N.H.), January 22, 1963, 10.

23. Carole Sloane, "Dave Garroway, 7.13.1913-7.21.1982," entry in SloaneView blog, July

13, 2015, http://sloaneview.blogspot.com/2015/07/dave-garroway-7131913-7211982.html.

24. Sloane, "Dave Garroway"; Harriet Van Horne, "Television News And Views: 'Talent Scouts' Best Of Lot," *Pittsburgh Press*, July 18, 1962, 58.

25. Sloane, "Dave Garroway."

26. Sloane, "Dave Garroway."

27. Sloane, "Dave Garroway."

28. Earl Wilson, "First For Robinson – And He's Sorry," *Philadelphia Daily News*, July 16, 1962, 26; Dean Gysel, "Garroway Cares Enough To Irritate You," *Dayton Daily News*, December 25, 1966, 82.

29. Flander, "Garroway Seems Too Yesterday For Today"; "Sun Gleams," *Brandon Sun* (Brandon, Manitoba, Canada), December 21, 1962, 4.

30. Dave Garroway Jr., written recollections, undated.

31. McManus, "Dave Garroway Has Spent Year Doing A Great Deal Of Thinking."; Elizabeth Sullivan, "Garroway Ends TV Sabbatical, Returns In June," *Boston Globe*, June 3, 1962, 94; Joan Crosby, "Meet Dave Garroway: Exploring Universe Without Any Misses," *Philadelphia Daily News*, July 11, 1962, 34.

32. "Dave Garroway To Speak At Whitfield Graduation," *St. Louis Post-Dispatch*, May 17, 1962, 73; "News Of Society: Julia Meier And Fiance Plan To Be Married Oct. 20," *St. Louis Globe-Democrat*, July 13, 1962, 11; Cynthia Lowry, "Garrulous Garroway Resumes His Career," *Tampa Tribune*, May 27, 1962, 7D; Sullivan, "Garroway Ends TV Sabbatical, Returns In June"; McManus, "Dave Garroway Has Spent Year Doing A Great Deal Of Thinking."

33. Donald Kirkley, "Look and Listen," *The Sun* (Baltimore, Md.), March 14, 1963, 26; "Garroway Is Coming Back To TV," *Tampa Times*, April 20, 1963, 20; Arthur Darack, "TV Is Now An Art, By Our Own Test," *Cincinnati Enquirer*, February 5, 1963, 30.

34. Percy Shain, "Egghead Looks Good On Dave Garroway," *Boston Globe*, January 30, 1963, 25; Harry Harris, "CBS Reports Study Of Supreme Court Overcomes Slow Start," *Philadelphia Inquirer*, February 21, 1963, 18; Alan Gill, "Television Today," *The Gazette* (Cedar Rapids, Iowa), February 7, 1963, 18.

35. Gee Mitchell, "TV Will Get Cleopatra First," *Dayton Daily News*, February 6, 1963, 39; "TV Review: Garroway Back In Tough Role," *Courier-Journal* (Louisville, Ky.), February 4, 1963, 17; Tony Fortuno, "Garroway Show Set For KUAT," *Arizona Daily Star* (Tucson, Ariz.), March 7, 1963, 36. "TV Talk," *Philadelphia Inquirer*, March 19, 1963, 25; N. Dean Evans, "Educational TV Isn't All Highbrow," *Delaware County Daily Times* (Chester, Pa.), September 17, 1963, 6; "Officials Hail WHYY On Channel 12 Debut," *Philadelphia Inquirer*, September 13, 1963, 14; Thomas J. Fleming, "The Trouble With Words," *American Weekly*, June 30, 1963, 2; Thomas J. Fleming, "Sticks, Stones and Words," *American Weekly*, July 21, 1963, 2; Thomas J. Fleming, "Beware Of Word Traps," *American Weekly*, July 28, 1963, 2; "5 From ASU Go To Parley On Semantics," *Arizona Republic* (Phoenix, Ariz.), August 11, 1963, 22.

37. Frank Gregory, "Names Make News," *Princeton Daily Clarion* (Princeton, Ind.), April 23, 1963, 3; clipping from Des Moines Register, June 11, 1963, in articles file, Dave Garroway Papers; "Headlines Around The World," *Honolulu Star-Bulletin*, June 11, 1963, 14.

38. Jim Crockett, "Long-Lost War On Obnoxious Ads," *San Francisco Chronicle Magazine*, May 17, 1970, 18.

39. Douglas Seymour, "Comedy Highlights Rockefeller Telethon," *Capital Journal* (Salem, Oregon), April 1, 1964, 17; Zan Stark, "Rocky's Acceptance Of Oregon Advice Big Factor In Victory," *Albany Democrat-Herald* (Albany, Ore.), May 19, 1964, 6.

40. Alex Freeman, "TV Closeup," *Star-Gazette* (Elmira, N.Y.), May 4, 1963, 22; Elizabeth L. Sullivan, "Tennis Matches Taped For Office Workers," *Boston Globe*, August 18, 1963, 70.

41. Dave Garroway, "Assets and Liabilities" document, 1964, Dave Garroway Papers.

42. Frances B. Murphey, "Dave's Drifting And Dreaming," *Akron Beacon Journal*, May 24, 1964, 2F; Earl Wilson, "In Bronx, He's Bernie Schwartz," *Honolulu Advertiser*, February 28, 1964, B3.

43. Dave Garroway, "Dave's On The Come-Back Trail," *Chicago Tribune*, July 5, 1964, 79.

CHAPTER 21

1. Advertisement in *New York Daily News*, March 2, 1964.

2. Barry Robinson, "Random Jottings," Asbury Park Press (Asbury Park, N.J.), April 28, 1964, 22; advertisement in *New York Daily News*, May 18, 1964, 23.

3. Kay Gardella, "Lodge In South Viet Nam; A TV Portrait Of Nehru," *New York Daily News*, May 19, 1964; advertisement in *New York Daily News*, August 31, 1964; Walter Winchell, "Jacqueline, Bobby Dine Quietly," *Indianapolis Star*, October 1, 1964, 33.

4. Advertisement in *Daily Times* (Salisbury, Md.), September 4, 1964, 19; Kay Gardella, "Producer Seeks to Improve Kaye's Emmy Award Show," *New York Daily News*, September 9, 1964, 86; John Rogers, "Expect Small Commodity Price Rise," *New York Daily News*, October 5, 1964; Larry Wolters, "TV To View Chicago With Pride And Love," *Chicago Tribune*, December 9, 1964, 79; advertisement in *New York Daily News*, November 25, 1964.

5. Lawrence Laurent, "Courage Dave Garroway's Future," *Arizona Republic* (Phoenix, Ariz.), December 19, 1964, 57.

6. Richard Doan, "Between Channels," *Salem News* (Salem, Ohio), April 20, 1965, 3.

7. Doan, "Between Channels."

8. Cynthia Lowry, "'Let's Go To The Fair' Tonight; Dave Garroway Starts ABC Stint," *North Adams Transcript* (North Adams, Mass.), April 21, 1965, 7; "TV Key, Highlights," *San Francisco Examiner*, April 22, 1965, 32; advertisement for KCRG-TV, *The Gazette* (Cedar Rapids, Iowa), April 23, 1965, 10.

9. Ben Gross, "TV: What's On?" *New York Daily News*, April 24, 1965; Donald Freeman, "Garroway's Back, Cooler Than Ever," *News-Pilot* (San Pedro, Calif.), May 15, 1965, 2; Paul Molloy, "That 'New Face' On ABC Deserves His Own Show," *Corpus Christi Caller-Times*, May 2, 1965, 9F.

10. Bettelou Peterson, "Our Personal Chat With Les Crane," *Detroit Free Press*, July 21, 1965, 22; Dorothy Stanich, "Around the Dial," *Corpus Christi Caller-Times*, June 27, 1965, 63.

11. Kay Gardella, "Once A TV Wise Guy, Crane Is Wiser Now," *New York Daily News*, June 30, 1965; Nadine Subotnik, "Channel Comment," *The Gazette* (Cedar Rapids, Iowa), July 4, 1965, 55; Gee Mitchell, "Let's Give Les Another Look," *Dayton Daily News*, June 30, 1965, 63.

12. Cindy Adams, "Garroway Prefers Night Show," *The Record* (Hackensack, N.J.) July 27, 1965, 18.

13. "'Nightlife' Show Moves To Seek Stars," *Courier-Journal* (Louisville, Ky.), August 22, 1965, F8; Richard Doan, "Between Channels," *Salem News* (Salem, Ohio), July 16, 1965, 5.

14. Richard K. Doan, "Agony Of Viet Nam War," *Kokomo Morning Times* (Kokomo, Ind.), August 7, 1965, 4; Barry Robinson, "Show Notes: Not A Good Time," *Asbury Park Press* (Asbury Park, N.J.), August 10, 1965, 22.

15. Robinson, "Show Notes: Not A Good Time."

16. Cindy Adams, "Cindy Says..." *Coney Island Times* (Brooklyn, N.Y.), October 9, 1964, 5; Dorothy Kilgallen, "The Voice Of Broadway," *Glens Falls Times* (Glens Falls, N.Y.), October 17, 1964, 4; Dave Garroway Jr., written recollections, undated; Laurent, "Courage Dave Garroway's Future"; Bettelou Peterson, "Mr. Garroway Drops In To Visit And Chat About A Few Things," *Detroit Free Press*, October 4, 1965, 37.

17. Dave Garroway Jr., written recollections, undated; "He Looked Very Tough," *Daily Reporter* (Dover, Ohio), July 29, 1961, 18.

18. Dave Garroway Jr., written recollections, undated; Taves, "Rumors 'Explain' Why Garroway Quit."

19. Peterson, "Mr. Garroway Drops In"; Dave Garroway Jr., written recollections, undated.

20. Peterson, "Mr. Garroway Drops In"; Dave Garroway Jr., written recollections, undated.

21. Dave Garroway Jr., written recollections, undated.

22. Dave Garroway Jr., written recollections, undated.

23. Dave Garroway Jr., written recollections, undated.

24. Feather, "Garroway – The Rest Has Been Silence."

25. Dave Garroway Jr., written recollections, undated.

26. Dave Garroway Jr., written recollections, undated.

27. Dave Garroway Jr., written recollections, undated; Dean Gysel, "Garroway Cares Enough To Irritate You," *Dayton Daily News*, December 25, 1966, 82.

28. Dave Garroway Jr., written recollections, undated.

29. Dave Garroway Jr., written recollections, undated.

30. Dave Garroway Jr., written recollections, undated.

31. Dave Garroway Jr., written recollections, undated.

32. Dave Garroway Jr., written recollections, undated.

33. Dave Garroway Jr., written recollections, undated.

34. Dave Garroway Jr., written recollections, undated.

35. Earl Wilson, "Oscar Crystal Ball In Buddy's Hands?" *Philadelphia Daily News*, April 17, 1969, 41; Dave Garroway Jr., written recollections, undated.

36. Jerry Gaghan, "Garroway Getting Feet Wet – Again," *Philadelphia Daily News*, September 29, 1965, 39; "TV Roundup: Three-Network Pool To Beam Pope's Visit Via Early Bird," *Philadelphia Inquirer*, September 29, 1965, 27; Peterson, "Mr. Garroway Drops In"; Phyllis Funke, "Garroway Tries To Catch Up," *Courier-Journal* (Louisville, Ky.), October 29, 1965, 26; Vince Leonard, "This Pair Hard To Beat," *Pittsburgh Press*, October 5, 1965, 58; Mark Beltaire, "Garroway In Politics?" *Detroit Free Press*, October 6, 1965, 46; Dickson Terry, "They Didn't Let The Old School Down," *St. Louis Post-Dispatch*, May 10, 1966, 49.

37. Dean Gysel, "Garroway's 'Waiting Period,'" *Des Moines Register*, December 25, 1966, 41; Dean Gysel, "Dave Garroway Hopes For A New Talk Show," *Philadelphia Inquirer*, January 3, 1967, 24.

38. "Quote Of The Week," *The Daily Item* (Sunbury, Pa.), January 27, 1967, 23; "Release Film On Tax Aids For Showing," *Sedalia Democrat* (Sedalia, Mo.), March 7, 1967, 1; "Observatory Fund Drive Announced," *Courier-News* (Bridgewater, N.J.), October 31, 1967, 9; "Richmond Forum Program Announced," *Progress-Index* (Petersburg, Va.), November 5, 1967, 19; "Eddie Sherman," *Honolulu Advertiser*, December 27, 1967, B-3.

39. Bill Mang, "The Heavenly Bodies," *The Times* (Scranton, Pa.), May 1, 1978, 13; Cecil Smith, "Afternoon Deejay – That's Garroway," *Los Angeles Times*, April 12, 1971, Sec. IV, 16; Norma Lee Browning, "Telescope Gives Dave Perspective," *Fort Lauderdale News*, July 23, 1971, 37F.

40. Mandel, "Remembering Dave Garroway," 17; Cynthia Lowry, "TV Idea Hunters Bat .500," *Kingston Daily Freeman* (Kingston, N.Y.), February 19, 1968, 25.

41. Joel H. Cohen, "150 Years Of Illinois – In 52 Minutes," *Chicago Tribune Magazine*, February 11, 1968, 36; Clay Gowran, "Special To Honor Illinois' Birthday," *Chicago Tribune*, July 9, 1967, TV-10; Mandel, "Remembering Dave Garroway," 17.

42. Advertisement in Hartford Courant, June 7, 1968, 24; "Garroway At Hershey Station," *Intelligencer Journal* (Lancaster, Pa.), June 25, 1968, 8.

43. Judith Adler Hennessee, "The Man Who Wouldn't Be King," *Esquire*, January 1984, 50-52+.

44. Paul Harvey, "Manhattan Island Bad Example," *Daily World* (Opelousas, La.), August 15, 1968, 4; "Action Line," *Independent* (Long Beach, Calif.), April 8, 1969, 1; "Garroway's Former Manager Arraigned," *Corpus Christi Caller-Times*, June 11, 1968, 6.

45. Harvey Pack, "Garroway, Manulis Compare Days Of Yore With Present," *The Record* (Hackensack, N.J.), October 16, 1968, 51.

CHAPTER 22

1. Frank Langley, "Anybody Need A TV Host?" *Courier-News* (Bridgewater, N.J.), November 5, 1968, 12; "Dialing Around With Television," *Daily Item* (Sunbury, Pa.), September 27, 1968, 19; Percy Shain, "Night Watch: 2 Hub Comedians Set For Guest Stint," *Boston*

Globe, November 1, 1968, 24; Hogan, "It's An Intimate Thing"; Pack, "Garroway, Manulis Compare Days Of Yore With Present"; Martin Hogan Jr., "The Laughs Have It," *Cincinnati Enquirer*, January 24, 1969, 41; Shain, "Garroway Returns To Be 'Young Again.'"

2. Shain, "Garroway Returns To Be 'Young Again.'"; Bob Thomas, "Garroway Trying Luck Out On Coast," *Boston Globe*, August 21, 1970, 2.

3. "USS Pueblo Officer Speaks Out: There's Still Much Left Unsaid," *Burlington Free Press* (Burlington, Vt.), April 29, 1969, 5.

4. "TV Highlights Today," *Boston Globe*, May 1, 1969, 50; Bud Collins, "It's A Man! It's A Bird! No, It's Super Hairpiece!" *Boston Globe*, May 17, 1969, 7.

5. "Comebacks: Peace, Old Tiger," *Time* July 18, 1969; Shain, "Garroway Returns To Be 'Young Again.'"

6. Percy Shain, "Night Watch: Finally, An Impossible Mission – Bain, Landau Firm On Pay Tiff," *Boston Globe*, June 17, 1969, 46; Percy Shain, "Full M-Day Coverage By Ch. 2," *Boston Globe*, October 16, 1969, 22; Percy Shain, "Night Watch: Social Problems Involve Emmy Judges," *Boston Globe*, May 27, 1969, 52; "Comebacks: Peace, Old Tiger."

7. Dave Garroway Jr., written recollections, undated.

8. Dave Garroway Jr., written recollections, undated.

9. Shain, "Garroway Returns To Be 'Young Again.'"

10. Percy Shain, "Changes In Exported 'Tempo-Boston,'" *Boston Globe*, November 12, 1969, 70.

11. Harry Harris, "Screening TV: Garroway Talk Show Debuts," *Philadelphia Inquirer*, November 25, 1969, 20; Kay Gardella, "Dave Garroway At Large Again," *New York Daily News*, December 7, 1969, S30.

12. Gardella, "Dave Garroway At Large Again."; Joe McGinniss, "Selling of 'Selling Of President,'" *Los Angeles Times* 4 Jan 1970.

13. Dick Adler, "Can Dave Come Back?" - July 1971 clipping in Dave Garroway Papers; "TV Roundup: Apollo To Carry 3d Camera," *Philadelphia Inquirer*, January 27, 1970, 16; Kay Gardella, "CBS' Mission: Impossible Warmed Up For Next Year," *New York Daily News*, February 14, 1970; Percy Shain, "Night Watch: TV Jugglers Leave Viewers Up In Air," *Boston Globe*, February 26, 1970, 42; Percy Shain, "Night Watch: Garroway's Departure Disappoints Viewers," *Boston Globe*, March 6, 1970, 44.

14. Shain, "Night Watch: TV Scene Keeps Shifting; Local Outlets Vary Slate."

15. Emery Wister, "Garroway: Outlook For TV Is Grim," *Charlotte News*, November 18, 1970, 6.

16. Lawrence Laurent, "TV's 'Tawny Tiger' Back On 'CBS Newcomers,'" *Florida Today* (Cocoa, Fla.), July 10, 1971, 3D; Dave Garroway Jr., written recollections, undated.

CHAPTER 23

1. Dorothy Manners, "Hollywood: Plus And Minus Jones Wedding," *San Francisco Exam-*

iner, September 15, 1970, 29; Robert Ward, "Slain Swindler Tried To Buy $70,000 Garroway Home," *Boston Globe*, January 6, 1972, 3; Bill Mang, "The Heavenly Bodies," *The Times* (Scranton, Pa.), May 1, 1978, 13.

2. Dave Garroway Jr., written recollections, undated.

3. Laurent, "TV's 'Tawny Tiger' Back On 'CBS Newcomers'"; Bob Thomas, "Garroway Trying Luck Out On Coast," *Boston Globe*, August 21, 2; Don Page, "Garroway's Peace Sign On KFI," *Los Angeles Times*, September 20, 1970.

4. Cecil Smith, "Afternoon Deejay – That's Garroway," *Los Angeles Times*, April 12, 1971, Sect. IV, 16; Harry Harris, "Old Timer Dave Garroway Returns With Young Hopefuls," *Philadelphia Inquirer TV Week*, July 11, 1971, 5.

5. Smith, "Afternoon Deejay – That's Garroway"; "Dave Garroway Back On Radio," *The Messenger* (Madisonville, Ky.), January 19, 1971, 2.

6. Smith, "Afternoon Deejay – That's Garroway"; Dave Garroway Jr., written recollections, undated.

7. Laurent, "TV's 'Tawny Tiger' Back On 'CBS Newcomers.'"

8. Lillian Hickey, "Dialer's Choice: CBS Will Introduce New Talent," *Sacramento Bee TV Magazine*, July 11, 1971, 6-7; Charles Witbeck, "TV Keynotes: Talent Hunt Has Twist," *Morning Call* (Allentown, Pa.), July 3, 1971, 18; Smith, "Afternoon Deejay – That's Garroway"; Bob Rose, "Garroway Finally Asked Back," *Minneapolis Star*, June 25, 1971, 19.

9. Don Page, "CBS Newcomers: Pro Talent Getting Into 'New Face' Act," *Los Angeles Times*, June 4, 1971, Sect. IV, 15.

10. Page, "CBS Newcomers: Pro Talent Getting Into 'New Face' Act"; Norma Lee Browning, "Garroway Happy To Be Back On TV," *Orlando Sentinel*, July 20, 1971, 23.

11. Rose, "Garroway Finally Asked Back"; Tom Green, "Whatever Happened To Dave Garroway?" *San Bernardino County Sun*, June 20, 1971, D1; Browning, "Telescope Gives Dave Perspective"; Page, "CBS Newcomers: Pro Talent Getting Into 'New Face' Act."

12. Harris, "Old Timer Dave Garroway Returns With Young Hopefuls"; Green, "Whatever Happened To Dave Garroway?"

13. Harris, "Old Timer Dave Garroway Returns With Young Hopefuls"; Don Freeman, "Dave Garroway The Ham," *Daily News-Post* (Monrovia, Ca.), August 7, 1971, 21; Cecil Smith, "Dave Garroway Back on CBS Newcomers," *Beckley Post-Herald* (Beckley, W. Va.), July 12, 1971, 4.

14. Don Freeman, "Unknowns Get A Chance On CBS Newcomers," *Clarion-Ledger* (Jackson, Miss.), June 25, 1971, 58; Bettelou Peterson, "The Bloom's Off 'Newcomers'; Hirt And 'Music' Enjoyable," *Detroit Free Press*, July 23, 1971, 24.

15. Charles Witbeck, "TV Keynotes: Talent Hunt Has Twist," *Morning Call* (Allentown, Pa.), July 3, 1971, 18; Terrence O'Flaherty, "Assignment Television," *Honolulu Star Bulletin*, July 19, 1971, 18.

16. Carolanne Griffith, "The CBS Newcomers: Garroway Offers Variety," *Fort Lauderdale News*, July 14, 1971, 79; Kay Gardella, "Merv's Talk With Rita Lacks Talk, Entertainment,"

New York Daily News, July 13, 1971; Dwight Newton, "Pray For Newcomers," *San Francisco Examiner*, July 13, 1971, 19; Don Freeman, "Unknowns Get A Chance On CBS Newcomers"; Dick Shippy, "Cavett's Very Serious Night," *Akron Beacon Journal*, July 15, 1971, 49; Terrence O'Flaherty, "Assignment Television," *Honolulu Star Bulletin*, July 19, 1971, 18; Clarence Petersen, "Talent: It Takes Some To Find Some," *Chicago Tribune*, July 19, 1971, 31.

17. Joyce Wagner, "Newcomers Came, But Brought Little Of Note," *Kansas City Times*, July 14, 1971, 35; Colby Sinclair, "'Newcomers' Talent Spread Too Thin," *Orlando Sentinel*, July 14, 1971, 19; Emery Winter, "Garroway Smells Like Mothballs," *Charlotte News*, July 13, 1971, 4.

18. Rick Du Brow, "Television In Review: New Talent Rather Flat," *Courier-Post* (Camden, N.J.), July 13, 1971, 10.

19. Judy Bachrach, "TV Notes: Rendered Speechless By CBS's Newcomers," *The Sun* (Baltimore, Md.) July 13, 1971, 17; Jack E. Anderson, "Foul-Mouthed Chicken Antics Brighten 'Newcomers' Show," *Miami Herald*, August 11, 1971, 44.

20. Bob Shiels, column in *Calgary Herald*, July 16, 1971, 68; Tom Hopkins, "CBS The Real Amateur In 'Newcomers' Production," *Daily News* (Dayton, Ohio), July 13, 1971, 32.

21. "Millie Tries To Serve Two Parties," *Corpus Christi Caller-Times*, July 26, 1971, 24; Peterson, "The Bloom's Off 'Newcomers'"; Percy Shain, "Night Watch: New Summer Show A Musical Success," *Boston Globe*, July 21, 1971, 44.

22. Cynthia Lowry, "Dave Garroway To Stay In Television," *Daily Mail* (Hagerstown, Md.), August 9, 1971, 11.

23. Lowry, "Dave Garroway To Stay In Television"; Leonard Feather, "Garroway's Many Worlds," *Los Angeles Times Calendar Magazine*, August 1, 1982, 57.

24. Lowry, "Dave Garroway To Stay In Television"; Don Freeman, "Dave Garroway The Ham," *Daily News-Post* (Monrovia, Ca.), August 7, 1971, 21.

25. Freeman, "Dave Garroway The Ham."

26. Jack E. Anderson, "Garroway Adds Nostalgia To Farewell Of Hugh Downs," *Miami Herald*, October 12, 1971, 27.

CHAPTER 24

1. "Today Show Marks 20th Year, Longest Running Daily Program," *Journal Times* (Racine, Wis.), January 15, 1972, 6; "Producer Watched For Future Moves," *Paducah Sun* (Paducah, Ky.), January 8, 1972, 28; Anderson, "Garroway Looks Back At Today"; Joan Crosby, "Of Cars and Things," *Journal Gazette* (Mattoon, Ind.), March 31, 1972, 12; "Today's TV Automotive-Trouble Quiz Should Entertain, Educate Viewers," *Great Falls Tribune* (Great Falls, Mont.), March 26, 1972, 79; Monahan, "Maybe I Belong In A Long-Gone Era."

2. Examples include a Bay View Federal Savings Bank advertisement in the *San Francisco Examiner*, January 8, 1973, 7; and such articles as "Race For Life Regatta Features Dave Garroway," *Redondo Reflex* (Redondo, Calif.), September 6, 1972, 51.

3. Crosby, "Of Cars and Things"; Monahan, "Maybe I Belong In A Long-Gone Era"; Cecil

Smith, "Dave Garroway Back on CBS Newcomers"; Shales, "'Coolest' TV Host Can't Find A Job."

4. Ernie Santosuosso, "Songwriters Have Their Night At Jazz Festival," *Boston Globe*, July 5, 1974, 13; Philip Elwood, "Flats And Sharps Of A Jazz Festival," *San Francisco Examiner*, July 5, 1974, 24; Harriet Choice, "Saluting The U.S. In Song," *Chicago Tribune*, July 5, 1974, 39.

5. Jack O'Brian, "The Lip'll Let 'Er Rip," *Paterson News* (Paterson, N.J.), January 20, 1975, 19; "Notables To Narrate 'Bicentennial Minutes,'" *Florence Morning News* (Florence, S.C.), March 1, 1975, 25; Flander, "Garroway Seems Too Yesterday For Today"; Val Adams, "Radio Roundup," *New York Daily News*, November 16, 1975, TV-8.

6. Joseph Finnegan, "TV Teletype: Hollywood," undated clipping in Dave Garroway Papers; Dave Garroway Jr., written recollections, undated. In his book *The Today Show*, Robert Metz cited a *New York Daily News* piece that said such responses were Silverman's way of gently letting down those who were considered "has-beens." As the piece stated, "The old-timers go away without a sale, but with their egos glowing." See Metz, 137-138.

7. Shales, "Garroway's Great Gift"; Finnegan, "TV Teletype: Hollywood," undated clipping; John South, "I've Been Blacklisted – I Can't Get a Job...Complains Dave Garroway, Ex-Host of TV's Today Show," *National Enquirer*, undated clipping, Dave Garroway Papers.

8. "Emmys – Some 25 Years After Shirley Dinsdale," *Montana Standard*, May 14, 1973, 16; Tom Riste, "Emmy's Splendor Doesn't Last Long," Arizona Daily Star (Tucson, Ariz.), May 29, 1975, 57; Feather, "Garroway – The Rest Has Been Silence."

9. Bill Granger, "A Soothing Voice of the Past, Dave Garroway, 63, Hunts Job," *News Journal* (Wilmington, Del.), October 12, 1976, 26.

10. Crosby, "Of Cars and Things."

11. Crosby, "Of Cars and Things"; Dave Garroway Jr., written recollections, undated.

12. Dave Garroway Jr., written recollections, undated.

13. Dave Garroway Jr., written recollections, undated.

14. Dave Garroway Jr., written recollections, undated.

15. Browning, "Telescope Gives Dave Perspective"; Dave Garroway Jr., written recollections, undated.

16. Dave Garroway Jr., written recollections, undated.

17. Feather, "Garroway's Many Worlds."

18. Stanley Meisler, "Eclipse 'Like Sex, Mystic,'" *Miami Herald*, July 4, 1973, 12A.

19. Dave Garroway Jr., written recollections, undated.

20. Dave Garroway Jr., written recollections, undated.

21. Dave Garroway Jr., written recollections, undated.

22. Dave Garroway Jr., written recollections, undated.

23. Sally Quinn, "Fundraising For Harry Reems," *Ottawa Citizen*, June 4, 1976, 60.

24. Dave Garroway Jr., written recollections, undated.

25. Feather, "Garroway's Many Worlds."

26. Monahan, "Maybe I Belong In A Long-Gone Era."

27. Dave Garroway Jr., written recollections, undated.

28. Dave Garroway Jr., written recollections, undated.

29. Dave Garroway Jr., written recollections, undated.

30. Feather, "Garroway's Many Worlds."

31. Dave Garroway Jr., written recollections, undated.

32. Dave Garroway Jr., written recollections, undated.

33. Dave Garroway Jr., written recollections, undated.

34. Dave Garroway Jr., written recollections, undated.

35. Dave Garroway Jr., written recollections, undated.

36. Dave Garroway Jr., written recollections, undated.

37. Garden Grove Community Church advertisement in *Los Angeles Times*, November 20, 1976, 35; "Hour of Power" advertisement in *Atlanta Constitution*, January 8, 1977, 3; "Nostalgia Radio," *Santa Ana Register* (Santa Ana, Calif.), January 13, 1977, 36.

38. Video recording of *Today*, January 14, 1977, author's collection; "Hard-Hitting Brokaw Bodes Well For Today," *Chicago Tribune*, January 12, 1977, 25.

39. Shales, "Garroway's Great Gift."

40. William Henry, "A TV Critic Switches Off His Set And Heads For New York," *Boston Globe*, August 31, 1980, B5.

41. Robert Taylor, "25 Years Of Todays For The Today Show," *Boston Globe*, August 3, 1977, 11.

42. "Today Show," *Democrat and Chronicle* (Rochester, N.Y.), January 13, 1977, 19; Jack E. Anderson, "Garroway Recalls Yesterday's Today," *Miami Herald*, January 12, 1977, 20A; Sheila McClear, "The Legacy of Dave Garroway," *San Francisco Examiner*, May 6, 1979.

43. Transcript of interview on "Extension 720," undated, Dave Garroway Papers.

44. Cleveland Amory, "Dave Garroway Looks At Today's TV," *The Pantagraph* (Bloomington, Ill.), July 28, 1976, 28; "TV Pioneer Garroway Retains His Sharp Wit," *Intelligencer Journal* (Lancaster, Pa.), March 8, 1977, 2.

45. Transcript of interview on "Extension 720," undated, Dave Garroway Papers.

46. Taylor, "TV's Outlook Is 'Glum,' Says Dave Garroway"; "TV Pioneer Garroway Retains His Sharp Wit"; Marilyn Beck, "Show Not Fair To Joe McCarthy," *Miami News*, February 17, 1977, 26; "TV Pioneer Garroway Retains His Sharp Wit"; Dick Lochte, "Book Notes: William Safire Takes The Plunge," *Los Angeles Times*, August 21, 1977.

47. Drafts of Garroway's unfinished memoirs are in the Lee Lawrence Papers, University of Maryland, and the Dave Garroway Papers, University of Wyoming. Dave Garroway Jr.

told the author during several conversations between 2018 and 2020 about why his father left the publication contract.

CHAPTER 25

1. "Stargazers, Dancers And Life Searches," *Philadelphia Inquirer*, September 26, 1980, 6A.

2. Terry Gross, recorded interview with Sarah Lippincott Garroway, Feb. 6, 1983, Dave Garroway Papers.

3. Gross, recorded interview with Sarah Lippincott Garroway.

4. "Chip Twists Ankle In Peanut Wagon Fall," *Detroit Free Press*, September 17, 1977, 44.

5. Gross, recorded interview with Sarah Lippincott Garroway.

6. One such ad for "Dave Garroway's Giant Garage Sale" can be found in the *Los Angeles Times*, July 10, 1977. Dave Garroway Jr.'s recollections are in personal documents, undated, provided to the author.

7. Jackson Brooks, *Cars I Could've, Should've, Kept: A Memoir of a Life Restoring Classic Cars* (Jefferson, N.C.: McFarland, 2007), 27-28. At the time this book was written, both the 1938 Jaguar and an XKE that Garroway later owned had been purchased by noted car collector Wayne Carini.

8. Gross, recorded interview with Sarah Lippincott Garroway.

9. Gross, recorded interview with Sarah Lippincott Garroway.

10. Gross, recorded interview with Sarah Lippincott Garroway; Marion Logue, "He Was 'Delightful As Always,'" *Delaware County Daily Times*, July 23, 1982, clipping in Dave Garroway Papers.

11. Marilyn Beck, "Herb Alpert Tries New 'Rise' To Fame," *Victoria Advocate* (Victoria, Tex.), October 26, 1979, 38; Dave Garroway Jr., written recollections, undated.

12. Lee Lawrence, letter to Pat Weaver, February 13, 1980, Lee Lawrence Papers.

13. Logue, "He Was 'Delightful As Always'"; Ruth Seltzer, "The Momjians Host A Capital Party," *Philadelphia Inquirer*, February 29, 1980, 50.

14. Craig R. McCoy and Burr Van Atta, "Dave Garroway, First 'Today' Host, Kills Himself At Swarthmore Home," *Philadelphia Inquirer*, July 22, 1982, 2A.

CHAPTER 26

1. "Dave Garroway, 69, Found Dead; First Host of 'Today' on NBC-TV," *New York Times*, July 22, 1982.

2. "First 'Today' Host Dave Garroway Ends Bittersweet Life With Suicide," *Miami Herald*, July 22, 1982.

3. Tom Shales, "Can Today's Mr. Nice Guy Boost Ratings?" *The Record* (Hackensack, N.J.), August 3, 1982, 32.

4. Video recording of *Today*, January 14, 1982, author's collection.

5. "Dave Garroway, 69, Found Dead," *New York Times*.

6. McCoy and Van Atta, "Dave Garroway, First 'Today' Host."

7. Logue, "He Was 'Delightful As Always.'"

8. Garroway, Wyoming draft, 115; McCoy and Van Atta, "Dave Garroway, First 'Today' Host."

9. Feather, "Garroway's Many Worlds."

10. Dave Garroway Jr., written recollections, undated.

11. Gary Deeb, "'Peace' - A Final Farewell To Dave Garroway," *Hawaii Tribune-Herald* (Hilo, Hawaii), July 29, 1982, 20.

12. Bud Wilkinson, "Friends Of TV Pioneer Say He Was Victimized," *Arizona Republic* (Phoenix, Ariz.) July 28, 1982, 61.

13. Shales, "Garroway's Great Gift."

14. Feather, "Garroway's Many Worlds."

15. Rundown sheet for *NBC News Overnight*, July 22, 1982.

16. Video clip of Barbara Walters at 1982 Emmy Awards, in author's collection.

17. "Garroway Buried In Private Service," *Democrat and Chronicle* (Rochester, N.Y.), July 29, 1982, 23.

18. Dave Bittan, "Jazz Stars To Shine For Dave Garroway," *Philadelphia Daily News*, February 4, 1983, 44; Kolson and Davis, "At Swarthmore, Jazz Greats Pay Tribute to Dave"; Bittan, "Singers' Sentimental Journey."

19. Kolson and Davis, "At Swarthmore, Jazz Greats Pay Tribute to Dave."

20. Bittan, "Singers' Sentimental Journey."

21. Kolson and Davis, "At Swarthmore, Jazz Greats Pay Tribute to Dave."

22. Bittan, "Singers' Sentimental Journey"; "A Tribute To Dave," *Philadelphia Daily News*, April 1, 1983, 58.

23. Dave Garroway Jr., written recollections, undated.

24. Darrell Sifford, "Isolating Causes Of Depression," *Philadelphia Inquirer*, December 11, 1983; *The Garroway Report*, Vol. 1, Winter 1986, copy in Dave Garroway Papers.

25. Dave Garroway Jr., written recollections, undated.

26. Dave Garroway Jr., written recollections, undated.

Index

Allen, Fred, 32, 90, 97, 111, 115, 130, 183, 236, 290
Allen, Steve, 127, 161, 170, 172, 176, 245
Alias Smith and Jones, 289
Andrews, Charlie, 69-70, 75, 80-81, 148, 159, 227-228, 295; background of, 63; as Garroway writer, 63-64, 71, 83-84, 87, 91, 154-155; European trip with Garroway (1951), 100-102, 322; and *Today*, 108-109, 144
Armour (sponsor), 100, 102
Armstrong, Louis, 79, 84, 165, 211

Babes in Toyland (1954 and 1955 *Producers Showcase* program, NBC), 160, 168
Baird, Bil and Cora, 150, 160
Bankhead, Tallulah, 78-81
Banner, Bob, 83, 88
Barstow, Edith, 84, 86, 155
Beebe, Phoebe B., 152
Belafonte, Harry, 69, 73, 74
Bell Telephone Hour ("Our Musical Ambassadors," 1960), 210
Bendick, Bob, 152, 203-204, 208; firing from *Today*, 213-214
Berg, Nancy, 130
Berle, Milton, 85, 86, 90, 147, 182, 195, 290
Bicentennial Minutes, 290
Biermann, Barbara, 29
Blair, Frank, 133, 143, 150, 159, 168, 172, 177, 178, 197, 201, 203, 204, 206, 224, 230, 238, 239, 305, 306, 308, 314, 317
The Blue Note (nightclub, formerly Lipp's Lower Level), 73, 75, 79
Bob (Elliott) and Ray (Goulding), 105, 142
Bobbs-Merrill (publishing company), 308
Boeke, Kees, 250, 270
Bradley, Lou, 193-195, 201, 236, 239
Broekman, David, 166, 182
Brokaw, Tom, 305, 306, 307, 318

Brooks, Jackson, 310-311
Brown, Oscar Jr., 224-225
Bullard, Eugene, 211

Caesar, Sid, 125, 165, 289, 290
Cain, Jackie, 69, 73, 290, 321
Camp Catlin (Hawaii), 54
Capp, Al, 98, 196
Cavett, Dick, 275, 288
The CBS Newcomers (1971 television series), 283-287, 289-290
Chance Piston Ring Company, 27
Chancellor, John, 171, 271, 315, 318-319; as *Today* host, 238-239
Chapel, Bette, 84, 145
Chicago Merchandise Mart, 56, 64, 83, 98, 272-273
"Chicago School," 82-83, 97-98, 109-110, 182, 183, 218, 249, 272
Clooney, Betty, 106
Clooney, Rosemary, 106-107, 130
Collingwood, Charles, 149-150
Collins, Bud, 276
Como, Perry, 171, 190, 199, 224, 240, 241, 259
Cook, Mike, 225-226
Congoleum-Nairn, 90, 99, 100
Corey, Dr. Irwin, 278
Corey, Jill, 145-146
The Cosmic View (book), 250, 270
Coward, Noel, 78, 80
Cox, Wally, 146, 160, 165
Crane, Les, 258-260
Cronkite, Walter, 149-150, 160
Crosby, John, 72, 85, 89, 92, 93, 115, 122, 131, 139, 146, 148, 150, 160, 163-164, 165, 174, 183, 184, 198, 209
Cross, Milton, 41-42, 145
Cullen, Bill, 171
Culligan, Matthew, 141-142

Daly, John Charles, 46, 231, 232, 238
Dann, Mike, 282
The Dave Garroway Show (NBC radio program), 72, 75
The Dave Garroway Show (NBC television series), 145-147, 149; cancellation, 154-155
Dave Garroway's Sports Spectaculars, 248
Dave's Place (1960 NBC television special), 218-219
Dave's Place (1975 radio program), 290
Dean, Jimmy, 181-182
USS *Devastator* (AM-318), 51-53, 317
Dial Dave Garroway, 100, 128, 129, 157
Divine, Father Jealous Major, 65
Doremus, Ralph, 87
Downs, Hugh, 69, 76, 242, 271, 288, 315
Duel, Peter, 289
Dumas, Major, 136, 233
Dunn, John, 212

Earhart, Amelia, 251
Edwards, Ralph, 248
Eisenhower, Dwight D., 187, 212, 215, 216
The 11:60 Club (WMAQ radio), 63-70, 71-73, 74, 75, 95, 268, 272, 290, 321
Ellerbee, Linda, 319
Ellington, Duke, 79, 84
Emerson, Faye, 136, 151
Engelbach, DeVere, 30
Exploring the Universe (1962 NET series), 245, 253-254

Feather, Leonard, 291, 301, 319, 320-321
Federal Bureau of Investigation (FBI): *Garroway at Large* investigation by, 93-95; Garroway's meeting with, 229-230
Federal Communications Commission (FCC), 240-241, 242
Fitzgerald, Ella, 74, 75, 190
Flagstad, Kirsten, 30-31
Fleming, James, 111-112, 116, 120, 124, 131-132, 133, 139, 142, 153, 163
Florman, Bernie, 194
FM Listeners' Guide, 246-248

Francis, Arlene, 238, 249
Frank, Reuven, 318
Freed, Fred, 221, 233
Friedman, Steve, 314, 316, 317
Fun On Wheels (book), 248
Furness, Betty, 130, 244, 317

Gallicchio, Joseph, 71, 84, 85
Gallico, Paul, 61, 99
Garroway (television program); see *Tempo Boston/Garroway*
Garroway, Adele (Dwyer; first wife), 26; marries Garroway, 45-46; joins Garroway in Massachusetts, 50-51; birth of daughter, 52; separation and divorce from Garroway, 59-60; friendship with Garroway, 130
Garroway, Alberta Isole Tanner (mother), 8-10, 12, 14, 19, 35
Garroway, Dave (David Cunningham Garroway VII):
 acting and, 21, 75, 289, 308
 ad-libbing ability of, 170, 212-213, 224
 ancestry, 7-8
 "assets and liabilities" lists of, 226, 255-256
 astronomy and, 15-16, 18, 25-26, 41, 252, 256, 272, 277, 281, 295-296, 309-310
 autobiography project, 308
 automobiles, 10, 21, 23, 35-36, 62, 76-77, 97, 114, 130, 179, 225-226, 260-262, 281, 310-311
 birth and early childhood, 8-12
 as book salesman, 27-29
 career difficulties, 243-245, 248, 255-256, 258, 260, 271-274, 279-280, 283, 287-288, 290-292, 307
 children of: see Garroway, David Cunningham VIII; Garroway, Paris; Garroway, Michael
 and civil rights, 73-75, 184-185, 211-212, 231-232,
 collections of, 250, 252-253, 292-294, 309-310, 311

concerns about atomic warfare/
bomb shelters, 161-163, 185, 186-
187, 196, 201-203, 216, 221,225, 242,
254-255
as concert promoter, 73
critical views of television, 190,
240-241, 242, 274, 288, 289-290,
307-308, 311
curiosity and interests of, 12-13,
14-15, 18, 20-21, 265-267, 269-270,
292-294, 298-299
death, 317; tributes, 317-320; memorial services, 320-322
depression and, 59-60, 96-97, 101,
157-158, 233, 301, 316-317
drug use: Dexedrine ("The Doctor"),
61-62, 73, 116-117, 200-201, 225, 228,
302, 303-304; Seconal, 181, 200
emotions and moods of, 212, 223,
226, 233, 297-298, 299-300, 313
fame and, 67-69, 78, 92-93, 95-96,
98, 111, 126-127, 261, 268, 299
first exposure to radio, 13-14, 16
golf and, 18-20, 23-25, 32, 42, 277
gambling and, 20, 172
health problems and injuries of, 42-
43, 149, 174-175, 193, 264, 300-301,
312-313, 316-317
income of, 75, 90, 95, 106, 109, 128,
171
introversion and shyness of, 15, 21-
22, 156-157, 311-312
legal problems, 246-248
marriages of: see *Garroway, Adele;
Garroway, Pamela; and Lippincott,
Sarah Lee*
military service of, 50-59
and J. Fred Muggs, 140, 143, 144, 152-
153, 177-178
musical abilities, 172, 253
as NBC announcer, 32-36
as NBC page/guide, 29-33
at NBC in Chicago, 44-45, 59, 62-110
parodies of, 170-171, 176
pets of, 76, 227
physical appearance, 21, 244, 273,
275, 289, 313, 314
as piston ring salesman, 27
political views of, 214-215, 225, 226,
241-242, 255
pranks of, 49, 148, 160, 195, 213, 263,
295
public relations efforts of, 199-200
radio style of, 55-56, 63-70, 71-72,
90-92, 153-155, 257-258, 281-282
religion and, 240, 304-305
as reporter, 46-49
resignation from NBC, 233-237
St. Louis tornado (1927) and, 17-18
schedule of, 72-73, 116-117, 128-130,
145, 156, 171-172, 173-174, 180-181,
194-195, 242
seasickness of, 52-54
as spokesman, 98-99, 126, 141-142,
144, 193-194, 198, 255, 271, 273, 289
strange behavior of, 225-226, 229-
230, 239, 273
television and, 83-84
television style of, 84-86, 88, 89-90,
126, 132-133, 148-149, 224, 233, 258-
260, 278-279, 285, 314
and *Today*, 107-109, 117-242, 305-
307, 314-316; as producer, 185-186,
221-226; videotape controversy,
204-209; staff changes and, 221-225
"unexplainables" of, 25
and women, 21-23, 45, 106-107, 130,
147, 172-173, 228; affairs, 52, 57, 59,
78-80; *see also individual entry on the
program itself*
wardrobe of, 68, 91, 95, 156
Washington University in St. Louis,
feelings toward: 26-27
See also titles of individual programs
Garroway, Dave Jr. (David Cunningham
Garroway VIII), 57, 74, 77, 180, 227,
229, 231, 232, 233, 239-240, 246,
247-248, 263-264, 277-278, 310, 320,
322; birth of, 187-189; relationship
with father, 251-253, 260-271, 282-
283, 288, 292-304, 318, 323; tribute
to, 325-330

Garroway, David Sr. (David Cunningham Garroway VI), 7-8, 12-14, 16, 17, 18-20, 23-25, 26, 27, 28, 51
Garroway, Grace Aitken (grandmother), 7
Garroway, Michael (stepson), 173, 188, 221, 227, 231, 242, 256, 278, 293, 320, 321, 326, 329
Garroway, Pamela (de Wilde; second wife), 172-174, 178-181, 187-189, 195, 199-200, 202, 227-231, 239, 242, 243, 319, 329
Garroway, Paris (Paris Grace Day, daughter), 52, 59, 60, 129, 135, 168, 189, 220, 226, 227, 231, 253, 261, 278, 293, 320; memories of her brother, 325-330
Garroway at Large (NBC television program), 83-90, 92, 96, 97, 108, 118, 128, 145, 182, 183, 190, 218, 219, 249, 268, 284, 285, 287, 290, 298, 315, 319; FBI investigation of, 93-95; commercial pressures on, 99-100; cancellation, 102-103, 106-107, 110
Gehman, Richard, 232-233
General Electric, 7, 13-14
Gibbs, Parker, 44, 71, 101
Gilbert, Carolyn, 63, 84, 85, 93-94
Godfrey, Arthur, 90, 92, 93, 105, 127, 146, 199, 258; Garroway as substitute host for, 218, 249-250, 257
Good Morning! (CBS, 1956), 169, 176, 181
Goodman, Julian, 94, 317
Goodman, Martin, 243, 249
Goodwin, Richard N., 205
Gould, Jack, 164, 170, 174, 197, 207, 254,
Graham, Billy, 244
Green, Gerald, 131-132, 134, 147, 151, 153
Gumbel, Bryant, 314-316

Harvey, Paul, 273
Haskell, Jack, 71, 84, 87, 91, 145, 183
Healion, Bill, 319
Hein, Jac, 131, 134, 147-148, 172, 178, 181, 186, 243, 319
Henderson, Florence, 201, 204, 212, 213, 316

Henderson, Skitch, 128, 145
Herbert, Don, 258
Herbuveaux, Jules, 44, 110
Hines, Earl "Fatha," 74, 78
Hobin, Bill, 88, 98, 283, 284, 285
Hoefer, George, 64
Holzfeind, Frank, 73
Horn, Dr. Henry, 229-231
Huntley, Chet, 142

I Surrender, Dear (1948 film), 75
Institute for the Advancement of Human Potential, 264-265
Internal Revenue Service, 247, 248, 272
Isaacs, Charlie, 284

Jack Frost (1979 Rankin/Bass television special), 308
Jessel, George, 147
Joiner, Earnest, 206, 212-213
Jones, Gene, 202, 212

KDKA (Pittsburgh radio station), 33-35, 37-44
Kelly, Mary, 135, 150, 151-152, 159, 169, 182, 192
Kelly, Pat, 33, 43, 154
Kempner Institute (Duke University), 275
Kennedy, John F., 220-221, 223, 232-233
Kennedy, Robert F., 241
KFI (Los Angeles radio station), 280, 281-282, 283, 287-288
KGU (Honolulu radio station), 54-57
Khrushchev, Nikita, 169, 190, 202-203, 272
Kicks & Co. (musical), 224-225
Kintner, Robert, 46, 214, 234-235; Garroway's suspicions of, 216-217, 232, 233
Kirkpatrick, Muriel, 134-135
Kokomo Jr. (chimpanzee), 177-178
Koppel, Ted, 273
Kral, Roy, 69, 73, 290, 321
Kukla, Fran and Ollie, 82, 83, 90, 92, 98, 109-110, 129, 145, 182
Kurtzman, Harvey, 202

Lawrence, Lee, 246, 251, 290, 312, 322
Lee, Peggy, 56, 78, 106, 321
Leonard, Jack, 221, 225
Lescoulie, Jack, 142, 150, 161, 172, 203, 207, 213, 230, 238-239, 305, 306, 317; hiring of, 112; and first *Today* broadcast, 117-118; role on program, 126, 133, 149, 159, 170, 192, 194; relationship with Garroway, 132, 224, 314; and Muggs, 177, 178; first departure from *Today*, 176-177; returns to *Today*, 182; second departure from *Today*, 237
Letterman, David, 315
Levin, "Biggie," 75, 102, 108, 109, 133, 160
Lewis, I.A. "Bud," 218, 219, 223,
Lights, Fred, 136, 151, 192, 200-201
Lippincott, Sarah Lee (third wife), 309-313, 316-322

Mad Magazine, 176
Mandel, Loring, 64; observations on Garroway's personality, 65-66, 272-273
McAvity, Tom, 109
McCall's, 242, 246
McGinniss, Joe, 279
Mennella, Buddy, 138-140, 151, 152, 153, 177-178
Meriwether, Lee Ann, 169, 174, 315, 316
Merklein, Frank, 114
Milkman's Music Hall, 48-49
Mills, Ted, 82-83, 98, 110, 223
Minow, Newton, 242
Miss Universe pageant, 1962, 249
Monitor (NBC radio series), 163-164, 167, 171, 173, 225
Moore, Garry, 238
Morgan, Henry, 84, 86, 92, 93
The Morning Show (CBS, 1954), 149-150
Mueller, Merrill, 133
Muggs, J. Fred, 138-141, 143-144, 147, 148, 149, 150-153, 159, 177-178, 305, 307, 315
Mulrony, Marion, 54-57
Murrow, Edward R., 241

National Association of Broadcast Engineers and Technicians (NABET), 197
National Automotive Trouble Quiz (1972), 289
National Broadcasting Company: Garroway in page program, 29-32; becomes announcer, 32-35; Garroway hired by NBC Chicago, 44; postwar career with network, 59; signs Garroway to long-term contract, 90; Garroway's value to, 147, 199; Garroway's separation from, 234-237, 243; *see also individual programs*
National Enquirer, 291
NBC News Overnight, 320
Nelson, Al, 34, 35
Nelson, Lindsey, 222, 226
Newman, Edwin, 238
Newport Jazz Festival, 290
Nightlife (ABC talk show), 258-260
North, Helen, 311, 312
Northshield, Robert "Shad," 218, 221
Norton, Cliff, 84, 87, 98, 103, 145, 218
Norwine, Jack, 22, 28

O'Brian, Jack, 110, 115, 121, 123, 146, 160, 164, 171, 176, 182, 187, 191
O'Connell, Helen, 174, 181, 192, 316
O'Gilvie, Sylvia, 287-288
Olson, Johnny, 106
Omnibus, 182, 190
Orbach, Jerry, 273
"Order of the Gold Brick," 57-58
Osgood, Charles, 273

Paar, Jack, 160, 168, 196-197, 207, 209-210, 224, 245, 258
Palmer, Betsy, 192, 193, 201, 213, 316
Parsons, Estelle, 132-133, 134, 135, 315
Pauley, Jane, 305, 307, 314, 315, 316
Peck, James, 231-232
Pegler, Westbrook, 215-216
Perkins, Marlin, 141
Person to Person, 181, 219
Petrillo, Joe, 66-67, 70
Pfizer, Beryl, 221-223, 224, 225, 230

Piazza, Marguerite, 158
Pinkham, Richard, 116, 117, 133, 134, 139, 141, 142, 172
Purdy, Ken, 244

Rapchak, Mike, 64
Rayburn, Gene, 105, 112, 249
Raye, Martha, 151
RCA Building, 31, 105, 108-109, 112, 117, 121, 134, 163, 191, 218-219
RCA Exhibition Hall, 112-114, 117-118, 126-127, 129, 191, 288, 315
Reems, Harry, 297
Reserved for Garroway, 90
Rhymer, Paul, 44-45
Riddle, Nelson, 284
Risser, Weeland, 87
RKO Television, 275, 278, 279
Rockefeller, Nelson A., 182, 255
Rogers, Will Jr., 168
Russell, Connie, 91, 145
Russell, Dan, 34, 35
Russell, Harold, 283
Russell, Nipsey, 259, 260

Safir, Len, 138, 139
Salk, Dr. Jonas, 270-271
Sarnoff, David, 31, 98, 167, 219, 222, 234
Sarnoff, Robert, 234, 235
Schechter, Abe, 46, 94, 116, 130
Scherer, Ray, 115, 238
Schneider, Burt, 299
Schuller, Dr. Robert, 304-305
Scott, Willard, 315
"Sentimental Journey," 72, 155, 237, 316, 320
Sevareid, Eric, 46
Shales, Tom, 120, 291, 306, 319
Shayon, Robert Lewis, 83, 237
Shepherd, Jean, 282
Sherman, Ransom, 43
Silverman, Fred, 290-291
Sinatra, Frank, 56, 127, 135, 155, 171, 180
Sloane, Carol, 249-251, 258
Sokolsky, George, 215
Speer, Charles, 105, 113, 138

Sproul, Derby, 34
Stabile, James, 235
Sterling, Jack, 257
Studs' Place, 83, 218
Sullivan, Ed, 85, 199, 232, 240, 241, 285,
Sunday with Garroway (*Friday with Garroway*), 153-154, 163
Swarthmore University, 309, 310, 312, 317, 320-322

Talent Scouts, 218, 250, 251, 283
Tallchief, Maria, 158
Tamplin, Robert, 283, 284
Tangora, Al, 54, 55
Tanner, Albert Brockelbank (grandfather), 7, 8-10, 14
Tempo Boston/Garroway (Boston talk show, 1969-70), 275-277, 278-279
Terkel, Studs, 73, 75, 83, 98
Texaco Star Theater, 86, 114, 147
Tilden, Fred, 27-28, 30
Tillstrom, Burr, 75, 82, 110, 145, 183
Today: origins of, 104-106, 107; preparations for first broadcast, 110-115; original studio, *see* RCA Exhibition Hall; debut broadcast, 116-124; breaking news and, 124, 169-170; prime-time special, 125; viewer response, 125-127, 148-149, 161; production and staff, 131-137, 159-160; ad sales, 141-142, 176; J. Fred Muggs, *see individual entry*; 1953 coronation and, 142-144; competitors: see *The Morning Show, Good Morning!*; board game, 175; format changes, 184, 185-187, 192; new studio, 191-192; "co-op" time, 193; anniversary shows: 195-196, 212, 220, 245, 272, 305-306, 314-316; remote shows: Paris (1959), 195-198; Rome (1960), 213-214; Washington (1960), 212; New York (1960), 214; videotape move, 203-210; renamed *The Dave Garroway Today Show*, 216; influence among decision-makers, 217; behind-the-scenes turmoil, 221-226;

Garroway's departure from, 233-237; Chancellor replaces Garroway, 238-239; *also see names of individual program personnel*
Tonight (Steve Allen), 131, 161, 176
Tonight! America After Dark (1957), 176-177, 182
Tonight (Jack Paar/Johnny Carson), 196, 207, 219, 245, 260
Torre, Marie, 176, 182, 193, 210, 217, 220, 239; Garroway and, 185-186
Toscanini, Arturo, 31-32, 218, 236
Truman, Harry S, 55, 144, 147
Truman, Margaret, 127
TV Guide, 203, 204, 208, 232, 244, 246
The TV Guide Awards (1962 television special), 248-249
2's Company with Dave Garroway (Boston TV show, 1970), 279

United States Information Agency (USIA), 241-242
University City High School, 20-21
Urquhart, Charlie, 45, 61

Van Damme, Art, 91
Van Doren, Charles, 182, 192, 193, 198, 240; firing from *Today*, 204-208
Vanocur, Sander, 238
Vaughan, Sarah, 63, 69-70, 73, 74, 94, 321-322

Waldron, Roy, 138-140, 151, 152, 153, 177-178

Wallace, Irving, 310
Wallace, Mike, 157, 171
Walters, Barbara, 279, 315, 318, 319-320
Washington University in St. Louis, 24-27, 45, 271
WCBS (radio station, New York), 257-258
Weiss, Lou, 242
Werner, Mort, 105-106, 108, 116, 118, 124, 131, 134, 159
Weaver, Sylvester "Pat," 104-105, 106, 107, 108-109, 110-111, 112-113, 119, 122, 123-124, 125, 141, 163-165, 166, 174, 288, 305, 312, 315
WGBH-TV (Boston), 279
Wide Wide World, 164-167, 170-171, 173, 174, 176, 182, 185, 187, 190-191, 219, 282, 320
Wilkinson, VAdm. Theodore, 57-58
William Morris Agency, 161, 200, 243
Winchell, Walter, 89, 110, 113, 124, 147, 209, 216
WMAQ (Chicago radio station), 43-44, 48-49, 56, 60-62, 67-68, 71-72, 73-75, 78
WNAC (Boston radio station), 16, 32
Wood, Barry, 174
Wood, Robert, 284

You Don't Say? (radio program), 37-38
You Don't Say...Or Do You? (book), 27-28, 36-37
Your Show of Shows, 125, 128, 145

Zeamer, Mike, 131, 134